Contributions to Economics

The series *Contributions to Economics* provides an outlet for innovative research in all areas of economics. Books published in the series are primarily monographs and multiple author works that present new research results on a clearly defined topic, but contributed volumes and conference proceedings are also considered. All books are published in print and ebook and disseminated and promoted globally. The series and the volumes published in it are indexed by Scopus and ISI (selected volumes).

Hasan Dinçer • Serhat Yüksel
Editors

Circular Economy and the Energy Market

Achieving Sustainable Economic Development Through Energy Policy

Springer

Editors
Hasan Dinçer
Istanbul Medipol University
Kadıköy, Istanbul, Turkey

Serhat Yüksel
Istanbul Medipol University
Besiktas, Istanbul, Turkey

ISSN 1431-1933 ISSN 2197-7178 (electronic)
Contributions to Economics
ISBN 978-3-031-13145-5 ISBN 978-3-031-13146-2 (eBook)
https://doi.org/10.1007/978-3-031-13146-2

This Springer imprint is published by the registered company Springer Nature Switzerland AG
The registered company address is: Gewerbestrasse 11, 6330 Cham, Switzerland

Contents

Chapter 1
The Improvements in Hydrogen Energy Investments

Hasan Dinçer, Çağatay Çağlayan, and Mutaliyeva Lyailya Maratovna

Abstract Hydrogen is the most easily found element in the universe. It also has a simple structure consisting of a proton and an electron. In addition, it is possible to produce electrical energy from hydrogen in some different ways. As a result of gasification of fossil fuels such as natural gas and coal, hydrogen and carbon monoxide gas are released. Low cost is one of the most important advantages of this method. On the other hand, carbon monoxide gas formed in this process causes air pollution. It is possible to obtain hydrogen energy by using renewable energy sources. In this context, electricity obtained from renewable energy sources is used in the electrolysis of water. Hydrogen and sulfur can be separated because of electrolysis of hydrogen sulfide gas. It is possible to say that hydrogen has many advantages compared to other types of energy. First of all, the energy obtained from hydrogen is much richer than oil and natural gas. On the other hand, no carbon gas is released into the atmosphere due to the combustion of hydrogen. Only water is produced in this process. In other words, hydrogen is an extremely environmentally friendly form of energy. It is predicted that hydrogen will be used much more actively in the future due to its many important advantages such as being efficient, environmentally friendly, and safe. Many countries have taken important steps towards the use of hydrogen energy. In this process, it is vital to increase technological investments in hydrogen energy, which is gaining importance day by day. To achieve this goal, priority should be given to research and development investments for the acquisition, storage, and transportation of hydrogen. In this way, it will be possible to obtain and use hydrogen energy at a lower cost. This will take the countries one step further in their energy policies.

Keywords Hydrogen · Energy investment · Clean energy · Carbon emission

H. Dinçer (✉) · Ç. Çağlayan
The School of Business, İstanbul Medipol University, İstanbul, Turkey
e-mail: hdincer@medipol.edu.tr

M. L. Maratovna
L.N. Gumilyov Eurasian National University, Nur-Sultan, Kazakhstan

H. Dinçer, S. Yüksel (eds.), *Circular Economy and the Energy Market*,
Contributions to Economics, https://doi.org/10.1007/978-3-031-13146-2_1

1.1 Introduction

Carbon gas is produced because of the use of fossil fuels in energy production. This situation causes significant environmental pollution (Yüksel et al., 2020). Countries are trying to take some measures to prevent this situation. However, each planned action has its own advantages and disadvantages (Liu et al., 2020). In this context, a detailed cost-benefit analysis of the applications to be carried out is required (Shang et al., 2021). Otherwise, the steps to be taken will not be preferred by businesses as they will not be efficient. This situation will not contribute to the solution of the carbon emission problem (Kou et al., 2022).

The use of hydrogen energy is one of the applications to be carried out to solve the carbon emission problem (Zhao et al., 2021). With the use of hydrogen, it is possible to produce much higher quality energy (Zhu et al., 2020). This contributes significantly to energy efficiency. Hydrogen can be stored in both liquid and gaseous form (Yüksel et al., 2021a, b, c). This makes it easier to use hydrogen. Hydrogen can be produced using any energy source (Shaikh et al., 2021). This provides significant advantages to hydrogen.

Due to these advantages, increasing hydrogen energy investments is important for the energy policies of countries. In this way, countries will be able to produce their own energy. This will reduce the energy dependency of countries. On the other hand, thanks to hydrogen, it will be possible for countries to produce clean energy (Li et al., 2020). This will help countries to reduce their health expenditures (Xie et al., 2021). In addition, its ability to produce clean energy will positively affect the image of countries (Zhong et al., 2020). This will contribute to the arrival of foreign investors to the countries.

1.2 The Needs for Clean Energy

The world population has been increasing day by day. In response to the increasing population, the need for energy has been increasing day by day. The main reason for the increase in energy needs in parallel with the increasing population is that energy is one of the basic needs of people. When it comes to every human need such as shelter, nutrition, and transportation, people's energy needs arise. In parallel with the increasing energy needs, states have to constantly increase their energy production. Because a power outage that may occur will have extremely negative consequences on both human life and the economy of the country (Chang et al., 2007). In this context, the amount of energy produced in the countries should be at a level that can meet the energy demand of the country in question. In parallel with this, various sources are used in energy production in the world. Fossil fuels are one of them. Fossil fuels are relatively cheap, easy to access and do not require advanced technology compared to other energy sources, but all fossil fuels are carbon-based fuels. Therefore, the combustion of every carbon-based energy source such as coal and natural gas produces a high amount of carbon emissions to nature. The carbon emission produced by each burning fossil fuel has various consequences on nature (Abas et al., 2015). For example, the burning of carbon-based fuels is among the main causes of air and water pollution. In addition, the burning of fossil fuels such as coal and natural gas accelerates global warming. The uncontrolled warming of the world causes dozens of negative consequences, such as shrinkage of agricultural areas, reduction of water resources, and loss of life from extreme heat (Luber & McGeehin, 2008).

One of the long-term effects of burning fossil fuels, such as global warming, is that it negatively affects human health in the long run. For example, various lung and respiratory diseases are more common in areas with intense carbon-based air pollution. The use of fossil fuels in these regions negatively affects human health and harms the country's economy (Kampa & Castanas, 2008). In these countries, health expenditures are constantly increasing, and a catastrophic amount of health expenditure is paid both from the budgets of the states and from the individual budgets. This situation reduces the living standard of people and makes the country's economies more fragile. Considering all these, an energy production based on fossil fuels with factors such as low cost increases social expenditures such as health and environmental expenditures, causing states to bear heavier costs in the long run. Thus, it can be said that the transition process from fossil fuels to cleaner and more efficient alternative energy sources should be faster (Uluer & Çağlayan, 2021).

Another energy source that meets the increasing energy demand is nuclear energy. Uranium, the element containing the most protons and neutrons, is used in nuclear power plants. The element uranium is broken down by the fission reaction, creating a large amount of heat. The resulting temperature reaches serious values. Therefore, the fission reaction, which takes place thanks to neutron traps, is kept under control. Uncontrolled fission reactions can cause nuclear power plant accidents that can cause serious loss of life and environmental damage (Yüksel & Çağlayan, 2020). The heat generated as a result of a controlled fission reaction turns the turbines by evaporating the water. Thus, the motion energy required for electrical energy is provided. The process of obtaining electricity from nuclear power plants is completely zero carbon. Since there is no carbon emission from nuclear power plants, it can be said that nuclear energy is an extremely clean type of energy (Xie et al., 2020). In addition to these, the advantages and disadvantages of nuclear energy can be mentioned.

One of the most important advantages of nuclear energy is that it produces electricity 24 hours a day. From this point of view, nuclear energy is a very efficient energy source. Another important factor is that the energy obtained from nuclear energy has the feature of being zero carbon. With this feature, nuclear energy is an extremely important energy source in the fight against global warming and environmental pollution (Dinçer et al., 2020). In addition to all these advantages, it is possible to talk about various disadvantages. First of all, it can be mentioned that the installation costs of nuclear energy are high. Since nuclear energy investments are big investments like all other energy investments, there may be problems in financing the investment (Yüksel et al., 2021a, b, c). Another disadvantage is the problems that can be experienced in waste management. The disposal of radioactive waste from nuclear power plants can be costly and harmful to the environment. Finally, one of the most important disadvantages of nuclear energy is the risk of the explosion of power plants. Considering the nuclear power plant accidents in the past, it is obvious that a possible accident will have serious consequences. The explosion risk of nuclear power plants due to various reasons such as human error, natural disasters, and terrorist attacks makes it difficult for the public to accept nuclear energy. Therefore, it would be the right choice to use various renewable energies, especially hydrogen energy, together with nuclear energy.

Considering the disadvantages of fossil fuels and nuclear energy, renewable energies come to the fore. The renewable energy source is defined as the energy source that can be available exactly the next day in the evolution of nature (Twidell, 2021). It can be said that renewable energies are sustainable since the potential for depletion of reserves seen in fossil fuel sources is not in question in renewable energies. Renewable energy sources can be listed as solar, wind, biomass, geothermal, hydraulic, hydrogen, and wave energy. These energy sources are reassuring energy sources, but they also have various advantages. One of the most important features of renewable energies is that it does not harm the environment in the energy production process. In this context, it can be said that renewable energies have an effective share in the fight against global warming by preventing carbon emissions. The fact that renewable energies will not run out over time, like fossil energy resource reserves, has been one of the biggest motivations for large investments made or to be made in this field. Another important advantage of renewable energies is their low maintenance costs. For example, since flammable fuels are not used in energy types such as solar and wind energy, the maintenance cost of these energy sources is relatively low (Dinçer et al., 2021a, b). It is possible to come across renewable energies in rural settlements or metropolitan living areas. For example, people make small investments in solar panels to produce hot water or electricity. Thanks to these small investments, people save on energy costs in the long run and reduce carbon emissions by using fewer fossil fuels. One of the important advantages of renewable energies is that it is an energy source with high acceptance by society. It is one of the energy sources with the highest acceptance by society because it is extremely environmentally friendly and has a low-risk rate.

In parallel with this, it is possible to talk about various disadvantages of renewable energies. First of all, since renewable energies are obtained from nature, the amount of energy produced is affected by various natural conditions or weather events. Although these energy sources are available worldwide, the energy obtained from these sources is not uninterrupted 24 hours a day, 7 days a week throughout the year (Yüksel et al., 2021a, b, c). The fact that the weather is cloudy on some days, the sun does not shine at night and the occurrence of dry periods can be given as examples of nature-based factors affecting renewable energy production. Therefore, changing weather events and climate are the leading conditions that affect the efficiency of renewable energy. Another important disadvantage is the lack of storage capability of renewable energy. Since some renewable energy sources do not promise 24-hour energy, it is important to store energy. As technology progresses, it seems possible that the energy storage capacity will increase and batteries will become more successful in accordance with the needs. Another important disadvantage that prevents the spread of renewable energies is the high installation costs of renewable energies. Therefore, there are problems in financing renewable energy projects. Considering all these conditions, it can be said that renewable energies are open to development and promising for the future, but it is a fact that the search for new energy sources will continue (Mohtasham, 2015).

1.3 The Advantages of Hydrogen Energy

Among renewable energies, especially hydrogen energy has a position that concerns all energy sources. The increase in prices with the decrease experienced after the excessive use of fossil fuel reserves and the damage these fuels cause to the environment have encouraged researchers to search for environmentally friendly alternative fuels that are abundant in nature. As a result of these studies, it is shown that hydrogen, the simplest and most common element in the universe, has most of the properties necessary for fuel. In parallel with this, researches are accelerating for hydrogen, which is promising to meet the energy needs of the current century (Momirlan & Veziroglu, 2002). Hydrogen, the first element of the periodic table, consists of a proton and an electron. It is the simplest and most common element on Earth. Hydrogen, which has an odorless, colorless, tasteless, and transparent structure, is the lightest chemical element in nature. Due to the instability in its hydrogen structure, it is not found in free form on earth and is included in different compounds. In the light of available information, it can be said that hydrogen has the highest energy content per unit of all known fuels. Apart from these, hydrogen is not a natural fuel. Hydrogen produced from sources such as water, biomass, nuclear and hydrocarbons is a synthetic fuel. For example, a water molecule consists of two hydrogen atoms and one oxygen atom. There are different numbers of hydrogen atoms in petroleum-derived organic compounds known as hydrocarbons. Hydrogen energy is chemical energy released in its molecules as a result of the decomposition of hydrogen in its pure form. This energy can be converted into heat and electrical forms by various methods (Veziroğlu & Şahi, 2008).

Production sources of hydrogen are plentiful and diverse. For example, it is possible to produce hydrogen from fossil fuels such as hydrocarbons, renewable energy sources such as biomass, and a wide variety of sources such as nuclear sources. There are many alternative hydrogen production technologies such as steam recovery, electrolysis during the production phase. Currently, most of the hydrogen is produced from fossil fuels, especially natural gas (labidine Messaoudani et al., 2016). Today, hydrogen is mainly obtained by the steam-methane method. In this production method, natural gas is exposed to steam at high temperature and hydrogen, carbon dioxide, and carbon monoxide are produced. In the next step, extra hydrogen and carbon dioxide are obtained by releasing carbon monoxide into the steam. As a result of this process, which is based on the production of hydrogen from fossil sources, a large number of greenhouse gases such as carbon dioxide are released. Integrating emerging technologies such as carbon capture in hydrogen production from fossil fuels into this production process will offer significant benefits in minimizing environmental impacts.

Another method is the electrolysis of water. By applying an electric current to the water, the water is separated into hydrogen and oxygen, and this process is called electrolysis. The electrolysis process is carried out in units called electrolysers. Electrolysers consist of two electrodes, the anode and the cathode. The hydrogen ion, one of the charged particles formed after the electric current is applied, has a positive electric charge and is collected at the negative electrode (cathode). Since oxygen has a negative charge, it collects at the positive electrode (anode). The breaking of the bonds of hydrogen and oxygen atoms basically occurs as a result of this process. If the electrolysis method is applied using renewable energy sources, it will make hydrogen energy zero carbon. Therefore, it can be said that this method is quite environmentally friendly. Since the cost of electricity consumed in the electrolysis process is sometimes higher than the price of the hydrogen produced, the electrolysis method has a very small share in hydrogen production. Although studies continue to make the electrolysis method more economical, hydrogen production can also be produced with different and more economical methods (Ursua et al., 2011).

Existing nuclear power plants can produce high-quality steam at lower costs than natural gas and can be used in many processes, including steam reforming. However, it is possible to obtain hydrogen in high yield when this high-quality steam is electrolyzed and decomposed into pure hydrogen and oxygen. Large amounts of hydrogen are produced by the high temperatures released from advanced nuclear reactors. Nuclear energy facilities are considered to have the potential to support hydrogen production both while providing electricity to the grid and thanks to this heat released. In addition, since nuclear power plants do not cause carbon emissions, they are seen as a green energy source, and the hydrogen to be produced through these reactors is considered as green hydrogen. Considering all these, it can be said that hydrogen can be obtained with fossil fuels, renewable energies, and nuclear energy. Therefore, hydrogen energy has a different position compared to other renewable energies (Sorgulu & Dincer, 2018). In parallel, there are various methods for obtaining energy from hydrogen. The first method is the burning method. Hydrogen gasoline is a combustible fuel like natural gas, but it has advantages over fossil fuels. The biggest advantage of hydrogen over fossil fuels is the low carbon emission. No carbon dioxide is produced during the hydrogen combustion process. Another method used to obtain energy from hydrogen is the fuel cell method. A fuel cell is the reverse of the electrolysis process. Electric current is obtained by combining hydrogen and oxygen. This method is one of the preferred methods in all applications, especially automobiles. It can be said that it is a more efficient method than burning hydrogen. It has almost no harmful emissions to the environment.

1.4 How to Improve Hydrogen Energy Investments

Hydrogen energy is used in many places from transportation to industry, from space rockets to oil production. Various advantages of hydrogen energy can be mentioned, especially its high efficiency and being an environmentally friendly resource. First, hydrogen can be produced using any energy source, including renewable energy sources. Hydrogen can be produced using electricity and converted into electricity with relatively high efficiency. In the end-use, hydrogen has the highest efficiency when transforming into energy to be used, and hydrogen is a more efficient fuel than fossil fuels. One of the most important advantages of hydrogen is that there are various methods for its storage and transportation after its production. The transportation process is done by compressing the hydrogen in gas form or converting it into liquid form in a pressurized environment and then loading it into tankers (Salvi & Subramanian, 2015). However, due to the increasing need for hydrogen in the coming years, it is possible to transport hydrogen through existing natural gas pipelines. Because the capacities of pipelines between countries are sufficient to transport hydrogen. For storage, the priority is concentrated on methods that allow transportation. Methods that prioritize transportation for storage of hydrogen; liquid hydrogen, gaseous hydrogen, metal hydride and chemical storage. Hydrogen does not have any harmful effects on the environment while being transported or stored. As a result of the combustion of hydrogen or its consumption in the fuel cell, only water is produced as the final product. With these properties, hydrogen can be used as energy for households or production sectors or as fuel in cars, ships, and airplanes.

Considering all these advantages of hydrogen energy, it should be said that hydrogen energy investments should be increased. Therefore, various improvements should be made to increase these investments and support existing investments. States should cooperate with the private sector to encourage hydrogen energy investments with tax breaks and various subsidies. Investments in hydrogen energy with subsidies will increase (Haghi et al., 2018). Government incentive packages should cover universities as well as the private sector. Universities should invest in research on the transportation, storage, and recovery of hydrogen and advance existing technology and literature. Hydrogen energy investments are big energy investments like other energy investments. Therefore, investors can be supported at the point of financing. Providing low-cost funds to investors will increase hydrogen energy investments (Bai & Zhang, 2020). Another important point in the development of hydrogen energy investments is the qualification of the employees who will work in these energy investments (Baş et al., 2022). The high competencies of the employees who will work in hydrogen energy investments will increase the efficiency of these investments. At the same time, informing the employees who will take part in hydrogen energy investments about new technologies related to hydrogen energy and organizing training programs will provide extra support to the progress of investments and increase efficiency by increasing the qualification of the employees. Taking all these steps will support the development of the hydrogen energy sector and literature, and will pave the way for the frequent use of hydrogen energy in the future.

1.5 Conclusion

Hydrogen energy contributes significantly to the solution of the carbon emission problem. In this way, the health expenditures of the countries will decrease significantly. Thus, the budget balances of the countries will be positively affected by this situation. The use of clean energy will also improve the image of countries in a positive way. This situation will contribute to the preference of foreign investors in these countries. Thus, it will be easier to solve many important problems such as unemployment. In addition, thanks to the use of hydrogen energy, countries will be able to produce their own energy. This will reduce the dependence of countries on other countries for energy.

On the other hand, there are some disadvantages in the use of hydrogen energy. For example, hydrogen gas is not easy to obtain. Hydrogen gas is actually abundant in nature. On the other hand, in order to obtain this gas, which is not in pure form, some applications such as electrolysis are required. This situation will also create extra costs. In addition, hydrogen occupies much more space, especially when compared to petroleum. Therefore, very large volumes are needed to store this gas. This leads to an increase in the costs of hydrogen energy investments.

As stated before, hydrogen energy investments need to be increased. In this case, it is important to eliminate these negativities. In this framework, priority should be given to research and development studies (Dincer et al., 2019). In this way, it will be possible to develop new techniques (Haiyun et al., 2021). This will contribute to reducing the costs of hydrogen energy production (Cheng et al., 2020; Yuan et al., 2021). In other words, thanks to developing technologies, it will be easier to decompose hydrogen and it will be possible to reduce the storage costs of this gas.

Another important issue for increasing hydrogen energy investments is qualified personnel. As can be seen, there are very comprehensive technical processes in hydrogen energy investments. In order for these processes to be carried out effectively, personnel who are experts in their work are needed (Zhou et al., 2020; Dinçer & Yüksel, 2019). Thanks to these personnel, it will be possible to solve the problems that may arise in investments effectively and quickly. This will help increase the efficiency of investments (Dinçer et al., 2021a, b). In this context, energy companies should pay attention to this issue in their personnel selection (Liu et al., 2021). In addition, the personnel working within the company should be provided with the training they need.

References

Abas, N., Kalair, A., & Khan, N. (2015). Review of fossil fuels and future energy technologies. *Futures, 69*, 31–49.

Bai, W., & Zhang, L. (2020). How to finance for establishing hydrogen refueling stations in China? An analysis based on fuzzy AHP and PROMETHEE. *International Journal of Hydrogen Energy, 45*(59), 34354–34370.

Baş, H., Eti, S., & Ersin, İ. (2022). Importance of renewable energy Investments for Qualified Workforce. In *Multidimensional strategic outlook on global competitive energy economics and finance*. Emerald Publishing Limited.

Chang, S. E., McDaniels, T. L., Mikawoz, J., & Peterson, K. (2007). Infrastructure failure interdependencies in extreme events: Power outage consequences in the 1998 ice storm. *Natural Hazards, 41*(2), 337–358.

Cheng, F., Lin, M., Yüksel, S., Dinçer, H., & Kalkavan, H. (2020). A hybrid hesitant 2-tuple IVSF decision making approach to analyze PERT-based critical paths of new service development process for renewable energy investment projects. *IEEE Access, 9*, 3947–3969.

Dinçer, H., & Yüksel, S. (2019). Multidimensional evaluation of global investments on the renewable energy with the integrated fuzzy decision-making model under the hesitancy. *International Journal of Energy Research, 43*(5), 1775–1784.

Dinçer, H., Lisin, A., Ubay, G. G., & Çağlayan, Ç. (2021a). Identifying the best financing sources for renewable energy companies in Latin American countries. In *Strategic approaches to energy management* (pp. 1–12). Springer.

Dincer, H., Yüksel, S., & Martinez, L. (2019). Balanced scorecard-based analysis about European energy investment policies: A hybrid hesitant fuzzy decision-making approach with quality function deployment. *Expert Systems with Applications, 115*, 152–171.

Dinçer, H., Yüksel, S., Çağlayan, Ç., & Uluer, G. S. (2020). The contribution of nuclear energy investment on sustainable financial and economic development. *Journal of Financial Economics and Banking, 1*(1), 39–51.

Dinçer, H., Yüksel, S., Tamer, İ., & Serezli, E. (2021b). The strategic importance of quality training given to personnel: An evaluation for nuclear energy companies. In *Management strategies to survive in a competitive environment* (pp. 349–365). Springer.

Haghi, E., Raahemifar, K., & Fowler, M. (2018). Investigating the effect of renewable energy incentives and hydrogen storage on advantages of stakeholders in a microgrid. *Energy Policy, 113*, 206–222.

Haiyun, C., Zhixiong, H., Yüksel, S., & Dinçer, H. (2021). Analysis of the innovation strategies for green supply chain management in the energy industry using the QFD-based hybrid interval valued intuitionistic fuzzy decision approach. *Renewable and Sustainable Energy Reviews, 143*, 110844.

Kampa, M., & Castanas, E. (2008). Human health effects of air pollution. *Environmental Pollution, 151*(2), 362–367.

Kou, G., Yüksel, S., & Dinçer, H. (2022). Inventive problem-solving map of innovative carbon emission strategies for solar energy-based transportation investment projects. *Applied Energy, 311*, 118680.

labidine Messaoudani, Z., Rigas, F., Hamid, M. D. B., & Hassan, C. R. C. (2016). Hazards, safety and knowledge gaps on hydrogen transmission via natural gas grid: A critical review. *International Journal of Hydrogen Energy, 41*(39), 17511–17525.

Li, X., Zhu, S., Yüksel, S., Dinçer, H., & Ubay, G. G. (2020). Kano-based mapping of innovation strategies for renewable energy alternatives using hybrid interval type-2 fuzzy decision-making approach. *Energy, 211*, 118679.

Liu, H., Yüksel, S., & Dinçer, H. (2020). Analyzing the criteria of efficient carbon capture and separation technologies for sustainable clean energy usage. *Energies, 13*(10), 2592.

Liu, Y., Gong, X., Yüksel, S., Dinçer, H., & Aydın, R. (2021). A multidimensional outlook to energy investments for the countries with continental shelf in East Mediterranean region with hybrid decision making model based on IVIF logic. *Energy Reports, 7*, 158–173.

Luber, G., & McGeehin, M. (2008). Climate change and extreme heat events. *American Journal of Preventive Medicine, 35*(5), 429–435.

Mohtasham, J. (2015). Renewable energies. *Energy Procedia, 74*, 1289–1297.

Momirlan, M., & Veziroglu, T. N. (2002). Current status of hydrogen energy. *Renewable and Sustainable Energy Reviews, 6*(1–2), 141–179.

Salvi, B. L., & Subramanian, K. A. (2015). Sustainable development of road transportation sector using hydrogen energy system. *Renewable and Sustainable Energy Reviews, 51*, 1132–1155.

Shaikh, Z. A., Moiseev, N., Mikhaylov, A., & Yüksel, S. (2021). Facile synthesis of copper oxide-cobalt oxide/nitrogen-doped carbon (Cu2O-Co3O4/CN) composite for efficient water splitting. *Applied Sciences, 11*(21), 9974.

Shang, H., Su, F., Yüksel, S., & Dinçer, H. (2021). Identifying the strategic priorities of the technical factors for the sustainable low carbon industry based on macroeconomic conditions. *SAGE Open, 11*(2), 21582440211016345.

Sorgulu, F., & Dincer, I. (2018). Cost evaluation of two potential nuclear power plants for hydrogen production. *International Journal of Hydrogen Energy, 43*(23), 10522–10529.

Twidell, J. (2021). *Renewable energy resources*. Routledge.

Uluer, G. S., & Çağlayan, Ç. (2021). The economic and environmental importance of Akkuyu nuclear power plant in Turkey. In *Handbook of research on strategic Management for Current Energy Investments* (pp. 300–319). IGI Global.

Ursua, A., Gandia, L. M., & Sanchis, P. (2011). Hydrogen production from water electrolysis: Current status and future trends. *Proceedings of the IEEE, 100*(2), 410–426.

Veziroğlu, T. N., & Şahi, S. (2008). 21st Century's energy: Hydrogen energy system. *Energy Conversion and Management, 49*(7), 1820–1831.

Xie, Y., Peng, Y., Yüksel, S., Dınçer, H., Uluer, G. S., Çağlayan, Ç., & Li, Y. (2020). Consensus-based public acceptance and mapping of nuclear energy investments using spherical and pythagorean fuzzy group decision making approaches. *IEEE Access, 8*, 206248–206263.

Xie, Y., Zhou, Y., Peng, Y., Dinçer, H., Yüksel, S., & an Xiang, P. (2021). An extended pythagorean fuzzy approach to group decision-making with incomplete preferences for analyzing balanced scorecard-based renewable energy investments. *IEEE Access, 9*, 43020–43035.

Yuan, G., Xie, F., Dinçer, H., & Yüksel, S. (2021). The theory of inventive problem solving (TRIZ)-based strategic mapping of green nuclear energy investments with spherical fuzzy group decision-making approach. *International Journal of Energy Research, 45*(8), 12284–12300.

Yüksel, S., & Çağlayan, Ç. (2020). The factors affecting the investors' decisions: A study on nuclear energy investments. *Economics Literature, 2*(2), 177–185.

Yüksel, S., Dinçer, H., Çağlayan, Ç., & Uluer, G. S. (2021a). Determining the optimal financial strategies for nuclear energy companies. In *Financial strategies in competitive markets* (pp. 1–16). Springer.

Yüksel, S., Dinçer, H., Çağlayan, Ç., & Uluer, G. S. (2021b). Strategy development to improve the business performance of nuclear energy companies. In *Management strategies to survive in a competitive environment* (pp. 33–46). Springer.

Yüksel, S., Dinçer, H., Karakuş, H., & Ubay, G. G. (2020). The negative effects of carbon emission on FDI: A comparative analysis between E7 and G7 countries. In *Handbook of research on sustainable supply chain management for the global economy* (pp. 20–35). IGI Global.

Yüksel, S., Mikhaylov, A., Ubay, G. G., & Uyeh, D. D. (2021c). The role of hydrogen in the Black Sea for the future energy supply security of Turkey. In *Handbook of research on strategic management for current energy investments* (pp. 1–15). IGI Global.

Zhao, Y., Xu, Y., Yüksel, S., Dinçer, H., & Ubay, G. G. (2021). Hybrid IT2 fuzzy modelling with alpha cuts for hydrogen energy investments. *International Journal of Hydrogen Energy, 46*(13), 8835–8851.

Zhong, J., Hu, X., Yüksel, S., Dinçer, H., & Ubay, G. G. (2020). Analyzing the investments strategies for renewable energies based on multi-criteria decision model. *IEEE Access, 8*, 118818–118840.

Zhou, P., Zhou, P., Yüksel, S., Dinçer, H., & Uluer, G. S. (2020). Balanced scorecard-based evaluation of sustainable energy investment projects with it2 fuzzy hybrid decision making approach. *Energies, 13*(1), 82.

Zhu, L., Hu, L., Yüksel, S., Dinçer, H., Karakuş, H., & Ubay, G. G. (2020). Analysis of strategic directions in sustainable hydrogen investment decisions. *Sustainability, 12*(11), 4581.

Chapter 2
The Problem of Depending on Fossil Fuels in the Energy Policies of the European Union: A Strategic Analysis in the Eastern Mediterranean Region

Mehmet Ali Alhan

Abstract The Eastern Mediterranean geographical area consists of an area surrounded by Europe in the North, Asia in the East, the Middle East in the Southeast, and Africa in the South. The Republic of Turkey is the country with the longest coastline in this area. Recently, the discovery of increasing hydrocarbon reserves in this geography has whetted the appetite of the European Union (EU) countries that cannot meet their energy needs. Federal Germany, which has the largest industrial capacity among the European Union countries with energy dependence on the Russian Federation, had an urgent and important need for an alternative, reliable, and clean energy supply, especially during the Russia-Ukraine crisis. In this study, the European Union's process of closing nuclear and hydro-electric power plants for alternative, reliable, and clean energy and the depletion of fossil fuels will be discussed. It will be argued that energy domination has a very strategic meaning. In the process of liberation from fossil fuel, the search for gas hydrate and the political, economic, and cultural relations of the Republic of Turkey with Europe will be discussed.

Keywords Carbon emission · Energy dependency · Eastern Mediterranean · Energy diplomacy · Gas hydrate

2.1 Introduction

Developing industrial production and rapidly growing societies increase their energy needs. Therefore, countries holding energy reserves such as oil and hydrocarbons become regional and global power. This situation increases the importance of renewable and sustainable energy sources (Dong et al., 2022; Zhang et al., 2022; Kou et al., 2022). It is considered that the Republic of Turkey wants to use these energy reserves in the Eastern Mediterranean basin as a means of political and

---

M. A. Alhan (✉)
The School of Business, İstanbul Medipol University, Istanbul, Turkey

H. Dinçer, S. Yüksel (eds.), *Circular Economy and the Energy Market*, Contributions to Economics, https://doi.org/10.1007/978-3-031-13146-2_2

economic pressure. Gas hydrate reserves in the Eastern Mediterranean attract all attention as the fuel of the future with its large methane volume. Soviet scientists discovered that gas hydrate reserves could also be found in cold and high-pressure sea areas. With the observation of solid natural gas in West Siberian gas sediments in the 1960s, the world's perspective on this area changed. Simultaneously, the need for a reliable energy supply for the high industrial power of the European Union countries is absolute. Therefore, the first outlines of the new era are already visible: renewable energies and energy efficiency (Mukhtarov et al., 2022; Kostis et al., 2022; Bhuiyan et al., 2022).

At the same time, a new era is being entered in the European Union, especially in Federal Germany. Recent strategic initiatives by the Federal Republic of Germany include the High-Tech Strategy 2025, the National Industrial Strategy 2030, and the Exit Coal Strategy. It is aimed to go beyond market fixation and lay the foundations for a more active state. We can trace the changes in ordoliberal principles in the successful energy transition policies of the 2000s. The post-World War II German economic model has been defined as an expansion-oriented policy that is stable in the production and dissemination of knowledge and increases the international competitiveness of its companies. An industrial strategy that requires tackling major challenges like the climate catastrophe requires a reinvigoration of both private and public investment, innovation and collaboration.

In this process, the Greek Cypriot Administration (GCA) claimed rights against the Republic of Turkey and Northern Cyprus according to the 1982 United Nations Convention on the Law of the Sea (UNCLOS) (www.ung.org). It also complicates the energy cooperation in the region by causing tension with the Turkish Republic, while at the same time Greece and the Greek Cypriot Administration are trying to persuade the EU to implement comprehensive sanctions against the Republic of Turkey (Merz, 2020). Ankara, on the other hand, rejects the legal authority of Greek Cypriot Administration to conduct exploration in the exclusive economic zone of the entire island (Axt, 2020).

On the other hand, it does not accept the existence of the Turkish Republic of Northern Cyprus and its rights under the 1960 United Nations Convention on the Law of the Sea (UNCLOS) (www.turkishgreek.org). The United States of America officially requested a military base in the south of the island from the Greek Cypriot Administration (www.tr.sputniknews.com). The start of negotiations in line with the demand caused the power balance in the region to be turned upside down. On the other hand, the European Union is developing various cooperation projects with the countries in the region, both in terms of its energy security and in terms of regional military security policies (Kısacık & Erenel, 2019). The European Union (EU), Israel, Greek Cypriot Administration, Egypt, Lebanon, and the United States of America (USA) left Ankara out and started new formations such as the "Eastern Mediterranean Natural Gas Forum" (www.petroleum.gov.eg). While carrying out natural gas transportation projects within the scope of the Eastern Mediterranean Gas Initiative, it also reveals a security perspective for the region with the Permanent Structured Cooperation Agreement (PESCO) initiative (Peternelj et al., 2018). Therefore, as of 2018, the Republic of Turkey has started to take steps to claim the

"Fair Share," one of the energy resources of the Eastern Mediterranean (Merz, 2020; Seufert, 2020).

In the ongoing cooperation negotiations between Israel, Southern Cyprus, and Greece, it has been concluded that the natural gas to be extracted from the Greek Cypriot Administration and Israel will be sent to Vienna via the Greek Island of Cyprus. The fact that the internal conflict that started in the Syrian Arab Republic in 2011 is still not over, the Russian Federation, the Islamic Republic of Iran, and the Republic of Turkey is accepted as the de facto guarantors of the ceasefire agreement in the Syrian Arab Republic by international law after the Astana Agreement. At the same time, it is predicted that the success of the PESCO Initiative initiated by NATO member EU countries and the reflections of the relations between the Republic of Turkey, an important NATO member, and EU countries, within the framework of the warming waters in the Eastern Mediterranean, will continue to constitute one of the remarkable problems of the international agenda in the coming periods.

This study aims to propose a strategic, applicable, reliable, and valid energy cooperation diplomacy within the framework of multiple diplomacies in the literature. In the first part of the study, the energy and security diplomacy experienced during the First World War due to the increasing energy dependence in the European Union and Federal Germany was investigated. In the second part, Russian Federation and Federal Germany's allied and commercial relations from past to present, energy dependency, Ukraine operation, and the tendency towards new energy sources as a result of the sanctions applied to the Russian Federation are examined. In the third chapter, the strategic and economic partnerships of the Republic of Turkey and the Federal Republic of Germany are explained. In the fourth and last chapter, the issue of political and strategic rapprochement of the European Union (EU) countries with the Republic of Turkey, in line with the energy demand expected to increase in the future is discussed.

2.2 The Problem of Energy Dependency of the European Union

The Russian Federation, with its strategic, geopolitical and military elements, is a fundamental actor in the international system together with the United States of America, the Republic of China, and the EU. The relations between the European Union and the Russian Federation are discussed from a geopolitical and geostrategic perspective. In particular, the new policies and strategies brought by the Russian Federation, where most of the natural gas shipments to Europe are carried out, in terms of the European Union and Federal Germany, will be expressed. The European Union has issued a total of five different sanctions packages to the Russian Federation (www.bafa.de).

Russian Federation and Federal Germany are two countries that have faced many times in crises and war periods in the past, especially during the Second World War.

Considering the support of the Russian Federation in the unification of East and West Federal Germany after World War II, and the economic support of Federal Germany after the collapse of the Union of Soviet Socialist Republics (S.S.C.B.), their debt of loyalty to each other is obvious. In the shadow of Ordoliberal rhetoric, German economic policy after the Second World War was based on implicit industrial and innovation policies and public-private partnerships. Such policies and alliances are focused on the gradual development of innovation and the dissemination of new knowledge and new practices through public research and educational institutions.

Today, however, it is problematic that the Federal Republic of Germany can ignore this relationship in view of the union as a whole. Federal Germany and the Russian Federation are two actors with almost equal power in the field of international diplomacy, deepening their relations when they were allies, and there were parties that faced each other in wars in their complexes (Le Renard, 2013: 103). The large-scale projects realized and planned with the increasing foreign trade and investment volume between the two countries continued to support each other in the field of economy and politics and continued to form a reliable basis for the development of bilateral relations (Turgunova, 2013: 1). As Shuster stated in his article published in 2019, the new natural gas pipeline of the Russian Federation with the Federal Republic of Germany, Nord Stream-2, will make Europeans more dependent on the energy of the Russian Federation. The Donald Trump administration, on the other hand, strongly opposed the Nord Stream-2 project, which is planned to transport Russian natural gas directly to the Federal Republic over the Baltic Sea, and accused Angela Merkel's government of being "a prisoner of Russia" (www.dw.com). The Federal Association of German Industries sees huge consequences for the German economy in the absence of oil, gas, and coal deliveries from the Russian Federation. He interprets the competitiveness of the industry as at risk (www.tagesschau.de).

On the Russia-Ukraine operation that threatened Europe while the project was under construction, Federal Germany said that it stopped the certification of the Nord Stream-2 gas pipeline after Moscow's actions in eastern Ukraine (www.edition.cnn.com). The foreign policy of Federal Germany is the unification of the eastern and western blocs after the Cold War, anti-militarist, multinational, economic factors are the progressive factor, and it has a civil power-centered structure focused on international influence (Oruç, 2020). In this respect, it will be insufficient to look at energy only from an economic point of view. Although there are various factors (history, foreign policy norms, public opinion, governments, opinion of business circles, etc.) that direct the foreign policy in the Federal Republic of Germany, the Eastern Policy (Ostpolitik) that it followed over time has also been continued steadily. Although the crises with the Russian Federation (the annexation of Crimea, conflicts in Eastern Ukraine, etc.) caused some changes in this policy, it continued to be implemented and the contacts between Federal Germany and the Russian Federation did not cease (Oruç, 2020).

In this direction, it is possible to continue to take initiatives for more diversification of the problems that may arise (Höhmann et al., 1998: 42). Federal Germany evaluates the solutions within the scope of international crises within the framework of Europe and tries to create outputs at the EU level (Büyükbay, 2017: 26). Therefore, in the realization of these goals, it is seen that the Union's authority over the member states in this area has a very flexible structure (Dyduch et al., 2012: 83, 94–95). The Ukraine-Russia crisis, which has been going on since 2014, has reached its peak with the recent operation, and while all eyes are wondering about the attitude of the European Union towards the Russian Federation, which has energy dependence, Federal Germany's role as a central intermediary in the Ukraine operation, the creation, and management of the EU policy in this regard by the Federal Republic of Germany has also proven one of the examples of the leadership role in the Union (Büyükbay, 2017: 27–29). As a result, it is seen that the Federal Republic of Germany has followed a mixed policy towards the common EU foreign energy policy in the last ten years (Duffield & Westphal, 2011: 169).

The fact that energy companies use energy goods as a foreign policy tool by the states they are affiliated with, especially because of their origins, shows that this state aims to have more power and prestige in the international arena and that it also desires to have a larger and stronger economy (Jirušek & Kuchyňková, 2018). Therefore, in this period, the Russian Federation did not paint a positive image not only in terms of energy but also in terms of freedoms and rights (Krause, 2006). It is the sense of exclusion from the West that pushes them to expand their bilateral relations and cooperate on regional issues (Isachenko, 2021).

2.3 Commercial Relations Between the Republic of Turkey and Germany

Federal Germany is the main trading partner of the Republic of Turkey. This is valid for both import and export products (Gumpel, 1986:43). The development of Turkish-German economic relations, especially since 1981, has been very pleasing (Gumpel, 1986:54). This view is supported by both the Republic of Turkey and the Federal Republic of Germany, because during the German Chancellor's visit to Ankara in July 1985, the wishes of both sides for further development of economic relations were clearly expressed.

It is necessary to look at the development of German-Turkish relations since the beginning of the twentieth century from this perspective. In the beginning, there was close German-Turkish cooperation in the military field (Adanır, 2021: 25). At the point reached today, approximately 5.7 million of our more than 6.7 million citizens living abroad reside in Western Europe (www.mfa.gov.tr), and in the last Bundestag elections, 2.8 million resident citizens of Turkish origin. Nearly 1.2 million of them have the right to vote as German citizens of Turkish origin (www.bbc.com). In this respect, the votes of German citizens of Turkish origin have reached a level that can be taken into account by German politicians.

Russia's operation against Ukraine on February 24, 2022, became a global turning point. Turkey's peaceful world policy approaches, such as the Republic of Turkey, which is a Muslim and pro-Western state, and its mediation role (Irzabek, 2009) between the Islamic Republic of Iran, which the United States considers positive, and the United States, is one of the important proofs of this. Federal Germany's focus is on the Eastern Mediterranean and in the short term, the Middle East and Central Asian Energy through the Republic of Turkey Baku-Tbilisi-Erzurum Natural Gas Pipeline (BTE), Eastern Anatolia Natural Gas Main Transmission Line (Islamic Republic of Iran–Turkey), Blue Stream Natural Gas, which is considered that it is making strategic moves as a future customer of the pipeline (Blue Stream), Russia–Turkey Natural Gas Pipeline (West Line) to Europe, and the Turkish Republic's reserves in the Eastern Mediterranean. As the Republic of Turkey does not yet have an ambitious decarbonization agenda, the biggest challenge for gas in its exclusive field is to stimulate hydrogen production primarily for export, without significant domestic demand. The political relations of the Russian Federation with the West are getting worse. While cooperation in the field of renewable energy and H2 remains one of the few promising areas, this cooperation can significantly contribute to the development of H2 value chains in both countries on behalf of both the Republic of Turkey and the Federal Republic of Germany.

Another important issue in this process is how the transfer will be made. It is problematic to transport the extracted gas from the energy reserves in the Eastern Mediterranean to Europe and other countries (Liu et al., 2021: 159). At this stage, the Republic of Turkey has policies aiming to be an energy security provider and energy corridor (Alhan, 2021). The biggest setback in this process is that the European Union is postponing the membership process of the Republic of Turkey for various excuses. In this direction, while the debates on how to deal with the Republic of Turkey continue in Europe, a clear chain of measures was discussed despite the progress made by the EU on the road to European democracy of the Republic of Turkey (Kramer, 2002). The issue of access to energy resources is a national and international security issue. In this regard, it is important to ensure national energy security, and in the same vein, countries have started to create functional areas (Talseth, 2012).

The Republic of Turkey-Federal Germany Joint Economy and Trade Commission (JETCO), Trade Minister Mehmet Mus, has recently experienced an increase in its trade with Federal Germany by 24% after the customs union agreement with the Republic of Turkey (Felbermayr et al., 2018). Peter Altmaier, Minister of Economy and Energy of the Federal Republic of Germany, was announced that the current trade volume of 37 billion dollars between the Republic of Turkey and Federal Germany will be increased to 50 billion dollars by a balanced increase (www.dunya.com).

Before the tensions in the Eastern Mediterranean, scenarios regarding the possible exit of the Republic of Turkey from NATO were being prepared. To keep them in the alliance, in July 2020, despite the fierce protests of Greece, the German government agreed to supply the Republic of Turkey with the basic components for the construction of six German-made submarines. According to experts, these submarines are further changing the balance of power in the Eastern Mediterranean in favor of the Republic of Turkey, thanks to their advanced propulsion technology (Seufert, 2021).

2.4 The Importance of Eastern Mediterranean Hydrocarbon Deposits to Minimize Energy Dependency

The nuclear disaster that occurred after the earthquake and tsunami at the Fukushima nuclear power plant in Japan in March 2011 led to an intensification of the discussions about the security of the energy system and the continuity of nuclear energy all over the world (Muradov, 2012). As a result of the disaster, countries like the United States have reviewed and updated their safety standards. Others, over time, decided to completely disable their existing nuclear power plants and give up nuclear energy. Namely, Federal Germany has decided to close all nuclear power plants until 2022 (Taner, 2021:35). Nuclear technology, which is used in a wide area such as health, industry, defense, agriculture, and livestock, has special importance for Federal Germany as well as for every country (Yuan et al., 2021; Meng et al., 2021; Yüksel & Dinçer, 2022). The reserve amount of natural gas fields belonging to Israel, Egypt, and the Greek Cypriot Administration is not sufficient for European Union member states (Erdemir, 2019). However, when the diversity of energy resources is evaluated, it has deposits equivalent to 30 billion barrels belonging to the Republic of Turkey (Yaycı, 2012).

In addition, Federal Germany acts from the perspective of great power within the European Union. Energy diplomacy both determines the foreign policies of energy importing countries and explains the political pressure tools of energy exporting countries. EU countries have contingency and prevention plans in place to respond early to supply crises. In the Federal Republic of Germany, large underground storage facilities act as a buffer to compensate for seasonal fluctuations and prevent bottlenecks. Their capacities have been expanding over the years.

In a report published by members of the European Parliament in May 2021, they concluded that unilateral measures in the Eastern Mediterranean region and provocative statements by European Union Member States have seriously affected European Union-Republic of Turkey relations (Kempin, 2021). Thus, the future German government will not only have to face the question of whether it wants and can continue to coordinate and significantly shape European policy towards the Republic of Turkey. The European Union will also have to find an answer to the question of how to act with the Republic of Turkey, a country that is dependent on cooperation in some areas, but whose foreign and domestic policies are increasingly less in line with European ideas (Seufert, 2021).

Despite a difficult situation for the Presidency of the German Council, the scientific service of the German Bundestag spoke about the violation of the "International Law of the Sea" regarding the Turkish-Libyan maritime agreement in

January 2020 (Mock & Dörr, 2008). Germany has traditionally not supported hardliners in the European Union (Greece, Cyprus, and France), curbing a tougher approach to the Republic of Turkey. However, the German government, in its role as President of the Council of the European Union, was only able to assume an intermediary position, although it could occasionally use a direct link. Merkel and Recep Tayyip Erdogan will, for example, persuade the Republic of Turkey to withdraw the drilling and exploration vessel "Oruç Reis" in late autumn 2020. In addition, the Presidency of the Council largely relinquished the field to the Union's High Representative for Foreign Affairs and Security Policy, Josep Borrell (Böttger & Jopp, 2021).

2.5 Conclusion

The economic power of the European Union is not taken into account much in the military field. For this reason, European Union countries always take this situation into account in international policies and establish relations. The reputation and position of Federal Germany in the European Union (EU) are mentioned. However, in terms of the countries in the union, the country with the highest energy needs simultaneously with industrial development is undoubtedly Federal Germany.

However, recent developments also highlight the dependence of Germany and Europe on fossil energy imports and Russia's dominant position as an energy supplier. At this stage, alternative energy suppliers of the European Union could be Azerbaijan, Egypt, the Syrian Arab Republic, the Republic of Iraq, and possibly Turkmenistan and the Islamic Republic of Iran, which further increases the importance of the Republic of Turkey for the West. It will also be very difficult to deal with the Ukraine problem, as the leadership of the United States of America has weakened, and no other option has taken its place (Turan, 2022).

In 2020, around 70 percent of all energy consumption in Germany was met by imported, mostly fossil fuels (hard coal, mineral oil, natural gas, and uranium) (Mikayilov et al., 2020; Yüksel et al., 2020; Du et al., 2020; Liu et al., 2020; Shang et al., 2021). Oil, which has a share of 28% in final energy consumption, is still the most important fossil primary energy source, followed by natural gas (27%) and hard coal (4%). For all three energy sources, Russia occupies a central market position as Germany's main supplier. In particular, the variable foreign policy of Federal Germany can be considered as an opportunity for the Republic of Turkey and the gas hydrate reserves in its natural gas fields can develop new strategies in terms of being a member of the union and foreign trade with the energy it will obtain from the Eastern Mediterranean.

It is known that the Republic of Turkey has a Muslim majority and is different from the Christian culture of Europe in this respect. A large number of Turkish citizens in the world live in Europe. For this reason, the Republic of Turkey, as a moderate Muslim state in Europe, forms a bridge between two great civilizations. Delaying the accession phase for a long time can lead to frustration and disappointment, ultimately to a reluctance and loss of confidence in the European identity and idea. It is considered that this will not be in the interest of the future of the European Union. In light of all this, the Republic of Turkey is not a country that can be negotiated with "Hard Power" diplomacy. This is why, based on the examples of the fifth fleet belonging to the United States of America (due to the commercial importance of the Strait of Hormuz) in the Persian Gulf, England (United Kingdom) activated Anglo-Persian oil companies to dominate the energy resources in the Middle East, it has over the Republic of Turkey. Strategic results will not be successful. As in the past, the relations between Federal Germany and the Republic of Turkey should be evaluated with the "Soft Power" energy diplomacy strategy of the energy to be obtained from the Eastern Mediterranean.

The Republic of Turkey established TPAO (Turkish Petroleum Corporation) in 1954, with law no. 6327, to carry out hydrocarbon exploration, drilling, production, refinery, and marketing activities on behalf of the public. Today, TPAO continues its activities as the national oil company that carries out hydrocarbon exploration and production projects (www.tpao.gov.tr). However, capitalism, together with neoliberal authoritarianism, re-evaluated the structural and functional aspects of the states, with the vision of an international company with high potential and having a say in the global energy markets that dominates liberal money, just before the collapse of the Union of Soviet Socialist Republics (USSR) on December 26, 1991. Based on the example of the Russian Federation, which was established as the Ministry of Industry and later transformed into a state natural gas company, its evaluation will also draw attention to energy security and support the political argument of the Republic of Turkey.

With the further intensification of the conflict with the Russian Federation or wider sanctions by the European Union and its partners, the reduction of fossil energy imports has acquired an entirely new urgency. For this reason, Federal Germany is not under the obligation to accept the regional policy vision of the Turkish Republic, but it has to come to terms with it as one of the new realities. Of all the states in the region, the Republic of Turkey is certainly the most desirable "model" to play such a central role in the diplomacy of this crucial region. The most basic example of this is undoubtedly the successful diplomacy traffic carried out during the Russia-Ukraine operation. Therefore, despite major changes in the region and the world, Federal Germany's relationship with the Republic of Turkey should remain strong and positive for the next decades.

References

Adanır, F. (2021). *Wandlungen des deutschen Türkeibildes in der ersten Hälfte des 20. Jahrhunderts* (pp. 23–42).

Alhan, M. A. (2021). Doğu Akdeniz enerji kaynakları ekseninde: Türkiye, Avrupa ve Amerika Birleşik Devletleri basınındaki haber başlıklarının karşılaştırmalı duygu analizi. *İstanbul Ticaret Üniversitesi Sosyal Bilimler Dergisi, 20*(42), 1438–1466. https://doi.org/10.46928/iticusbe.932569

Axt, H. J. (2020). Nervenkrieg um Energie-Ressourcen im östlichen Mittelmeer. *Südosteuropa Mitteilungen, 01-02*, 83–98.

Bhuiyan, M. A., Dinçer, H., Yüksel, S., Mikhaylov, A., Danish, M. S. S., Pinter, G., et al. (2022). Economic indicators and bioenergy supply in developed economies: QROF-DEMATEL and random forest models. *Energy Reports, 8*, 561–570.

Böttger, K., & Jopp, M. (2021). Die deutsche EU-Ratspräsidentschaft 2020: selektive Föderalisierung des Integrationsprozesses. *integration, 44*(1), 3–22.

Büyükbay, C. (2017). Federal Almanya'nın AB İçerisindeki Liderlik Rolü: Uluslararası Krizler Bağlamında Dış Politikada Süreklilik ve Değişim. *Ege Stratejik Araştırmalar Dergisi., 8*(1), 19–38.

Dong, W., Zhao, G., Yüksel, S., Dinçer, H., & Ubay, G. G. (2022). A novel hybrid decision making approach for the strategic selection of wind energy projects. *Renewable Energy, 185*, 321–337.

Du, L., Dinçer, H., Ersin, İ., & Yüksel, S. (2020). IT2 fuzzy-based multidimensional evaluation of coal energy for sustainable economic development. *Energies, 13*(10), 2453.

Duffield, J. S., & Westphal, K. (2011). Germany and EU energy policy: Conflicted champion of integration? In *Toward a common European Union energy policy* (pp. 169–186). Springer.

Dyduch, J., Klimowicz, M., & Michalewska-Pawlak, M. (2012). Evolution in the context of the treaty of Lisbon and European 2020 strategy. University of Wroclaw. *Faculty of Social Sciences.*, 83–115.

Erdemir, E. (2019). Avrupa Birliği'nin enerji Güvenliğinde Doğu Akdeniz: Hidrokarbon Kaynaklarının Kıbrıs Sorunun Çözümüne Etkisi. *EURA Politika, 3*(2), 37–38.

Felbermayr, G., Gröschl, J. K., Kohler, W., Brändle, T., & Koch, A. (2018). *Auswirkungen der Marktöffnung im Außenhandel für Wirtschaft, Wachstum und Arbeitsplätze in Deutschland (1990–2014)* (No. 92). ifo Forschungsberichte.

Gumpel, W. (1986). Die Wirtschaftsbeziehungen zwischen der Türkei und der Bundesrepublik Deutschland. *Comparative Southeast European Studies, 35*(1), 43–55.

Höhmann, H. H., Meier, C., & Timmermann, H. (1998). Russia and Germany in Europe: Recent trends in political and economic relations. *Journal of Communist Studies and Transition Politics, 14*(3), 24–57.

Irzabek, J. (2009). Pożegnanie Europy. *Newsweek Polska, 35*, 56.

Isachenko, D. (2021). Türkei und Russland: die Logik einer konfliktträchtigen Zusammenarbeit.

Jirušek, M., & Kuchyňková, P. (2018). The Conduct of Gazprom in Central and Eastern Europe: A Tool of the Kremlin, or Just an Adaptable Player? *32*(4), 818–844.

Kempin, R. (2021). Frankreich und die Türkei–Machtpoker ohne Sieger. *integration, 44*(3), 177–188.

Kısacık, S., & Erenel, F. (2019). Doğu Akdeniz Güvenlik Algılamaları Bağlamında, Kalıcı Yapılandırılmış İş birliği Savunma Anlaşması (The Permanent Structured Cooperatıon-Pesco) ve Enerji Güvenliği Meselelerinin Avrupa Birliği-Türkiye İlişkilerine Olası Yansımalarını Anlamak. *Türkiye Siyaset Bilimi Dergisi, 2*(1), 51–76.

Kostis, P., Dinçer, H., & Yüksel, S. (2022). Knowledge-based energy investments of European Economies and Policy Recommendations for Sustainable Development. *Journal of the Knowledge Economy*, 1–33.

Kou, G., Yüksel, S., & Dinçer, H. (2022). Inventive problem-solving map of innovative carbon emission strategies for solar energy-based transportation investment projects. *Applied Energy, 311*, 118680.

Kramer, H. (2002). Die Türkei und die Kopenhagener Kriterien.

Krause, H. (2006). Sekizler Grubu'nun yeni başkanı Rusya. DW.

Le Renard, C. (2013). External actors and national preference formation: European Energy Security Policy and Relations with Russia. A Dissertation submitted in partial fulfillment of the requirements for the degree of Doctor of Philosophy at George Mason University. 389.

Liu, H., Yüksel, S., & Dinçer, H. (2020). Analyzing the criteria of efficient carbon capture and separation technologies for sustainable clean energy usage. *Energies, 13*(10), 2592.

Liu, Y., Gong, X., Yüksel, S., Dinçer, H., & Aydın, R. (2021). A multidimensional outlook to energy investments for the countries with continental shelves in East Mediterranean region with hybrid decision making model based on IVIF logic. *Energy Reports, 7*, 158–173.

Meng, Y., Dincer, H., & Yüksel, S. (2021). Understanding the innovative developments with two-stage technology S-curve of nuclear energy projects. *Progress in Nuclear Energy, 140*, 103924.

Merz, F. (2020). Tumult im östlichen Mittelmeerraum. *CSS Analysen zur Sicherheitspolitik, 275.*

Mikayilov, J. I., Mukhtarov, S., Dinçer, H., Yüksel, S., & Aydın, R. (2020). Elasticity analysis of fossil energy sources for sustainable economies: A case of gasoline consumption in Turkey. *Energies, 13*(3), 731.

Mock, M., & Dörr, B. (2008). *Wissenschaftlicher Dienst des Deutschen Bundestags* (pp. 8–11). Fragen zu den Goldbeständen der Deutschen Bundesbank.

Mukhtarov, S., Yüksel, S., & Dinçer, H. (2022). The impact of financial development on renewable energy consumption: Evidence from Turkey. *Renewable Energy.*

Muradov, E. (2012). Federal Almanya'nın Nükleer Enerji Politikasını Etkileyen Faktörler. *Öneri Dergisi, 10*(38), 105–111.

Oruç, K. (2020). *Neo-klasik realist teori bağlamında Federal Almanya ve Rusya arasındaki ilişkilerin AB enerji politikasına yansıması* (Master's thesis, Sosyal Bilimler Enstitüsü).

Peternelj, B., Kurecic, P., & Kozina, G. (2018). The Permanent Structured Cooperation Initiative (PESCO) as a step towards the European Defense Union. *Economic and Social Development: Book of Proceedings*, 38–48.

Seufert, G: Störenfried aus Ankara, in: Zeit Online, 28. August 2020.

Seufert, G. (2021). Die Türkeipolitik der künftigen Bundesregierung: Konfliktlinien und Kooperationsfelder.

Shang, H., Su, F., Yüksel, S., & Dinçer, H. (2021). Identifying the strategic priorities of the technical factors for the sustainable low carbon industry based on macroeconomic conditions. *SAGE Open, 11*(2), 21582440211016345.

Shuster, S. (18 Şubat 2019). Russia and China are driving a wedge between estranged U.S. and Europe.

Talseth, L. U. C. (2012). The EU-Russia Energy Dialogue. *Travelling Without Moving. German In-stitute for International and Security Affairs.*

Taner, A. C. (2021). *Onuncu yılında Fukushima Daiichi Nükleer Santral Kazası*, TMMOB, *Ankara.* 32–44 ISBN: 978–605–01-1400-3.

Turan, İ. (2022). Liderlik yokluğunda Rusya'ya karşı koymak kolay olmayacak gibi. *Dünya Gazetesi.*

Turgunova, V. (2013). The nexus of politics and the economy: A Case Study of RussianGerman Relations. University of Tampere. *International Relations. Master's Thesis.* 85.

Yaycı, C. (2012). Doğu Akdeniz'de Yetki Alanlarının Paylaşılması Sorunu ve Türkiye. *Bilge Strateji, 4*(6), 1–70.

Yuan, G., Xie, F., Dinçer, H., & Yüksel, S. (2021). The theory of inventive problem solving (TRIZ)-based strategic mapping of green nuclear energy investments with spherical fuzzy group decision-making approach. *International Journal of Energy Research, 45*(8), 12284–12300.

Yüksel, S., & Dinçer, H. (2022). Identifying the strategic priorities of nuclear energy investments using hesitant 2-tuple interval-valued Pythagorean fuzzy DEMATEL. *Progress in Nuclear Energy, 145*, 104103.

Yüksel, S., Dinçer, H., Karakuş, H., & Ubay, G. G. (2020). The negative effects of carbon emission on FDI: A comparative analysis between E7 and G7 countries. In *Handbook of research on sustainable supply chain management for the global economy* (pp. 20–35). IGI Global.

Zhang, Y., Zhang, Y., Gong, C., Dinçer, H., & Yüksel, S. (2022). An integrated hesitant 2-tuple Pythagorean fuzzy analysis of QFD-based innovation cost and duration for renewable energy projects. *Energy, 123561.*

Chapter 3
Strategy Recommendations for Increasing Solar Energy Investments

Buse Kevser Günoğlu, Kader Ulakçı, and Zehra Akçe

Abstract The aim of this study is to determine the right strategies for increasing solar energy investments. In this context, articles with "solar energy" in their titles for 2020 and 2021 in the Web of Science database are included in the review. In this context, 933 articles are identified. After that, the abstracts of the mentioned articles are analyzed by data mining method. To achieve this aim, the N-gram application over the KNIME program has been taken into consideration. In this process, the most frequent double words and triple words are determined. Thanks to these prominent word groups, it has been tried to determine the factors that are important for solar energy investments. The biggest contribution of this study to the literature is the simultaneous consideration of very comprehensive studies to present correct policy recommendations to solar energy investors. By examining all current studies on solar energy investments, it will be possible to determine the right strategy proposals.

Keywords Solar Energy · Solar Energy Investments · Renewable Energy · KNIME · N-gram · Data Mining · Investment Strategies

3.1 Introduction

Energy is a necessity that countries cannot give up, both socially and economically. Therefore, regardless of the price, countries have an obligation to meet this need. The energy need is mostly supplied from fossil fuels such as coal and oil around the world (Dong et al., 2022). Low cost is the biggest advantage of these energy types. On the other hand, there are some disadvantages of using fossil fuels in energy production (Zhang et al., 2022). For example, a significant amount of carbon gas is emitted into the atmosphere as a result of the use of fossil fuels. This situation causes

---

B. K. Günoğlu (✉) · K. Ulakçı · Z. Akçe
The School of Business, İstanbul Medipol University, Istanbul, Turkey
e-mail: bkgunoglu@medipol.edu.tr; kader.ulakci@medipol.edu.tr; zakce@medipol.edu.tr

H. Dinçer, S. Yüksel (eds.), *Circular Economy and the Energy Market*, Contributions to Economics, https://doi.org/10.1007/978-3-031-13146-2_3

serious environmental pollution. If this problem is not eliminated, the lives of many living things will be in danger (Kou et al., 2022).

The use of renewable energy is one of the applications that can be considered in solving this problem mentioned above. Increasing environmental pollution due to the increase in the use of natural resources and the widespread use of fossil fuels has increased the importance of renewable energy use (Liang, 2020). Renewable energy means producing energy from natural sources such as the sun and wind. These types of energy have some advantages. First of all, the carbon gas released into the air as a result of the use of renewable energy is reduced to minimum levels (Mukhtarov et al., 2022). With the development of renewable energy technology, carbon emissions released into the atmosphere due to fossil fuel use will decrease (Evans, 2011). Due to this mentioned point, renewable energies are accepted as an environmentally friendly type of energy. Another advantage of renewable energy types is that countries produce their own energy. This situation reduces the foreign dependency of countries on energy (Kostis et al., 2022). Thanks to the policies aimed at increasing the renewable energy resources of the countries, it helps to reduce the foreign dependency in energy and to increase the environmental sustainability of the countries (Jiankun, 2012). In this way, it will be much easier for the country to achieve its sustainable economic development goals.

Solar energy is one of the most popular types of renewable energy. Solar energy means generating electricity by evaluating the rays coming from the sun. This type of energy has many contributions to the social and economic development of the country. Since only the sun's rays are taken into account in this process, there is no carbon gas emission to the atmosphere (Bhuiyan et al., 2022). In this way, the energy produced is environmentally friendly. Photovoltaic solar energy, a renewable energy source, is seen as an alternative to cope with the challenges of energy scarcity from traditional sources (Sampaio, 2017). On the other hand, it is possible to talk about some negative aspects of solar energy investments. For example, the initial cost of solar energy investments is very high. In this case, it creates serious financial problems for investors. In addition, the technical competence of the company that can make solar energy investments must be high. Otherwise, it will be very difficult to achieve success in these investments. Due to these negativities, it becomes difficult to increase solar energy investments.

Considering the above-mentioned issues, it is seen that solar energy investments have both positive and negative aspects. Therefore, it is essential to develop the right strategies in order to increase these investments (Yüksel & Dinçer, 2022). Another important issue for the success of solar energy investments is the quality of the working personnel. The literature review supports that the lack of qualified personnel is one of the biggest problems in this sector (Meijer, 2019). In his work, he emphasized the lack of qualified, competent, and knowledgeable personnel who can handle complex technologies. Since these investment types are projects with a complex structure, qualified personnel are needed to a great extent. Another strategy that can be developed to increase solar energy investments is for technical competencies. In order for these projects to be successful, the investor company must have the necessary technical equipment (Wan et al., 2022). As a result, there are different types of strategies to achieve success in solar energy investments. The important point here is to determine the most correct one among these strategy alternatives (Dinçer et al., 2022).

Considering the situation in Turkey, since the energy resources in the country are insufficient to meet the energy needs of the society, more than half of its energy needs are met by importing. Turkey's diversification of energy resources and the necessity of domestic renewable energy production are also necessary for the development of the country (Bulut & Muratoglu, 2018). Wind energy is the most preferred renewable energy source in Turkey; it was observed that solar energy, hydraulic energy, biomass energy, geothermal energy, and wave energy followed it (Çolak & Kaya, 2017). It is thought that the renewable energy resource increase target in Turkey's 2023 targets is uncertain due to costs, but this target will be achieved with incentives to the private sector and costs will be reduced (Deveci & Güler, 2020; Yüksel et al., 2022a, b).

In this study, it is aimed to examine the solar energy and investment problems in the articles and to determine the most effective strategies to increase solar energy investments. It is aimed to examine the factors that play the most role in increasing solar energy investments and to offer solutions for these factors. For this purpose, all articles with the phrase "Solar Energy" in the title and included in the Web of Science search engine from the last two years were included in the review. Data mining analysis was carried out by using the summary sections of these articles. In this process, the KNIME program was used. The most common double and triple word groups in these articles were determined by the N-gram approach. Considering the contents of these word groups, it is possible to determine effective strategies for solar energy investors. The biggest contribution of this study to the literature is the determination of the right strategies with an original method in order to increase solar energy investments, which contribute significantly to the social and economic development of countries. The analysis results to be obtained will help the investors to make the right decision.

This study consists of five parts. After the introduction, the second part includes a literature review. The third part of the study gives information about the method used in the analysis process. In the fourth chapter, the results of the analysis are shared. The fifth part of the study includes the conclusion part.

3.2 Theoretical Information

There are many different studies in the literature on solar energy investments. In a significant part of these studies, it is aimed to determine the right strategies to increase the success of solar energy investments. A significant part of these studies emphasized the importance of technological development in order to increase the efficiency of solar energy investments. Solar energy investments are complex projects that involve quite extensive processes. Therefore, the costs of solar energy investments are quite high (Zhang et al., 2020). Companies need to have the necessary technological competence to overcome this problem (Kabir et al., 2018). Solar energy investment companies with advanced technology can implement processes at lower cost (Lehtola & Zahedi, 2019). This situation contributes to increasing the efficiency of solar energy projects (Creutzig et al., 2017). Raina and Sinha (2019) aimed to produce the right strategies to increase the efficiency of solar energy investments in India. In this context, they emphasized that technological development is an important strategy and that the Paris Agreement will contribute to the development of this strategy. Similarly, Li et al. (2017) also emphasized the importance of technological investment in order to increase the efficiency of solar energy investments. Quitzow et al. (2017) examined the factors affecting the performance of solar energy investments in China. In order to achieve this aim, the necessity of technological investments has been underlined.

In some of the studies, the importance of personnel quality was emphasized in order to increase the efficiency of solar energy investments. Solar energy projects are investments that include extensive engineering knowledge. Therefore, qualified personnel are needed to increase the performance of these investments (Adalı et al., 2022). In case of employment of incompetent personnel, a possible malfunction in these projects will not be eliminated in a short time. In this case, it will reduce the efficiency of investments. Sindhu et al. (2016) stated that personnel who are not experts in the installation, maintenance, and operation of solar energy equipment will be insufficient in case of malfunctions. They also mentioned the lack of educational institutions suitable for training qualified personnel and experts in this field. In another study, it was stated that one of the obstacles to such investments is the lack of qualified human resources. As a result of the analyses made in the field of renewable energy, the incompatibility between the education system and the sector demand has been shown as one of the reasons for this deficiency (Lucas et al., 2018). Similarly, Boamah (2020) also mentioned in his study the importance of maintaining solar energy systems and the difficulty of finding competent personnel to provide system maintenance.

It has been emphasized that high investment costs and decreasing profit margins in the solar energy sector reduce labor costs. The importance of the role of states in promoting the acquisition of human capital in employing knowledgeable and skilled workers has been underlined (Dicce & Ewers, 2021; Haiyun et al., 2021). Zhang et al. (2017) stated that the installation of solar energy systems becomes difficult due to the lack of qualified personnel. The lack of skilled personnel leads to the necessity of employing personnel with expertise in fields such as electrical and electronics. They stated that employing non-expert personnel will cause distrust in potential customers and this will reduce the demand for solar energy technology. In many studies, the importance of qualified personnel for increasing solar energy investments has been mentioned. It was also mentioned that governments should support the employment of qualified personnel in the field of renewable energy. It is stated that state supports such as corporate tax reductions for these investments, customs tax reductions on items used in investments, and the supply of qualified personnel in this field may attract the attention of investors (Wang et al., 2019).

On the other hand, in some of the studies, it has been stated that customer satisfaction is necessary to increase the success of solar energy investments. Solar energy investments ultimately aim for customers to use energy more efficiently. In this context, it is vital to clearly define customer expectations. In order to achieve this goal, it is necessary to conduct comprehensive analyses to understand the demands of different types of customers. This will contribute to increasing customer satisfaction (Zhao et al., 2021; Yuan et al., 2021). Thus, solar energy companies will be preferred more and this will help to increase the profitability of the companies. Since customers who prefer renewable energy are diverse, their expectations also differ. Therefore, the separation of customers as commercial and non-commercial will ensure more effective after-sales support. Thus, providing special services for the special needs of customers will contribute to increasing customer satisfaction (Li et al., 2021). Reducing the cost and achieving a higher user experience were seen as the key to supporting the sustainable transition. It has been stated that customer satisfaction is of key importance for solar energy businesses to establish long-term relationships with customers (Yadav et al., 2019). Rigo et al. (2021) emphasized the need for businesses to define their relationships with their customers.

Services and procedures designed for different customer segments will strengthen the customer–business relationship. It is stated that this will increase customer satisfaction in a positive way (Li et al., 2021). Ding et al. (2021) mentioned that it is important to increase the environmental awareness of the public and to have information about the advantages of renewable energy in energy saving and environmental protection, especially in developing countries where solar energy investments are still new. They emphasize that since such steps taken to inform the public will lead to a good relationship of trust with potential customers, the trust gained will have a positive effect on customer satisfaction. Peng (2018) argued that company behaviors towards customer satisfaction, such as technical support and after-sales support, increase customer satisfaction and competitiveness. In another study, it was stated that sustainable consumption opportunities are an important criterion in the dimension of customer satisfaction (Li et al., 2020).

3.3 Methodology

Data mining is an interdisciplinary subfield of computer science and statistics with the general aim of extracting information (intelligently) from a data set and converting the information into an understandable structure for later use. Data mining, also known as knowledge discovery in data (KDD), is the process of extracting patterns and other valuable information from large data sets. The purpose of data mining is to extract needed patterns and information from large amounts of data. Data analysis and data mining are different from each other. Regardless of the amount of data, data analysis is used to test models and hypotheses in the dataset. Data mining is the use of machine learning and statistical models to uncover hidden patterns in large amounts of data.

Data mining is important because of its ability to uncover hidden patterns, trends, correlations, and anomalies in datasets. This information obtained by data mining is used together with traditional data analysis to improve decision-making processes and strategic planning. In the data-centric world we live in, it is important to gain as many advantages as possible. Data mining plays an important role in helping data scientists and companies find the information they need by helping to discover hidden patterns of automated behavior and trends.

KNIME (Konstanz Information Miner) is a free and open source data analysis, reporting and integration platform. KNIME allows users to visually create data streams (or pipelines), selectively execute some or all of the analysis steps, then examine results and models using interactive widgets and views. N-gram models are a statistical language model used to predict the next element of a sequential sequence using the (n-1) format Markov chain. N-grams (or ngrams) is the general name given to sequential arrays of n elements. In the context of natural language processing and computational linguistics, the elements that make up ngrams can be selected as words, syllables, phonemes, or letters in a spoken text or written text, depending on the need and application area.

The N-gram algorithm is used to find the repetition rate in a sequential sequence. The variable expressed with N represents the value for which the repetition is controlled, while the gram corresponds to the weight of this repeated value in the array. Today, N-gram models are frequently used in fields such as statistical based natural language processing, computational linguistics, linguistic modeling, statistics, and communication theory. N-gram models have gained popularity because they are scalable and much simpler compared to other algorithms and models that do the same job. For this reason, it has been used in many different studies in the literature.

Experiments in the life sciences include tools from various fields. Passing data between these tools often results in complex scripts to control data flow, data conversion, and statistical analysis. Such scripts are not only platform dependent, but they tend to grow as the experiment progresses. This hinders the reproducibility of the experiment. KNIME aims to solve these problems by providing a platform to connect tools graphically and guaranteeing the same results in different operating systems (Fillbrunn et al., 2017). Varsou et al. (2018) stated that access and data mining for multiple chemical databases can be done through the KNIME interface. In another study, KNIME (Konstanz Information Miner) is defined as a well-known, Java-based, modular data mining application that facilitates easy assembly, testing and operation of data mining pipelines (Adekitan & Salau, 2019). Mohasseb et al. (2020) argued that examining the increasing cyber security attacks in recent years with text analysis and data mining techniques will play an important role in detecting and preventing future security threats. In another study using the KNIME N-gram method, an examination was made for the strategies that countries should develop in order to achieve their sustainable development goals. As a result, he stated what kind of activities can make important contributions to achieve sustainable developments (Sebestyén et al., 2020).

3.4 Key Determinants to Improve Solar Energy Investments

In this study, in order to determine the right strategies for increasing solar energy investments, articles with "solar energy" in the titles of 2020 and 2021 in the Web of Science database were included in the scope of the review. In this context, 933 articles were identified and data mining analysis was carried out using the summary sections of these articles. The most common double words and triple words in the abstracts of the mentioned articles were determined. Thanks to these prominent word groups, it has been tried to determine the factors that are important for solar energy investments.

Reach with the "solar energy" keyword and 2020–2021 filters made on the Web of Science site. The summary sections of 933 articles were printed as Excel documents. The received Excel document was read through the Excel Reader node in the KNIME program. Arrays of columns specified by the Strings to Document node are used as titles, authors, and full text. Alphanumeric characters are converted to lowercase with the Case Converter node. With the Punctuation Erasure node, all punctuation in the document has been removed. With the Stop Word Filter node, pause words such as "and" and "or" are filtered out. With the Bag Of Words Creator node, columns were created from the terms in the file. With the TF node, the relative term frequency of each term was calculated and a column containing the values was created. After these stages, NGram Creator was used to determine the most used 2-word and 3-word words. Excel Writer was used to export the resulting outputs to Excel.

As a result of data mining using the N-gram application of the KNIME program, the most repeated binary words (Table 3.1) and the most repeated triplet words (Table 3.2) are determined. As can be seen in the tables, it has been observed that the articles published in the last two years mostly focus on energy storage and energy efficiency.

Table 3.1 The most repeated binary words

	Corpus frequency	Document frequency	Sentence frequency
Energy storage	32064	95	264
Photovoltaic Pv	15660	76	155
Energy conversion	15458	63	150
Energy harvesting	13412	52	127
Solar cells	11706	45	108
Energy efficiency	11430	47	109
Thermal conductivity	9404	30	77

Table 3.2 The most repeated triplet words

	Corpus frequency	Document frequency	Sentence frequency
Solar energy conversion	9996	46	104
Solar energy harvesting	8912	39	91
Thermal energy storage	8696	38	88
Solar energy storage	5720	23	54
Solar Photovoltaic Pv	4732	22	45
Energy storage system	4307	17	42
Photovoltaic solar energy	2930	12	28
Energy storage systems	2716	12	26
Solar energy technology	2444	9	22
Photovoltaic Pv systems	2340	12	24
Dye-sensitized solar cells	2292	13	26
Energy conversion storage	2206	11	25

3.5 Conclusion

Energy is a need that countries must meet, regardless of its price. This necessity causes countries to prefer fossil fuels with lower costs. However, as it is known, in addition to the cost advantage, there are also disadvantages of using fossil fuels. The amount of carbon gas emitted into the atmosphere because of the use of fossil fuels is very high and this leads to serious environmental pollution. It is predicted that this situation, the effects of which we can see even today, will endanger the lives of many living things in the long run. One of the solutions to this problem is to ensure the widespread use of renewable energy. Renewable energy means producing energy from natural sources such as the sun and wind. Renewable energies, which have advantages such as minimizing the carbon gas released into the air, are accepted as environmentally friendly energy types. Another advantage of renewable energy types is that countries can produce their own energy. This situation reduces the foreign dependency of countries on energy. Solar energy is one of the most popular types of renewable energy. Solar energy means generating electricity by evaluating the rays coming from the sun. On the other hand, renewable energy investments also have some disadvantages. For example, the initial cost of such investments is very high. This situation creates serious financial problems for investors.

In this study, it is aimed to examine the solar energy and investment problems in the articles and to determine the most effective strategies to increase solar energy investments. The factors that play the most role in increasing solar energy investments will be examined and solution proposals will be presented regarding these factors. For this purpose, 933 articles were identified, and data mining analysis was carried out using the summary sections of these articles. The most common double words and triple words in the abstracts of the mentioned articles were determined. Thanks to these prominent word groups, it has been tried to determine the factors that are important for solar energy investments. As a result of data mining using the

N-gram application of the KNIME program, the most repeated binary words (Table 3.1) and the most repeated triplet words (Table 3.2) were determined.

It is possible to determine effective strategies for solar energy investors by considering the contents of these word groups. As seen in the tables, it has been observed that the articles published in the last two years mostly focus on energy storage and energy efficiency. Based on the results of the analysis, we can say that the two biggest obstacles to the increase of renewable energy investments and especially solar energy investments are high cost and lack of technological infrastructure. It is seen that to increase solar energy investments, it is necessary to reduce costs and invest in technology. Investors should attach importance to technological investments so that energy can be stored or produced more efficiently, that is, less costly. Increasing technological investments will indirectly reduce costs.

Basically, in this research article, it was examined which strategic targets should be determined to increase solar energy investments. Solar energy technologies have become well-established and popular technologies around the world. It is expected that investments to be made in the field of solar energy and developing solar energy technologies will attract the attention of many more investors soon. For this reason, it is important to carry out more comprehensive studies on how to increase solar energy investments in future studies.

Acknowledgement This study is derived from the master thesis of Buse Kevser Günoğlu in İstanbul Medipol University.

References

Adalı, Z., Dinçer, H., Eti, S., Mikhaylov, A., & Yüksel, S. (2022). Identifying new perspectives on geothermal energy investments. In *Multidimensional strategic outlook on global competitive energy economics and finance*. Emerald Publishing Limited.

Adekitan, A. I., & Salau, O. (2019). The impact of engineering students' performance in the first three years on their graduation result using educational data mining. *Heliyon*, e01250.

Bhuiyan, M. A., Dinçer, H., Yüksel, S., Mikhaylov, A., Danish, M. S. S., Pinter, G., et al. (2022). Economic indicators and bioenergy supply in developed economies: QROF-DEMATEL and random forest models. *Energy Reports, 8*, 561–570.

Boamah, F. (2020). Desirable or debatable? Putting Africa's decentralised solar energy futures in context. *Energy Research & Social Science*, 101390.

Bulut, U., & Muratoglu, G. (2018). Renewable energy in Turkey: Great potential, low but increasing utilization, and an empirical analysis on renewable energy-growth nexus. *Energy Policy*, 240–250.

Çolak, M., & Kaya, İ. (2017). Prioritization of renewable energy alternatives by using an integrated fuzzy MCDM model: A real case application for Turkey. *Renewable and Sustainable Energy Reviews*, 840–853.

Creutzig, F., Agoston, P., Goldschmidt, J. C., & Pietzcker, R. (2017). The underestimated potential of solar energy to mitigate climate change. *Nature Energy*, 1–9.

Deveci, K., & Güler, Ö. (2020). A CMOPSO based multi-objective optimization of renewable energy planning: Case of Turkey. *Renewable Energy*, 578–590.

Dicce, R., & Ewers, M. C. (2021). Solar labor market transitions in the United Arab Emirates. *Geoforum*, 54–64.
Dinçer, H., Yüksel, S., & Martínez, L. (2022). Collaboration enhanced hybrid fuzzy decision-making approach to analyze the renewable energy investment projects. *Energy Reports, 8*, 377–389.
Ding, L., Shi, Y., He, C., Dai, Q., Zhang, Z., Li, J., & Zhou, L. (2021). How does satisfaction of solar PV users enhance their trust in the power grid? - Evidence from PPAPs in rural China. *Energy, Sustainability and Society*, 1–19.
Dong, W., Zhao, G., Yüksel, S., Dinçer, H., & Ubay, G. G. (2022). A novel hybrid decision making approach for the strategic selection of wind energy projects. *Renewable Energy, 185*, 321–337.
Evans, V. S. A. (2011). Optimization methods applied to renewable and sustainable energy: A review. *Renewable and Sustainable Energy Reviews.*
Fillbrunn, A., Dietz, C., Pfeuffer, J., Rahn, R., Landrum, G. A., & Berthold, M. R. (2017). KNIME for reproducible cross-domain analysis of life science data. *Journal of Biotechnology*, 149–156.
Haiyun, C., Zhixiong, H., Yüksel, S., & Dinçer, H. (2021). Analysis of the innovation strategies for green supply chain management in the energy industry using the QFD-based hybrid interval valued intuitionistic fuzzy decision approach. *Renewable and Sustainable Energy Reviews, 143*, 110844.
Jiankun, O. Y. Z. (2012). China's strategy for energy development and climate change mitigation. *Energy Policy.*
Kabir, E., Kumar, P., Kumar, S., Adelodun, A. A., & Kim, K.-H. (2018). Solar energy: Potential and future prospects. *Renewable and Sustainable Energy Reviews*, 894–900.
Kostis, P., Dinçer, H., & Yüksel, S. (2022). Knowledge-based energy investments of European economies and policy recommendations for sustainable development. *Journal of the Knowledge Economy*, 1–33.
Kou, G., Yüksel, S., & Dinçer, H. (2022). Inventive problem-solving map of innovative carbon emission strategies for solar energy-based transportation investment projects. *Applied Energy, 311*, 118680.
Lehtola, T., & Zahedi, A. (2019). Solar energy and wind power supply supported by storage technology: A review. *Sustainable Energy Technologies and Assessments*, 25–31.
Li, M.-J., Zhu, H., Guo, J.-Q., Wang, K., & Tao, W.-Q. (2017). The development technology and applications of supercritical CO 2 power cycle in nuclear energy, solar energy and other energy industries. *Applied Thermal Engineering*, 255–275.
Li, X., Zhu, S., Yüksel, S., Dincer, H., & Ubay, G. (2020). Kano-based mapping of innovation strategies for renewable energy alternatives using hybrid interval type-2 fuzzy decision-making approach. *Energy, 211*, 118679.
Li, Y. X., Wu, Z. X., Dinçer, H., Kalkavan, H., & Yüksel, S. (2021). Analyzing TRIZ-based strategic priorities of customer expectations for renewable energy investments with interval type-2 fuzzy modeling. *Energy Reports, 7*, 95–108.
Liang, Z. B. C. Q. (2020). Metal–organic frameworks as a platform for clean energy applications. *EnergyChem.*
Lucas, H., Pinnington, S., & Cabeza, L. F. (2018). Education and training gaps in the renewable energy sector. *Solar Energy*, 449–455.
Meijer, L. L. (2019). Barriers and drivers for technology commercialization by SMEs in the Dutch sustainable energy sector. *Renewable and Sustainable Energy Reviews, 112*, 114–126.
Mohasseb, A., Aziz, B., Jung, J., & Lee, J. (2020). Cyber security incidents analysis and classification in a case study of Korean enterprises. *Knowledge and Information Systems*, 29–35.
Mukhtarov, S., Yüksel, S., & Dinçer, H. (2022). The impact of financial development on renewable energy consumption: Evidence from Turkey. *Renewable Energy.*
Peng, H.-C. (2018). *Discussion of the competitive performance and competitive strategies of Solar PV manufacturers.* DEStech Transactions on Economics, Business and Management.

Quitzow, R., Huenteler, J., & Asmussen, H. (2017). Development trajectories in China's wind and solar energy industries: How technology-related differences shape the dynamics of industry localization and catching up. *Journal of Cleaner Production*, 123–133.

Raina, G., & Sinha, S. (2019). Outlook on the Indian scenario of solar energy strategies: Policies and challenges. *Energy Strategy Reviews*, 331–341.

Rigo, P. D., Siluk, J., Lacerda, D. P., & Spellmeier, J. P. (2021). Competitive business model of photovoltaic solar energy installers in Brazil. *Renewable Energy*, 39–50.

Sampaio, P. G. (2017). Photovoltaic solar energy: Conceptual framework. *Renewable and Sustainable Energy Reviews, 74*, 590–601.

Sebestyén, V., Domokos, E., & Abonyi, J. (2020). Focal points for sustainable development strategies-Text mining-based comparative analysis of voluntary national reviews. *Journal of Environmental Management*, 110414.

Sindhu, S., Nehra, V., & Luthra, S. (2016). Recognition and prioritization of challenges in growth of solar energy using analytical hierarchy process: Indian outlook. *Proceedings of the ICE - Energy*, 332–348.

Varsou, D.-D., Nikolakopoulos, S., Tsoumanis, A., Melagraki, G., & Afantitis, A. (2018). Enalos+ KNIME nodes: New cheminformatics tools for drug discovery: Methods and protocols. *Rational Drug Design*. (s. 113-138). içinde.

Wan, Q., Zhao, X., Liu, H., Dinçer, H., & Yüksel, S. (2022). Assessing the new product development process for the industrial decarbonization of sustainable economies. *SAGE Open, 12*(1), 21582440211067231.

Wang, S., Li, W., Dincer, H., & Yüksel, S. (2019). Recognitive approach to the energy policies and investments in renewable energy resources via the fuzzy hybrid models. *Energies, 12*, 43–56.

Yadav, P., Davies, P. J., & Sarkodie, S. A. (2019). The prospects of decentralised solar energy home systems in rural communities: User experience, determinants, and impact of free solar power on the energy poverty cycle. *Energy Strategy Reviews*, 10024.

Yuan, G., Xie, F., Dinçer, H., & Yüksel, S. (2021). The theory of inventive problem solving (TRIZ)-based strategic mapping of green nuclear energy investments with spherical fuzzy group decision-making approach. *International Journal of Energy Research, 45*(8), 12284–12300.

Yüksel, S., & Dinçer, H. (2022). Identifying the strategic priorities of nuclear energy investments using hesitant 2-tuple interval-valued Pythagorean fuzzy DEMATEL. *Progress in Nuclear Energy, 145*, 104103.

Yüksel, S., Dinçer, H., Çağlayan, Ç., Uluer, G. S., & Lisin, A. (2022b). Bitcoin Mining with Nuclear Energy. In *Multidimensional strategic outlook on global competitive energy economics and finance*. Emerald Publishing Limited.

Yüksel, S., Dinçer, H., Mikhaylov, A., Adalı, Z., & Eti, S. (2022a). Key issues for the improvements of shallow geothermal investments. In *Sustainability in energy business and finance* (pp. 183–194). Springer.

Zhang, S., Chen, Y., Liu, X., Yang, M., & Xu, L. (2017). Employment effects of solar PV industry in China: A spreadsheet-based analytical model. *Energy Policy*, 59–65.

Zhang, Y., Ren, J., Pu, Y., & Wang, P. (2020). Solar energy potential assessment: A framework to integrate geographic. *Renewable Energy an International Journal*, 577–586.

Zhang, Y., Zhang, Y., Gong, C., Dinçer, H., & Yüksel, S. (2022). An integrated hesitant 2-tuple Pythagorean fuzzy analysis of QFD-based innovation cost and duration for renewable energy projects. *Energy*, 123561.

Zhao, Y., Xu, Y., Yüksel, S., Dinçer, H., & Ubay, G. G. (2021). Hybrid IT2 fuzzy modelling with alpha cuts for hydrogen energy investments. *International Journal of Hydrogen Energy, 46*(13), 8835–8851.

Chapter 4
The Ways to Improve Nuclear Cybersecurity for Zero Emission

Serhat Yüksel, Esma Nur Atasoy, Esma Vatandaş, and Sergey Prosekov

Abstract Cybersecurity is another important issue for nuclear power plants. Modification of data by unauthorized persons can cause serious problems in nuclear power plants. In this context, it is vitally important to take the necessary precautions by producing the most accurate strategy. This chapter aims to generate appropriate strategies for the nuclear energy investors to enhance cybersecurity. In the analysis process, DEMATEL approach is taken into consideration. Increasing technological investments plays the most significant role to improve cybersecurity in nuclear power plants. Hence, the priorities should be given for the technological investments. This situation helps to create more effective nuclear energy investments. It is necessary to ensure the cybersecurity of nuclear power plants by making technological investments. Better technological investments will help to better provide the infrastructure to be protected from these risks. Otherwise, power outages may occur as a result of changing the data of nuclear power plants. This will reduce the efficiency of the electricity generation process. On the other hand, as a result of cyberattacks, it is possible that nuclear reactions cannot be stopped. This increases the probability of an explosion at the nuclear power plant.

Keywords Nuclear Energy · Energy Investments · Zero Emission, KNIME

S. Yüksel (✉)
The School of Business, İstanbul Medipol University, Istanbul, Turkey
e-mail: serhatyuksel@medipol.edu.tr

E. N. Atasoy
The School of Business, İstanbul Sabahattin Zaim University, Istanbul, Turkey

E. Vatandaş
The School of Business, İstanbul University, Istanbul, Turkey

S. Prosekov
Financial University under the Government of the Russian Federation, Moscow, Russia

H. Dinçer, S. Yüksel (eds.), *Circular Economy and the Energy Market*,
Contributions to Economics, https://doi.org/10.1007/978-3-031-13146-2_4

4.1 Introduction

Clean and efficient energy is one of the most important needs of today. The carbon emission problem arises as a result of the use of fossil fuels. This situation is considered as one of the most important problems of global warming. Therefore, it is necessary to find some alternatives other than fossil fuels in energy consumption (Bhuiyan et al., 2022). Renewable energy and nuclear energy sources can meet this need. There is no carbon emission in both types of energy. This situation also contributes to the solution of the global warming problem (Kou et al., 2022).

On the other hand, renewable energy types have some disadvantages. The amount of energy produced in renewable energy types depends on climatic conditions. In other words, the amount of energy produced due to the change in air temperatures varies during the day. This will cause instability in the amount of energy obtained. This is considered as one of the most important negative aspects of renewable energy types (Meng et al., 2021).

Nuclear energy is not affected by climatic conditions. It is possible to produce electricity at any time of the day in nuclear power plants. This helps to stabilize the amount of energy produced. This factor is considered to be the greatest advantage of nuclear energy compared to renewable energy sources. In summary, it is possible to produce both efficient and clean energy thanks to nuclear energy. Therefore, it is necessary to increase nuclear energy investments by producing the necessary strategies (Yüksel & Dinçer, 2022).

However, there are some negativities in nuclear energy investments. Radioactive waste generated as a result of nuclear energy is one of the most criticized issues. Moreover, the explosion risk of nuclear power plants is another important problem in this process. This is an issue that needs to be taken care of because it threatens people's lives. Cybersecurity is another important issue for nuclear power plants. Modification of data by unauthorized persons can cause serious problems in nuclear power plants. In this context, it is vitally important to take the necessary precautions by producing the most accurate strategy.

4.2 Theoretical Information

The word cyber refers to an area that covers all devices and networks that provide digital data storage and processing, such as computers, internet, and information technologies, which are the communication tools of the modern world. In this area, which is named as cyber universe or cyber space, data storage, data calculation, data analysis, multimedia items storage, and playback activities are carried out (Jang et al., 2022). It also includes the activities of exchanging data between devices with the internet network, sharing electronic messages and content, and establishing audio, video, or written communication. As a result of the rapid spread of technology and its transformation into a consumer society, the cyber universe has spread unpredictably with the penetration of devices such as telephone, computer, and internet into almost every home. However, the rapid spread of the cyber universe and the fact that it is accessible to everyone has also revealed security problems in this field.

The concept of security, in its simplest form, means being away from all dangers and threats. Cybersecurity, on the other hand, refers to all processes and actions followed by institutions or states to protect the confidentiality and integrity of data stored, processed, and transferred in the cyber universe from unauthorized persons or organizations. Although anti-virus programs have been developed for security problems related to personal data in the cyber universe, companies, universities, banks, etc. There is a greater need for cybersecurity for many areas that contain corporate data. On the other hand, today, cyber threats and attacks against critical infrastructures or strategic industrial sectors are carried out more frequently and in a more organized manner (Pazouki et al., 2021).

Cyber security is important because it is a system that prevents personal data or large volumes of data on the digital platforms of institutions from falling into the hands of unauthorized persons or organizations or being damaged. Cybersecurity is also essential as it provides network security, endpoint security, authentication, database and infrastructure security, cloud security, mobile security, and disaster recovery (Yohanandhan et al., 2022). Cyber security becomes even more important, especially in sectors with critical infrastructure, as threats and attacks on data are more common. As technology, artificial intelligence, machines, and IT industry tools continue to evolve, the issue of cybersecurity will become even more important.

4.3 The Importance of Nuclear Cybersecurity

Rosch-Grace and Straub (2022) discussed the effects of quantum computing technology on cyber, national and military security. Especially in nuclear armament, which gained momentum after the Cold War, it was emphasized how cybersecurity provides mutual trust and deterrence between nation states. While making these studies, historical analysis method was used. In the study, the quantum computing system is analyzed in terms of mutually guaranteed destruction. As a result of the study, it was concluded that nation states should implement cryptographic methods, which are a secure solution against cyber vulnerability and quantum computing attacks.

Judge et al. (2022) examined various smart grid frameworks, their multidimensional effects, energy trading and integration of renewable energy sources made between 2015 and 2021. In the study, the survey method was preferred. On the main axis, there are the long-term environmental and economic benefits, challenges, and suggestions for the future process of Renewable Energy Resources (RES) integration and Energy Storage Systems (ESS). As a result of the study, it is concluded that RES integration has some problems, such as high cost, noise pollution, etc. It has been determined that there are difficulties in this regard.

For this reason, the potential to lead to green energy has been discovered, since the choice of PEV and ESS penetration both reduces high power demand and minimizes carbon dioxide emissions.

Salvi et al. (2022) conducted for the objectives of measuring the durability of critical cyber infrastructures in the electrical energy sector and identifying the risks that these infrastructures may pose from communication, computing, and physical integrations. It offers a model proposal that provides minimal time cyber protection and includes advanced intervention methods. The analyses are based on the EU's electrical energy sector. The method of the study is action design research. As a result, after analyzing the failures of critical cyber infrastructures, a conceptual model based on the implementation of an integrated digital twin is designed.

Lin et al. (2022) dealt with the Built-in Self-Test (BIST) method, which was developed to detect and correctly operate the failed aspects of the steps used in the operating systems of nuclear power plants. As the object of the method, the CPR1000 chooses NPP's FPGA-based reactor protection subsystem. The aim of the study is to solve the safety problems of nuclear power plants in a short time and at low cost. While BIST simplifies the testing processes with its automatic partitioning strategy, it has achieved 100% success for protection reliability.

Priyadarshini et al. (2021) examined the issue of cybersecurity in the energy and space sector and the classification of cyber vulnerabilities. A new model is needed because the purpose of cloud computing, which is used in infrastructure protection in the energy sector, has changed and smart grids cannot protect them sufficiently. It included the Analytical Hierarchy Process (AHP), which is a Multi-Criteria Decision Making (MCDM) tool, in order to eliminate these insecurities and resolve cybersecurity.

Yohanandhan et al. (2022) focused on the importance and current status of the Cyber-Physical Power System (CPPS) in the energy sector, and the trial tests about it. Sustainable cybersecurity solutions must be provided in order for CPPS to progress smoothly on the basis of control and information flow. Maintaining maximum flexibility and reliability of the power grid is critical. In order to achieve this control, CPPS test environments that provide cybersecurity beyond traditional power grid network systems are required. Historical analysis and correlation method are used as methods in the study. Finally, the importance of CPPS test beds is explained using the history of cyber-physical attacks in the energy sector. The solution proposal of the study is that a NIST defined CPPS field should be presented over the problems of CPPS.

Eggers and Le Blanc (2021), based on the need for advanced cyber risk analysis methods, examined the efficient and effective cyber protection of nuclear power plants. Questionnaire was preferred in the method of the research. In the study, the constraints of the nuclear industry and all aspects of cyber risk analysis techniques were examined. It has been determined that the existing techniques benefit the nuclear industry by 53%. By analyzing ICS, the increasing security vulnerabilities and the complexity of cyber threats as the years progressed necessitated prioritizing risk mitigation measures to be taken. For this reason, it has been determined that cyber risk analysis is an ongoing challenge in all industries. It was concluded that it would be difficult to implement techniques that increase the complexity and cost of a cybersecurity program without providing an increased benefit over current NRC or NEI guidance.

Leszczyna (2021) aimed to comprehensively determine the cybersecurity assessment methods in the current scientific literature and present them in terms of applicability. In this context, 32 methods are presented about cybersecurity. Literature research and retrospective data analysis were used in the research method. As a result of the study, instead of suggesting a solution to a specific cyber risk situation, improvements in the applicability of existing methods, incorporation of efficient techniques into cybersecurity systems and their design are suggested.

Nedeljkovic and Jakovljevic (2022) examined cyberattacks on communication networks between smart devices to ensure cybersecurity. In the research method, comparative analysis and case study method were used. Considering the structure of ICS, the devices in the control system also analyze the applicability of the intrusion detection algorithm application. As a result of the study, the algorithmic method that detects these attacks is based on Convolutional Neural Networks (CNN). The method, validated by two case studies, automatically selects the appropriate CNN design for detecting online intrusions into cyber networks.

Pazouki et al. (2021) examine the vulnerability of CPPS to cybersecurity attacks, the strengthening of smart grids, and the economic impact of cyberattacks on energy centers. In the study, a cybersecurity attack based on the maximum-minimum method against distributed energy sources and integrated energy centers is discussed. Simulation and data analysis methods were used in the research. In the study, it is aimed to prepare action plans to proactively reduce the economic impact of cyberattacks on energy centers. The results show that separation of energy centers from electricity networks and integrating thermal storage into the system during a cyberattack reduces the increasing costs. At this point, it is important to reduce the cost and increase the reliability of DERs.

El-Genk et al. (2021) studied the pressurizing dynamic model and similar protection models for the protection of nuclear power plants from cyberattacks. The burden created by the increasing digitalization in nuclear power plants in working transitions over scram carries the risk of turning into a cyberattack by directing the sensor data to Programmable Logic Controllers (PLC). PLC's task in nuclear power plants is to ensure the operational safety of the plant. The aims of the study are to develop a three-zone pressurizing model integrated with the PWR plant model to design ad hoc cyber operations without scram.

A comprehensive review on nuclear data infrastructure was carried out by Herman et al. (2021). Econometric modeling was preferred as the research method. In the study, it is aimed to propose a new model for nuclear data evaluation. They concluded that the model should be performed using a combination of differential and integral experiments, and that its hardware is built on ML techniques and computer power. Lee et al. (2022) also analyzed the method of responding to cyberattacks on nuclear power plants with the Markov decision process model. Case study was used in the method of the research. The target of the study are operators who are not familiar with cybersecurity actions. The goal of these operators to provide maximum time for cyberattack defense and facility security is based on the use of temporal response margin analysis. As a result of the study, it is determined that with the Monte-Carlo tree search algorithm method, the operators protect the operating structure in the maximum time and the most appropriate intervention environments are created to ensure facility safety.

Chowdhury and Gkioulos (2021a, 2021b) examined existing cyber training modules for the protection of critical cyber infrastructures, focusing on the energy, nuclear, and aviation sectors. In the method of the research, literature review and data collection were preferred. The study aims to identify the inadequacy of simulation-based training options and to create key performance indicators (KPIs) integrated with advanced technology. Eggers (2021) evaluated the security of the global economy and the expanding supply chain. The main axis of the research is to make a risk analysis of the nuclear cyber supply chain and to identify security vulnerabilities. After the risk analysis, it proposes a digital I&C system as a solution proposal. E&K system, unit, system, factory acceptance, site acceptance, etc. It is a complex supply chain that includes systems. It has been determined that this supply chain is an important indicator in developing cyberattack surface diagram and cyber supply chain tools.

Kumar et al. (2021) discussed the cybersecurity of nuclear power plants and smart grids through cryptographic hardware chip design. The target group of the research is power plants, smart grid, and nuclear application areas. In the continuation of the study, it has been proposed to solve the security facility of smart grid and nuclear power plants with the integration of Field Programmable Gate Array (FPGA). They then determined that the cryptographic chip should be a Time Authenticated Cryptographic Identity Transmission (TACIT) encryption algorithm. Econometric modeling was used in the research method.

Based on the critical importance of I&C systems in nuclear power plants, Singh and Singh (2021) offered suggestions for researching and improving the reliability of these systems. In the study, industry practitioners were interviewed. The aim of this research is to reach senior managers, engineers, and politicians, as well as being a guide to those who design NPP and I&C systems. As a result of the interviews, access security of NPP and I&C systems, failsafe testing, software development on open-source platforms, robust documentation, secure software, functional defense techniques development etc. themes were presented by practitioners.

Bıçakcı and Evren (2022) studied the cybersecurity issue of the Turkish Akkuyu NPP. The causal comparative method is used in the method of the study. The issue of nuclear safety does not have a deep history, due to the multinational and multicultural nature of the Turkish Akkuyu NPP and its newness in the nuclear energy sector. In the study, Hofstede's national culture has been tried to be explained by establishing a relationship with the issue of security. The NPP's involvement in a multinational consortium raises the issue of nuclear safety culture. The study aims to identify the differences in the working cultures of Turkey and Russia and to examine their reflections on nuclear safety. As a result, he says that a cooperation model should be established that will combine cyber and physical security units.

Yadav and Paul (2021) examined the importance of protecting and monitoring critical infrastructures through SCADA systems. The transformation of modern SCADA systems into open and complex has brought many problems in the energy sector. In the study, the structure of SCADA systems and the applied protocols were analyzed. Then, security attacks on this system were tried to be detected. As a result of the study, it is aimed to bring a new approach for the security of SCADA systems by expanding the research problems over IoTization SCADA. An investigation was made on the multifaceted effects of cyberattacks through the Asherah nuclear power plant simulator by E Silva et al. (2021). The simulator produces the dynamic behavior of a 2,772 MWt pressurized water reactor, testing results such as cyberattack resilience, network flexibility, and data capture for posterior analysis. With the simulation, the ways of establishing security in nuclear digital systems are shown.

Maccarone and Cole (2022) emphasized that nuclear power plants, as they are critical infrastructure, may be exposed to cyber threats during the integration process and it is necessary to take precautions. They examined how to determine the best strategy when taking cybersecurity measures. In this direction, as a method, Bayesian game theory approach is preferred to secure the critical infrastructure, since the features of the competitors are uncertain, and they have incomplete information about each other. The Stackelberg game and the Nash equilibrium of two simultaneous games are determined and discussed. Accordingly, they argue that a security team at a nuclear power plant can choose the most appropriate strategy to protect the plant from possible cyber threats.

Alagappan et al. (2022) aimed to investigate ways to increase cybersecurity, improve precautions, and prevent cyber threats in virtual power plants. As a method, they used the Zero Trust Network Architecture application, which is gaining popularity in the ICT industry. As a result of the study, it has been determined that the implementation of zero trust architecture is still in its early stages and there are various test problems. In addition, it has been argued that while the zero trust network contributes to an additional layer of security, zero trust is not immune to cybersecurity risks. Moving towards zero-security security, unlike other data center security layers, is not complex and may require additional research. This study will contribute to establishing the basis or future scope of further research on the convergence of zero trust networks with other technologies.

Yang et al. (2022) revealed that a comprehensive indicator system should be established in order to understand the energy security situation in China and make a scientific assessment. They examined the relationship between social and economic development and energy security in five dimensions: driving forces, pressures, state, effects, and reactions. As a method, they created an index system with the DSPR model and used the entropy weight TOPSIS model to comprehensively evaluate the index system. As a result of their analysis, they found that there is heterogeneity in the field of energy security among various provinces in China. In addition, they concluded that although the general energy security level was low, the "basic security" level could be reached and gradually improved. Finally, they presented three policy proposals: diversifying energy import channels, developing renewable energy, and increasing energy efficiency.

Levy and Gafni (2021) aimed to introduce the concept of cybersecurity footprint. However, they sought to offer suggestions for future research by exploring ways to measure and reduce the cybersecurity footprint. They preferred documented case-based analysis (phenomenological approach as a qualitative research method) and interpretation analysis as methods. The method of the study, its examination with illustrated cases, also constitutes the originality of the study and its contribution to the literature. As a result of their research and analysis, they determined that while smaller structures have a large cybersecurity footprint, unlike larger structures, they can have a smaller cybersecurity footprint. In addition, they concluded that cyberattacks focus on individuals or small organizations that are part of larger organizations that cause domino effects.

Chowdhury and Gkioulos (2021a, b) aimed to make a systematic literature review of published research articles on critical infrastructure cybersecurity. In this direction, they used literature review and comparative interpretation analysis method. As a result of their studies, they revealed that some skills and competencies, which they gathered in four categories as technical, managerial, practical, and social skills, are necessary for providing cybersecurity in critical infrastructures. However, they have determined that there is no consensus yet about the most critical of these skills and competencies. Another important finding is that the informatics syllabus in academia is not fully aligned with the skills and competencies in the industry and more effort is needed. The originality of this study is that it provides a mapping that is missing from previous studies on skills and competencies found critical in cybersecurity.

Gyllensten and Torner (2021) aimed to investigate the effect of value conflicts in nuclear power generation and related sector on information security. As a method, they preferred the mixed method design, which includes both qualitative research and quantitative research. Accordingly, one-on-one interviews were conducted with 24 employees of two organizations in Sweden, and survey data on information security were requested from 667 employees (62%) in the same institutions. In the qualitative research part of the study, five different types of value conflicts were identified that affect information security behavior. As a result of the quantitative data, it has been revealed that value conflicts related to information security have a negative relationship with rules-compliant behaviors. In addition, it was stated that a robust information security climate is positively related to both rules-compliant and participatory information security behavior. In this study, organizational contextual conditions that affect the skills and motivation of employees in managing information security and value conflicts in organizations with high risks are emphasized.

Bechara and Schuch (2020) aimed to objectively define the ways in which international cooperation and global regulations can be made more operational. A multi-disciplinary analysis was made, and the deductive analysis method was used. As a result of the study, it has been argued that cybersecurity, which is a global and multidimensional issue, requires the participation of the private sector and civil society as well as international cooperation. Another important finding is that a more accurate and precise good management that is more compatible with the system in decision-making processes is required.

Gyllensten and Torner (2021) discussed the relationship between Swedish nuclear power generation and information security. Accordingly, they aimed to examine the organizational and social prerequisites for the behavior of the employees in the relevant sector in accordance with the rules. Interview technique was used as the method and individual in-depth interviews were conducted with 24 employees in two organizations in the nuclear energy industry in Sweden. As a result of the study, it has been suggested that the prerequisites for the information security behavior of the employees can be considered in three categories as structural, social, and individual. With the field work it offers, this study can enable organizations to better create and encourage the necessary conditions for information security.

Kim et al. (2021) aimed to investigate the role of nuclear power plant life extensions for deep decarbonization in the US energy system. They used Pacific Northwest National Laboratory's Global Change Assessment Model (GCAM) as a method. For this analysis, they developed two climate scenarios, a Ref scenario without climate policy and a climate scenario limiting the global carbon emissions pathway. As a result of the study, they suggested that the longevity of existing nuclear energy has a significant carbon value and will reduce the peak and fall behavior of nuclear energy investments. In addition, they found that decisions regarding the continued operation of existing nuclear reactors include the tangible and significant carbon emission prevention value that the US nuclear fleet provides today. Another key finding is to consider the capital inventory turnover ratios and realistic timelines required for the deployment and decommissioning of all carbon-neutral technology options to address climate change. Jang et al. (2022) aimed to investigate the nuclear safety of the Kudankulam nuclear power plant (KNPP) in India after the cyberattack. In this study, it is stated that one of the important issues in the context of cybersecurity is technological investment.

4.4 An Evaluation for the Improvement of Cybersecurity for Nuclear Energy Investments

In this chapter, it is aimed to generate appropriate strategies for the nuclear energy investors to enhance cybersecurity. For this purpose, the strategies are defined in Table 4.1.

In the analysis process, DEMATEL approach is taken into consideration. This methodology is used to compute the significance weights of the factors (Yuan et al., 2021; Yüksel et al., 2022a, b). Many scholars preferred this methodology for different purposes (Zhe et al., 2021; Zhao et al., 2021; Zhang et al., 2022). The weights of the factors are given in Table 4.2.

Table 4.1 Strategies to enhance nuclear cybersecurity

Strategies	References
Evaluating the expectations of the customers	Adalı et al. (2022), Dong et al. (2022), Li et al. (2021)
Increasing technological investments	Du et al. (2020), Haiyun et al. (2021), Mukhtarov et al. (2022)
Making appropriate trainings to the personnel	Kostis et al. (2022), Kou et al. (2022), Liu et al. (2021)
Using effective equipment to increase security	Li et al. (2020), Meng et al. (2021), Wan et al. (2022)

Table 4.2 The weights of the criteria

Strategies	Weights
Evaluating the expectations of the customers	0.2231
Increasing technological investments	0.2819
Making appropriate trainings to the personnel	0.2358
Using effective equipment to increase security	0.2592

Increasing technological investments plays the most significant role to improve cybersecurity in nuclear power plants. Hence, the priorities should be given for the technological investments. This situation helps to create more effective nuclear energy investments.

4.5 Conclusion

Nuclear energy has some superiorities over other energy types. For instance, it is not affected by climatic conditions. Electricity can be produced at any time of the day in nuclear power plants. This contributes to stabilize the amount of energy produced which is accepted as the greatest advantage of nuclear energy compared to renewable energy sources. It is possible to produce both efficient and clean energy thanks to nuclear energy. Hence, it is necessary to increase nuclear energy investments by producing the necessary strategies.

Despite these issues, there are some negativities in nuclear energy investments. Radioactive waste generated because of nuclear energy is one of the most criticized issues. Furthermore, the explosion risk of nuclear power plants is another important problem in this process. This is an issue that needs to be taken care of because it threatens people's lives. Cyber security is another important issue for nuclear power plants. Modification of data by unauthorized persons can cause serious problems in nuclear power plants. In this context, it is vitally important to take the necessary precautions by producing the most accurate strategy.

In this chapter, it is aimed to generate appropriate strategies for the nuclear energy investors to enhance cybersecurity. In the analysis process, DEMATEL approach is taken into consideration. This methodology is used to compute the significance weights of the factors. Many researchers preferred this methodology for different purposes. Increasing technological investments plays the most significant role to improve cybersecurity in nuclear power plants. Hence, the priorities should be given for the technological investments. This situation helps to create more effective nuclear energy investments.

It is necessary to ensure the cybersecurity of nuclear power plants by making technological investments. Better technological investments will help to better provide the infrastructure to be protected from these risks. Otherwise, power outages may occur because of changing the data of nuclear power plants. This will reduce the efficiency of the electricity generation process. On the other hand, as a result of cyberattacks, it is possible that nuclear reactions cannot be stopped. This increases the probability of an explosion at the nuclear power plant.

References

Adalı, Z., Dinçer, H., Eti, S., Mikhaylov, A., & Yüksel, S. (2022). Identifying new perspectives on geothermal energy investments. In *Multidimensional strategic outlook on global competitive energy economics and finance*. Emerald Publishing Limited.

Alagappan, A., Venkatachary, S. K., & Andrews, L. J. B. (2022). Augmenting Zero Trust Network Architecture to enhance security in virtual power plants. *Energy Reports, 8*, 1309–1320.

Bechara, F. R., & Schuch, S. B. (2020). Cybersecurity and global regulatory challenges. *Journal of Financial Crime*.

Bhuiyan, M. A., Dinçer, H., Yüksel, S., Mikhaylov, A., Danish, M. S. S., Pinter, G., et al. (2022). Economic indicators and bioenergy supply in developed economies: QROF-DEMATEL and random forest models. *Energy Reports, 8*, 561–570.

Bıçakcı, A. S., & Evren, A. G. (2022). Thinking multiculturality in the age of hybrid threats: Converging cyber and physical security in Akkuyu nuclear power plant. *Nuclear Engineering and Technology, 54, 2467.*

Chowdhury, N., & Gkioulos, V. (2021a). Cyber security training for critical infrastructure protection: A literature review. *Computer Science Review, 40*, 100361.

Chowdhury, N., & Gkioulos, V. (2021b). Key competencies for critical infrastructure cybersecurity: a systematic literature review. *Information & Computer Security*.

Dong, W., Zhao, G., Yüksel, S., Dinçer, H., & Ubay, G. G. (2022). A novel hybrid decision making approach for the strategic selection of wind energy projects. *Renewable Energy, 185*, 321–337.

Du, L., Dinçer, H., Ersin, İ., & Yüksel, S. (2020). IT2 Fuzzy-based multidimensional evaluation of coal energy for sustainable economic development. *Energies, 13*(10), 1–21.

e Silva, R. B., Piqueira, J. R. C., Cruz, J. J., & Marques, R. P. (2021). Cybersecurity assessment framework for digital interface between safety and security at nuclear power plants. *International Journal of Critical Infrastructure Protection, 34*, 100453.

Eggers, S. (2021). A novel approach for analyzing the nuclear supply chain cyber-attack surface. *Nuclear Engineering and Technology, 53*(3), 879–887.

Eggers, S., & Le Blanc, K. (2021). Survey of cyber risk analysis techniques for use in the nuclear industry. *Progress in Nuclear Energy, 140*, 103908.

El-Genk, M. S., Altamimi, R., & Schriener, T. M. (2021). Pressurizer dynamic model and emulated programmable logic controllers for nuclear power plants cybersecurity investigations. *Annals of Nuclear Energy, 154*, 108121.

Gyllensten, K., & Torner, M. (2021). The role of organizational and social factors for information security in a nuclear power industry. *Organizational Cybersecurity Journal: Practice, Process and People*.

Haiyun, C., Zhixiong, H., Yüksel, S., & Dinçer, H. (2021). Analysis of the innovation strategies for green supply chain management in the energy industry using the QFD-based hybrid interval valued intuitionistic fuzzy decision approach. *Renewable and Sustainable Energy Reviews, 143*, 110844.

Herman, M., Brown, D. A., Capote, R., Chadwick, M. B., Haeck, W., Hutchinson, J. D., et al. (2021). Infrastructure for the new paradigm of nuclear reaction evaluation. *Annals of Nuclear Energy, 163*, 108494.

Jang, K. B., Baek, C. H., & Woo, T. H. (2022). Analysis of cyber nuclear terrorism by DTrack consequences in the civilian nuclear power plant. *Journal of Nuclear Science and Technology, 59*(2), 207–215.

Judge, M. A., Khan, A., Manzoor, A., & Khattak, H. A. (2022). Overview of smart grid implementation: Frameworks, impact, performance and challenges. *Journal of Energy Storage, 49*, 104056.

Kim, S. H., Taiwo, T. A., & Dixon, B. W. (2021). The carbon value of nuclear power plant lifetime extensions in the United States. *Nuclear Technology*, 1–19.

Kostis, P., Dinçer, H., & Yüksel, S. (2022). Knowledge-based energy investments of European Economies and Policy Recommendations for Sustainable Development. *Journal of the Knowledge Economy*, 1–33.

Kou, G., Yüksel, S., & Dinçer, H. (2022). Inventive problem-solving map of innovative carbon emission strategies for solar energy-based transportation investment projects. *Applied Energy, 311*, 118680.

Kumar, N., Mishra, V. M., & Kumar, A. (2021). Smart grid and nuclear power plant security by integrating cryptographic hardware chip. *Nuclear Engineering and Technology, 53*(10), 3327–3334.

Lee, C., Han, S. M., Chae, Y. H., & Seong, P. H. (2022). Development of a cyberattack response planning method for nuclear power plants by using the Markov decision process model. *Annals of Nuclear Energy, 166*, 108725.

Leszczyna, R. (2021). Review of cybersecurity assessment methods: Applicability perspective. *Computers & Security, 108*, 102376.

Levy, Y., & Gafni, R. (2021). Introducing the concept of cybersecurity footprint. *Information & Computer Security*.

Li, X., Zhu, S., Yüksel, S., Dinçer, H., & Ubay, G. G. (2020). Kano-based mapping of innovation strategies for renewable energy alternatives using hybrid interval type-2 fuzzy decision-making approach. *Energy, 211*, 1–16.

Li, Y. X., Wu, Z. X., Dinçer, H., Kalkavan, H., & Yüksel, S. (2021). Analyzing TRIZ-based strategic priorities of customer expectations for renewable energy investments with interval type-2 fuzzy modeling. *Energy Reports, 7*, 95–108.

Lin, Z., Wang, L., Cai, Y., Wang, F., & Wu, Y. (2022). Implementation of a built-in self-test for nuclear power plant FPGA-based safety-critical control systems. *Annals of Nuclear Energy, 165*, 108644.

Liu, J., Lv, J., Dinçer, H., Yüksel, S., & Karakuş, H. (2021). Selection of renewable energy alternatives for green blockchain investments: A hybrid IT2-based Fuzzy Modelling. *Archives of Computational Methods in Engineering, 28*, 3687–3701.

Maccarone, L. T., & Cole, D. G. (2022). Bayesian games for the cybersecurity of nuclear power plants. *International Journal of Critical Infrastructure Protection, 37*, 100493.

Meng, Y., Zhou, R., Dinçer, H., Yüksel, S., & Wang, C. (2021). Analysis of inventive problem-solving capacities for renewable energy storage investments. *Energy Reports, 7*, 4779–4791.

Mukhtarov, S., Yüksel, S., & Dinçer, H. (2022). The impact of financial development on renewable energy consumption: Evidence from Turkey. *Renewable Energy, 187, 169*.

Nedeljkovic, D., & Jakovljevic, Z. (2022). CNN based method for the development of cyber-attacks detection algorithms in industrial control systems. *Computers & Security, 114*, 102585.

Pazouki, S., Naderi, E., & Asrari, A. (2021). A remedial action framework against cyberattacks targeting energy hubs integrated with distributed energy resources. *Applied Energy, 304*, 117895.

Priyadarshini, I., Kumar, R., Sharma, R., Singh, P. K., & Satapathy, S. C. (2021). Identifying cyber insecurities in trustworthy space and energy sector for smart grids. *Computers & Electrical Engineering, 93*, 107204.

Rosch-Grace, D., & Straub, J. (2022). Analysis of the likelihood of quantum computing proliferation. *Technology in Society, 68*, 101880.

Salvi, A., Spagnoletti, P., & Noori, N. S. (2022). Cyber-resilience of critical cyber infrastructures: Integrating digital twins in the electric power ecosystem. *Computers & Security, 112*, 102507.

Singh, P., & Singh, L. K. (2021). Instrumentation and control systems design for nuclear power plant: An interview study with industry practitioners. *Nuclear Engineering and Technology, 53*(11), 3694–3703.

Wan, Q., Zhao, X., Liu, H., Dinçer, H., & Yüksel, S. (2022). Assessing the new product development process for the industrial decarbonization of sustainable economies. *SAGE Open, 12*(1), 21582440211067231.

Yadav, G., & Paul, K. (2021). Architecture and security of SCADA systems: A review. *International Journal of Critical Infrastructure Protection, 34*, 100433.

Yang, B., Ding, L., Zhan, X., Tao, X., & Peng, F. (2022). Evaluation and analysis of energy security in China based on the DPSIR model. *Energy Reports, 8*, 607–615.

Yohanandhan, R. V., Elavarasan, R. M., Pugazhendhi, R., Premkumar, M., Mihet-Popa, L., & Terzija, V. (2022). A holistic review on Cyber-Physical Power System (CPPS) testbeds for secure and sustainable electric power grid–Part–I: Background on CPPS and necessity of CPPS testbeds. *International Journal of Electrical Power & Energy Systems, 136*, 107718.

Yuan, G., Xie, F., Dinçer, H., & Yüksel, S. (2021). The theory of inventive problem solving (TRIZ)-based strategic mapping of green nuclear energy investments with spherical fuzzy group decision-making approach. *International Journal of Energy Research, 45*(8), 12284–12300.

Yüksel, S., & Dinçer, H. (2022). Identifying the strategic priorities of nuclear energy investments using hesitant 2-tuple interval-valued Pythagorean fuzzy DEMATEL. *Progress in Nuclear Energy, 145*, 104103.

Yüksel, S., Dinçer, H., Çağlayan, Ç., Uluer, G. S., & Lisin, A. (2022b). Bitcoin mining with nuclear energy. In *Multidimensional Strategic Outlook on Global Competitive Energy Economics and Finance*. Emerald Publishing Limited.

Yüksel, S., Dinçer, H., Mikhaylov, A., Adalı, Z., & Eti, S. (2022a). Key Issues for the improvements of shallow geothermal investments. In *Sustainability in Energy Business and Finance* (pp. 183–194). Springer.

Zhang, Y., Zhang, Y., Gong, C., Dinçer, H., & Yüksel, S. (2022). An integrated hesitant 2-tuple Pythagorean fuzzy analysis of QFD-based innovation cost and duration for renewable energy projects. *Energy, 248*, 123561.

Zhao, Y., Xu, Y., Yüksel, S., Dinçer, H., & Ubay, G. G. (2021). Hybrid IT2 fuzzy modelling with alpha cuts for hydrogen energy investments. *International Journal of Hydrogen Energy, 46*(13), 8835–8851.

Zhe, L., Yüksel, S., Dinçer, H., Mukhtarov, S., & Azizov, M. (2021). The positive influences of renewable energy consumption on financial development and economic growth. *Sage Open, 11*(3), 1–9.

Chapter 5
Investigating the Role of Export Diversification, Remittances, and Environmental Sustainability in Accordance with Clean Energy and Zero Emission

Ibrahim Nandom Yakubu, Ayhan Kapusuzoglu, and Nildag Basak Ceylan

Abstract In recent decades, scholars have attempted to unearth the key factors driving environmental degradation, with conflicting results. This study seeks to contribute to the unending debate on the determinants of environmental quality by examining the influence of export diversification and remittances on ecological footprint using data from the MINT (Mexico, Indonesia, Nigeria, and Turkey) countries. The study applies the Fully Modified OLS (FMOLS) and Dynamic OLS (DOLS) techniques, with the Pooled Mean Group (PMG) estimator as an alternative method to check for robustness. From the econometric analysis, the FMOLS and DOLS long-run estimates show that export diversification and remittance inflows exert a negative significant influence on ecological footprint, indicating that they contribute significantly to enhancing environmental sustainability in the MINT countries. We also evidence that while financial development aids in curtailing environmental pollution, the economic growth of the MINT economies significantly exacerbates environmental degradation. The findings hold with the alternative analytical technique (PMG estimator) except for remittance inflows which exhibit a positive influence on environmental degradation. We provide some recommendations for policy in light of these findings.

Keywords Energy market · Sustainability · Environmental issues · Energy investments · Carbon emission

---

I. N. Yakubu
Graduate School of Social Sciences, Ankara Yildirim Beyazit University, Ankara, Turkey

A. Kapusuzoglu (✉) · N. B. Ceylan
Faculty of Business, Ankara Yildirim Beyazit University, Ankara, Turkey
e-mail: akapusuzoglu@ybu.edu.tr; nbceylan@ybu.edu.tr

H. Dinçer, S. Yüksel (eds.), *Circular Economy and the Energy Market*,
Contributions to Economics, https://doi.org/10.1007/978-3-031-13146-2_5

5.1 Introduction

Climate change over the years has emerged as a critical threat and a persistent stumbling block to achieving sustainable development (Yang et al., 2021). Researchers contend that carbon dioxide emissions have been the most prevalent source of greenhouse gas emissions contributing to climate change. The rapid increase in the emission of greenhouse gases (GHG) has prompted widespread concern among governments and international institutions in both emerging and developed countries. In this regard, international treaties and accords have reiterated the importance of environmental sustainability, advocating the implementation of policies that would help in the reduction of greenhouse gas emissions (Yakubu et al., 2021a). The Kyoto Protocol and the United Nations Framework Convention on Climate Change are notable accords championing the environmental sustainability agenda. Despite these treaties, achieving an optimal decline in the level of environmental pollution is still a long way off.

In light of this backdrop, studies into the factors that contribute to environmental quality have garnered increasing attention across the globe. The literature has presented numerous factors as drivers of environmental quality. These factors encompass institutional, social, and economic variables. The literature however has documented inconclusive findings and therefore requires more research efforts.

In this study, we rely on two economic variables that have not been adequately investigated in the literature on environmental quality determinants. We look at the impact of export diversification and remittance inflows on environmental quality. A country's trade and development structures are reflected in its export diversification, therefore understanding the environmental effect of this metric is crucial (Liu et al., 2019). Countries centered on the export of specialized and hazardous products contribute significantly to increasing environmental degradation. The World Bank in 2021 urges nations to increase the diversification of their products in order to limit over-reliance on certain commodities and also generate sustainable revenues from exports (Rehman et al., 2021). Export diversification is seen as a crucial aspect of structural growth and its implications on environmental quality must be carefully considered (Jebli et al., 2016; Ali, 2017).

Remittances are progressively becoming an integral part of many economies and serve as a possible income-generating source (Yang et al., 2021). Remittance inflows also play a significant role in enhancing several economic outcomes such as the development of the financial sector (Olayungbo & Quadri, 2019). Notwithstanding the economic benefits of remittances provided to the recipient country, they can potentially trigger environmental pollution. That is to say, increased remittance inflows may increase the purchasing power of individuals which makes the acquisition of accessories such as vehicles and other electronic gadgets quite easier. This, as a consequence, increases energy consumption and contributes to environmental pollution.

Given the foregoing, this study seeks to examine how export diversification and remittance inflows affect environmental quality in the MINT (Mexico, Indonesia,

Nigeria, and Turkey) countries. The MINT economies in the next few decades are poised to be among the largest economies in the world. As part of their economic agenda, these countries continue to strive to reach fully industrialized status. Achieving these goals requires a solid infrastructural base and an efficient energy system to reduce any inimical environmental outcomes. Also, the fact that Mexico, Indonesia, and Nigeria are among the top 25 countries in terms of remittance inflows makes this study worthwhile.

This study contributes significantly to the environmental economics literature in many ways. Firstly, it can be noted that carbon dioxide emission is widely employed in the literature as a measure of environmental degradation (see Salahuddin et al., 2015; Zaman et al., 2017; Khan et al., 2020a, b; Osobajo et al., 2020; Isaeva et al., 2022; Le & Nguyen, 2021; Yakubu et al., 2021b; Liguo et al., 2022; Ma et al., 2022; Usman et al., 2022; Weili et al., 2022). This proxy however is criticized as not being an appropriate measure given that it does not deliberate resources such as oil, forest, mining, soil, and fishing. Hence, this study employs ecological footprint which accounts for these resources as a measure of environmental quality. Second, we provide an initial attempt to investigate the relationship between export diversification, remittance inflows, and environmental quality in the MINT economies using ecological footprint as a proxy for environmental sustainability. Finally, the study employs different panel techniques to provide more robust results.

The remainder of the chapter is outlined as follows: The second section reviews the literature. The third section covers the data and methods. Section 4 presents the empirical findings, and Section 5 concludes the chapter.

5.2 Overview of Existing Literature

The current literature on international trade and environmental performance has mostly centered on how trade openness affects the environment. The environmental impact of diversification, whether in terms of exports or imports, has not been sufficiently explored. Likewise, remittances have been included as a predictor of environmental quality in recent research, though its impact is still inconclusive. Accordingly, this study extends the sparse literature on export diversification and remittance inflows in the examination of environmental sustainability drivers. In this section, we discuss the extant literature on the impact of export diversification and remittance inflows on environmental quality.

5.2.1 The Relationship Between Export Diversification and Environmental Degradation

Despite the fact that this nexus is still relatively new in the literature, there have been several studies that have deliberated the link between export diversification and environmental performance. For instance, Gozgor and Can (2016) investigated the impact of export diversification on CO_2 emissions in Turkey within the environmental Kuznets curve. Using the DOLS approach, the results suggested that diversifying exports increases CO_2 emissions. Shahzad et al. (2020) investigated the link between export diversification and carbon dioxide emissions in a sample of developed and developing nations over the period 1971–2014. Utilizing several panel methodologies, the authors discovered that diversifying exports reduces emissions in the selected economies. In the G7 economies, Wang et al. (2020) found that CO_2 emission level increases with growth in export diversification. Mania (2020) observed a positive link between the diversification of exports and emissions levels in some developed and developing economies. Using data from Regional Comprehensive Economic Partnership (RCEP) economies, Khan et al. (2021) revealed that export diversification positively drives emission levels. In the instance of China, Li et al. (2021) discovered that increasing export diversity leads to a reduction of CO_2 emissions. Applying the augmented mean group (AMG) technique, Iqbal et al. (2021) evidenced a positive effect of export diversification on pollution in the OECD countries. Employing the ARDL approach, Sheikh and Hassan (2021) indicated that a poorly diversified export portfolio contributes to water pollution in India. Adopting the generalized quantile regression method, Zafar et al. (2021) established that diversifying exports decrease CO_2 emissions in the world's top remittance-receiving nations. According to Haq et al. (2022), varying export dramatically reduces short-term environmental pollution in Pakistan.

5.2.2 The Relationship Between Remittances and Environmental Degradation

Remittances' influence on environmental degradation has been highlighted in recent years. Sharma et al. (2019) examined the impact of remittances and foreign aid on Nepal's emissions levels. The results of the ARDL technique indicated that boosting remittance inflows greatly slows emissions. Using the NARDL approach, Ahmad et al. (2019) demonstrated that the influence of remittances on CO_2 emissions is dependent on the pattern of remittances over time. That is, a swift decrease in remittance inflows results in a reduction in CO_2 emissions and vice versa. In the case of Asian nations, Rahman et al. (2019) revealed a long-term positive correlation between CO_2 emissions and remittances. Neog and Yadava (2020) indicated that whereas positive shocks in the inflows of remittance result in a rise in emissions of CO_2, adverse shocks significantly impede emissions in India. Similar results are documented by Ahmad et al. (2022) and Kibria (2022) in the case of Pakistan and Bangladesh, respectively. Wang et al. (2021) established that remittances contribute to CO_2 emission reductions in Egypt and some selected Asian nations. By employing the DOLS and FMOLS methodologies, Jamil et al. (2021) discovered that remittance inflows into the G20 nations contribute considerably to rising levels of CO_2 emissions. In a global sample, Yang et al. (2021) demonstrated that CO_2 emissions in both developing and developed nations rise with a thriving level of remittances. Khan et al. (2020a, b) empirically found that remittance inflows cause pollution (CO_2) within the BRICS bloc. A study conducted by Jafri et al. (2022) using the NARDL technique demonstrated that decreasing the amount of remittance inflows positively drives CO_2 emissions in China. Remittance inflows, according to the findings of Karasoy (2021), undermine long-term environmental performance in the Philippines.

The empirical studies on export diversification, remittances, and pollution nexus reveal inconsistent findings and a lack of conclusive evidence. Thus, this study complements existing research on the effect of export diversification and remittances on environmental degradation.

5.3 Research Methodology

5.3.1 Data and Variables

Panel dataset from member countries in the MINT group is used, which spanned the period 1980–2017. Ecological footprint is the dependent variable, whereas export diversification and remittances are the key explanatory factors in the study. We controlled for the influence of financial development and economic growth. Ecological footprint (ECF) is captured as "a composite of six dimensions comprising carbon, build-up land, grazing land, fishing grounds, forest land, and cropland" in gha per person terms. The Global Footprint websites provide the data for this variable. Export diversification (EXD) is estimated based on the Theil Index and the data is gleaned from the International Monetary Fund. Remittances (REM) are the aggregate amount of personal remittances received (in current US dollars). In terms of the control factors, domestic credit by the financial sector as a percentage of GDP gauges financial development (FID), whereas economic growth (ECG) is GDP per capita (Constant 2010 US dollars). We retrieved the data for remittances, financial development, and economic growth from the World Bank.

5.3.2 Empirical Model

Two different models are estimated in the study. To begin, we investigate export diversification's influence on environmental quality. The second model examines the remittances-environmental performance nexus. In both scenarios, we take into account the effects of financial development and economic growth. Given these objectives, the following are the primary empirical models:

$$ln\,\mathrm{ECF_{it}} = \alpha_0 + \beta_1\, ln\,\mathrm{EXD_{it}} + \beta_2\, ln\,\mathrm{FID_{it}} + \beta_3\, ln\,\mathrm{ECG_{it+}}\ \varepsilon_{it} \tag{5.1}$$

$$ln\,\mathrm{ECF_{it}} = \alpha_0 + \beta_1\, ln\,\mathrm{REM_{it}} + \beta_2\, ln\,\mathrm{FID_{it}} + \beta_3\, ln\,\mathrm{ECG_{it+}}\ \varepsilon_{it} \tag{5.2}$$

ECF, EXD, REM, FID, and ECG from the equations denote ecological footprint, export diversification, remittances, financial development, and economic growth in a specific country i at period t, respectively. ε signifies the error term. To reduce the issue of heteroscedasticity, the variables are transformed to a logarithm form (Yang et al., 2021).

5.3.3 Analytical Approach

The study performs several baseline tests to ensure that an appropriate technique is selected and the model estimates are accurate. The CD test by Pesaran (2004) is first employed to determine whether or not the selected variables show cross-sectional dependence. This is followed by unit root tests and then determining if the variables are cointegrated.

The fully modified ordinary least squares (FMOLS) and dynamic ordinary least squares (DOLS) which are panel cointegration techniques are used to examine the relationship among the variables.

The FMOLS estimator for a panel dataset is presented as:

$$\widehat{\alpha}^*_{\mathrm{GFM}} = \mathrm{N}^{-1}\sum_{\mathrm{n}=1}^{\mathrm{N}} \widehat{\alpha}^*_{\mathrm{FM,n}} \tag{5.3}$$

where $\widehat{\alpha}^*_{\mathrm{GFM}}$ is the FMOLS estimator which is applied to the individual countries in the panel.

The DOLS estimator is also derived as follows.

$$y_{it} = z'_{it-1}\beta + \sum_{j=-p1}^{j=p2} c_{ij}\Delta z_{it+j} + v_{it} \tag{5.4}$$

The coefficient of lag of the first differenced variables is represented by c_{ij}. Generally, the traditional OLS regression estimates are considered to be biased because of endogeneity issues. The FMOLS and DOLS estimators are apt for modelling long-run relationships (Balsalobre-Lorente et al., 2019). These techniques are also fit for dealing with endogeneity issues through semi-parametric correction of the OLS (Phillips & Hansen, 1990). Additionally, the study applies the pooled mean group (PMG) approach to ensure that the findings are robust.

5.4 Empirical Results

5.4.1 Descriptive Statistics

Table 5.1 shows the non-logarithmic summary statistics for the variables. Ecological footprint has an average value of 1.954 in terms of gha per person. The mean of export diversification is 3.476 and it ranges from 1.812 to 6.152 0. For the Theil index, a lower value indicates a higher degree of export diversification and vice versa. Given the average value, we deduce that the MINT economies have a moderate level of export diversification. Averagely, remittance inflow for the study period is $6,038.573 million. Domestic credit by the financial sector is averaged at 37.816% and GDP per capita has an average value of US$5,357.289.

5.4.2 Cross-Sectional Dependence (CD) Test

In the first step of our analysis, we check for cross-sectional dependency (CD), which is a prevalent issue in panel data analysis. The results of the CD tests are summarized in Table 5.1. From the three CD test methods employed, the null

Table 5.1 Descriptive statistics and cross-sectional dependence (CD) test results

Variables	ECF	EXD	REM	FID	ECG
Mean	1.954	3.476	6038.573	37.816	5357.289
Median	1.842	2.803	2003.000	37.061	4553.443
Maximum	3.818	6.152	32270.510	80.604	14975.090
Minimum	0.952	1.812	0.000	4.909	1231.195
Std. Dev.	0.791	1.568	8139.603	15.692	3668.011
Skewness	0.289	0.745	1.520	0.356	0.448
Kurtosis	1.616	1.888	3.955	2.857	1.988
Jarque-Bera	14.240	21.896	64.339	3.346	11.566
Probability	0.001	0.000	0.000	0.188	0.003

Variables	Breusch-Pagan LM	Pesaran scaled LM	Bias-corrected scaled LM
lnECF	70.758***	18.694***	18.640***
lnEXD	138.428***	38.229***	38.175***
lnREM	107.186***	29.210***	29.156***
lnFID	42.134***	10.431***	10.377***
lnECG	164.144***	45.652***	45.598***

Note: *** indicates 1% significance level.

hypothesis that the series exhibit cross-sectional independence is rejected based on the significance level of the variables. As a result, the analysis gives definitive evidence of cross-sectional dependence, suggesting that an upheaval in a member country in the bloc will transcend to the others.

5.4.3 Panel Unit Root Test

The cross-sectional augmented Dickey-Fuller (CADF) method of panel unit root test by Pesaran (2007) is adopted in this study. This method accounts for cross-sectional dependency which is evident in our data. The order of integration of the series is depicted in Table 5.2. The results indicate that at level (I(0)), only economic growth has a unit root, suggesting non-stationarity. However, at first difference (I(1)), all the variables are stationary.

5.4.4 Results of Panel Cointegration Test

After affirming the unit root properties of the series, we use Pedroni's (1999) panel cointegration method to determine the cointegration level of the variables. Pedroni (1999) proposed different test statistics for determining whether or not cointegration exists, and these are either within-dimension (Panel test statistics) or between-dimension (Group test statistics) estimates. The cointegration test is performed for the two models as shown in Table 5.2. In both scenarios, the variables are cointegrated in the long term given that most of the test statistics are significant.

5.4.5 Regression Estimates

The empirical findings for FMOLS, DOLS, and the PMG estimation techniques are presented in Table 5.2. In Model 1, the effect of export diversification on ecological footprint is depicted while Model 2 examines the impact of remittances on ecological footprint. In both models, we control for the influence of financial development and economic growth.

From the econometric analysis, the FMOLS and DOLS long-run estimates show that export diversification exerts a significant negative influence on ecological footprint. Considering this, as export diversification accelerates by a percentage, environmental degradation is lowered by 0.202–0.273%. The finding implies that the MINT countries are pursuing the World Bank's recommendation for economies to diversify their exports in order to achieve sustainable development. Therefore, promoting export diversification through viable trade policies will aid in enhancing long-term environmental sustainability in the MINT countries. The result

Table 5.2 Panel unit root/panel cointegration/FMOLS–DOLS-PMG regression test results

Variables	Level I(0)	First Difference I(1)
	z (t-bar)	z (t-bar)
lnECF	1.921	−3.186***
lnEXD	0.490	−2.088**
lnREM	−0.347	−1.771**
lnFID	0.313	−4.087***
lnECG	−2.024**	−1.446*

Pedroni test Stats.	f(Y ~ EXD, FID, ECG)		f(Y ~ REM, FID, ECG)	
	Panel	Group	Panel	Group
v-Statistic	1.491*	–	0.755	-
Rho-Statistic	−3.500***	−2.563***	−3.504***	−2.569***
PP-Statistic	−4.473***	−4.250***	−4.525***	−4.353***
ADF-Statistic	−0.976	−1.088	−1.049	−1.610**

Variables	FMOLS Model 1	FMOLS Model 2	DOLS Model 1	DOLS Model 2	PMG Model 1	PMG Model 2
lnEXD	−0.202** (0.012)		−0.273** (0.043)		−0.206** (0.039)	
lnREM		−0.017** (0.032)		−0.021* (0.056)		0.029* (0.062)
lnFID	−0.056** (0.027)	−0.092*** (0.005)	−0.065* (0.076)	−0.152*** (0.007)	−0.063** (0.045)	−0.069** (0.030)
lnECG	0.289*** (0.000)	0.507*** (0.000)	0.276*** (0.001)	0.526*** (0.0000)	0.462*** (0.000)	0.573*** (0.000)
Short-run estimates ECT_{t-1}					−0.388* (0.061)	−0.355* (0.089)
lnEXD					−0.120 (0.489)	
lnREM						−0.036 (0.220)
lnFID					−0.024 (0.316)	−0.041 (0.200)
lnECG					0.340** (0.025)	0.392** (0.010)
C					−0.473* (0.061)	−0.708* (0.089)

Model 1 = f(Y ~ EXD, FID, ECG) **Model 2 = f(Y ~ REM, FID, ECG)**

Notes: *P*-values are in parentheses. ***, **, and * indicate 1%, 5%, and 10% significance level, respectively.

corroborates previous research (for example, Mania, 2020; Wang et al., 2020; Iqbal et al., 2021; Khan et al., 2021).

The effect of remittances on ecological footprint is documented to be negative and significant. Precisely, environmental degradation is abated by 0.017–0.021% for any percentage growth in the inflows of remittance. This indicates that remittance influxes bolster the efforts to mitigate environmental pollution in the MINT. A plausible implication is that due to escalating costs of traditional energy sources, remittance recipients are perhaps judiciously using their remittances to obtain renewable energy or acquire energy-efficient and environmentally friendly appliances. Our finding aligns with the results of Sharma et al. (2019), Jafri et al. (2022), and Zafar et al. (2021).

As a control variable in both models, financial development negatively and significantly drives ecological footprint. This suggests that the development of the financial sector of the MINT economies lessens pollution in the bloc. The implication is that financial development contributes significantly to the financing and promotion of research and development which facilitates the advancement of environmentally friendly technologies, thus limiting environmental pollution (Amin et al., 2022). Financial development also helps to curb pollution by directing the financial sector to lend to corporations who are poised to invest in ecological friendly initiatives. Our finding is similar to prior studies (see Zafar et al., 2019; Usman & Hammar, 2021; Abid et al., 2022).

Economic growth shows a positive significant influence on ecological footprint, suggesting that a boom in economic activities in the MINT economies triggers environmental pollution. This result sync with the findings of prior studies (see Lu, 2018; Kahia et al., 2019; Naz et al., 2019; Anwar et al., 2021; Hundie, 2021; Yakubu et al., 2022).

Turning to the PMG estimates, it can be observed that export diversification, financial development, and economic growth maintain their respective coefficient signs and are statistically significant. However, remittances tend to positively drive environmental degradation with the PMG method. In a nutshell, we conclude that aside from the impact of remittances the findings obtained from the FMOLS and DOLS techniques are robust to an alternative estimator.

Similar to the long-run estimates via the FMOLS and DOLS techniques, the PMG results indicate that export diversification, remittances, and financial development enhance environmental sustainability in the short term, given their negative relationship with ecological footprint. Nonetheless, the impacts are negligible as they demonstrate statistical insignificance. Economic growth maintains its inimical effect on environmental sustainability in the short term.

5.5 Conclusion and Discussion

Considering that climate change is among the fundamental debates in contemporary literature, the achievement of carbon neutrality is one of the most pertinent issues facing the world's economic system today. Several attempts have been made to determine the influence of various economic variables on environmental performance. The role of export diversification and remittances in promoting environmental quality, on the other hand, has received relatively little attention. Hence, this study augments the few research on this nexus by looking at the effect of export diversification and remittance inflows on ecological footprint in the MINT countries over the years 1980–2017. To accomplish the study's goal, we performed various preliminary tests. We first examine if the variables have cross-sectional dependence (CD) which prevalence may lead to inaccurate findings if an appropriate technique is not employed. Second, the panel series are examined for unit root using the cross-sectional augmented Dickey-Fuller (CADF) method. We also determine if the variables are cointegrated via the Pedroni (1999) panel cointegration method. Based on these preliminary tests, the study applies the FMOLS and DOLS techniques and employs the PMG technique as an alternative method to check for robustness.

From the econometric analysis, the FMOLS and DOLS long-run estimates show that export diversification and remittance inflows exert a negative significant influence on ecological footprint, indicating that they contribute significantly to environmental sustainability in the MINT countries. We also evidence that while financial development aids in curtailing environmental pollution, the economic growth of the MINT states significantly exacerbates environmental degradation. The findings hold with the alternative analytical technique (PMG estimator) except for remittance inflows which exhibit a positive influence on environmental degradation. The PMG short-run estimates further demonstrate that export diversification, remittances, and financial development enhance environmental sustainability in the short run, albeit insignificantly. Economic growth dramatically deteriorates the environment in the short term.

The findings of the study lead to several key policy implications. First, given that export diversity improves environmental quality, we advocate for more trade liberalization efforts in the MINT economies. Reducing bureaucratic hurdles to trade will greatly assist in the achievement of this trade liberalization agenda. In boosting the export potentials of the member nations, incentives might be provided to stimulate research and innovation in these countries. Firms engaged in export activities should be eligible for subsidies aimed at increasing export diversification. Secondly, to enhance the beneficial impact of remittances on environmental quality, remittance recipient households might be offered incentives and discounts to utilize their remitted funds to acquire environmentally friendly equipment and appliances. Remittance-related taxes must also be reduced or eliminated to boost remittance inflows in the MINT bloc. Additionally, financial institutions in the MINT countries should be strengthened and encouraged to promote and finance environmentally sustainable initiatives. This study is primarily based on panel analysis and individual country analysis may bolster policy formulation. Therefore, we recommend future studies to explore the link amid export diversification, remittances, and environmental quality for each of the countries in the MINT to establish whether the country-specific analyses are coherent with the findings of this study.

References

Abid, A., Mehmood, U., Tariq, S., & Haq, Z. U. (2022). The effect of technological innovation, FDI, and financial development on CO_2 emission: Evidence from the G8 countries. *Environmental Science and Pollution Research, 29*(8), 11654–11662.

Ahmad, M., Ul Haq, Z., Khan, Z., Khattak, S. I., Ur Rahman, Z., & Khan, S. (2019). Does the inflow of remittances cause environmental degradation? Empirical evidence from China. *Economic research-Ekonomska istraživanja, 32*(1), 2099–2121.

Ahmad, W., Ozturk, I., & Majeed, M. T. (2022). How do remittances affect environmental sustainability in Pakistan? *Evidence from NARDL approach. Energy, 243*, 122726.

Ali, M. (2017). Determinants of related and unrelated export diversification. *Economies, 5*(4), 50.

Amin, A., Ameer, W., Yousaf, H., & Akbar, M. (2022). Financial development, institutional quality, and the influence of various environmental factors on carbon dioxide emissions: Exploring the nexus in China. *Frontiers in Environmental Science, 9*, 838714.

Anwar, A., Chaudhary, A. R., Malik, S., & Bassim, M. (2021). Modelling the macroeconomic determinants of carbon dioxide emissions in the G-7 countries: The roles of technological innovation and institutional quality improvement. *Global Business Review*, September. https://doi.org/10.1177/09721509211039392

Balsalobre-Lorente, D., Driha, O. M., Bekun, F. V., & Osundina, O. A. (2019). Do agricultural activities induce carbon emissions? The BRICS experience. *Environmental Science and Pollution Research, 26*(24), 25218–25234.

Gozgor, G., & Can, M. (2016). Export product diversification and the environmental Kuznets curve: evidence from Turkey. *Environmental Science and Pollution Research, 23*(21), 21594–21603.

Haq, I. U., Mehmed, B., Naradda Gamage, S. K., Allayarov, P., Khan, D., & Khattak, Z. Z. (2022). Nexus between export variety and carbon emissions in Pakistan: The role of FDI and technological development. *PloS one, 17*(1), e0263066.

Hundie, S. K. (2021). Income inequality, economic growth and carbon dioxide emissions nexus: empirical evidence from Ethiopia. *Environmental Science and Pollution Research, 28*(32), 43579–43598.

Iqbal, N., Abbasi, K. R., Shinwari, R., Guangcai, W., Ahmad, M., & Tang, K. (2021). Does exports diversification and environmental innovation achieve carbon neutrality target of OECD economies? *Journal of Environmental Management, 291*, 112648.

Isaeva, A., Salahodjaev, R., Khachaturov, A., & Tosheva, S. (2022). The impact of tourism and financial development on energy consumption and carbon dioxide emission: Evidence from post-communist countries. *Journal of the Knowledge Economy, 13*(1), 773–786.

Jafri, M. A. H., Abbas, S., Abbas, S. M. Y., & Ullah, S. (2022). Caring for the environment: measuring the dynamic impact of remittances and FDI on CO_2 emissions in China. *Environmental Science and Pollution Research, 29*(6), 9164–9172.

Jamil, K., Liu, D., Gul, R. F., Hussain, Z., Mohsin, M., Qin, G., & Khan, F. U. (2021). Do remittance and renewable energy affect CO_2 emissions? An empirical evidence from selected G-20 countries. *Energy & Environment*. https://doi.org/10.1177/0958305X211029636

Jebli, M. B., Youssef, S. B., & Ozturk, I. (2016). Testing environmental Kuznets curve hypothesis: The role of renewable and non-renewable energy consumption and trade in OECD countries. *Ecological Indicators, 60*, 824–831.

Kahia, M., Ben Jebli, M., & Belloumi, M. (2019). Analysis of the impact of renewable energy consumption and economic growth on carbon dioxide emissions in 12 MENA countries. *Clean Technologies and Environmental Policy, 21*(4), 871–885.

Karasoy, A. (2021). How do remittances to the Philippines affect its environmental sustainability? Evidence based on the augmented ARDL approach. *Natural Resources Forum, 45*(2), 120–137. Oxford, UK: Blackwell Publishing Ltd.

Khan, M. I., Teng, J. Z., & Khan, M. K. (2020a). The impact of macroeconomic and financial development on carbon dioxide emissions in Pakistan: Evidence with a novel dynamic simulated ARDL approach. *Environmental Science and Pollution Research, 27*(31), 39560–39571.

Khan, Z. U., Ahmad, M., & Khan, A. (2020b). On the remittances-environment led hypothesis: Empirical evidence from BRICS Economies. *Environmental Science and Pollution Research, 27*(14), 16460–16471.

Khan, Z., Murshed, M., Dong, K., & Yang, S. (2021). The roles of export diversification and composite country risks in carbon emissions abatement: Evidence from the signatories of the Regional Comprehensive Economic Partnership agreement. *Applied Economics, 53*(41), 4769–4787.

Kibria, M. (2022). Environmental downfall in Bangladesh: Revealing the asymmetric effectiveness of remittance inflow in the presence of foreign aid. *Environmental Science and Pollution Research, 29*(1), 731–741.

Le, T. H., & Nguyen, C. P. (2021). The impact of tourism on carbon dioxide emissions: Insights from 95 countries. *Applied Economics, 53*(2), 235–261.

Li, M., Ahmad, M., Fareed, Z., Hassan, T., & Kirikkaleli, D. (2021). Role of trade openness, export diversification, and renewable electricity output in realizing carbon neutrality dream of China. *Journal of Environmental Management, 297*. https://doi.org/10.1016/j.jenvman.2021.113419

Liguo, X., Ahmad, M., & Khattak, S. I. (2022). Impact of innovation in marine energy generation, distribution, or transmission-related technologies on carbon dioxide emissions in the United States. *Renewable and Sustainable Energy Reviews, 159*. https://doi.org/10.1016/j.rser.2022.112225

Liu, H., Kim, H., & Choe, J. (2019). Export diversification, CO_2 emissions and EKC: Panel data analysis of 125 countries. *Asia-Pacific Journal of Regional Science, 3*(2), 361–393.

Lu, W. C. (2018). The impacts of information and communication technology, energy consumption, financial development, and economic growth on carbon dioxide emissions in 12 Asian countries. *Mitigation and Adaptation Strategies for Global Change, 23*(8), 1351–1365.

Ma, Q., Tariq, M., Mahmood, H., & Khan, Z. (2022). The nexus between digital economy and carbon dioxide emissions in China: The moderating role of investments in research and development. *Technology in Society, 68*. https://doi.org/10.1016/j.techsoc.2022.101910

Mania, E. (2020). Export diversification and CO_2 emissions: An augmented environmental Kuznets curve. *Journal of International Development, 32*(2), 168–185.

Naz, S., Sultan, R., Zaman, K., Aldakhil, A. M., Nassani, A. A., & Abro, M. M. Q. (2019). Moderating and mediating role of renewable energy consumption, FDI inflows, and economic growth on carbon dioxide emissions: Evidence from robust least square estimator. *Environmental Science and Pollution Research, 26*(3), 2806–2819.

Neog, Y., & Yadava, A. K. (2020). Nexus among CO_2 emissions, remittances, and financial development: a NARDL approach for India. *Environmental Science and Pollution Research, 27*(35), 44470–44481.

Olayungbo, D. O., & Quadri, A. (2019). Remittances, financial development and economic growth in sub-Saharan African countries: Evidence from a PMG-ARDL approach. *Financial Innovation, 5*(1), 1–25.

Osobajo, O. A., Otitoju, A., Otitoju, M. A., & Oke, A. (2020). The impact of energy consumption and economic growth on carbon dioxide emissions. *Sustainability, 12*. https://doi.org/10.3390/su12197965

Pedroni, P. (1999). Critical values for cointegration tests in heterogeneous panels with multiple regressors. *Oxford Bulletin of Economics and Statistics, 61*(S1), 653–670.

Pesaran, M. H. (2004). General diagnostic tests for cross section dependence in panels. *IZA Discussion Paper* (No. 1240), The Institute for the Study of Labor, Bonn.

Pesaran, M. H. (2007). A simple panel unit root test in the presence of cross-section dependence. *Journal of Applied Econometrics, 22*(2), 265–312.

Phillips, P. C., & Hansen, B. E. (1990). Statistical inference in instrumental variables regression with I(1) processes. *The Review of Economic Studies, 57*(1), 99–125.

Rahman, Z. U., Cai, H., & Ahmad, M. (2019). A new look at the remittances-FDI-energy-environment nexus in the case of selected Asian nations. *The Singapore Economic Review*, 1–19.

Rehman, M. A., Fareed, Z., Salem, S., Kanwal, A. & Pata, U. K. (2021). Do diversified export, agriculture, and cleaner energy consumption induce atmospheric pollution in Asia? Application of method of moments quantile regression. *Frontiers in Environmental Science*, https://doi.org/10.3389/fenvs.2021.781097.

Salahuddin, M., Gow, J., & Ozturk, I. (2015). Is the long-run relationship between economic growth, electricity consumption, carbon dioxide emissions and financial development in Gulf Cooperation Council Countries robust? *Renewable and Sustainable Energy Reviews, 51*, 317–326.

Shahzad, U., Ferraz, D., Doğan, B., & do Nascimento Rebelatto, D. A. (2020). Export product diversification and CO_2 emissions: Contextual evidences from developing and developed economies. *Journal of Cleaner Production*. https://doi.org/10.1016/j.jclepro.2020.124146

Sharma, K., Bhattarai, B., & Ahmed, S. (2019). Aid, growth, remittances and carbon emissions in Nepal. *The Energy Journal, 40*(1), 129–141.

Sheikh, A., & Hassan, O. I. (2021). Investigating the relationship between export diversification and river water pollution: a time series analysis of the Indian experience. *Arthaniti: Journal of Economic Theory and Practice*. https://doi.org/10.1177/09767479211040135

Usman, M., & Hammar, N. (2021). Dynamic relationship between technological innovations, financial development, renewable energy, and ecological footprint: fresh insights based on the STIRPAT model for Asia Pacific Economic Cooperation countries. *Environmental Science and Pollution Research, 28*(12), 15519–15536.

Usman, M., Kousar, R., Makhdum, M. S. A., Yaseen, M. R., & Nadeem, A. M. (2022). Do financial development, economic growth, energy consumption, and trade openness contribute to increase carbon emission in Pakistan? An insight based on ARDL bound testing approach. *Environment, Development and Sustainability*. https://doi.org/10.1007/s10668-021-02062-z

Wang, L., Chang, H. L., Rizvi, S. K. A., & Sari, A. (2020). Are eco-innovation and export diversification mutually exclusive to control carbon emissions in G-7 countries? *Journal of Environmental Management, 270*. https://doi.org/10.1016/j.jenvman.2020.110829

Wang, Z., Zaman, S., & Rasool, S. F. (2021). Impact of remittances on carbon emission: Fresh evidence from a panel of five remittance-receiving countries. *Environmental Science and Pollution Research, 28*(37), 52418–52430.

Weili, L., Khan, H., & Han, L. (2022). The impact of information and communication technology, financial development, and energy consumption on carbon dioxide emission: Evidence from the Belt and Road countries. *Environmental Science and Pollution Research*. https://doi.org/10.1007/s11356-021-18448-5

Yakubu, I. N., Kapusuzoglu, A., & Ceylan, N. B. (2021a). Environmental Impact of Economic Globalization and Renewable Energy Consumption in the OPEC Countries. In S. Yuksel & H. Dincer (Eds.), *Strategic Approaches to Energy Management, Contributions to Management Science* (pp. 155–171). Springer.

Yakubu, I. N., Kapusuzoglu, A., & Ceylan, N. B. (2021b). Urbanization, fossil fuel consumption and carbon dioxide emission in Ghana: The STIRPAT model approach. In S. Yuksel & H. Dincer (Eds.), *Strategic Approaches to Energy Management, Contributions to Management Science* (pp. 201–216). Springer.

Yakubu, I. N., Kapusuzoglu, A., & Ceylan, N. B. (2022). ICT trade and energy transition in the BRICS economies. In H. Dincer & S. Yuksel (Eds.), *Sustainability in energy business and finance, contributions to finance and accounting* (pp. 13–24). Springer.

Yang, B., Jahanger, A., & Ali, M. (2021). Remittance inflows affect the ecological footprint in BICS countries: Do technological innovation and financial development matter? *Environmental Science and Pollution Research, 28*(18), 23482–23500.

Zafar, M. W., Saleem, M. M., Destek, M. A., & Caglar, A. E. (2021). The dynamic linkage between remittances, export diversification, education, renewable energy consumption, economic growth, and CO_2 emissions in top remittance-receiving countries. *Sustainable Development.* https://doi.org/10.1007/s11356-022-18622-3

Zafar, M. W., Saud, S., & Hou, F. (2019). The impact of globalization and financial development on environmental quality: Evidence from selected countries in the Organization for Economic Co-operation and Development (OECD). *Environmental Science and Pollution Research, 26*(13), 13246–13262.

Zaman, K., Moemen, M. A. E., & Islam, T. (2017). Dynamic linkages between tourism transportation expenditures, carbon dioxide emission, energy consumption and growth factors: Evidence from the transition economies. *Current Issues in Tourism, 20*(16), 1720–1735.

Chapter 6
The Role of Green Energy Investments in Energy Supply Security

Ahmet Murat Ermiş and Muhammed Emrullah Güven

Abstract Renewable energy sources provide the management and control of energy production. The increase in the share of renewable energy sources in the energy portfolio ensures that the renewable energy obtained from local sources is controlled nationally. Since energy is obtained by using local resources, control can be achieved completely. Ensuring the control of energy resources constitutes a priority step towards ensuring supply security. An important element of energy supply security is to ensure continuity of access to energy while meeting energy needs. If the continuity of access to energy is affected by any political, political, or economic factor and dragged into a negative direction, it is a risk factor for energy supply security. Reducing or eliminating the current risk will be possible by focusing on renewable energy sources. Investments in renewable energy resources will reduce foreign dependency as it will ensure energy supply stability through energy management and control. The fragility of access to energy will decrease. Energy supply security will be ensured by reducing the vulnerability of energy access. In this context, renewable energy investments are a factor that needs to be increased to ensure energy supply security.

Keywords Renewable energy · Green energy · Energy supply · Energy investment

6.1 Introduction

Energy has become one of the most important and indispensable elements of today's world, with its place in every aspect of life in micro and macro dimensions. Energy has a place in many areas from production to transportation, from daily use to health and many more. Energy sources can simply be divided into two classes, renewable energy and non-renewable energy sources. Non-renewable energy sources are also divided into two as fossil fuels and nuclear energy. Energy sources such as natural

A. M. Ermiş (✉) · M. E. Güven
The School of Business, İstanbul Medipol University, Istanbul, Turkey
e-mail: mermis@medipol.edu.tr; meguven@medipol.edu.tr

H. Dinçer, S. Yüksel (eds.), *Circular Economy and the Energy Market*,
Contributions to Economics, https://doi.org/10.1007/978-3-031-13146-2_6

gas, oil, and coal are examples of fossil fuels. These fuels consist of living remains and are formed over a very long time. One of the characteristic features of fossil fuels is that they are not sustainable because they are non-renewable (Dong et al., 2022). In addition, fossil fuels are not available in every region of the world. Another non-renewable energy source is nuclear energy sources. Nuclear energy source is obtained from the atomic nucleus.

There are some advantages and disadvantages of energy resources in terms of production and use. Fossil fuels are one of the most harmful fuels for the environment in terms of their use. Climate change can be mentioned at the beginning of these damages. Fossil fuels cause the global temperature to be above the average, thus causing regional drought or excessive precipitation and frost. Another harm of fossil fuels is the loss of biodiversity. This means the disappearance and extinction of many plant and animal species (Zhang et al., 2022). Another harm caused by fossil fuel consumption is chemical pollution.

Fossil fuels cause the emission of various gases harmful to the environment because of their use. This situation causes air pollution and leads to various social problems. Studies on this subject show that pollution triggers respiratory tract, lung cancer, and cardiovascular diseases. The increase in health problems also increases the expenditures made in this field (Kou et al., 2022). Especially in countries with budget deficits such as Turkey, this situation results in a worsening of the budget. In addition, the increase in health problems is one of the factors that negatively affect the workforce. The damage to the workforce negatively affects production and therefore welfare and income distribution. All these negative situations constitute a social cost that a society must overcome.

Renewable energy resources can be defined as energy resources that remain in a natural cycle and do not decrease as they are consumed. Wind, solar, biomass, hydraulic, tidal wave, and hydrogen are examples of renewable energy sources. The characteristic features of renewable energy sources are that they do not decrease due to consumption, that they are sustainable and environmentally friendly. Renewable energy sources differ from fossil fuels in terms of their production. Countries can produce the energy they need by establishing the necessary facilities from renewable energy sources (Mukhtarov et al., 2022). This is not the case for fossil energy sources. In addition, renewable energy sources can meet the energy needed today without consuming the energy that future generations will need. In this respect, it is also referred to as sustainable energy.

The fact that countries produce their own energy using renewable energy sources is an element that provides political advantage to countries. Especially for countries with high energy dependency, energy resources can be a political handicap. At this point, energy production with renewable energy sources can be a factor that strengthens the hand of countries in international relations. The tension between Russia and Ukraine, which we have witnessed recently, and the worries experienced by European countries at the point of imposing sanctions on Russia can be given as examples.

With the increase in industrialization, energy has become the most important input of production. Another advantage of renewable energy sources is the reduction of exchange rate risks and the preservation of financial stability. As it is known, foreign currency is used in energy import and export. For this reason, in case of exchange rate shocks, this may adversely affect financial stability and may also burden the economy as inflation. While this situation negatively affects the current account balance for energy-dependent countries, it positively affects the current transactions of the countries that produce the energy they need.

6.2 Energy Dependence Problem

From the industrial revolution to the present, the use of energy has been increasing its weight by intensifying in every phase of life. From the needs in our daily lives to the most strategic points of the countries as a production factor, the need for energy emerges as an indispensable element. With the developments in information communication technologies, blockchain technology, and robotization, it is seen that energy is now moving towards the point of becoming almost the life itself rather than a necessity. The fact that energy has become so important brings with it some difficulties. Ensuring the demand and supply balance of energy, which is not technologically possible to store yet, emerges as a national security factor for countries. In this context, energy dependency is of vital importance (Yüksel et al., 2022).

Energy dependency is mainly due to the difference between energy demand and energy supply. Although there are different definitions of energy dependence in the literature, to put it simply, it is the situation where the energy deficit, which arises because of the energy demand being higher than the energy production, must be closed. If the required amount of energy cannot be met by national means, the energy deficit must be met by supplying it somehow. This situation also includes many risk factors for countries. The risk of not providing a vital factor gives an idea of how deep the addiction can be (Kostis et al., 2022). It is possible to classify the risks posed by energy dependence under four headings. The risks posed by energy dependence are defined as political risk, economic risk, uncertainty, and security of supply.

Energy dependency makes the country, which must supply the energy deficit, politically dependent on the country from which it supplies energy. Policy makers, who must meet the energy deficit that can have devastating economic and social effects, must follow a moderate and harmonious policy towards the countries from which they import energy in terms of both the future of the country and the course of their political life. With the effect of globalization, which is a pillar of the economic and financial architecture created after the Second World War, it must follow policies close to the country it is dependent on, even in matters not directly related to it (Bhuiyan et al., 2022). Although in the short term, it seems profitable to follow policies close to the country of dependence in the context of the country's economy and social order, since it will destroy the environment for independent policy development and action in the long run, it leaves countries with a problem that is not easy to get out of on the level of existence-independence. As a result of energy dependence, it is not possible to reject the political and economic demands coming from the energy importing country, even if it is not compatible with national interests. Political instability arises, causing wrong economic decisions to be made.

The need for energy will not only cause problems in political decisions, but also prevent the implementation of the principle of reciprocity in international law. The principle of reciprocity in international law expresses the right to respond in kind to an act, policy, or sanction applied. With the spread of international trade and transnational companies and the globalization of competition, companies have started to act in the international arena from a national basis. Countries may engage in restrictive attitudes and behaviors towards international companies in line with their own interests. Applications such as quotas, legal restrictions, and holding at customs on imported products affect companies negatively, and due to this attitude, they also negatively affect the country where the company is headquartered (Yüksel & Dinçer, 2022). It is especially common in agricultural products. Even though such applications are relatively low in high-tech products, they can be observed in the context of strategic policies and in the name of developing baby industries. The country exposed to such a situation will be affected both economically and socio-politically as the internal market conditions will change. The most deterrent factor when countries resort to such practices is the principle of reciprocity in international law. However, the implementation of the principle of reciprocity becomes very difficult in countries with energy dependence. This situation emerges as a political risk factor.

One of the elements that form the foundations of modern economies is industry. The most important input of the industrial sector is energy. Energy dependence can directly affect industrial production and cause the country's economy to suffer. The decrease in industrial production causes a decrease in the growth and development of the country. Although growth does not mean development, an increase in production and an increase in exports mean an increase in per capita income. The increase in national income per capita will also bring about an increase in the level of welfare. The increase in the welfare level will also contribute to the increase in the level of economic development (Wan et al., 2022). A problem in the supply of energy will reverse the process and cause economic shrinkage, and economic development will decrease with the decrease in the welfare level. Energy dependence causes countries to become dependent on economic growth and development through industrial production. Ensuring the energy deficit while creating an economic policy presents itself as an obstacle that must be overcome to create an effective and efficient policy.

Another economic risk of energy dependence is unemployment. Any negative situation that will occur in industrial production will cause a decrease in production and therefore a decrease in the required workforce. Although the decrease in labor demand will be delayed for a while with the effect of employment contracts and unions, it will show itself as unemployment (Zhao et al., 2022). The deterioration in the labor market will cause social problems. Increasing unemployment is a factor that can have serious social consequences. The economic activities of the unemployed agents will change, and this will affect the entire market. This deterioration in the balance of the domestic market will not only cause unemployment but also negatively affect other economic factors (Li et al., 2022). In addition, the increase in the unemployment rate may cause deterioration in the budget balance by causing an increase in the payments made within the scope of unemployment benefits and social assistance. As a result of energy dependence, the economic cost of a problem with the country from which energy is supplied can be very heavy.

Another risk of energy dependence is uncertainty. The deepening of financial markets, the transformation in the instruments used, and the expectations of economic agents are very effective on countries and the policies they implement. One of the most important triggers of economic dynamics is expectations. Uncertainty in the economy may cause the behavior of agents and the balance to change. Possible problems arising from energy dependence will be an indicator that markets, which price the possibilities in advance, will consider in their expectations. The resulting perception affects the economic variables and has negative consequences on the country's economy (Dinçer et al., 2022). Energy dependency will create the opinion that the country's economy is fragile. It will have a negative impact on direct investors as well as on financial markets. Country risk premiums will increase and direct investments to the country will decrease. The most obvious indicator of the negative externality created by energy dependence is the risk of uncertainty.

The negative externality of energy dependence in the context of uncertainty is not only on perceptions, but also directly affects concrete economic indicators. Problems that may occur in energy flow for any reason can directly affect production. The decrease in production is reflected to the domestic and foreign markets as changes in prices. Changes in prices cause inflation and negatively affect the country's economy. The increase in inflation has a direct impact on the consumption and investment decisions of economic agents. In addition to inflation, the inability to import energy in local currency brings exchange rate uncertainty. Currency fluctuations can cause very difficult conditions to be compensated for those who have foreign currency debt. Exchange rate fluctuations can cause damage to the society with inflation. Problems may occur in the current account balance due to the use of a currency other than the local currency in trade. The foreign exchange deficit, which occurs outside of national possibilities, poses a risk as a situation that needs to be closed somehow (Haiyun et al., 2021). The problem that will occur in the current balance creates a risk regarding the budget and the whole planning of the country. Policy makers, who must act with the sensitivity of a surgeon in the economic system where all elements are interconnected, have to reduce the uncertainty environment as much as possible in order to carry both economic welfare and social factors in a balanced way. Energy dependence causes an environment of uncertainty.

Energy dependence is also an important risk factor in terms of supply security. In some periods, energy importing countries may impose various restrictions on energy exports due to both their internal dynamics and external reasons. Sometimes the elimination of the destruction in the energy transportation channels, sometimes the maintenance and repair works, and sometimes the obstacles to energy export due to unpredictable reasons pose a serious problem for energy importing countries. The interruption of the energy they export because of such events occurring in the internal dynamics of energy-exporting countries creates a supply security risk for energy importing countries. In addition to internal dynamics, there may also be problems caused by external dynamics (Yuan et al., 2021). The cost of a problem that will occur at the point of energy supply can be very heavy for energy importing countries. Energy supply security is a strategic issue for all countries. The supply security risk of energy dependence is an important risk factor that cannot be ignored.

6.3 The Role of Renewable Energy Investments in Energy Supply Security

Energy refers to the physical ability to do work. It is the thing that occurs because of the change in matter and provides the opportunity to do work. Energy is needed in all the work we do in our daily life. Resources that produce energy using certain techniques are also called energy resources. Although energy sources are diverse, they have become more diverse with the development of technology. Especially with the increase in environmental problems and the importance of the concept of sustainability, the search for different energy sources has become inevitable. In this context, there is a need to classify energy sources (Zhou et al., 2021). It is important to make the classification correctly so that policy makers can take a more active role. Energy sources are divided into two as renewable energy sources and non-renewable energy sources.

Non-renewable energy sources are energy sources that are depleted as they are used and cannot renew themselves. These resources are found in certain proportions and amounts on earth. When they are used for energy production, they cannot be recycled and reused. They are not sustainable. They harm the environment and cause global warming. They cause serious negative externalities while meeting their energy needs. Today, non-renewable energy sources are widely used in energy supply. The most important reason for this is that it is cheap and does not require new technological investments. It is more stable than renewable energy sources. Non-renewable energy sources are fossil fuels and nuclear energy (Meng et al., 2021). Fossil fuels are the energy source formed by the death of living organisms and their decay by being in an oxygen-free environment for many years. Fossil fuels contain high levels of carbon. When they are burned, they release a high amount of carbon to the nature together with energy and harm the environment. Coal, oil, and natural gas are some of the fossil resources. Nuclear energy is the energy obtained from the nucleus of the atom. Energy is obtained by splitting atoms. It causes the release of heavy radioactive substances. These substances can cause devastating effects on living things that will last for generations.

Renewable energy is self-renewing and environmentally friendly energy. We can classify renewable energy sources as solar energy, wind energy, geothermal energy, biomass energy, hydroelectric energy, wave energy, and hydrogen energy. Solar energy is the energy obtained by using the rays coming from the sun. Throughout history, the sun has been used for different purposes (Levenda et al., 2021). The sun was used in determining the time, war technologies, and some other fields. The sun not only illuminates our world, but also has effects both sociologically and physically. Sun rays are an important source of energy. When we say solar energy as a renewable energy source, it is meant to convert the rays from the sun into electrical energy through thermal and photovoltaic systems. In photovoltaic systems, it is done by means of photovoltaic batteries placed on the solar panel. Electricity is obtained through batteries by taking the sun's rays. In thermal systems, the sun's rays are first converted into heat. Heat energy is converted into electrical energy (Sebestyén, 2021). It is possible to store solar energy with certain methods. Studies have shown that solar energy can be stored for years.

The sun's rays heat different regions at different levels according to the position of our world, the difference in distance and the angle of incidence of the rays. Pressure differences due to temperature differences cause the formation of winds. These winds are also a source of energy, as are the sun's rays. Wind turbines are used to convert winds into energy. Kinetic energy is obtained because of the movement of wind turbines by the effect of the wind. Kinetic energy is converted to mechanical energy and mechanical energy is converted to electrical energy (Panagopoulos, 2021). The process is completed with the conversion of wind into electrical energy. The blowing speed and duration of the winds affect the energy obtained. Wind turbines, also called wind vane, are divided into two as horizontal axis wind turbines and vertical axis wind turbines.

Heat accumulation takes place on the earth due to both the sun and other reasons. The heat accumulated in the earth's crust is called geothermal. It was created by combining the words geo meaning earth and thermal meaning heat. There are temperature and pressure differences at various levels of the earth's crust. Hot water, steam, and gases collected in the earth's crust form geothermal fluids. The energy created by geothermal fluids is called geothermal energy. It is an environmentally friendly energy source. Combustion method is not used. It produces zero carbon emissions (Pietrzak et al., 2021). It is very easy to use because it does not carry any risk factors. It is an energy source with a very high efficiency and does not require a large facility area. Energy and electricity are obtained by separating the fluids obtained from the drilled wells. Geothermal energy is one of the renewable energy sources.

Biomass energy, one of the renewable energy sources, is an energy source whose importance is increasing day by day as the fourth largest energy source among existing energy sources. Biomass is expressed as the total mass of living organisms belonging to a species or a community of various species in a certain period. It is also considered as organic carbon. Biomass is converted into energy by going through various processes. Biomass is burned (decomposed) into energy and then into electricity (Opeyemi, 2021). Energy is obtained by burning biomass in biomass power plants. Although there are different processes, motion energy is obtained by performing the rotation process with the gas, which is basically separated because of burning the biomass. This energy is then converted into electrical energy. While some of the generated electrical energy is used in the facility, the remaining portion is sent to the grid.

Another renewable energy source is hydroelectric energy. It is defined as the energy obtained from running water. The potential energy of water is used by converting it to kinetic energy and kinetic energy to electrical energy. This process we are talking about is carried out in hydroelectric power plants. In order to benefit from hydroelectric energy more efficiently, it is necessary to pay attention to the climate structure of the region where the power plant will be established and the speed of the flowing water. The hydroelectric power plant also creates a positive externality socially and economically in the region where it is built (Ivanovski et al., 2021). The prevention of floods, the creation of irrigation channels, the improvement of the quality of life, the development of fisheries, and the creation of recreational facilities are some of the positive externalities we can count. Hydroelectric power plants are long-lasting. The size of the hydroelectric power plant varies according to the amount of energy needed or the conditions of the region.

Wave energy, one of the renewable energy sources, is the energy obtained by utilizing the waves that occur in the seas and oceans. Waves occur in the seas and oceans due to earthquakes, tides, and winds. Wave energy is obtained from the wave surface or below the wave surface. Energy is provided through wave energy conversion systems. Hydrogen energy is another renewable energy source. Hydrogen is the most abundant element on earth. It is an odorless, light, and non-toxic substance, but it is not a source of energy (Gernaat et al., 2021). To be used as an energy source, it must go through various transformations. With hydrogen energy systems, energy is obtained from hydrogen.

There are various reasons for turning to renewable energy sources, which we mentioned above. One of the biggest problems of our world, perhaps the most important, is undoubtedly limited resources. While meeting our energy needs, renewable energy aims to turn to resources that can renew themselves and do not harm the environment instead of limited resources. The use of renewable energy sources is an important element for a sustainable system, as it will not cause any scarcity problems. Although conventional energy, which is widely used today, is sufficient to meet the needs of current generations, it causes serious concerns about meeting the needs of future generations. Developments in information and communication technologies in our age, population growth, and lifestyles increase our demand for energy. With the changing conditions, the possibility of accessing and using energy gains new dimensions. Our energy approach needs to be reviewed in the light of all these. We need to consider environmental and social factors not only to transfer resources to future generations, but also to leave livable conditions.

6.4 Conclusion

Renewable energy is basically a structure built on two columns. It is based on two foundations. They are sustainable and environmentally friendly. As with all elements of the sustainability concept, the concept of green energy is an approach that basically prevents the unlimited use of resources that future generations will need and aims not to deprive humanity of energy resources in the future while meeting our own needs. The fact that energy resources are renewable means that resource consumption and relatively waste of resources come to an end. The problem of scarcity comes to an end with renewable resources and the obstacle to energy shortage is eliminated. Sustainable and predictable energy needs can be supplied from renewable energy sources. The energy supply problem may come to an end for both our world and future generations.

Another element of renewable energy is that it is environmentally friendly. Renewable energy aims to meet our energy needs without harming the environment. The effects of global warming are felt more intensely every day. The damage caused by fossil fuels to the environment has reached an irreparable level. Carbon emissions, greenhouse gases, and other harmful things can be prevented by the renewable energy approach. While meeting the energy needs, it does not harm the ecological system and the risks are reduced to the lowest level. Climate change causes serious problems. The renewable energy approach focuses on increasing energy efficiency. Technological developments that will increase efficiency are an important element of the renewable energy approach. Developments in the field of energy technology will enable us to reach safe and long-lasting energy. Increasing energy efficiency will ensure that the need for energy is met with less resources. In this way, possible damage to the environment will be reduced.

Renewable energy has both positive and negative aspects. The most important negative side of renewable energy is its high investment costs. Whichever renewable energy source will be preferred for access to renewable energy, appropriate investments should be made in suitable regions. The high cost of the investments needed is the most important obstacle to renewable energy. Although the costs are high, the long-term gains will bring a return beyond the costs. Renewable energy sources will make a positive contribution to ensuring energy supply security. When the cost of the risks posed by the energy supply security is compared with the investment cost, it will undoubtedly be profitable to invest. Investments made in renewable energy resources will ensure energy supply security with energy diversity, management of energy production, and sustainability of access to energy.

The more effective and active use of renewable energy sources is important in terms of creating energy diversity. Renewable energy sources can be used together with non-renewable energy sources to meet the energy needs. Increasing the share of renewable energy use in energy supply and consumption will provide energy diversification and support the security of energy supply. It is necessary to increase the use of renewable energy in order to diversify energy sources and meet energy needs in different ways. The increase in renewable energy supply and consumption will be possible by increasing the investment in renewable energy sources. Reducing the problem of access to energy with energy diversity will increase the security of energy supply. Increasing energy supply security is also a strategic issue of vital national importance. It is aimed to increase the investments made in renewable energy sources with various supports. Investors are tried to be directed to renewable energy investments by developing policies in order to increase energy diversity and increase renewable energy sources.

Another factor to be created by the increase in renewable energy investments is sustainability. As a constant need, energy appears in every moment of both economic and social life. The resources and methods used in energy supply must be sustainable. Perhaps the energy need can be met today from unsustainable sources, but it will not be possible to meet the energy need in the coming years. Renewable energy sources are sustainable as they are not scarce and can be renewed. In this respect, it will support the provision of energy supply security. Renewable energy sources are not only sustainable in terms of resources, but also a sustainable energy source as a method used in obtaining energy. Just being sustainable is not enough. If the method used to access the energy source is not sustainable, it will not be possible to use it continuously due to the negative externality that will arise. Such a situation will also create an energy supply risk. Negative externality will disappear as it is obtained through renewable clean and environmentally friendly methods. Investments in renewable energy sources will ensure energy supply security with this dimension.

References

Bhuiyan, M. A., Dinçer, H., Yüksel, S., Mikhaylov, A., Danish, M. S. S., Pinter, G., et al. (2022). Economic indicators and bioenergy supply in developed economies: QROF-DEMATEL and random forest models. *Energy Reports, 8*, 561–570.

Dinçer, H., Yüksel, S., & Martínez, L. (2022). Collaboration enhanced hybrid fuzzy decision-making approach to analyze the renewable energy investment projects. *Energy Reports, 8*, 377–389.

Dong, W., Zhao, G., Yüksel, S., Dinçer, H., & Ubay, G. G. (2022). A novel hybrid decision making approach for the strategic selection of wind energy projects. *Renewable Energy, 185*, 321–337.

Gernaat, D. E., de Boer, H. S., Daioglou, V., Yalew, S. G., Müller, C., & van Vuuren, D. P. (2021). Climate change impacts on renewable energy supply. *Nature Climate Change, 11*(2), 119–125.

Haiyun, C., Zhixiong, H., Yüksel, S., & Dinçer, H. (2021). Analysis of the innovation strategies for green supply chain management in the energy industry using the QFD-based hybrid interval valued intuitionistic fuzzy decision approach. *Renewable and Sustainable Energy Reviews, 143*, 110844.

Ivanovski, K., Hailemariam, A., & Smyth, R. (2021). The effect of renewable and non-renewable energy consumption on economic growth: Non-parametric evidence. *Journal of Cleaner Production, 286*, 124956.

Kostis, P., Dinçer, H., & Yüksel, S. (2022). Knowledge-based energy investments of european economies and policy recommendations for sustainable development. *Journal of the Knowledge Economy*, 1–33.

Kou, G., Yüksel, S., & Dinçer, H. (2022). Inventive problem-solving map of innovative carbon emission strategies for solar energy-based transportation investment projects. *Applied Energy, 311*, 118680.

Levenda, A. M., Behrsin, I., & Disano, F. (2021). Renewable energy for whom? A global systematic review of the environmental justice implications of renewable energy technologies. *Energy Research & Social Science, 71*, 101837.

Li, J., Yüksel, S., Dinçer, H., Mikhaylov, A., & Barykin, S. E. (2022). Bipolar q-ROF hybrid decision making model with golden cut for analyzing the levelized cost of renewable energy alternatives. *IEEE Access.*

Meng, Y., Wu, H., Zhao, W., Chen, W., Dinçer, H., & Yüksel, S. (2021). A hybrid heterogeneous Pythagorean fuzzy group decision modelling for crowdfunding development process pathways of fintech-based clean energy investment projects. *Financial Innovation, 7*(1), 1–34.

Mukhtarov, S., Yüksel, S., & Dinçer, H. (2022). The impact of financial development on renewable energy consumption: Evidence from Turkey. *Renewable Energy.*

Opeyemi, B. M. (2021). Path to sustainable energy consumption: The possibility of substituting renewable energy for non-renewable energy. *Energy, 228*, 120519.

Panagopoulos, A. (2021). Water-energy nexus: desalination technologies and renewable energy sources. *Environmental Science and Pollution Research, 28*(17), 21009–21022.

Pietrzak, M. B., Igliński, B., Kujawski, W., & Iwański, P. (2021). Energy transition in Poland—assessment of the renewable energy sector. *Energies, 14*(8), 2046.

Sebestyén, V. (2021). Renewable and sustainable energy reviews: Environmental impact networks of renewable energy power plants. *Renewable and Sustainable Energy Reviews, 151*, 111626.

Wan, Q., Zhao, X., Liu, H., Dinçer, H., & Yüksel, S. (2022). Assessing the new product development process for the industrial decarbonization of sustainable economies. *SAGE Open, 12*(1), 21582440211067231.

Yuan, G., Xie, F., Dinçer, H., & Yüksel, S. (2021). The theory of inventive problem solving (TRIZ)-based strategic mapping of green nuclear energy investments with spherical fuzzy group decision-making approach. *International Journal of Energy Research, 45*(8), 12284–12300.

Yüksel, S., & Dinçer, H. (2022). Identifying the strategic priorities of nuclear energy investments using hesitant 2-tuple interval-valued Pythagorean fuzzy DEMATEL. *Progress in Nuclear Energy, 145*, 104103.

Yüksel, S., Dinçer, H., Eti, S., & Adalı, Z. (2022). Strategy improvements to minimize the drawbacks of geothermal investments by using spherical fuzzy modelling. *International Journal of Energy Research.*

Zhang, Y., Zhang, Y., Gong, C., Dinçer, H., & Yüksel, S. (2022). An integrated hesitant 2-tuple Pythagorean fuzzy analysis of QFD-based innovation cost and duration for renewable energy projects. *Energy, 248*, 123561.

Zhao, Y., Korsakienė, R., Dinçer, H., & Yüksel, S. (2022). Identifying significant points of energy culture for developing sustainable energy investments. *SAGE Open, 12*(1), 21582440221087262.

Zhou, P., Luo, J., Cheng, F., Yüksel, S., & Dinçer, H. (2021). Analysis of risk priorities for renewable energy investment projects using a hybrid IT2 hesitant fuzzy decision-making approach with alpha cuts. *Energy, 224*, 120184.

Chapter 7
Investigation of the Nexus Between the Electricity Consumption and the Ecological Footprint

Zafer Adalı and Mir Sayed Shah Danish

Abstract Among the footprint, the ecological footprint has been accepted as one of the most comprehensive indexes to indicate the human demand for natural resources. Within this scope, the world encounters a massive challenge consisting of sharp rising energy demand, environmental degradation, and sustainability. The electricity demand is a prime indicator reflected in production, urbanization, and consumption patterns. However, fossil sources predominantly generate electricity, which contributes to environmental degradation. In this study, it is aimed to investigate the causality link between the electricity consumption and the ecological footprint in emerging countries. Within this aim, Panel VAR Granger Causality analysis is performed on data for 1971–2014. The study's objective is to provide insight into the policymakers to guide the energy management policies. The samples are selected from important emerging countries: Turkey, China, India, Brazil, Indonesia, Malaysia, and Mexico. The considered samples are that the urbanizations, higher populations, and the industrialization efforts for achieving higher economic welfare have a vital matter for the considered countries. The electricity consumption is directly related to all mentioned events. According to the findings, it is found that electricity consumption is the cause of the ecological footprint. As can be understood from the above-mentioned issues, the use of fossil fuels causes significant damage to the environment. In this context, it is necessary to consider different alternatives in energy use. In this context, it is important to increase investments in renewable energy and nuclear energy, which are considered clean energy. It is important to make technological investments for the development of renewable energy projects. In this way, it will be possible to reduce the initial costs of these projects. As a result, renewable energy projects will become competitive with fossil fuels. It is of vital importance to take some measures to prevent the risk of explosion in nuclear power plants. In this context, it is necessary to prevent this risk by using new technologies.

Z. Adalı (✉)
Department of Economics, Artvin Coruh University, Artvin, Turkey
e-mail: zaferadali@artvin.edu.tr

M. S. S. Danish
Strategic Research Projects Center, University of the Ryukyus, Nishihara, Japan

H. Dinçer, S. Yüksel (eds.), *Circular Economy and the Energy Market*,
Contributions to Economics, https://doi.org/10.1007/978-3-031-13146-2_7

On the other hand, radioactive wastes occur as a result of energy production in nuclear power plants. These wastes need to be disposed of effectively. In this process, effective disposal methods need to be considered. Otherwise, nuclear energy investments will become quite inefficient.

Keywords Electricity consumption · Economic growth · Ecological footprint · Energy Economics

7.1 Introduction

The industrial age labelling the last 300 years of human history has changed the standard of human-being life, the scale of production, and consumption. The industrialization has initially occurred in a few countries located in Europe, but the last few decades have marked all countries' efforts and attempts to develop their economic structure or protect their economic welfare in the world league. Within these competitions among the countries, energy has seemed to be one of the most irreplaceable tools to achieve higher economic welfare. Primarily, the recent structure of the energy sources used for meeting the development and growth efforts of the countries is based on fossil fuels. According to EIA (2021), approximately 80 percent of the energy emanates from fossil fuels, with coal for 26.8%, natural gas for 23.2%, and oil for 30.9%.

As for the reflection of the humans' energy needs for meeting production and standard of life, electricity is accepted as a comprehensive indicator as the manufacturing sector is laboriously conditional on electricity availability. According to Our World in Data (2022), approximately 64 percent of global electricity is derived from fossils sources, and renewable energy sources generate 26.3 percent. However, the electricity demand continues to increase day by day. The EIA (2021) documents that the electricity demand grows at 2.7% per year to 2040, and the major reason for the increasing demand is driven by the developing countries, especially China and India. It is obvious that the pressure of human activities on the planet will be more visible regarding this scenario. Moreover, the economies should tend to increase the share of renewable energy in total energy generation because the nonrenewable energy sources are finite. Besides, the usage of nonrenewable energy sources produces detrimental products degrading the environment, especially greenhouse emissions.

Since the last few centuries, all transformations and changes in society, production, urbanization, and consumption have induced massive pressure on the world. The only increase in 1 Celsius in the world temperature leads to huge *catastrophes* events consisting of melting icefield, drought, flood, vanishing the species of plants and animals. All environmental degradations may be aggregated in terms named as climate changes or global warming. Historically, highly industrialized developed countries have been in charge of a large percentage of greenhouse emissions, while the growth rate in developing countries has been much higher recently (Balsalobre-Lorente et al., 2018).

In addition, climate change is mainly driven by the greenhouse emissions covering six sub gases, and CO2 emissions account for seventy percent of the greenhouse emissions. However, EIA (2021) affirms that 80 percent of CO2 emissions results from energy consumption, and CO2 emissions are the primary source of global warming. Hence, many intergovernmental organizations and governments have set targets and defined the implications to reduce CO2 emissions (Bélaïd & Youssef, 2017). Notwithstanding, the effects of the Anthropogenic on the world are not limited to the atmosphere. Anthropogenic activities have induced various degradations involving a reduction in biodiversity, depletion of the ozone layer, global warming, deforestation, air, and water pollution. As a result, more comprehensive indicators are required to set environmental targets, implement energy and environmental management, and path a way for sustainable development. Within this purpose, various footprints are developed, and a specific footprint is a reliable way of indicating the burden of human activities and their effects on sustainability. The burden of human activities on specific areas can be expressed through related footprints such as the financial footprint, the energy footprint, the carbon footprint, the chemical footprint, the biodiversity footprint, etc. (Čuček et al., 2012).

Among the footprint, the ecological footprint has been accepted as one of the most comprehensive indexes to indicate the human demand for natural resources. The ecological footprint is introduced by Rees (1992) and then developed by Wackernagel and Rees (1998). The ecological footprint comprehensively addresses environmental problems because it comprises six subcomponents: cropland, grazing land, carbon, forest products, built-up land, and fishing ground. Along with these six subcomponents, the ecological footprint effectively replies to how much nature countries possess and how much they utilize productive areas in nature (Galli et al., 2012). Furthermore, the ecological footprint is also a comprehensive indicator of global warming. The carbon footprint is situated in the ecological footprint, and the carbon footprint accounts for more than half of the ecological footprint. Thus, the ecological footprint also firmly mirrors the impacts of GHG emissions. Furthermore, the ecological footprint is one of the most important indicators for sustainability since it measures how much of the renewable capacity of the biosphere is used by human activities, meaning the pressure of humans on the environment, shows the ecological cost of goods and services provided to the human. In another expression, the ecological footprint defines environmental boundaries and how people exceed these boundaries (Solarin, 2019).

Within this scope, the world encounters a massive challenge consisting of sharp rising energy demand, environmental degradation, and sustainability. The electricity demand is a prime indicator reflected in production, urbanization, and consumption patterns. However, fossil sources predominantly generate electricity, which contributes to environmental degradation. Consequently, we aim to investigate the causality link between the electricity consumption and the ecological footprint in emerging countries. Within this aim, Panel VAR Granger Causality analysis is performed on data for 1971–2014. The study's objective is to provide insight into the policymakers to guide the energy management policies.

7.2 Theoretical Information About Environmental Issues

The concern about environmental degradation has induced a reflection shaping and changing the academic fields' perspective. A large number of the studies related to directly or indirectly the environment has been conducted by the researchers in the light of the different aims. As for the economy, the studies have been aimed to determine the effects of various factors involving economic growth, urbanization, trade, etc. on the environment. Although the investigations have been made using different econometric methodologies, different countries or regions, and various proxies, the pathing ways for sustainable development and preventing the environmental degradations caused by the economic activities have been summarized as the primary objectives of the efforts. Within this scope, the nexus between energy consumption and environmental degradation has been one of the leading topics in the literature because energy consumption is considered the essential indicator providing insight information on the economic growth, industrializations, urbanizations, and the ordinary human being's standard of lives.

Furthermore, defining environmental degradations seem to be another challenging issue in the literature. The pressure of human activities on the planet may be observed in different parts of the planet, such as the sea, river, forest, and atmosphere. However, climate change and global warming can be considered the most significant outcome of human activities and the essential factors causing various catastrophic events involving floods, deforestation, fauna, flora, and animals' extinction. Therefore, CO2 emissions have been the most valuable variables since climate change and global warming are driven by greenhouse emissions, of which CO2 accounts for 70% of greenhouse emissions. Thus, various studies in the literature have been conducted to investigate the connection between energy consumption and CO2 emissions. Energy consumption is disaggregated into renewable and nonrenewable energy sources; the former is mainly used to detect its ability to prevent environmental degradation.

The latter is primarily used to determine its effects on environmental degradation. Various research topics range from the EKC hypothesis, the pollution halo, to the pollution haven hypothesis. Besides, the causality analysis has been one of the leading hypotheses because its implication plays a vital role in establishing energy management and environmental policies. However, there is no finding reaching an agreement. For example, some studies confirm a unidirectional causality link moving from energy consumption to CO2 emissions (Lotfalipour et al., 2010; Farhani et al., 2014). In addition, a one-way causality nexus operating from CO2 emissions to energy consumption is also affirmed by some studies (Soytas et al., 2007; Farhani & Rejeb, 2012). Besides, a bidirectional causality relationship between energy consumption and CO2 emissions is another consequence of the investigations (Sbia et al., 2014; Alkhathlan & Javid, 2013; Ben Mbarek et al., 2018). Finally, the absence of the causality association between energy consumption and CO2 emissions is also revealed (Soytas & Sari, 2009; Ghosh, 2010).

The connection between electricity consumption and environmental quality has been one of the cornerstone research topics in the literature. CO2 emissions have the most usage appears used as a proxy for the environmental quality. Besides, the electricity consumption is categorized as two sub lines consisting of the electricity consumption generated from fossil-fuel-based energy sources and the electricity consumption generated from renewable energy sources. Within this context, many studies confirm that electricity consumption from fossil-fuel-based energy sources increases CO2 emissions, in which the environmental quality has deteriorated (Salahuddin et al., 2015; Bélaïd & Youssef, 2017; Rahman, 2020). Furthermore, various researchers affirm that electricity consumption from renewable energy sources improves ecological quality by diminishing CO2 emissions (Bélaïd & Youssef, 2017; Balsalobre-Lorente et al., 2018).

Furthermore, some studies try to find the causality link between electricity consumption and CO2 emissions. For example, Farhani and Shahbaz (2014) indicate a piece of evidence that electricity consumption derived from nonrenewable and renewable sources causes CO2 emissions. Various studies also confirm a one-way causality link operating from electricity consumption to CO2 emissions (Saint Akadiri et al., 2020). A feedback causality between electricity consumption and CO2 emissions is affirmed by Shahbaz et al. (2014). Kahouli (2018) also achieves a piece of evidence confirming the feedback relationship between electricity consumption and environmental degradation.

In addition to the studies employing CO2 emissions as the environmental degradation indicators, the ecological footprint has surged new attention in the same research topics. Though the ecological footprint is a more comprehensive index than CO2 emissions, the study volume has been limited. Langnel and Amegavi (2020) strive to discover the connection between electricity consumption and the ecological footprint in Ghana for 1971–2016. The empirical evidence is achieved from the Autoregressive Distribute Lag (ARDL) bound test, accounting for the structural breaks. In the study, electricity consumption from fossil-fuel-based energy sources is employed. The finding affirms the long-run connection between electricity consumption and the ecological footprint and the feedback causality between the considered variables.

Furthermore, it is also concluded that electricity consumption performs as a deteriorating factor affecting the environmental quality. Bello et al. (2018) use four environmental degradation indicators involving CO2 emission, carbon footprint, water footprint, and ecological footprint to determine the role of electricity consumption generated by hydro sources in Malaysia. The VECM Granger causality technique is applied between 1971 and 2016. The implications of the result show that hydroelectricity consumption abates environmental degradation. Moreover, the unidirectional causality from hydroelectricity and fossil fuel consumption to environmental degradation indicators is affirmed. Topcu (2021) applies the Johansen Cointegration test, FMOLS, DOLS, and CCR model to determine the connection between renewable energy consumption and the ecological footprint in Turkey for 1990–2015. The study approves that renewable energy consumption leads to a decline in the ecological footprint. Baz et al. (2020) try to discover the asymmetric effects of nonrenewable energy consumption and economic growth on the ecological footprint in Pakistan for 1971–2014. According to the evidence, two-way asymmetric causality between nonrenewable energy consumption and the ecological footprint is confirmed.

Besides, another causality investigation between nonrenewable energy consumption and the ecological footprint is conducted by Udemba (2020) for Nigeria, and the finding affirms a one-way causality link operating from nonrenewable energy consumption to the ecological footprint. Nathaniel et al. (2020) analyze the role of renewable and nonrenewable energy consumption in the ecological footprint in MENA countries. The Augmented Mean Group algorithm is applied to data over the period of 1990 to 2016. As a consequence of the analysis, it is confirmed that nonrenewable energy consumption leads to higher environmental degradation. In contrast, the effects of renewable energy are not influential factors affecting environmental quality.

Alper et al. (2022) apply the Fourier bootstrap ARDL cointegration and the Fourier bootstrap Toda-Yamamoto causality method to detect the impacts of energy consumption on the ecological footprint in the top 10 countries contributing to the most significant carbon dioxide emissions in the world. The estimation reveals the presence of a long-run connection between the variables for seven of the ten countries. Moreover, energy consumption has a significantly positive effect on the ecological footprint in China, Germany, Iran, and Saudi Arabia. However, the result of the causality analysis is mixed. Li et al. (2022) try to answer whether renewable energy sources improve the environmental quality without preventing economic growth for 120 countries. They affirm that renewable energy sources play a pivotal role in improving environmental quality and promoting economic growth.

7.3 An Evaluation for Emerging Economies

This part aims to determine the causality relationship between electricity consumption and the ecological footprint. Within this objective, Panel VAR Granger causality analysis is employed on the data spanning from 1971 to 2014. The samples are selected from important emerging countries: Turkey, China, India, Brazil, Indonesia, Malaysia, and Mexico. The considered samples are that the urbanizations, higher populations, and the industrialization efforts for achieving higher economic welfare have a vital matter for the considered countries. The electricity consumption is directly related to all mentioned events. The ecological footprint data is achieved from Global Footprint Network's data stream (https://data.footprintnetwork.org/#/exploreData), and the ecological footprint is chosen as gha. The electricity consumption is obtained from the World Bank data streams, and it is based on kWh per capita. Before analysis, the logarithm of the variable was made.

The first-generation panel unit root tests are conducted to determine the stationarity properties of the variables. The results of the unit root tests are presented

Table 7.1 The results of the panel unit tests

	Level		The First Differences	
	Electricity consumption	The ecological footprint	Electricity consumption	The ecological footprint
Levin, Lin & Chu t*	−0.82623	0.17789	−6.54312***	−6.34973***
Breitung t-stat	2.00714	0.48309	−5.86369***	−5.82290***
Im, Pesaran and Shin W-stat	1.59305	−0.66473	−7.27461***	−9.26454***
ADF-Fisher Chi-square	9.61630	17.1371	77.0063***	99.4040***
PP-Fisher Chi-square	9.83309	30.4814***	123.182***	462.859***

Notes:***, and * present significance level at 1% and 10%

Table 7.2 The result of the panel VAR Granger causality analysis

Electricity consumption → The ecological footprint			The ecological footprint→ Electricity consumption		
Chi-sq	df	Prob.	Chi-sq	df	Prob.
3.977991	1	0.0461	3.423947	1	0.0643

in Table 7.1. The tests show that electricity consumption and the ecological footprint are stationary at the first differences.

In order to detect the causality link between the variables, Panel VAR Granger causality analysis is performed. The optimal lag is selected as 1, considering the Serial Correlation and Heteroscedasticity Tests. The results of the causality analysis are posed in Table 7.2. According to the findings, it is found that electricity consumption is the cause of the ecological footprint.

7.4 Conclusion

In the process of electricity consumption, mostly fossil fuels are preferred all over the world. The main reason for this is the lower cost of fossil fuels compared to other alternatives. This is an important source of motivation for investors (Haiyun et al., 2021). Low cost also means high profitability. Therefore, investors may prefer fossil fuels to ensure cost efficiency. This situation creates a serious problem for the country (Li et al., 2021). It is obvious that fossil fuels create social and economic problems for countries. When electricity is produced using these fuels, a significant amount of carbon gas is released into the atmosphere. This situation both pollutes the air and causes significant environmental problems (Kou et al., 2022). As a result, there is an increase in the number of people who are sick. This will lead to an increase in health costs in countries. This will have a negative effect on the budget balance of the countries. Another negative aspect of fossil fuel use is that it leads to an increase in the workforce in the country (Bhuiyan et al., 2022). People who become ill as a result of air pollution will not be able to continue their work. This situation leads to a significant decrease in production in the countries. Less labor force participation will also negatively affect the economies of countries (Du et al., 2020). On the other hand, the fact that people are constantly sick is also accepted as a factor that reduces their quality of life.

As can be understood from the above-mentioned issues, the use of fossil fuels causes significant damage to the environment (Dong et al., 2022). In this context, it is necessary to consider different alternatives in energy use. In this context, it is important to increase investments in renewable energy and nuclear energy, which are considered clean energy. Natural resources such as wind and sun are taken into account in renewable energy projects (Adalı et al., 2022). In other words, no element is burned in the energy production process. Therefore, the carbon emission problem is minimized (Zhe et al., 2021). For these reasons, renewable energy alternatives are considered environmentally friendly. Therefore, one way to reduce the negative impact of energy production on the environment is to increase renewable energy projects (Kostis et al., 2022). However, the initial cost of these projects is very high (Li et al., 2020). This situation prevents investors from turning to this area. In summary, it is important to make technological investments for the development of renewable energy projects. In this way, it will be possible to reduce the initial costs of these projects. As a result, renewable energy projects will become competitive with fossil fuels.

Another way to develop clean energy projects is to increase investments in nuclear energy. It is possible to produce electricity at any time of the day in nuclear energy projects. This also contributes to the stability of the amount of energy produced. This positive aspect does not apply to renewable energy projects (Liu et al., 2021). For example, the amount of electricity produced in wind energy projects depends on the strength of the blowing wind. In other words, in case the wind blows less, there will be a decrease in the amount of electricity obtained (Yüksel et al., 2022a, b). Similarly, the amount of energy obtained from solar energy projects will decrease at night and during the winter months (Mukhtarov et al., 2022; Zhao et al., 2021). However, these problems do not exist in nuclear energy projects. On the other hand, no carbon emissions occur in electricity production with nuclear energy. This allows nuclear energy to be accepted as environmentally friendly energy.

It is clear that nuclear energy projects need to be developed. However, these projects also have some disadvantages. For example, nuclear power plants are at risk of explosion. Past bad experiences show that this explosion is very risky (Meng et al., 2021). In this process, many people lost their lives and the region became uninhabitable. As can be understood from this situation, it is of vital importance to take some measures to prevent the risk of explosion in nuclear power plants (Yuan et al., 2021; Yüksel & Dinçer, 2022). In this context, it is necessary to prevent this risk by using new technologies. On the other hand, radioactive wastes occur as a result of energy production in nuclear power plants. These wastes need to be disposed of effectively (Wan et al., 2022). In this process, effective disposal methods need to be considered. Otherwise, nuclear energy investments will become quite inefficient. In this context, it is necessary to increase the performance in the disposal process of radioactive waste, especially by following up-to-date technologies (Zhang et al., 2022).

References

Adalı, Z., Dinçer, H., Eti, S., Mikhaylov, A., & Yüksel, S. (2022). Identifying new perspectives on geothermal energy investments. In *Multidimensional strategic outlook on global competitive energy economics and finance*. Emerald Publishing Limited.

Alkhathlan, K., & Javid, M. (2013). Energy consumption, carbon emissions and economic growth in Saudi Arabia: An aggregate and disaggregate analysis. *Energy Policy, 62*, 1525–1532.

Alper, A. E., Alper, F. O., Ozayturk, G., & Mike, F. (2022). Testing the long-run impact of economic growth, energy consumption, and globalization on ecological footprint: New evidence from Fourier bootstrap ARDL and Fourier bootstrap Toda–Yamamoto test results. *Environmental Science and Pollution Research*, 1–16.

Balsalobre-Lorente, D., Shahbaz, M., Roubaud, D., & Farhani, S. (2018). How economic growth, renewable electricity and natural resources contribute to CO2 emissions? *Energy Policy, 113*, 356–367.

Baz, K., Xu, D., Ali, H., Ali, I., Khan, I., Khan, M. M., & Cheng, J. (2020). Asymmetric impact of energy consumption and economic growth on ecological footprint: Using asymmetric and nonlinear approach. *Science of the Total Environment, 718*, 137364.

Bélaïd, F., & Youssef, M. (2017). Environmental degradation, renewable and non-renewable electricity consumption, and economic growth: Assessing the evidence from Algeria. *Energy Policy, 102*, 277–287.

Bello, M. O., Solarin, S. A., & Yen, Y. Y. (2018). The impact of electricity consumption on CO2 emission, carbon footprint, water footprint and ecological footprint: The role of hydropower in an emerging economy. *Journal of Environmental Management, 219*, 218–230.

Ben Mbarek, M., Saidi, K., & Rahman, M. M. (2018). Renewable and non-renewable energy consumption, environmental degradation and economic growth in Tunisia. *Quality & Quantity, 52*(3), 1105–1119.

Bhuiyan, M. A., Dinçer, H., Yüksel, S., Mikhaylov, A., Danish, M. S. S., Pinter, G., et al. (2022). Economic indicators and bioenergy supply in developed economies: QROF-DEMATEL and random forest models. *Energy Reports, 8*, 561–570.

Čuček, L., Klemeš, J. J., & Kravanja, Z. (2012). A review of footprint analysis tools for monitoring impacts on sustainability. *Journal of Cleaner Production, 34*, 9–20.

Dong, W., Zhao, G., Yüksel, S., Dinçer, H., & Ubay, G. G. (2022). A novel hybrid decision making approach for the strategic selection of wind energy projects. *Renewable Energy, 185*, 321–337.

Du, L., Dinçer, H., Ersin, İ., & Yüksel, S. (2020). IT2 fuzzy-based multidimensional evaluation of coal energy for sustainable economic development. *Energies, 13*(10), 1–21.

EIA (2021). Annual energy outlook. Technical report, U.S. Energy Information Administration.

Farhani, S., & Rejeb, J. B. (2012). Energy consumption, economic growth and CO2 emissions: Evidence from panel data for MENA region. *International Journal of Energy Economics and Policy, 2*(2), 71–81.

Farhani, S., & Shahbaz, M. (2014). What role of renewable and non-renewable electricity consumption and output is needed to initially mitigate CO2 emissions in MENA region?. *Renewable and Sustainable Energy Reviews*, 40, 80–90.

Farhani, S., Chaibi, A., & Rault, C. (2014). CO2 emissions, output, energy consumption, and trade in Tunisia. *Economic Modelling, 38*, 426–434.

Galli, A., Wiedmann, T., Ercin, E., Knoblauch, D., Ewing, B., & Giljum, S. (2012). Integrating ecological, carbon and water footprint into a "footprint family" of indicators: Definition and role in tracking human pressure on the planet. *Ecological Indicators, 16*, 100–112.

Ghosh, S. (2010). Examining carbon emissions economic growth nexus for India: A multivariate cointegration approach. *Energy Policy, 38*(6), 3008–3014.

Haiyun, C., Zhixiong, H., Yüksel, S., & Dinçer, H. (2021). Analysis of the innovation strategies for green supply chain management in the energy industry using the QFD-based hybrid interval valued intuitionistic fuzzy decision approach. *Renewable and Sustainable Energy Reviews, 143*, 110844.

Kahouli, B. (2018). The causality link between energy electricity consumption, CO2 emissions, R&D stocks and economic growth in Mediterranean countries (MCs). *Energy, 145*, 388–399.

Kostis, P., Dinçer, H., & Yüksel, S. (2022). Knowledge-based energy investments of European Economies and Policy Recommendations for sustainable development. *Journal of the Knowledge Economy*, 1–33.

Kou, G., Yüksel, S., & Dinçer, H. (2022). Inventive problem-solving map of innovative carbon emission strategies for solar energy-based transportation investment projects. *Applied Energy, 311*, 118680.

Langnel, Z., & Amegavi, G. B. (2020). Globalization, electricity consumption and ecological footprint: An autoregressive distributive lag (ARDL) approach. *Sustainable Cities and Society, 63*, 102482.

Li, R., Wang, X., & Wang, Q. (2022). Does renewable energy reduce ecological footprint at the expense of economic growth? An empirical analysis of 120 countries. *Journal of Cleaner Production, 131207.*

Li, X., Zhu, S., Yüksel, S., Dinçer, H., & Ubay, G. G. (2020). Kano-based mapping of innovation strategies for renewable energy alternatives using hybrid interval type-2 fuzzy decision-making approach. *Energy, 211*, 1–16.

Li, Y. X., Wu, Z. X., Dinçer, H., Kalkavan, H., & Yüksel, S. (2021). Analyzing TRIZ-based strategic priorities of customer expectations for renewable energy investments with interval type-2 fuzzy modeling. *Energy Reports, 7*, 95–108.

Liu, J., Lv, J., Dinçer, H., Yüksel, S., & Karakuş, H. (2021). Selection of renewable energy alternatives for green blockchain investments: A hybrid IT2-based fuzzy modelling. *Archives of Computational Methods in Engineering, 28*, 3687–3701.

Lotfalipour, M. R., Falahi, M. A., & Ashena, M. (2010). Economic growth, CO2 emissions, and fossil fuels consumption in Iran. *Energy, 35*(12), 5115–5120.

Meng, Y., Zhou, R., Dinçer, H., Yüksel, S., & Wang, C. (2021). Analysis of inventive problem-solving capacities for renewable energy storage investments. *Energy Reports, 7*, 4779–4791.

Mukhtarov, S., Yüksel, S., & Dinçer, H. (2022). The impact of financial development on renewable energy consumption: Evidence from Turkey. *Renewable Energy.*

Nathaniel, S., Anyanwu, O., & Shah, M. (2020). Renewable energy, urbanization, and ecological footprint in the Middle East and North Africa region. *Environmental Science and Pollution Research, 27*(13), 14601–14613.

Our World in Data (2022). https://ourworldindata.org/energy-access.

Rahman, M. M. (2020). Environmental degradation: The role of electricity consumption, economic growth and globalisation. *Journal of Environmental Management, 253*, 109742.

Rees, W. E. (1992). Ecological footprints and appropriated carrying capacity: What urban economics leaves out. *Environment and Urbanization, 4*(2), 121–130.

Saint Akadiri, S., Alola, A. A., Olasehinde-Williams, G., & Etokakpan, M. U. (2020). The role of electricity consumption, globalization and economic growth in carbon dioxide emissions and its implications for environmental sustainability targets. *Science of the Total Environment, 708*, 134653.

Salahuddin, M., Gow, J., & Ozturk, I. (2015). Is the long-run relationship between economic growth, electricity consumption, carbon dioxide emissions and financial development in gulf cooperation council countries robust? *Renewable and Sustainable Energy Reviews, 51*, 317–326.

Sbia, R., Shahbaz, M., & Hamdi, H. (2014). A contribution of foreign direct investment, clean energy, trade openness, carbon emissions and economic growth to energy demand in UAE. *Economic Modelling, 36*, 191–197.

Shahbaz, M., Sbia, R., Hamdi, H., & Ozturk, I. (2014). Economic growth, electricity consumption, urbanization and environmental degradation relationship in United Arab Emirates. *Ecological Indicators, 45*, 622–631.

Solarin, S. A. (2019). Convergence in CO 2 emissions, carbon footprint and ecological footprint: Evidence from OECD countries. *Environmental Science and Pollution Research, 26*(6), 6167–6181.

Soytas, U., & Sari, R. (2009). Energy consumption, economic growth, and carbon emissions: Challenges faced by an EU candidate member. *Ecological Economics, 68*(6), 1667–1675.

Soytas, U., Sari, R., & Ewing, B. T. (2007). Energy consumption, income, and carbon emissions in the United States. *Ecological Economics, 62*(3–4), 482–489.

Topcu, B. A. (2021). The impact of export, import, and renewable energy consumption on Turkey's ecological footprint. *Journal of Economics Finance and Accounting, 8*(1), 31–38.

Udemba, E. N. (2020). A sustainable study of economic growth and development amidst ecological footprint: New insight from Nigerian perspective. *Science of the Total Environment, 732*, 139270.

Wackernagel, M., & Rees, W. (1998). *Our ecological footprint: Reducing human impact on the earth* (Vol. 9). New society publishers.

Wan, Q., Zhao, X., Liu, H., Dinçer, H., & Yüksel, S. (2022). Assessing the new product development process for the industrial decarbonization of sustainable economies. *SAGE Open, 12*(1), 21582440211067231.

Yuan, G., Xie, F., Dinçer, H., & Yüksel, S. (2021). The theory of inventive problem solving (TRIZ)-based strategic mapping of green nuclear energy investments with spherical fuzzy group decision-making approach. *International Journal of Energy Research, 45*(8), 12284–12300.

Yüksel, S., & Dinçer, H. (2022). Identifying the strategic priorities of nuclear energy investments using hesitant 2-tuple interval-valued Pythagorean fuzzy DEMATEL. *Progress in Nuclear Energy, 145*, 104103.

Yüksel, S., Dinçer, H., Çağlayan, Ç., Uluer, G. S., & Lisin, A. (2022b). Bitcoin mining with nuclear energy. In *Multidimensional strategic outlook on global competitive energy economics and finance*. Emerald Publishing Limited.

Yüksel, S., Dinçer, H., Mikhaylov, A., Adalı, Z., & Eti, S. (2022a). Key issues for the improvements of shallow geothermal investments. In *Sustainability in energy business and finance* (pp. 183–194). Springer.

Zhang, Y., Zhang, Y., Gong, C., Dinçer, H., & Yüksel, S. (2022). An integrated hesitant 2-tuple Pythagorean fuzzy analysis of QFD-based innovation cost and duration for renewable energy projects. *Energy, 123561*.

Zhao, Y., Xu, Y., Yüksel, S., Dinçer, H., & Ubay, G. G. (2021). Hybrid IT2 fuzzy modelling with alpha cuts for hydrogen energy investments. *International Journal of Hydrogen Energy, 46*(13), 8835–8851.

Zhe, L., Yüksel, S., Dinçer, H., Mukhtarov, S., & Azizov, M. (2021). The positive influences of renewable energy consumption on financial development and economic growth. *SAGE Open, 11*(3), 1–9.

Chapter 8
The Role of Environmental Journalism in Raising Awareness on Energy Efficiency

Başak Gezmen

Abstract Forming public opinion and education functions, which are among the functions of the media, are an issue that should be given great sensitivity today. What should be understood from media education is that the content of the broadcasts should be aimed at informing the public and meeting the information needs, rather than the direct education given in educational institutions, as well as culture, art, environment, politics, economy, etc. It is necessary to raise awareness about the issues. As human beings, we can sustain our lives by using natural resources. We provide all our needs directly or indirectly by living from nature. At this point, environmental education plans are needed for people's well-being and survival. Today, the importance of environmental education has become very important in the development of awareness and sensitivity towards the environment in individuals, identifying environmental problems and acquiring skills for them. Creating awareness and raising awareness about energy saving in energy efficiency can also be achieved through the media. In particular, public opinion can be formed by ensuring the correct flow of information on the subject. Within the scope of the study, the role of environmental education and environmental journalism on energy and energy efficiency will be discussed, and what kind of awareness areas can be created for the problems within the framework of news and journalism briefs will be discussed in the axis of suggestions.

Keywords Energy efficiency · Environmental education · Media · News · Environmental journalism

---

B. Gezmen (✉)
The School of Communication, İstanbul Medipol University, Istanbul, Turkey
e-mail: bgezmen@medipol.edu.tr

H. Dinçer, S. Yüksel (eds.), *Circular Economy and the Energy Market*,
Contributions to Economics, https://doi.org/10.1007/978-3-031-13146-2_8

8.1 Introduction

Energy refers to a mobility that can be transformed into many various forms with continuity. The concepts of energy efficiency and energy saving are closely related to each other. Using energy more rationally also defines energy efficiency in general (Mukhtarov et al., 2022; Liu et al., 2021). Various studies are carried out to ensure efficient and effective use of energy, and some practices related to this issue are made compulsory. And at this point, both international and national legal regulations have been made (Xie et al., 2021; Kou et al., 2022; Zhou et al., 2021).

The phenomenon of consumption, which has become the most important occupation of human beings today, is an indispensable part of the system that legitimizes the capitalist system. Due to the system, the individual has come to produce much more than his needs. As a result of all these, there is a continuous increase in waste production. By constantly consuming energy, more energy is needed (Zhe et al., 2021; Meng et al., 2021). The problems that have arisen with all these have become the problem areas that the whole world concentrates on and tries to solve. Societies have now increasingly destroyed nature for energy.

In the digital world, individuals who can access information very easily can share information very easily and quickly. At this point, important duties fall on the media. Providing accurate information and creating public opinion, especially in the field of environment and health, are among the most important duties of the media. Expert opinions on the subject for the purpose of awareness in the field of correct energy use, consumption and efficiency, international developments should be conveyed to individuals quickly, the harms of excessive consumption, efficient energy use, environmental ecology, sustainability, and environmental awareness should be raised (Dinçer et al., 2022; Ding et al., 2021). In the study, the importance of news and journalism is examined and the role of environmental journalism in raising awareness about energy efficiency is discussed and evaluated with solution suggestions (Haiyun et al., 2021; Dong et al., 2022; Li et al., 2022; Zhao et al., 2021).

8.2 Developing News and Journalism on the Axis of Journalism

In the early periods of history, the concept of news was used instead of the concept of communication. When we look at the emergence process of the news, it is seen that there is an instinct of curiosity and a search for people's information and information needs. At this point, one of the first concepts that comes to mind when the history of communication is mentioned is news. Human beings have communicated with each other in line with their basic needs. Even in the earliest periods of history, the first people felt the need to use captions to communicate (Gezmen & Gürkan, 2016).

As a dictionary meaning, the press means all the newspapers and magazines published at certain times. At this point, the press generally includes newspapers and magazines. In a broad sense, the press is the whole of the mass media that conveys all kinds of news and ideas to the society. Over time, the press has become an indispensable part of societies with an increasing power of influence (Bülbül, 2001). In Caesar's time Rome had a newspaper. The Acta Diurna (acts of the day) inscribed on the tablet was poured onto a wall after each meeting of the Senate. However, people always wanted to know what was going on and that others helped us. The newspapers we know today have their roots in seventeenth-century Europe. Corantos, single-page news pages about specific events, were published in English in the Netherlands in 1620, and were messages by English booksellers who were eager to satisfy the public's demand for information about events taking place on the continent, important to England and eventually leading to what we call the Thirty Years' War (Baran, 2006). Journalism, which started in Europe for the first time, later spread to other countries of the world. In the seventeenth century, the first real newspaper came into play, and the American War of Independence and the French Revolution changed the course of journalism and added new dimensions to the content. Newspaper numbers have increased, and new methods have been developed in the function of reporting.19. With the Industrial Revolution that started in England in the nineteenth century, it started a period in which radical changes took place in terms of the institutionalization and development of newspapers (Bülbül, 2001). In the early twentieth century, journalist Finley Peter Dunne said that the purpose of journalism was to comfort the sick and upset the comfortable. At best, journalism can expose injustices that affect those without money or power or expose corruption or other wrongdoings of governments and corporations. In some cases, it can do both at the same time. Journalism overthrew presidents, helped end practices of apartheid, and warned the public about potentially dangerous cars, drugs, and other products (Foust, 2011). Along with psychological and cultural factors, technological developments and scientific discoveries, industrialization and urbanization, people have had the opportunity to look at life from different perspectives through the products of mass media. Differences, in diversity, have become curious about the lives of others besides their own lives. While he wants to learn about the events in the world, he feels that he is in a lively environment, communicates with his surroundings, and does not remain indifferent to the events happening around him. At this point, it would not be wrong to say that the effect of newspapers and mass media on the formation of individuals who look to the future with hope is undeniable. Since the seventeenth century, in the process of the emergence of newspapers, the concept of news, which is an indispensable factor in people's lives, has become a mass media tool identified with newspaper and journalism (Cereci, 2012). As mentioned, collecting and transferring some of the later news information is based on the beginning of social life. New inventions and discoveries have further stimulated the curiosity of individuals, and hand-written news has been replaced by news bulletins printed under the news. Since the seventeenth century, collecting and compiling some information, especially in Europe, and publishing it to be marketed for a fee has turned into a periodical form. This practice, which spread to the international area of the mid-nineteenth century, has continued to the present day (Girgin & Özay, 2013).

The changes that have occurred in journalism in the 100th year are no less staggering than those affecting many other aspects of human life. Journalists today publish news using techniques and sources unthinkable in the early 1900s. Online journalists were doing the unknown just 15 years ago. Yet the function of journalists has not changed drastically (Craig, 2005). Experimental news operations have popped up all over the internet since Journalism 2.0 was first released. Some quickly became sustainable businesses. Others are finding new ways of dealing with issues and communities while still pursuing validity. In short, the demand for journalism has not diminished from its audience. But models are starting to look very different (Briggs, 2016). Writing for the web is just a change of medium from paper to screen, so despite all the talk, writing does not change, traditional news media use the internet as an additional outlet for their news, and reporters use the internet as a research tool. An important implication is that the internet allows various media print and publications to do more than just file news stories in their own formats (text, graphics, audio, and video) onto websites (Starr & Dunsford, 2014). Most of the content of a daily newspaper is prepared before the day's edition, with only the front page and a few inside pages filled as close to the deadline as possible.

Newspapers can't compete with electronic media on speed, so their approach should be to come up with something different to entice people to buy them. National tabloids tend to rely on brash headlines and big dramatic pictures to entice their readers. They are written in simple and direct language to appeal to as wide a readership as possible, and they tend to focus too much on stories about human interests beyond the front page. Gossip and show business news are indispensable (Fleming, 2006).

Referring to the vital role of the news, Cereci states that the news absolutely covers all kinds of subjects in life, contains information that directly concerns human life, and that in some cases it warns, teaches, directs, and in some cases, it entertains and encourages. Due to this social structure, the news that everyone can find something from a part of their own life is a tidy summary of life. In fact, it makes people's lives easier in this sense (Cereci, 2012).

By referring to the educational function of the news, Botton (2014) states that modern societies talk about education too much, but at this point, communities are negligent in examining the most effective tool in education so far. Much more powerful and continuous than the education in schools and classrooms is realized by the media organs through our screens, we are subject to the training of news organizations much more than any academic institution. After your formal education, the news becomes our teacher. News is the only significant force that sets the mood for public life and shapes our impressions of society. The power of the news, which is the primary creator of political and social reality, to create public opinion, consciousness, and awareness is revealed (Botton, 2014). The news serves a vital democratic function in each situation, whether anyone is listening or not. The news constructs a symbolic world with some sort of priority, a certificate of legitimate significance. And this symbolic world, supposedly and practically, becomes the property of all, in its easily accessible, cheap, material form. Ours. This is a significant lesson in democracy. It makes the news a source when people are ready to take political action, whether they are ordinary citizens, lobbyists, leaders of social movements, or self-sacrificing judges. It is the necessity and promise of public knowledge that we call news and the political culture of which it is an indispensable part (Shudson, 2003).

Park states that having knowledge is a term that is used as a part of social heritage as well as being scientific. Having knowledge is not just accumulated experience, but results revealed by the systematic investigation of nature. It is to be aware of the work of different researchers in each branch of science. In this totality, news has its own place. News is not a systematic information like in the natural sciences. The news is not history, its facts are not historical reality, its resemblance to history is because it is about events. The subject of the news is specific and isolated events. A commodity that loses its freshness quickly appears as alive until it reaches the target audience, and as a date after it is printed (Park, 2009).

With the word news used for news in English, it is emphasized that the news is primarily about new facts. In addition, accurate and understandable information and important or interesting information are also effective in news formation (Shneider & Raue, 2002). News is primarily a product produced with social responsibility concerns. The news should perform important functions such as informing and educating under the umbrella of social responsibility. In other words, news is a product that the newspaper industry manufactures and markets to its consumers. At this point, the journalist uses his authority to ask questions, research, and investigates according to the answers he receives, and then transfers them to the society (Çağlar & Porghamrezaeieh, 2012).

Among the newsworthy topics are confusion, tension, proximity to the country, etc., locality, success, being new and up-to-date, unusualness, and attractiveness. In a very general sense, it is the transfer of various events that took place in a certain place and time to those who do not know. These are the events that occur in every direction in the opening of the words North, East, West, South, which are the initials of the word News (Girgin & Özay, 2013).

8.3 Environmental History, Environmental Impact, and Importance of Environmental Education

Environmental history emerges as a human-based research field. Approaches in the field of environmental history focus on people's thoughts on nature and study the way these thoughts are equated through literature and art. In fact, at this point, it can be considered as a sub-branch of intellectual history. In Clarence Glacken's approaches, three main environmental ideas that dominate Western literature are mentioned. These can be summarized as the thoughts that the universe was designed, that the environment shapes human beings, that humans change nature for better or worse. The general opinion of researchers is that environmental changes occur because of changes that can last for tens of hundreds of years. Climate changes have recently been the subject of research by two historians. The first book published in France, of Feast, Times of Famine: A history of Climate since The Year 100- is among the most successful examples. In addition, reliable records of the weather have been kept for the last 200–300 years. Historical climate information can be obtained from tree rings in hot regions and snow layer particles in cold regions. On the subject, Hubert H. Lamb and the Climate Research Institute in the United Kingdom, headed by him, conducted pioneering research (Hughes, 2019).

Since it is not possible to see the environment separately from human beings, environmental history deals with the relationship between human beings and other communities in nature, which are subject to sudden and profound changes over time (Hughes, 2019). It is possible to talk about the three basic functions of the environment for all living things. First of all, the environment provides the necessary resources for life, such as water, clean air, food and shelter, as well as natural resources used in industrial economies. Secondly, it eliminates or minimizes the damage of wastes produced in resource consumption. Finally, it provides a place for all living things to live. The environment provides the "habitat" of our foreheads, where we carry out all kinds of living practices, from our living spaces to our working areas (Bozdemir, 2019).

In its most general definition, ecological footprints, which can be explained by associating with the biocapacity, which is the level of carrying the human impact of a living environment, are the effects of human activities on natural life. It is expressed as the total land size (hectares) needed to meet the needs of the current population and to dispose of wastes. Ecological footprints, which are the amount of biocapacity used to meet human needs, are the size of the impact of human activities on nature. In short, biocapacity is the limit of the opportunities that nature offers us, and the extent to which we use these opportunities is our ecological footprints (Özdemir, 2019).

On the axis of the order of nature, ecology does not isolate any element from its environment. According to environmental science, everything is evaluated together with the living system. An ecosystem is defined as all the interrelationships in a relative harmony and organization that connect living beings living together and their environment. Simonnet likens ecosystems to intertwined Russian dolls. Each of them continues to trade with others (Simonnet, 1993).

Environmental education is all the educational efforts carried out to increase the level of knowledge and awareness of students about the environment they live in. Only in this way can the new generation take an active role in protecting and developing the environment in which they live and will live for their own future. Children and young people can develop solution-oriented approaches in line with their own views over time, as they have knowledge about the environment. Environmental education not only improves the quality of daily life, but also contributes to both physical and psychological health. Of course, the perspective that examines the diversity, resources, functioning, problems, and solutions of the environment we live in will also contribute to finding meaning in life. Rather than perceiving nature as an unknown force, environmental education emphasizes evaluating its laws, possibilities, and problems, rather than individuals who are disconnected from the environment we live in. When it comes to living together, it is becoming increasingly important to gain awareness of nature and the environment, which is necessary for living together to be possible. To have a higher level of awareness, an efficient environmental education is necessary (Cansaran, 2019).

In 1970, an International Working Meeting on environmental education was held by UNESCO and the International Union for Conservation of Nature (IUCN). The first definition of environmental education made at this meeting draws attention. According to this definition, environmental education is the process of recognizing values and clarifying concepts in order to develop the skills and attitudes necessary to understand and adopt the relationships between man, his culture and his biophysical environment (Cansaran, 2019).

Considering the factors that increase the effectiveness of environmental education, no environmental problem can be understood and solved as a single field of knowledge, so there is a necessity to make associations in scientific fields. Although it is necessary to act with a global mentality in an effective understanding of environmental problems, it is also very important to act locally. Awareness and solution-oriented approaches to local environmental events of the region where the training is held are also required. The effort to gain student-centered movement and problem-solving skills in education, to gain critical thinking practices and to learn in life are among the factors that increase the effectiveness in environmental education. In addition, parent participation is beneficial in strengthening the desired results of the training given.

Apart from all these, another important factor is values education. Concepts such as that other living things have the right to live together with other living things, and the responsibility to protect and develop the environment gain importance in values education. In addition, artists, politicians, etc., whom we take as role models that we constantly see in the media. The fact that people come across as strong and effective role models is also among the factors that increase the effectiveness of education. The work of public institutions and non-governmental organizations in this regard is also very effective in today's digital world. Activities such as social responsibility campaigns and public service announcements are awareness-raising and educational activities (Cansaran, 2019, s. 57–60).

Corporate social responsibility (CSR) projects have also started to appear frequently in our mix, as their awareness of the environment has started to increase. Considering the importance of CSR projects in perception management, the primary reason why institutions attach importance to these practices is the idea that corporate social responsibility projects positively affect consumer perception. Each institution has focused its differentiation efforts on reputation. Technological developments, the increase in the number and variety of products have brought a new face to the consumer profile and consumer expectations have also changed (Gündüz Kalan, 2012). In this context, corporate social responsibility campaigns on the environment are gaining more and more importance.

8.4 Environmental Education and Environmental Journalism in Creating Energy Efficiency Awareness

The issue of energy efficiency, which has an important place in the public today, is frequently on the policy agenda of many developed countries. The importance of energy efficiency as a policy objective is associated with commercial, industrial competitiveness and energy security benefits, as well as environmental benefits such as reducing CO2 emissions increasingly. There are also many reports and books written on the subject. Despite this growing policy interest, and despite the writing and research on "energy efficiency," what has been noticed is that little attention has been paid to the precise definition of the term. Patterson critically reviews and discusses the range of energy efficiency definitions and how they can be operationalized using indicators (Yüksel et al., 2021). Energy efficiency is a general term and there is no precise quantitative measure of energy efficiency. Instead, a set of indicators should be relied upon to measure changes in energy efficiency (Serezli et al., 2021). It is striking that the definition of energy efficiency is not made in the published reports on energy efficiency. In a general definition, energy means using less energy to produce the same amount of service or useful output (Kostis et al., 2022). As an example, energy efficiency in the industrial sector can be measured by the amount of energy required to produce one tonne of product (Bhuiyan et al., 2022; Patterson, 1996).

While the increasing share of renewable energy is on the policy agenda in countries around the world, some governments have set ambitious targets for the issue. In these countries, support programs aimed at facilitating the market have also started to be implemented. Although the success of these policies differs between countries, it is observed that wind energy stands out with the most impressive growth in some countries (Wüstenhagen et al., 2007).

The term "efficiency" is widely used not only in engineering, building design or product development, but also in management, organization, economics, and policy making of all kinds. Establishing energy efficiency Since efficiency relates to "more services for the same energy input or the same services for less energy input," identifying improvements depends on specifying the "service" and measuring the amount of energy involved. In the energy world, efficiency is considered as a "fuel" (Shove, 2018).

The issue of energy efficiency, which is an important target for health, is gradually increasing its importance. Efficient use of energy is an ostensibly attractive tool for reducing energy-related impacts on the environment and health. To achieve the same services with less energy use, it should theoretically reduce burdens on infrastructure, reduce occupational risks, reduce costs, reduce emissions of local pollutants and greenhouse gases, and reduce harmful exposures. At this point, higher energy efficiency, i.e., the ratio of higher useful energy output to input energy, essentially means more efficient technology, although behavioral factors do play a role in this type of use.

Considering the ratio of energy use to gross national income (GNI) in the twentieth century, significant developments have been seen in global energy efficiency. However, the energy consumption as a total and as a single individual has increased a lot. Such evidence should not be interpreted as implying that energy efficiency is the main driver of increased energy use. However, productivity gains typically appear to go together with economics. Growth, rising expectations, social changes, and population growth are the main components. As the world gets richer, devices that use energy are developed and used to meet our productivity, entertainment, safety, comfort, and health needs. The point to be carefully considered here is that if society wants to reduce energy-related emissions of greenhouse gases and other combustion pollutants, mechanisms are needed to ensure that all costs of energy use, including damage to health and the environment, are reflected in the choices made. It refers to individuals as well as society (Wilkinson et al., 2007).

Environmental education is of primary importance at this point. Environmental education should start from a very young age with the aim of creating an environmentally conscious society. An important part of environmental education can be carried out in education and training institutions. Experiencing first-hand the real ecosystem is always an effective way to foster empathy, and students can become environmental stewards by researching to better understand their local environment. Collecting data and monitoring data by working with relevant people about certain species in the environment will guide the system in recognizing and adapting. By teaching students to develop their critical thinking and problem-solving skills, as well as to have more empathy for the ecosystems in which they work, a lasting impression and impact on students can be created. It structures fieldwork and outdoor classroom experiences. These will have a positive effect on students' long-term memory and may improve attitudes towards the environment. In addition, at this point, individuals learn by having fun. It is valid not only for juniors, but also for adult students. Projects are important in this regard. With sufficient awareness, facilitation, and positive experiences in the environment, students can be encouraged to design and implement their own research projects (Singh & Rahman, 2012).

Within the scope of environmental sociology, in most of the nineteenth-century social thought, the influence of nature on society is perceived as decisive. Those working on social thought of the period are guided by the view that environments shape culture. Within the scope of this view, not only the cultural features determined by geographical factors, but also the discourse that these factors have a direct effect on cultures emerge as an integrating element. This geographical or environmental determinism, which spread and settled over time, considered several questions about how cultural traits emerge, change, adapt, and function. In line with this view, it was possible to explain all cultural characteristics and to explain cultural diversity by referring to the effects of the natural environment. Thus, according to some thinkers in the late nineteenth century, the primary ecological problem with the material environment was less about the origins of environmental degradation and environmental problems, but how societies were kept under control by their natural environment. Also, a formal subdiscipline of "environmental sociology" emerged only after what is commonly referred to as "public environmental awareness" emerged in North America in the 1970s. Environmental sociology, which tries to theorize the connection between human societies and the natural environment, cannot help us understand environmental problems and disasters due to its one-dimensional environmental determinist definitions. According to Heinz Bonfadelli, who looks at environmental communication from a wider perspective, it is necessary to define communication within a broader discipline. At this point, beyond citizen participation and stakeholder cooperation in governance contexts, mass media play an important role for social communication, especially on often abstract and complex environmental issues. Environmental sustainability poses a challenge for media and journalism because the long-term and integrative perspective does not fit immediately into journalistic routines (Heinrichs & Gross, 2009).

Today, climate change and global warming are recognized as one of the main challenges of humanity. There are constant calls for action by scientists and activists, and the issue is widely reported in the news media. In this case, the media and journalism have been identified as key actors in the work towards a sustainable society and bear a special responsibility in informing and engaging the public. Public participation and other measures have been considered important to tackle the great challenge posed by climate change, and research shows that media reporting and climate change frameworks can increase public interest and participation (Appelgren & Jönsson, 2021).

The 1980s caused environmental problems to remain in the background in the economy. However, the environment continues to be at the top of the public, corporate, and media agendas. The purpose of the media environmental agenda is important because research suggests it has a significant media agenda-setting effect for environmental issues. The public relies heavily on the media for information about the environment, and a strong correlation has been found between the media and public agendas. In contrast, the media's environmental agenda is highly dependent on the agenda-setting efforts of sources that provide information subsidies to the media to ultimately influence public and policy agendas. Early research on the subject reveals that 85% of environmental reporters trust press releases for information, and 82% trust brochures and other reports. Twenty years later, Griffin and Dunwoody confirm that local media environmental reporting often uses the least costly, most easily accessible sources of information (Curtin & Rhodenbaugh, 2001). In this context, it is considered that the researcher, environment, and health journalism network should be developed.

The traditional journalistic model has been to follow interesting stories, uncover scandals, and explore conflicts. It would not be wrong to say that this approach is very relevant to the political process. This situation, which is not applicable to the currently critical relationship between humanity and the Earth, will of course fall short in raising awareness in the field of energy use. Today's communities must understand the links between energy use, climate, and food in order to transition to an efficient, resilient, and sustainable society. As a more integrative approach, this process includes people from all sectors such as businesses, citizen groups, farmers and foresters, students and teachers, state government officials, politicians and voters. It requires an informed public with access to a wide range of reliable information on local and global environmental issues. As environmental concerns have grown, the need for a well-informed public has become a necessity and critical. The biggest challenge is how to convey complex concepts and give a sense of the urgency of these challenges in a way that engages the reader. Climate change, for example, is a fascinating and important story, but it is not adequately told by traditional media. The founders of the online journalistic collaboration Climate Desk (http://theclimatedesk.org/ about) point to several reasons for this. Some of these include the slow progress of climate change, the large and overwhelming situation for news organizations to contend with, the science, technology, policy and business aspects being handled by different teams, often culminating debates over endangered wildlife, political games, or the existence of climate change. is to be taken (Betts & Gibson, 2012).

When it comes to the theoretical approach, the informative approach about environmental problems in the media allows the buyer to learn unknown facts about the environmental problem in one way or another. It is known that environmental journalism is a special kind of journalism, but it should not be contented with just reporting and glossing over a relevant fact. The most important goal of environmental journalism should be to propose alternatives, solutions, strategies, or conclusions about the reported environmental problem or reality. Here it is necessary to avoid both disaster and lack of knowledge. Where possible, it is necessary to complement the presentation of intervention possibilities and solution alternatives (Rodríguez et al., 2021).

8.5 Conclusion

The issue of energy efficiency is gaining more and more importance today, to prevent the widespread belief that the earth will serve mankind forever with its unlimited resources. Industrialization, the understanding of continuous production within the framework of the capitalist system, and the changes in consumption habits bring individuals face to face with a great danger. Energy efficiency awareness depends, first, on a basic awareness of environmental problems. Unfortunately, there is not enough awareness in the national and international arena about the generation that is worried about the future of their own kind and will create a healthy future. Awareness of environmental problems primarily depends on sound environmental education. This training gains functionality in different areas of our life practices. Environmental education focused on awareness and sensitivity towards the environment should start at a very young age. The family, which constitutes the first and most important pillar of socialization, is an important part of this education. For this reason, trainings on environment and energy consumption for each of the adult family members should be increased both in private institutions and in the public area, and studies should be carried out on the importance of the subject.

The role of the media in forming public opinion and education shows that news and journalism are among the most important tools in this regard. The influence of the media is an undeniable fact. Technological developments and new applications in the digital arena now enable everyone to be instantly informed about everything. At this point, the media is responsible for providing the right information flow to the public. Individuals obtain all kinds of information about the environment and health, which are the most sensitive issues, through the media. The media can also raise awareness on this sensitive issue with the agenda they create. Environmental journalists should adopt a publishing approach that does not serve profit-oriented institutions and organizations, which considers the public interest in terms of limiting energy consumption, sustainability, and efficient energy use, in order to eliminate the services of industrial enterprises that harm nature. At this point, based on ethical principles, it should be focused on solution-oriented research news supported by interviews with both academic and field experts. Comprehensive environmental education issues including adults should be included frequently from childhood. Publications for experiential activities and research activities should be increased. Environmental reports should be constantly included, and practices for informing the public about energy efficiency, indoor and other living spaces, and publications on environmental education policies handled with sustainable integrative approaches should be supported.

References

Appelgren, E., & Jönsson, A. M. (2021). Engaging citizens for climate change—Challenges for journalism. *Digital Journalism, 9*(6), 755–772.

Baran, J. S. (2006). *Introduction to mass communication media literacy and culture*. McGraw-Hıll International Edition.

Betts, A. K., & Gibson, E. (2012). Environmental journalism revisited. Environmental leadership: a Reference Handbook.

Bhuiyan, M. A., Dinçer, H., Yüksel, S., Mikhaylov, A., Danish, M. S. S., Pinter, G., et al. (2022). Economic indicators and bioenergy supply in developed economies: QROF-DEMATEL and random forest models. *Energy Reports, 8*, 561–570.

Botton, A. (2014). *Haberler Bir Kullanma Kılavuzu*. Sel Yayıncılık.

Bozdemir, H. (2019). Çevresel Değerler ve Eğitimi. In S. Yalmancı Gürbüzoğlu & S. Aydın (Eds.), *Çevre Etiği: Temel İlkeleri ve Eğitimi* (pp. 37–56). Nobel Akademik Yayıncılık.

Briggs, M. (2016). *Journalism next a practical guide to digital reporting and publishing*. Sage.

Bülbül, R. (2001). *Haberin Anatomisi ve Temel Yaklaşımlar*. Nobel Yayın Dağıtım.

Çağlar, Ş., & Porghamrezaeieh, S. (2012). *Şövalyelik Mesleği Gazeteciliğin Keskin Kılıcı*. Anonim Yayıncılık.

Cansaran, D. (2019). *Sürdürülebilir Kentler İçin Çevre Bilinci*. Gece Kitaplığı.

Cereci, S. (2012). *Medya Yapımları ve Yapım Teknikleri*. Nobel Akademik Yayıncılık.

Craig, R. (2005). *Reporting writing and editing for new media online journalism*. Thomson Wadsworth.

Curtin, P. A., & Rhodenbaugh, E. (2001). Building the news media agenda on the environment: A comparison of public relations and journalistic sources. *Public Relations Review, 27*(2), 179–195.

Dinçer, H., Yüksel, S., & Martínez, L. (2022). Collaboration enhanced hybrid fuzzy decision-making approach to analyze the renewable energy investment projects. *Energy Reports, 8*, 377–389.

Ding, Z., Yüksel, S., & Dincer, H. (2021). An integrated Pythagorean fuzzy soft computing approach to environmental management systems for sustainable energy pricing. *Energy Reports, 7*, 5575–5588.

Dong, W., Zhao, G., Yüksel, S., Dinçer, H., & Ubay, G. G. (2022). A novel hybrid decision making approach for the strategic selection of wind energy projects. *Renewable Energy, 185*, 321–337.

Fleming, C. (2006). *An introduction to journalism*. Sage Publications.

Foust, C. J. (2011). *Online journalism principles and practices of news for the web*. Holcomb Hathaway Publishers.

Gezmen, B., & Gürkan, H. (2016). *Haber Uygulamaları*. Es Yayınları.

Girgin, A., & Özay, S. (2013). *Haber Yazmak*. Der Yayınları.

Gündüz Kalan, Ö. (2012). Çevre Bilinci, Tüketim ve Sosyal Sorumluluk İlişkisi: NTV Yeşil Ekran Örneği. In S. Kırlı & Ü. Sarı (Eds.), *Medya ve Gündelik Yaşamda Çevre Gerçeği* (pp. 91–107). Aya Kitap Yayınları.

Haiyun, C., Zhixiong, H., Yüksel, S., & Dinçer, H. (2021). Analysis of the innovation strategies for green supply chain management in the energy industry using the QFD-based hybrid interval valued intuitionistic fuzzy decision approach. *Renewable and Sustainable Energy Reviews, 143*, 110844.

Heinrichs, H., & Gross, M. (2009). Introduction: New trends and interdisciplinary challenges in environmental sociology. In M. Gross & H. Heinrichs (Eds.), *Environmental sociology European perspectives and interdisciplinary challenges* (pp. 1–16). Springer.

Hughes, J. ç. (2019). *Çevresel Tarih Nedir?* (F. M. Çalışır, translator.) İstanbul: Tarih Vakfı Yurt Yayınları.

Kostis, P., Dinçer, H., & Yüksel, S. (2022). Knowledge-based energy Investments of European Economies and Policy Recommendations for sustainable development. *Journal of the Knowledge Economy*, 1–33.

Kou, G., Yüksel, S., & Dinçer, H. (2022). Inventive problem-solving map of innovative carbon emission strategies for solar energy-based transportation investment projects. *Applied Energy, 311*, 118680.

Li, J., Yüksel, S., Dınçer, H., Mikhaylov, A., & Barykin, S. E. (2022). Bipolar q-ROF hybrid decision making model with golden cut for analyzing the levelized cost of renewable energy alternatives. *IEEE Access, 10*, 42507–42517.

Liu, J., Lv, J., Dinçer, H., Yüksel, S., & Karakuş, H. (2021). Selection of renewable energy alternatives for green blockchain investments: A hybrid IT2-based fuzzy modelling. *Archives of Computational Methods in Engineering, 28*(5), 3687–3701.

Meng, Y., Wu, H., Zhao, W., Chen, W., Dinçer, H., & Yüksel, S. (2021). A hybrid heterogeneous Pythagorean fuzzy group decision modelling for crowdfunding development process pathways of fintech-based clean energy investment projects. *Financial Innovation, 7*(1), 1–34.

Mukhtarov, S., Yüksel, S., & Dinçer, H. (2022). The impact of financial development on renewable energy consumption: Evidence from Turkey. *Renewable Energy, 187*, 169–176.

Özdemir, O. (2019). Gündelik Yaşam Pratikleri ve Çevre Eğitimi. In S. Yalmancı, Gürbüzoğlu, & S. Aydın (Eds.), *Çevre Etiği: Temel İlkeleri ve Eğitimi* (pp. 23–35). Nobel Akademik Yayıncılık.

Park, R. (2009). Bilgi Formu Olarak Haber: Bilgi Sosyolojisinde Bir Bölüm. (E. Erkebay translator). In N. Rigel & Ş. Çağlar (Eds.), *Matriksi Şimşek Olan Metinler Gazetecilik I* (pp. 37–40). Anonim Yayıncılık.

Patterson, M. G. (1996). What is energy efficiency?: Concepts, indicators and methodological issues. *Energy Policy, 24*(5), 377–390.

Rodríguez, C. M. A., Rodríguez, M. J. A., & Villalba, C. G. (2021). Environmental journalism in the Latin American digital press. *Centro Sur, 5*(2), 1–20.

Serezli, E., Yüksel, S., Tamer, İ., & Dinçer, H. (2021). The role of innovative renewable energy investment strategies on macroeconomic stability. In *Financial strategies in competitive markets* (pp. 165–178). Springer.

Shneider, W., & Raue, P. (2002). *Gazetecinin El Kitabı*. İstanbul: İstanbul Üniversitesi İletişim Fakültesi Yayınları-16.

Shove, E. (2018). What is wrong with energy efficiency? *Building Research & Information, 46*(7), 779–789.

Shudson, M. (2003). *The power of news*. Harward University Press.

Simonnet, D. (1993). *Çevrecilik*. İletişim Yayınları.

Singh, H. R., & Rahman, S. A. (2012). An approach for environmental education by non-governmental organizations (NGOs) in biodiversity conservation. *Procedia-Social and Behavioral Sciences, 42*, 144–152.

Starr, D., & Dunsford, D. (2014). *Working the story a guide to reporting and news writing for journalists and public relations professionals*. Rowman&Littlefield.

Wilkinson, P., Smith, K. R., Beevers, S., Tonne, C., & Oreszczyn, T. (2007). Energy, energy efficiency, and the built environment. *The Lancet, 370*(9593), 1175–1187.

Wüstenhagen, R., Wolsink, M., & Bürer, M. J. (2007). Social acceptance of renewable energy innovation: An introduction to the concept. *Energy Policy, 35*(5), 2683–2691.

Xie, Y., Zhou, Y., Peng, Y., Dinçer, H., Yüksel, S., & an Xiang, P. (2021). An extended pythagorean fuzzy approach to group decision-making with incomplete preferences for analyzing balanced scorecard-based renewable energy investments. *IEEE Access, 9*, 43020–43035.

Yüksel, S., Mikhaylov, A., Ubay, G. G., & Uyeh, D. D. (2021). The role of hydrogen in the Black Sea for the future energy supply security of Turkey. In *Handbook of research on strategic management for current energy investments* (pp. 1–15). IGI Global.

Zhao, Y., Xu, Y., Yüksel, S., Dinçer, H., & Ubay, G. G. (2021). Hybrid IT2 fuzzy modelling with alpha cuts for hydrogen energy investments. *International Journal of Hydrogen Energy, 46*(13), 8835–8851.

Zhe, L., Yüksel, S., Dinçer, H., Mukhtarov, S., & Azizov, M. (2021). The positive influences of renewable energy consumption on financial development and economic growth. *SAGE Open, 11*(3), 21582440211040133.

Zhou, P., Luo, J., Cheng, F., Yüksel, S., & Dinçer, H. (2021). Analysis of risk priorities for renewable energy investment projects using a hybrid IT2 hesitant fuzzy decision-making approach with alpha cuts. *Energy, 224*, 120184.

Chapter 9
Clean Energy Technologies and Renewable Energy Risks

Konstantin Panasenko and Fi-John Chang

Abstract The paper presents a target vision of the new energy sector in Russia, based on the analysis of promising areas of its development in the field of energy technology economics and assessment of energy risks of using renewable energy sources. Financial and commercial indicators for various types of power plants under construction or under reconstruction are presented, showing that the new economic basis for the widespread use of renewable energy allows building new energy with a lower specific investment per 1 kW of installed capacity and obtaining cheaper electric energy. To assess the prospects for full inclusion of renewable energy facilities in the energy complex of our country and expand their use, a description of the risks arising in the renewable energy sector and their management methods is given. Based on the analysis of calculation results and data on electricity production at solar power plants commissioned in the Altai Republic, the effectiveness of the proposed methodology for assessing natural resource risks in renewable energy is shown. The construction of large hydroelectric power plants, which account for ~20% of the country's total energy balance, is also associated with a negative impact on the environment. Reservoirs necessary for regulating the productivity of hydroelectric power plants occupy significant territories that are excluded from agricultural turnover. The construction of reservoirs is associated with a violation of the hydrogeological regime of rivers, changes in the properties of ecosystems, and the species composition of hydrobionts. It should be noted that large hydroelectric power plants are not considered to be objects operating on the basis of renewable energy sources. According to the existing classification, such facilities include small hydroelectric power plants with a capacity of up to 25 MW and microhpps. The sulfur and nitrogen oxides contained in TPP emissions lead to acid rain and have a detrimental effect on human and animal health, as well as on plants. Serious

K. Panasenko (✉)
Financial Research Institute of Ministry of Finance of the Russian Federation, Moscow, Russian Federation

F.-J. Chang
Department of Bioenvironmental Systems Engineering, National Taiwan University, Taipei, Taiwan
e-mail: changfj@ntu.edu.tw

H. Dinçer, S. Yüksel (eds.), *Circular Economy and the Energy Market*,
Contributions to Economics, https://doi.org/10.1007/978-3-031-13146-2_9

problems are also associated with ash and slag from thermal power plants. The discharge of heated water from the cooling systems of thermal power plants to surface water sources causes their thermal pollution, leading to a decrease in water saturation with oxygen.

Keywords Energy technologies · Future energy · Risk management · Clean energy

9.1 Introduction

Against the background of the recently aggravated global crisis processes associated with the recession of the world economy against the background of a pandemic, the inevitability of a high-quality restructuring of the energy sector, which is transformed from an industry structure into a socially oriented energy information system for ensuring the life of a new society, is becoming more and more obvious.

The goal-oriented vision of new energy requires a comprehensive scientific study of the future, followed by the formation of a new energy strategy for Russia and a "road map" for the transition to a new energy civilization. The new energy sector will be based on a comprehensive study of promising areas of development in the field of energy technology economics and energy risk assessment.

Currently, in the Russian Federation, the needs for electric and thermal energy are mainly met by three sources of generation: thermal power plants (TPPs) and installations running on fossil fuels; hydroelectric power plants (HPPs); and nuclear power plants (NPPs).

Traditional thermal energy, which accounts for the largest share in the total energy balance of the Russian Federation—about 70%—is also the largest man-made source of harmful emissions into the atmosphere, soil, water sources, and greenhouse gas emissions, the main of which is carbon dioxide. The largest reserves of organic fuel both abroad and in Russia are hard and brown coals. But coal-fired thermal power plants are characterized by the greatest harmful emissions. The efficiency of most of the existing large steam turbine thermal power plants is 38–40%, while new thermal power plants using combined-cycle technologies have an efficiency of 38–40%. The efficiency reaches 55–60%. That is, 40–60% of the energy of fuel burned at thermal power plants is released into the environment.

9.2 Literature Review

Construction of nuclear power plants is 2.0–2.5 times more expensive than coal-fired steam turbine thermal power plants and 3.0–3.5 times more expensive than modern thermal power plants with combined-cycle technologies. In the report of the International Energy Agency (IEA) "Updated assessment of capital expenditures of power generating plants," back in 2010, the specific investment in new nuclear power plants was estimated at $ 5,339/kW. The need to take into account the costs of decommissioning plants, which are comparable to the costs of their construction, in calculating the cost of NPP energy, leads to the fact that the actual cost of electricity production at an NPP is shown to be higher than at thermal power plants, hydroelectric power plants, and power plants based on renewable energy sources (Bhuiyan et al., 2021; Dong et al., 2021, Mikhaylov, 2021b; Baboshkin et al., 2022; Barykin et al., 2022; Baig et al., 2022a; Liu et al., 2022a; Liu et al., 2022b; Bhuiyan et al., 2022b; Danish et al., 2022; Baig et al., 2022b; Saqib et al., 2021; Yüksel et al., 2021a, b, c; Mukhametov et al., 2021, Candila et al., 2021; Mikhaylov & Grilli, 2022).

Many countries refuse to use nuclear power plants. Italy closed all existing nuclear power plants in 1987–1990 after the Chernobyl accident and completely abandoned nuclear power. In 2010, Sweden eliminated its last nuclear reactor. Belgium, Germany, Spain, the Netherlands, Taiwan, and Switzerland are taking measures to systematically close nuclear power plants (Meng et al., 2021; Dinçer et al., 2022; Ding et al., 2021). Lithuania and Kazakhstan have temporarily stopped using nuclear power. Austria, Cuba, Libya, North Korea, and Poland after the accident at the Fukushima-1 nuclear power plant in Japan did not begin to complete the construction of their first nuclear power plants. Also, Australia, Azerbaijan, Denmark, Greece, Georgia, Ireland, Latvia, Norway, Portugal, and a number of other countries refused to develop nuclear energy.

The share of nuclear power in global electricity production decreased from 17.6% in 1996 to 10.7% in 2015. Bloomberg New Energy Finance predicts a total decline in the share of nuclear power plants in the world to 4% by 2040.

At the same time, today there is a significant increase in energy capacity using renewable energy sources, which in the last 5–7 years is associated with a sharp drop in prices for equipment used at these stations. Especially dramatic is the drop in prices for silicon cells (panels), which are the basis of most modern solar power plants being built (Denisova et al., 2019; Nyangarika et al., 2019b; Nyangarika et al., 2019a; Huang et al., 2021a; Huang et al., 2021b; Mikhaylov, 2018a; Mikhaylov, 2018b; Mikhaylov et al., 2019; Conteh et al., 2021; Mikhaylov, 2022a, b; Sediqi et al., 2022, Khan et al., 2021; Bhuiyan et al., 2022a; Liu et al., 2021a; Liu et al., 2021b; Daniali et al., 2021).

In recent years, renewable energy generation has established itself in the world not only as the fastest-growing and fastest-paying energy sector, but also as the main energy sector. In 2013, more than 150 GW of new solar and wind capacities were put into operation in the world—for the first time more than traditional energy facilities. In 2018, a solar power plant with a total capacity of more than 120 GW was commissioned, and a wind farm with a total capacity of 60 MW was commissioned. Prices of about $ 0.03/(kW) have become common for electric energy at renewable energy installations created without state support. As an example, the price of wind farm electricity in Saudi Arabia was 0.0234 USD/(kW·h), the price of $ 0.0197/(kW) is fixed at Mexican solar power plants): today, installations using renewable energy sources are confidently reaching self-sufficiency (An et al., 2019a; An et al., 2019b; Mikhaylov, 2020a, b, c; Mikhaylov & Tarakanov, 2020; An et al., 2020a, b, c; Moiseev et al., 2020; Moiseev et al., 2021; Grilli et al., 2021; Gura et al., 2020; Dooyum et al., 2020; Mikhaylov et al., 2022; Mikhaylov, 2021a; Varyash et al., 2020; Zhao et al., 2021a, b; An & Mikhaylov, 2020; Alwaelya et al., 2021; Yumashev & Mikhaylov, 2020; Yumashev et al., 2020; Mutalimov et al., 2021; Morkovkin et al., 2020a; Morkovkin et al., 2020b; An & Mikhaylov, 2021).

9.3 Economics of Advanced Energy Technologies

The new economic basis for the widespread use of renewable energy allows us to build a new energy sector with a lower specific investment per 1 kW of installed capacity and with cheaper electricity generation.

As a basis for comparison, a conditional nuclear power plant with an installed capacity of 1000 MW is used, operating in the basic mode with an average installed capacity utilization factor (CIUM) of 70%. This corresponds to the annual usage time of the installed capacity of 6132 hours. The estimated electricity supply of a conventional NPP is 5825.4 TWh·b/year. For an adequate comparison, the same estimated power supply is accepted for all other types of power plants compared. In order to meet this condition with a significant difference in the CIM for different generation technologies, it was necessary to take the following values of the installed electrical capacities: for coal-fired TPPs—1097.2 MW, for natural gas TPPs—1647.1 MW, for hydroelectric power plants—1758.8 MW, for wind farms—2000.0 MW, for solar power plants—2800.0 MW.

However, despite the fact that the required capacity of wind farms and SES is much larger than for all other power plants, the construction of wind farms and SES requires, nevertheless, in the current market situation, the smallest investment. At the same time, it is important that the cost of electricity supplied to wind farms and SES also has the lowest values.

Under these conditions, only wind farms and SES will have acceptable payback periods that do not exceed half of the plant's service life. All other power generation technologies do not provide payback over the entire lifetime of these facilities, which is usually 40 years. At the same time, for all power facilities, except for wind farms and SES, net income for the entire period of operation is negative. With such values of economic criteria, there is no interest in investing capital in such projects.

Acceptable financial and commercial indicators for power plants under construction or under reconstruction are provided in practice at the expense of state subsidies. Budget dating for the capacity provided to the power system is carried out using capacity supply agreements (PDAs). In practice, this means additional payments from the budget for the capacity produced in order to reduce electricity tariffs for consumers to acceptable values.

At the same time, the best and most satisfactory payback will occur when investing in the construction of wind farms and SPP. These types of power plants also provide the highest net return on invested capital, the highest return on investment index, and the highest return on investment. To date, many energy companies have come to the conclusion that it makes no sense, for economic reasons, to build nuclear power plants, thermal power plants, and large hydroelectric power plants, and preference should be given to renewable energy technologies.

It is significant that such a world-famous company as SIEMENS It is already reducing production of its high-efficiency gas turbines due to a significant decline in demand for them.

9.4 Risk management in the Russian Renewable Energy Sector

Speaking about the prospects for full inclusion of renewable energy facilities in the energy complex of our country and expanding their use, it is necessary to consider the risks arising in the renewable energy sector and their management methods (Mukhtarov et al., 2022; Liu et al., 2021a, b, c; Xie et al., 2021). When analyzing the main types of risks, risks should also be distinguished by the stages of operation of renewable energy facilities: design, construction, and operation. During the design phase, the greatest danger is caused by the risks associated with errors in assessing the potential of resources in the area of creating an object, errors in choosing the site of placement, and errors in choosing equipment are compounded. This is especially important in the wind power industry, where the power received varies in proportion to the cubic value of the wind speed, and the optimal choice of equipment depending on the wind power characteristics determines the value of the installed capacity utilization factor and how much of the wind power flow will be effectively converted into electricity (Kou et al., 2022; Zhou et al., 2021; Zhe et al., 2021). That is why a necessary condition for obtaining investment for the project, for insuring construction works and further operation of wind farms is to conduct long-term monitoring (at least a year) of the wind regime at various heights according to a strictly defined methodology that provides a full amount of statistical data on wind power characteristics. Solar power engineering does not require pre-project monitoring and allows for the design of solar power plants based on international databases compiled from the data of remote sensing and long-term series of actinometric measurements (Yüksel et al., 2022; Adalı et al., 2022; Dayong et al., 2020; Mikhaylov et al., 2018; Nyangarika et al., 2018; Danish et al., 2020; Danish et al., 2021; An et al., 2021; Uyeh et al., 2021; Tamashiro et al., 2021; Shaikh et al., 2021).

9.5 Conclusion

Today, the modernization of Russian thermal power plants based on traditional technologies, with the replacement of turbines and boilers that have spent their life, with new ones, even with slightly better parameters, will only lead to an even greater lag of our energy sector from the world level (Haiyun et al., 2021; Dong et al., 2022; Li et al., 2022). By installing new steam turbine equipment to replace worn-out ones, we are condemning ourselves to using outdated energy technologies for at least another 40 years—a period equal to the service life of this equipment. And if only 3–4 years ago these issues were not so acute, now it is unacceptable to waste time without introducing new technologies based on renewable energy sources (Zhao et al., 2021a, b; Yüksel et al., 2021a, b, c; Kostis et al., 2022).

It becomes obvious that the current "Energy Strategy of the Russian Federation for the period up to 2035" and "General Layout of electric power facilities up to 2035," in which the prospective structure of energy capacities is maintained at the current level with a greater share of electricity production from fossil fuels, no longer meet global trends, socio-economic needs of the country and require a radical revision.

Recall that, in accordance with the decisions of the UN Paris Climate Conference, the world community has set a goal: to limit the increase in temperature on the planet by 2050 within 2°With. This goal can only be achieved if no more than 10% of the existing hydrocarbon fuel reserves are used by 2050.

If these approaches are valid, then the costs of exploration and development of new deposits of fossil fuels do not make sense. It is necessary to finance not the exploration and development of new deposits of natural fuels, but research aimed at creating new methods of generating energy without using these fuels.

Today, the main items of State Budget revenue are deductions from the profits of corporations that sell gas, oil, and coal abroad. However, demand for fossil fuels will rapidly decline. Russia has no more than 10–15 years at its disposal to find sources of income other than the export of natural hydrocarbons.

The main share of Russian hydrocarbon exports falls on the EU countries. The economic development of these countries leads to a significant increase in the demand for electric energy and biofuels. Therefore, the solution suggests itself: to plan sources of budget income precisely at the expense of production in Russia and export abroad of energy products instead of raw materials. In this light, in our opinion, it is advisable to implement the following program of actions:

- Conducting market research to determine possible sales volumes of electric energy and biofuels abroad.
- Conducting scientific research to improve the efficiency of photovoltaic modules, develop new technologies for the production of FEM in order to maximize their cost reduction, develop fundamentally new schemes for solar power plants, and transfer the energy generated by them over long distances. Russian research institutes that have a large scientific and technical background, but little implemented in practice, can be involved in this work.
- Creation of landfills for conducting large-scale experimental studies in the field of renewable energy use. Such landfills can be created in Dagestan on the basis of the Institute of Geothermal Problems of the Dagestan Scientific Center of the Russian Academy of Sciences, in Sevastopol on the basis of Sevastopol State University, in Dubna, Moscow region on the basis of the International University

of Nature, Society and Man "DUBNA." These polygons may have different technological orientation depending on their geographical location.

- Conducting R & D to create efficient technologies for converting various types of biomass into electric and thermal energy, technologies for the production of cheap solid, liquid, and gaseous biofuels.
- Design and construction of new large enterprises for the production of biofuels. Organization of sales of biofuels to foreign and Russian consumers, as well as to consumers in the CIS countries.
- Construction of solar power plants abroad with their subsequent sale or supply of electricity to local consumers.

The use of renewable energy sources has already become the norm almost all over the world. In the CIS countries, however, it still causes some distrust. This has led to a serious lag in the CIS and, in particular, the Russian Federation in creating a modern base for energy development.

Abandoning the use of fossil fuels is the general direction of global energy development. Currently, there is a widespread replacement of traditional energy production technologies with the use of renewable sources. The transition from the export of fossil fuels to the export of electricity produced using renewable sources will allow us to get significant budget preferences for our country.

There are significant reserves of peat and wood in our country. It is this resource base that can play a decisive role in the transition to new energy technologies in our country. Currently, there are no effective industrial technologies for energy utilization of biomass in the world. The existing domestic developments of new technologies for the energy use of biomass allow us to count on leading positions in the modernization of the energy industry in this direction.

The comparison of the results of risk analysis guaranteed the production of electricity with solar power by conducting assessments of the variability of insolation using the method of calculation of the coefficients of variation of mean monthly and daily values of receipt of direct solar radiation and the data about the efficiency of existing SES in the Republic of Altai on the calculation of the coefficient of utilization of installed capacity showed a favorable allocated according to the location of SES areas by using GIS-technologies and areas of the SES with higher values of capacity factor. The conducted studies have shown the possibility and prospects of using this methodology for assessing the natural resource risks of using solar energy resources. Further developments are planned to refine the methodology and conduct assessments in other regions of Russia with high potential for solar resources.

References

Adalı, Z., Dinçer, H., Eti, S., Mikhaylov, A., & Yüksel, S. (2022). Identifying new perspectives on geothermal energy investments. In H. Dinçer & S. Yüksel (Eds.), *Multidimensional strategic outlook on global competitive energy economics and finance* (pp. 1–11). Emerald Publishing Limited. https://doi.org/10.1108/978-1-80117-898-320221002

Alwaelya, S. A., Yousif, N. B. A., & Mikhaylov, A. (2021). Emotional development in preschoolers and socialization. *Early Child Development and Care, 191*, 16.

An, J., & Mikhaylov, A. (2021). Analysis of energy projects financial efficiency and renewable energy generation in Russia. *Finance: Theory and Practice, 25*(5), 79–91.

An, J., & Mikhaylov, A. (2020). Russian energy projects in South Africa. *Journal of Energy in Southern Africa, 31*, 3.

An, J., Mikhaylov, A., & Jung, S.-U. (2020a). The strategy of South Korea in the global oil market. *Energies, 13*(10), 2491.

An, J., Mikhaylov, A., & Jung, S.-U. (2021). A linear programming approach for Robust network revenue management in the airline industry. *Journal of Air Transport Management, 91*, 101979.

An, J., Mikhaylov, A., & Kim, K. (2020b). Machine learning approach in heterogeneous group of algorithms for transport safety-critical system. *Applied Sciences, 10*(8), 2670.

An, J., Mikhaylov, A., & Moiseev, N. (2019a). Oil price predictors: Machine learning approach. *International Journal of Energy Economics and Policy, 9*(5), 1–6.

An, J., Mikhaylov, A., & Richter, U. H. (2020c). Trade war effects: Evidence from sectors of energy and resources in Africa. *Heliyon, 6*, e05693. https://doi.org/10.1016/j.heliyon.2020.e05693

An, J., Mikhaylov, A., & Sokolinskaya, N. (2019b). Machine learning in economic planning: Ensembles of algorithms. *Journal of Physics: Conference Series, 1353*, 012126.

Baboshkin, P., Mikhaylov, A., & Shaikh, Z. A. (2022). Sustainable cryptocurrency growth is not possible? Impact of network power demand on bitcoin price. *Financial Journal, 14*(2), 39–55.

Baig, U., Hussain, B. M., Khan, A. A., Shaikh, Z. A., Mikhaylov, A., Chao, C.-C., & Barykin, S. E. (2022b). Research on investors of the reginal stock exchange: An influence of behavioral finance on investment decision making. *Risks, 10*(4), 116.

Baig, U., Khan, A. A., Abbas, M. G., Shaikh, Z. A., Mikhaylov, A., Laghari, A. A., & Hussain, B. M. (2022a). Crucial causes of delay in completion and performance management of the construction work: study on the base of relative importance index. *Journal of Tianjin University Science and Technology, 55*, 6.

Barykin, S., Mikheev, A., Kiseleva, E., Putikhin, Y., Alekseeva, N., & Mikhaylov, A. (2022). An empirical analysis of russian regions' debt sustainability. *Economies, 10*(4), 296.

Bhuiyan, M. A., Dinçer, H., Yüksel, S., Mikhaylov, A., Danish, M. S. S., Pinter, G., Uyeh, D. D., & Stepanova, D. (2022a). Economic indicators and bioenergy supply in developed economies: QROF-DEMATEL and random forest models. *Energy Reports, 8*(2022), 561–570.

Bhuiyan, M. A., Khare, V., Mikhaylov, A., Pinter, G., Zhang (2022b) Does renewable energy consumption affect economic growth? A systematic literature review. Frontiers in Environmental Science.

Bhuiyan, M. A., An, J., Mikhaylov, A., Moiseev, N., & Danish, M. S. S. (2021). Renewable energy deployment and COVID-19 measures for sustainable development. *Sustainability, 13*, 4418.

Candila, V., Maximov, D., Mikhaylov, A., Moiseev, N., Senjyu, T., & Tryndina, N. (2021). On the relationship between oil and exchange rates of oil-exporting and oil-importing countries: from the great recession period to the Covid-19 era. *Energies, 14*, 8065.

Conteh, F., Takahashi, H., Hemeida, A. M., Krishnan, N., Mikhaylov, A., & Senjyu, T. (2021). Hybrid grid-connected renewable power generation for sustainable electricity supply in Sierra Leone: Case study Lungi Town. *Sustainability, 13*, 18.

Daniali, S. M., Barykin, S. E., Kapustina, I. V., Khortabi, F. M., Sergeev, S. M., Kalinina, O. V., Mikhaylov, A., Veynberg, R., Zasova, L., & Senjyu, T. (2021). Predicting volatility index according to technical index and economic indicators on the basis of deep learning algorithm. *Sustainability, 2021*(13), 14011.

Danish, M. S. S., Bhattacharya, A., Stepanova, D., Mikhaylov, A., Grilli, M. L., Khosravy, M., & Senjyu, T. (2020). A systematic review of metal oxide applications for energy and environmental sustainability. *Metals, 10*(12), 1604.

Danish, M. S. S., Senjyu, T., Sabory, N. R., Khosravy, M., Grilli, M. L., Mikhaylov, A., & Majidi, H. (2021). A forefront framework for sustainable aquaponics modeling and design. *Sustainability, 13*, 9313.

Danish, M. S. S., Estrella-Pajulas, L. L., Alemaida, I. M. A., Grilli, M. L., Mikhaylov, A., & Senjyu, T. (2022). Green synthesis of silver oxide nanoparticles for photocatalytic environmental remediation and biomedical applications. *Metals, 12*, 4.

Dayong, N., Mikhaylov, A., Bratanovsky, S., Shaikh, Z. A., & Stepanova, D. (2020). Mathematical modeling of the technological processes of catering products production. *Journal of Food Process Engineering, 43*(2), 1–9.

Denisova, V., Mikhaylov, A., & Lopatin, E. (2019). Blockchain infrastructure and growth of global power consumption. *International Journal of Energy Economics and Policy, 9*(4), 22–29.

Dinçer, H., Yüksel, S., & Martínez, L. (2022). Collaboration enhanced hybrid fuzzy decision-making approach to analyze the renewable energy investment projects. *Energy Reports, 8*, 377–389.

Ding, Z., Yüksel, S., & Dincer, H. (2021). An Integrated Pythagorean fuzzy soft computing approach to environmental management systems for sustainable energy pricing. *Energy Reports, 7*, 5575–5588.

Dong, B., Ikonnikova, I., Rogulin, R., Sakulyeva, T., & Mikhaylov, A. (2021). Environmentaleconomic approach to optimization of transport communication in megacities. *Journal of Environmental Science and Health, Part A, 56*(6), 660–666.

Dong, W., Zhao, G., Yüksel, S., Dinçer, H., & Ubay, G. G. (2022). A novel hybrid decision making approach for the strategic selection of wind energy projects. *Renewable Energy, 185*, 321–337.

Dooyum, U. D., Mikhaylov, A., & Varyash, I. (2020). Energy security concept in Russia and South Korea. *International Journal of Energy Economics and Policy, 10*(4), 102–107.

Grilli, M. L., Valerini, D., Rizzo, A., Yilmaz, M., Song, C., Hu, G., Chierchia, R., Mikhaylov, A., & Rinaldi, A. (2021). A comparative study of the mechanical and tribological properties of thin Al2O3 coatings fabricated by atomic layer deposition and radiofrequency sputtering. *Physica Status Solidi (A), 218*(24), 1–25.

Gura, D., Mikhaylov, A., Glushkov, S., Zaikov, M., & Shaikh, Z. A. (2020). Model for estimating power dissipation along the interconnect length in single on-chip topology. *Evolutionary Intelligence*, s12065.

Haiyun, C., Zhixiong, H., Yüksel, S., & Dinçer, H. (2021). Analysis of the innovation strategies for green supply chain management in the energy industry using the QFD-based hybrid interval valued intuitionistic fuzzy decision approach. *Renewable and Sustainable Energy Reviews, 143*, 110844.

Huang, Y., Masrur, H., Shigenobu, R., Hemeida, A. M., Mikhaylov, A., & Senjyu, T. (2021a). A comparative design of a campus microgrid considering a multi-scenario and multi-objective approach. *Energies, 14*, 2853.

Huang, Y., Yona, A., Takahashi, H., Hemeida, A. M., Mandal, P., Mikhaylov, A., Senjyu, T., & Lotfy, M. E. (2021b). Energy management system optimization of drug store operate electric vehicles charging station. *Sustainability, 14*, 1217836.

Khan, A. A., Shaikh, Z. A., Baitenova, L., Mutaliyeva, L., Moiseev, N., Mikhaylov, A., Laghari, A. A., Idris, S. A., & Alshazly, H. (2021). QoS-ledger: Smart contracts and metaheuristic for secure Quality-of-Service and cost-efficient scheduling of medical-data processing. *Electronics, 10*, 3083.

Kostis, P., Dinçer, H., & Yüksel, S. (2022). Knowledge-based energy investments of european economies and policy recommendations for sustainable development. *Journal of the Knowledge Economy*, 1–33.

Kou, G., Yüksel, S., & Dinçer, H. (2022). Inventive problem-solving map of innovative carbon emission strategies for solar energy-based transportation investment projects. *Applied Energy, 311*, 118680.

Li, J., Yüksel, S., Dınçer, H., Mikhaylov, A., & Barykin, S. E. (2022). Bipolar q-ROF hybrid decision making model with golden cut for analyzing the levelized cost of renewable energy alternatives. *IEEE Access, 10*, 42507–42517.

Liu, L., Kato, T., Mandal, P., Mikhaylov, A., Hemeida, A. M., Takahashi, H., & Tomonobu, S. (2021a). Two cases studies of Model Predictive Control approach for hybrid Renewable Energy Systems. *AIMS Energy, 9*(6), 1241–1259.

Liu, J., Lv, J., Dinçer, H., Yüksel, S., & Karakuş, H. (2021b). Selection of renewable energy alternatives for green blockchain investments: A hybrid IT2-based fuzzy modelling. *Archives of Computational Methods in Engineering, 28*(5), 3687–3701.

Liu, L., Kato, T, Mandal, P., Mikhaylov, A, Hemeida, A.M. and Senjyu T. (2021c). Multi-area power system load frequency control by using model predictive control by introducing renewable energy sources. 2021 International Conference on Science & Contemporary Technologies (ICSCT), 1–6, https://doi.org/10.1109/ICSCT53883.2021.9642521

Liu, Z., Panfilova, E., Mikhaylov, A., & Kurilova, A. (2022b). Assessing stability in the relationship between parties in crowdfunding and crowdsourcing projects during the COVID-19 crisis. *Journal of Global Information Management (JGIM), 30*(4), 1–18. https://doi.org/10.4018/JGIM.297905

Liu, Z.-J., Panfilova, E., Mikhaylov, A., & Kurilova, A. (2022a). COVID-19 crisis impact on the stability between parties in crowdfunding and crowdsourcing. *Wireless Personal Communications, 122*, 915–930.

Meng, Y., Wu, H., Zhao, W., Chen, W., Dinçer, H., & Yüksel, S. (2021). A hybrid heterogeneous Pythagorean fuzzy group decision modelling for crowdfunding development process pathways of fintech-based clean energy investment projects. *Financial Innovation, 7*(1), 1–34.

Mikhaylov, A. (2018a). Volatility spillover effect between stock and exchange rate in oil exporting countries. *International Journal of Energy Economics and Policy, 8*(3), 321–326.

Mikhaylov, A. (2018b). Pricing in oil market and using probit model for analysis of stock market effects. *International Journal of Energy Economics and Policy, 8*(2), 69–73.

Mikhaylov, A. (2020a). Cryptocurrency market analysis from the open innovation perspective. *Journal of Open Innovation: Technology, Market, and Complexity, 6*(4), 197.

Mikhaylov, A. (2020b). Geothermal energy development in Iceland. *International Journal of Energy Economics and Policy, 10*(4), 31–35.

Mikhaylov, A. (2020c). Cryptocurrency market development: hurst method. *Finance: Theory and Practice, 24*(3), 81–91.

Mikhaylov, A. (2021a). Development of Friedrich von Hayek's theory of private money and economic implications for digital currencies. *Terra Economicus, 19*, 1.

Mikhaylov, A. (2021b). Lichens as indicators of atmospheric pollution in urban ecosystems. *Israel Journal of Ecology & Evolution, 67*(1–2), 60–68. https://doi.org/10.1163/22244662-bja10016

Mikhaylov, A. (2022a). Efficiency of renewable energy generation in Russia. *Annals of the Brazilian Academy of Sciences, 94*, 3.

Mikhaylov, A. (2022b). Sustainable development and renewable energy: A new view to a global problem. *Energies, 15*, 1397. https://doi.org/10.3390/en15041397

Mikhaylov, A., & Grilli, M. L. (2022). Machine learning methods and sustainable development: metal oxides and multilayer metal-oxides. *Metals, 12*, 4.

Mikhaylov, A., & Tarakanov, S. (2020). Development of Levenberg-Marquardt theoretical approach for electric network. *Journal of Physics: Conference Series, 1515*, 052006.

Mikhaylov, A., Burakov, D., & Didenko, V. (2019). Relationship between oil price and macroeconomic indicators in Russia. *Finance: Theory and Practice, 23*(2), 105–116. https://doi.org/10.26794/2587-5671-2019-23-2-105-116

Mikhaylov, A., Sokolinskaya, N., & Nyangarika, A. (2018). Optimal carry trade strategy based on currencies of energy and developed economies. *Journal of Reviews on Global Economics, 7*, 582–592.

Mikhaylov, A., Yumashev, A., & Kolpak, E. (2022). Quality of life, anxiety and depressive disorders in patients with extrasystolic arrhythmia. *Archives of Medical Science, 18*, 2. https://doi.org/10.5114/aoms.2020.101359

Moiseev, N., Mikhaylov, A., Varyash, I., & Saqib, A. (2020). Investigating the relation of GDP per capita and corruption index. *Entrepreneurship and Sustainability Issues, 8*(1), 780–794.

Moiseev, N., Sorokin, A., Zvezdina, N., Mikhaylov, A., Khomyakova, L., & Danish, M. S. S. (2021). Credit risk theoretical model on the base of DCC-GARCH in time-varying parameters framework. *Mathematics, 9*, 2423. https://doi.org/10.3390/math9192423

Morkovkin, D. E., Gibadullin, A. A., Kolosova, E. V., Semkina, N. S., & Fasehzoda, I. S. (2020b). Modern transformation of the production base in the conditions of Industry 4.0: problems and prospects. *Journal of Physics: Conference Series, 1515*, 032014.

Morkovkin, D., Lopatkin, D., Sadriddinov, M., Shushunova, T., Gibadullin, A., & Golikova, O. (2020a). Assessment of innovation activity in the countries of the world. *E3S Web of Conferences, 157*, 04015. https://doi.org/10.1051/e3sconf/202015704015

Mukhametov, A., Bekhorashvili, A., Avdeenko, A., & Mikhaylov, A. (2021). The impact of growing legume plants under conditions of Biologization and Soil Cultivation on Chernozem fertility and productivity of rotation crops. *Legume Research, 44*, 12.

Mukhtarov, S., Yüksel, S., & Dinçer, H. (2022). The impact of financial development on renewable energy consumption: Evidence from Turkey. *Renewable Energy, 187*, 169–176.

Mutalimov, V., Kovaleva, I., Mikhaylov, A., & Stepanova, D. (2021). Assessing regional growth of small business in Russia. *Entrepreneurial Business and Economics Review, 9*(3), 119–133. https://doi.org/10.15678/EBER.2021.090308

Nyangarika, A., Mikhaylov, A., & Richter, U. (2019a). Influence oil price towards economic indicators in Russia. *International Journal of Energy Economics and Policy, 9*(1), 123–129.

Nyangarika, A., Mikhaylov, A., & Richter, U. (2019b). Oil price factors: Forecasting on the base of modified auto-regressive integrated moving average model. *International Journal of Energy Economics and Policy, 9*(1), 149–159.

Nyangarika, A., Mikhaylov, A., & Tang, B.-J. (2018). Correlation of oil prices and gross domestic product in oil producing countries. *International Journal of Energy Economics and Policy, 8*(5), 42–48.

Saqib, A., Chan, T.-H., Mikhaylov, A., & Lean, H. H. (2021). Are the responses of sectoral energy imports asymmetric to exchange rate volatilities in Pakistan? Evidence from recent foreign exchange regime. *Frontiers in Energy Research, 9*, 614463. https://doi.org/10.3389/fenrg.2021.614463

Sediqi, M. M., Nakadomari, A., Mikhaylov, A., Krishnan, N., Lotfy, M. E., Yona, A., & Senjyu, T. (2022). Impact of Time-of-Use demand response program on optimal operation of Afghanistan real power system. *Energies, 15*, 296.

Shaikh, Z. A., Moiseev, N., Mikhaylov, A., & Yüksel, S. (2021). Facile synthesis of copper oxide-cobalt oxide/nitrogen-doped carbon (Cu2O-Co3O4/CN) composite for efficient water splitting. *Applied Sciences, 11*, 9974. https://doi.org/10.3390/app11219974

Tamashiro, K., Alharbi, T., Mikhaylov, A., Hemeida, A. M., Krishnan, N., Lotfy, M. E., & Senjyu, T. (2021). Investigation of home energy management with advanced direct load control and optimal scheduling of controllable loads. *Energies, 14*, 7314. https://doi.org/10.3390/en14217314

Uyeh, D. D., Asem-Hiablie, S., Park, T., Kim, K.-M., Mikhaylov, A., Woo, S., & Ha, Y. (2021). Could Japonica rice be an Alternative variety for increased global food security and climate change mitigation? *Food, 10*, 1869. https://doi.org/10.3390/foods10081869

Varyash, I., Mikhaylov, A., Moiseev, N., & Aleshin, K. (2020). Triple bottom line and corporate social responsibility performance indicators for Russian companies. *Entrepreneurship and Sustainability Issues, 8*(1), 313–331.

Xie, Y., Zhou, Y., Peng, Y., Dinçer, H., Yüksel, S., & an Xiang, P. (2021). An extended pythagorean fuzzy approach to group decision-making with incomplete preferences for analyzing balanced scorecard-based renewable energy investments. *IEEE Access, 9*, 43020–43035.

Yüksel, S., Dinçer, H., Mikhaylov, A., Adalı, Z., & Eti, S. (2022). Key issues for the improvements of shallow geothermal investments. In H. Dinçer & S. Yüksel (Eds.), *Sustainability in energy business and finance. Contributions to finance and accounting*. Springer. https://doi.org/10.1007/978-3-030-94051-5_16

Yüksel, S., Mikhaylov, A., & Ubay, G. G. (2021a). Factors causing delay in the installation of nuclear power plants. In S. Yüksel & H. Dinçer (Eds.), *Strategic approaches to energy management. Contributions to management science*. Springer. https://doi.org/10.1007/978-3-030-76783-9_7

Yüksel, S., Mikhaylov, A., Ubay, G. G., & Uyeh, D. D. (2021b). The role of hydrogen in the Black Sea for the future energy supply security of Turkey. In *Handbook of research on strategic management for current energy investments* (pp. 1–15). IGI Global.

Yüksel, S., Mikhaylov, A., Ubay, G. G., & Uyeh, D. D. (2021c). The role of hydrogen in the black sea for the future energy supply security of Turkey. In S. Yüksel & H. Dinçer (Eds.), *Handbook of research on strategic management for current energy investments (pp. 1–15)*. IGI Global. https://doi.org/10.4018/978-1-7998-8335-7.ch001

Yumashev, A., & Mikhaylov, A. (2020). Development of polymer film coatings with high adhesion to steel alloys and high wear resistance. *Polymer Composites, 41*(7), 2875–2880.

Yumashev, A., Ślusarczyk, B., Kondrashev, S., & Mikhaylov, A. (2020). Global indicators of sustainable development: Evaluation of the influence of the human development index on consumption and quality of energy. *Energies, 13*, 2768.

Zhao, Q., Cherkasov, S., Avdeenko, A., Kondratenko, L., & Mikhaylov, A. (2021a). Integral estimate of the added value of agricultural crops in the synergetic agriculture on the example of Vicia faba (Vicia faba L.). *Polish Journal of Environmental Studies, 30*(5), 1–9. https://doi.org/10.15244/pjoes/131949

Zhao, Y., Xu, Y., Yüksel, S., Dinçer, H., & Ubay, G. G. (2021b). Hybrid IT2 fuzzy modelling with alpha cuts for hydrogen energy investments. *International Journal of Hydrogen Energy, 46*(13), 8835–8851.

Zhe, L., Yüksel, S., Dinçer, H., Mukhtarov, S., & Azizov, M. (2021). The positive influences of renewable energy consumption on financial development and economic growth. *Sage Open, 11*(3), 21582440211040133.

Zhou, P., Luo, J., Cheng, F., Yüksel, S., & Dinçer, H. (2021). Analysis of risk priorities for renewable energy investment projects using a hybrid IT2 hesitant fuzzy decision-making approach with alpha cuts. *Energy, 224*, 120184.

Chapter 10
Technological Innovations in Russian Renewable Energy Projects

Miraj Ahmed Bhuiyan and Nora Hegedusne Baranyai

Abstract Since 2011, 34 technology platforms have been created within the framework of Russia's industrial policy in key areas: medicine and biotechnology, information and communication technologies, photonics, aerospace, nuclear technologies, energy, transport, new materials and metallurgy, natural resource extraction, production technologies, and ecology. Despite the fact that they were initiated during the difficult post-crisis period, they represent roadmaps for accelerated development in the context of the Russian economy until 2030. In this article, we discuss ideas for global technological innovations in the following areas: bioenergy, hydropower, geothermal energy, wind energy, solar energy, and marine energy. According to the Organization for Economic Cooperation and Development, global research and development expenditures amount to $1200 billion annually. National figures vary greatly, for example, the amount of R&D in Russia is 1% of GDP, and in the Republic of Korea—2.7% of GDP. About $10 billion. US $0.8% of the total amount is allocated to research and development in the field of renewable energy sources. In order to effectively channel these funds both for commercial purposes and through the state budget, it is necessary to identify technological priorities in the field of renewable energy sources. Renewable energy sources (RES) are a modern high-tech innovative sector with double-digit annual growth rates with significant potential for improvement and the emergence of new technologies, attracting domestic and international investment. In the potentially vast Russian market, this is a window of opportunity. The main question is whether Russian technology platforms correspond to global trends in promoting renewable energy. Since 2011, 34 technology platforms have been created as part of Russia's industrial policy. Despite the fact that they were initiated during a difficult post-crisis period, they represent a significant number of challenges.

M. A. Bhuiyan (✉)
School of Economics, Guangdong University of Finance and Economics, Guangzhou, China

N. H. Baranyai
University of Pannonia, Veszprém, Hungary

H. Dinçer, S. Yüksel (eds.), *Circular Economy and the Energy Market*,
Contributions to Economics, https://doi.org/10.1007/978-3-031-13146-2_10

Keywords Renewable energy sources · Technological innovations · Wind power · Solar power

10.1 Introduction

There are two broad groups of investments: governments and private corporations. Until 2015, R & D expenditures were distributed evenly between these two participants—50% each. More recently, government R & D has started to decline, and now corporate R & D accounts for 70% of the total amount (US $5.5 billion per year in absolute terms in 2016).

Geographically, the European Union (EU) continues to be the leader in renewable energy R & D, followed by China. By industry breakdown, most of the funding goes to solar energy research, up to 50% of the total (US $3.6 billion in 2016), followed by biofuels—US $1.7 billion (23% of total investment).

Public investment in solar and wind power has fallen by 30–40% since the early 2010s. The share of R & D expenditures in total investment decreased from 5% in 2010 to less than 3% in 2018. Despite this trend, the increase in installed capacity of renewable energy sources has continued since 2011, which is a clear indicator of the maturity of an industry that can successfully develop with reduced R & D costs (Denisova et al., 2019; Nyangarika et al., 2019a, b; Huang et al., 2021a, b; Mikhaylov, 2018a, b, 2022a, b; Mikhaylov et al., 2019; Conteh et al., 2021; Sediqi et al., 2022; Khan et al., 2021; Bhuiyan et al., 2022a; Liu et al., 2021a, b; Daniali et al., 2021).

10.2 National Renewable Energy Goals in Russia

The first national target programs for renewable energy sources were established in 2009. According to the federal program "Energy Efficiency and Development of the Energy Sector," 6.2 GW of new generating capacities based on renewable sources were to be installed in Russia by 2020. The deployment of 6.2 GW renewable energy capacity corresponds to an annual investment of US $2 billion per year. The average investment in renewable energy in Russia in 2005–2019 is estimated at $100 million per year, which is 10 times less than the stated level. Thus, the share of renewable energy sources in the national energy balance, instead of reaching 2.5%, was 0.8% at present.

The introduction and expansion of the set of renewable energy technologies described above leads to a less carbon-oriented energy system. Early signs of the so-called "great transition" to this new system are occurring in the area of energy investment (Mukhtarov et al., 2022; Liu et al., 2021a, b, c; Xie et al., 2021; Kou et al., 2022).

The share of fossil fuels in total energy investment declined sharply in 2014–2016, approaching only 50% (10 years ago it was about 70%). Growth has shifted towards renewables, grids, storage, and energy efficiency. They increase their share due to stable growth.

The share of renewable energy sources increased from 16% to 19%, networks from 12% to 16%, and investments in efficiency improvements accounted for 14% of the total in 2018, compared to 10% in 2014.

In 2018, investments in energy efficiency reached $281 billion. Investments in oil and gas exploration and production decreased by 44% in 2014–2016. In absolute terms, energy investment in the global economy totaled US $1830 billion in 2018, down 8% from 2014, mainly due to reduced oil and gas production. Electricity generation costs reached 420 billion US dollars, of which about 70% are renewable energy sources, or 288 billion US dollars.

Costs for all renewable energy sources, including biofuels for transport and solar thermal installations, totaled US $313 billion as part of a broad shift in investment towards low-carbon energy sources.

In China, the largest energy investor by size, new energy investment is dominated by spending on renewables, grids, and energy efficiency. Thus, in 2018, 25% less coal-fired capacity was commissioned compared to 2015.

Given the 5–7-year time lag, in the mid-2020s, we should experience the establishment of a new energy balance structure on a global scale, as well as in individual countries. The structure of the global energy sector is strongly diversified in the next decade, which will contribute to the development of competition between different types of energy, between countries and regions. There will be corresponding economic and social consequences.

Renewable energy production continued to grow strongly, reaching almost 22% of global output by 2018, up from 18% in 2007. Investment in new renewable energy capacity exceeded US $270 billion worldwide in 2016 and is likely to remain strong.

10.3 Literature Review

The level of investment in renewable energy sources in Russia should be significantly increased. On average, the volume of investment in renewable energy in Russia in 2005–2014 is estimated at $100 billion per year, which is much less than the required level stated in the government's forecast. To achieve the goals of renewable energy development, Russian industry must follow global trends in research and development (R & D) in this sector (Zhou et al., 2021; Zhe et al., 2021; Meng et al., 2021; Dinçer et al., 2022; Ding et al., 2021; Haiyun et al., 2021).

The article provides an overview of current trends in the development of "green" energy technologies and sustainable development of the energy complex in the Arctic zone of Russia. The problems and prospects of using renewable energy technologies in the harsh natural conditions of the Arctic and their possible role in improving the efficiency of generating capacity use are considered (Yüksel et al., 2022; Adalı et al., 2022; Dayong et al., 2020; Mikhaylov et al., 2018; Nyangarika et al., 2018; Danish et al., 2020, 2021; An et al., 2021; Uyeh et al., 2021; Tamashiro et al., 2021; Shaikh et al., 2021).

The development of natural resources in the Arctic zone of the Russian Federation (AZRF) is of strategic importance for the country's socio-economic development. In this regard, there is a need to further explore new opportunities for developing and implementing methods for building a distributed energy infrastructure for autonomous energy supply in the Arctic territories of Russia. An assessment of their energy and socio-economic efficiency is also required. Russia is a northern power: more than 60% of its territory is located in the northern regions, where about 12 million people live. The importance of the North for the Russian economy is great, because these territories are exceptionally endowed with nature: over half of the forest, water resources, more than 80% of natural gas, oil, 50% of business wood, 80% of gold, copper and nickel; almost all diamonds, cobalt and many rare earth metals. The Arctic (especially the Russian one) is now the largest oil and gas province on Earth, capable of safely providing hydrocarbons to the needs of all mankind in the twenty-first century. The Northern Sea Route is a global transport system capable of providing the shortest possible transportation: transit to the United States and Japan from Europe is cheaper than through the Suez Canal (An et al., 2019a, b, 2020a, b, c; Mikhaylov, 2020a, b, c; 2021a; Mikhaylov & Tarakanov, 2020; Moiseev et al., 2020, 2021; Grilli et al., 2021; Gura et al., 2020; Dooyum et al., 2020; Mikhaylov et al., 2022; Varyash et al., 2020; Zhao et al., 2021a, b; An & Mikhaylov, 2020, 2021; Alwaelya et al., 2021; Yumashev & Mikhaylov, 2020; Yumashev et al., 2020; Mutalimov et al., 2021; Morkovkin et al., 2020a, b).

The current state of energy supply in the Arctic territories cannot be considered satisfactory. The main problem of transport supply in the Arctic territories is the seasonality of its operation. Fuel delivery for the operation of local power supply systems can only be carried out periodically (Dong et al., 2022; Li et al., 2022; Zhao et al., 2021a, b; Kostis et al., 2022; Serezli et al., 2021). To date, water transport provides up to 80% of supplies, in particular, to Yakutia. The duration of operation of water transport does not exceed 120–150 days during the year. It is necessary to develop technologies that provide local energy supply to the Arctic territories using local fuel and energy resources. Various types of waste, including solid and liquid household waste, should also be used as local fuel and energy resources (Bhuiyan et al., 2021, 2022b; Dong et al., 2021; Mikhaylov, 2021b; Baboshkin et al., 2022; Barykin et al., 2022; Baig et al., 2022a, b; Liu et al. 2022a, b Liu et al., 2022b; Danish et al., 2022; Saqib et al., 2021; Yüksel et al., 2021a, b, c; Mukhametov et al., 2021; Candila et al., 2021; Mikhaylov & Grilli, 2022).

The results of assessing the energy and socio-economic efficiency of the prospective development of energy infrastructure based on renewable energy sources in areas of permanent residence of people and labor activity were obtained. They showed that the Russian Arctic has both significant potential and a significant need for the use of renewable energy sources.

Within the framework of this study, the principles of building an energy infrastructure in the Arctic were considered, taking into account the characteristic features of the region—the remoteness and small number of settlements, the development of large transport, logistics and production hubs, climatic conditions, etc. It is shown that compliance with the principles of sustainable development is a necessary condition for the future efficiency of the energy complex in the Russian Arctic. Important results obtained in the course of the study can be grouped into three main thematic areas: (1) geographical analysis of the general population and the state of the AZRF energy complex in terms of the use of various energy resources; (2) assessment of renewable energy potential and environmental efficiency of renewable energy installations; (3) the impact of climate change on the development of energy infrastructure within the life cycle of both existing and projected power plants. The results obtained, aimed at solving current problems of energy infrastructure development in the Arctic region of Russia, will help optimize the composition and structure of the energy economy of the Arctic territories in areas of permanent residence, reducing the burden on natural ecosystems and sustainable economic and social development of the region as a whole. Based on the data of, recommendations were formulated for adapting the energy infrastructure to changing climatic and environmental conditions, and the basic principles for building the AZRF energy complex from the point of view of complexity and sustainable development were developed.

Due to the relatively high gross and technical potential of renewable energy sources in the Arctic region, it is possible to introduce appropriate technologies to ensure a more sustainable energy supply. Solutions that combine traditional and renewable energy technologies are able to meet the basic requirements of reliability, while contributing to the sustainability of the oil and gas industry.

10.4 Main Economic Interests of the Arctic States

The main economic interests of the Arctic states are still more focused around natural resources and new transit opportunities. For the Russian Arctic (RA), this interest is determined by the high traditional and unconventional hydrocarbon potential of the region, as well as other natural resources and new transport and logistics routes, such as the Northern Sea Route. However, the future socio-economic development of the region largely depends not only on the exploitation of natural resources, but also on the development of energy and transport infrastructure. Currently, transportation and delivery of traditional energy resources to the Arctic regions account for a significant part of the total cost of electricity generation and maintenance of existing infrastructure. Local and renewable energy sources are the most promising way to ensure reliable and affordable energy supply to the developing Arctic region. Such solutions for energy supply in the Arctic region are possible due to the availability of new technologies and materials that significantly affect its efficiency and reliability. Their successful implementation will contribute to: sustainable development of energy infrastructure and energy supply in the Russian Arctic in line with climate and environmental challenges. More widespread adoption of decentralized energy production solutions based on the sharing of traditional and local renewable energy sources is needed. This is especially important for developing the infrastructure of the Northern Sea Route and providing remote decentralized energy consumers. Increased adoption of decentralized combined energy solutions will provide the foundation for sustainable regional development.

The Arctic is a specific geographical region with extreme climatic conditions, a vulnerable natural environment, but rather intensive industrialization. This region is also the most sensitive to global climate change. The average annual temperature anomaly in the Arctic from October 2019 to September 2020 was 1.9 °C warmer than the 1981–2010 average for land areas between 60 and 90°N. Since 2000, the average temperature anomalies in the Arctic are more than twice as high as global anomalies.

The specifics of the Arctic require alternative solutions to ensure energy supply to consumers of energy resources, which is due to the growing demand for energy carriers and the small-scale decentralized nature of energy supply. Currently, most of the energy consumption in the region is covered by hydrocarbon energy resources supplied from the mainland. Renewable energy technologies can be effectively implemented to meet the needs of small, decentralized energy consumers in the Russian Arctic, but they are currently being applied on a very modest scale. Environmental challenges and threats associated with climate change, their interrelation and impact on the technological choice of the future energy supply of the region, should be considered from the point of view of ensuring the future sustainable development of the Russian Arctic. At the current stage in Russia, until 2024, the main mechanism in place to support the development of renewable energy is the conclusion (based on the results of competitive selection of projects) of long-term contracts for the provision of capacity for the supply of electricity by generating facilities based on renewable energy to the wholesale electricity market (PDM RES) and mandatory priority purchase of electricity produced by qualified generating facilities based on renewable energy. Capacity supply agreements guarantee investors a return on investment in construction and operation property, as well as receiving income on the invested capital. This support mechanism provides investors with a return of 12% per annum (in addition to the return on capital and operating costs) under PDM agreements valid for 15 years. By supporting a multi-year subsidy program, the state acts as an additional guarantor for investors. This support mechanism significantly reduces the financial risks of investing in large competitive projects.

Additional risks and costs arise during the operation of renewable energy facilities. An analysis of the experience of foreign renewable energy projects has shown that non-financial and financial risk management mechanisms can be distinguished when solving risk management problems. Risk management by non-financial methods is carried out by the developer by reducing them during design and operation high professional level of projects, technically reliable equipment, development of regulatory documents, training of personnel to reduce the risks of the human factor, use of high-quality raw materials in bioenergy. Risks accepted by insurance companies usually include those developed for traditional industries. These include: technological risks (equipment failure), organizational risks (delays in deliveries), natural disasters, human factors, as well as some legal and financial risks. The most common type of insurance is the insurance of technological and organizational risks that arise during the delivery of equipment and operation: delays in deliveries, risks of breakdowns during delivery equipment, risks of malfunctions and fires of turbines during operation. With the development of technology, the equipment also changes. Thus, the blade length of modern wind power plants can reach more than 100 m. Transportation and installation of such equipment in hard-to-reach places in fields and mountains to unprepared sites expand the list of risks that need to be considered. International practice shows the need to take into account the risks associated with theft of solar panels and acts of vandalism in insurance. Natural fires also pose a great danger to Russia. Forest fires are also spreading in open, grass-covered areas where renewable energy facilities can be located. When designing new facilities, it is necessary to take into account long-term statistics on natural fires.

In the vast territory of Russia with a high variety of natural and climatic conditions, resource risks are especially important, since the used solar, wind, and hydroelectric resources are subject to climate variability and significant fluctuations over time. The characteristics of time variability depend on the geographical location of the power facility in a particular climate zone. This variability also leads to significant fluctuations in the output of power plants, which increase the risks of a stable supply of EE to the grid and lead to risks of higher project costs in the future. There is no need to install energy storage devices. For example, the analysis of electricity production at solar power plants commissioned in the Altai Republic by calculating the average installed capacity utilization factor for a certain period showed large differences both in time and depending on the location of the SES. The average annual Cim values vary from 17.04% at Kosh-Agach SES-2 to 11.6% at Maiminskaya SES, for the autumn-winter period this figure is even lower—10.63% and 4.90%, respectively.

10.5 Conclusions

Changes in climatic characteristics inevitably have an impact on the operating conditions and on the efficiency of power facilities. The degree of this dependence is investigated for different types of fuel and energy infrastructure facilities. The results of the assessment of the impact of global climate change on the fuel and energy sector infrastructure and the possibilities for its adaptation are presented, which include: (1) the impact on power generation facilities; (2) the impact on energy transportation; (3) problems of permafrost thawing; (4) climate impacts on electricity consumption and socio-economic indicators; (5) the role of distributed energy and RES in climate change adaptation. It is shown that for the territories of Armenia with isolated energy supply, the development of energy-efficient systems and renewable energy sources will reduce climate risks for the sustainable growth of this sector of the economy and the economic complex as a whole by both better adapting them to the consequences of climate change and reducing man-made greenhouse gas emissions.

The Northern territories play a significant role in the national economy, in ensuring Russia's security and geopolitical interests. As part of the new strategy for the development of the northern territories until 2035, it is planned to create fuel and energy industry enterprises that meet the current level of development and do not have a negative impact on the unique northern environment. For the practical implementation of this program, it is necessary to develop new local energy supply technologies that can be used in the Arctic zone. It is necessary to provide the northern regions of the country with environmentally friendly energy and motor fuel based on local raw materials, limit and, ultimately, completely exclude the expensive northern import of petroleum products. To solve this problem, it is necessary to develop methods for a comprehensive assessment of the socio-economic efficiency of the development of environmentally safe renewable energy in remote sparsely populated areas of the North, including for the infrastructure support of the Northern Sea Route and specially protected natural areas.

References

Adalı, Z., Dinçer, H., Eti, S., Mikhaylov, A., & Yüksel, S. (2022). Identifying new perspectives on geothermal energy investments. In H. Dinçer & S. Yüksel (Eds.), *Multidimensional strategic outlook on global competitive energy economics and finance* (pp. 1–11). Emerald Publishing Limited. https://doi.org/10.1108/978-1-80117-898-320221002

Alwaelya, S. A., Yousif, N. B. A., & Mikhaylov, A. (2021). Emotional development in preschoolers and socialization. *Early Child Development and Care, 191*, 16.

An, J., & Mikhaylov, A. (2020). Russian energy projects in South Africa. *Journal of Energy in Southern Africa, 31*(3), 58–64.

An, J., & Mikhaylov, A. (2021). Analysis of energy projects financial efficiency and renewable energy generation in Russia. *Finance: Theory and Practice, 25*(5), 79–91.

An, J., Mikhaylov, A., & Moiseev, N. (2019a). Oil price predictors: Machine learning approach. *International Journal of Energy Economics and Policy, 9*(5), 1–6.

An, J., Mikhaylov, A., & Sokolinskaya, N. (2019b). Machine learning in economic planning: Ensembles of algorithms. *Journal of Physics: Conference Series, 1353*, 012126.

An, J., Mikhaylov, A., & Jung, S.-U. (2020a). The strategy of South Korea in the global oil market. *Energies, 13*(10), 2491.

An, J., Mikhaylov, A., & Kim, K. (2020b). Machine learning approach in heterogeneous group of algorithms for transport safety-critical system. *Applied Sciences, 10*(8), 2670.

An, J., Mikhaylov, A., & Richter, U. H. (2020c). Trade war effects: Evidence from sectors of energy and resources in Africa. *Heliyon, 6*, e05693. https://doi.org/10.1016/j.heliyon.2020.e05693

An, J., Mikhaylov, A., & Jung, S.-U. (2021). A linear programming approach for Robust network revenue management in the airline industry. *Journal of Air Transport Management, 91*, 101979.

Baboshkin, P., Mikhaylov, A., & Shaikh, Z. A. (2022). Sustainable cryptocurrency growth is not possible? Impact of network power demand on bitcoin price. *Financial Journal, 14*(2), 39–55.

Baig, U., Hussain, B. M., Khan, A. A., Shaikh, Z. A., Mikhaylov, A., Chao, C.-C., & Barykin, S. E. (2022a). Research on investors of the reginal stock exchange: An influence of behavioral finance on investment decision making. *Risks, 10*(4), 116.

Baig, U., Khan, A. A., Abbas, M. G., Shaikh, Z. A., Mikhaylov, A., Laghari, A. A., & Hussain, B. M. (2022b). Crucial causes of delay in completion and performance management of the construction work: Study on the base of relative importance index. *Journal of Tianjin University Science and Technology, 55*(6).

Barykin, S., Mikheev, A., Kiseleva, E., Putikhin, Y., Alekseeva, N., & Mikhaylov, A. (2022). An empirical analysis of Russian regions' debt sustainability. *Economies, 10*(4), 296.

Bhuiyan, M. A., An, J., Mikhaylov, A., Moiseev, N., & Danish, M. S. S. (2021). Renewable energy deployment and COVID-19 measures for sustainable development. *Sustainability, 13*, 4418.

Bhuiyan, M. A., Dinçer, H., Yüksel, S., Mikhaylov, A., Danish, M. S. S., Pinter, G., Uyeh, D. D., & Stepanova, D. (2022a). Economic indicators and bioenergy supply in developed economies: QROF-DEMATEL and random forest models. *Energy Reports, 8*, 561–570.

Bhuiyan, M. A., Khare, V., Mikhaylov, A., Pinter, G., & Zhang. (2022b) Does renewable energy consumption affect economic growth? A systematic literature review. *Frontiers in Environmental Science.*

Candila, V., Maximov, D., Mikhaylov, A., Moiseev, N., Senjyu, T., & Tryndina, N. (2021). On the relationship between oil and exchange rates of oil-exporting and oil-importing countries: From the great recession period to the Covid-19 era. *Energies, 14*, 8065.

Conteh, F., Takahashi, H., Hemeida, A. M., Krishnan, N., Mikhaylov, A., & Senjyu, T. (2021). Hybrid grid-connected renewable power generation for sustainable electricity supply in Sierra Leone: Case study Lungi Town. *Sustainability, 13*(18), 1–20.

Daniali, S. M., Barykin, S. E., Kapustina, I. V., Khortabi, F. M., Sergeev, S. M., Kalinina, O. V., Mikhaylov, A., Veynberg, R., Zasova, L., & Senjyu, T. (2021). Predicting volatility index according to technical index and economic indicators on the basis of deep learning algorithm. *Sustainability, 2021*(13), 14011.

Danish, M. S. S., Bhattacharya, A., Stepanova, D., Mikhaylov, A., Grilli, M. L., Khosravy, M., & Senjyu, T. (2020). A systematic review of metal oxide applications for energy and environmental sustainability. *Metals, 10*(12), 1604.

Danish, M. S. S., Senjyu, T., Sabory, N. R., Khosravy, M., Grilli, M. L., Mikhaylov, A., & Majidi, H. (2021). A forefront framework for sustainable aquaponics modeling and design. *Sustainability, 13*, 9313.

Danish, M. S. S., Estrella-Pajulas, L. L., Alemaida, I. M. A., Grilli, M. L., Mikhaylov, A., & Senjyu, T. (2022). Green synthesis of silver oxide nanoparticles for photocatalytic environmental remediation and biomedical applications. *Metals, 12*(4), 769.

Dayong, N., Mikhaylov, A., Bratanovsky, S., Shaikh, Z. A., & Stepanova, D. (2020). Mathematical modeling of the technological processes of catering products production. *Journal of Food Process Engineering, 43*(2), 1–9.

Denisova, V., Mikhaylov, A., & Lopatin, E. (2019). Blockchain infrastructure and growth of global power consumption. *International Journal of Energy Economics and Policy, 9*(4), 22–29.

Dinçer, H., Yüksel, S., & Martínez, L. (2022). Collaboration enhanced hybrid fuzzy decision-making approach to analyze the renewable energy investment projects. *Energy Reports, 8*, 377–389.

Ding, Z., Yüksel, S., & Dincer, H. (2021). An Integrated Pythagorean fuzzy soft computing approach to environmental management systems for sustainable energy pricing. *Energy Reports, 7*, 5575–5588.

Dong, B., Ikonnikova, I., Rogulin, R., Sakulyeva, T., & Mikhaylov, A. (2021). Environmental economic approach to optimization of transport communication in megacities. *Journal of Environmental Science and Health, Part A, 56*(6), 660–666.

Dong, W., Zhao, G., Yüksel, S., Dinçer, H., & Ubay, G. G. (2022). A novel hybrid decision making approach for the strategic selection of wind energy projects. *Renewable Energy, 185*, 321–337.

Dooyum, U. D., Mikhaylov, A., & Varyash, I. (2020). Energy security concept in Russia and South Korea. *International Journal of Energy Economics and Policy, 10*(4), 102–107.

Grilli, M. L., Valerini, D., Rizzo, A., Yilmaz, M., Song, C., Hu, G., Chierchia, R., Mikhaylov, A., & Rinaldi, A. (2021). A comparative study of the mechanical and tribological properties of thin

Al2O3 coatings fabricated by atomic layer deposition and radiofrequency sputtering. *Physica Status Solidi (A), 218*(24), 1–25.
Gura, D., Mikhaylov, A., Glushkov, S., Zaikov, M., & Shaikh, Z. A. (2020). Model for estimating power dissipation along the interconnect length in single on-chip topology. *Evolutionary Intelligence*.
Haiyun, C., Zhixiong, H., Yüksel, S., & Dinçer, H. (2021). Analysis of the innovation strategies for green supply chain management in the energy industry using the QFD-based hybrid interval valued intuitionistic fuzzy decision approach. *Renewable and Sustainable Energy Reviews, 143*, 110844.
Huang, Y., Masrur, H., Shigenobu, R., Hemeida, A. M., Mikhaylov, A., & Senjyu, T. (2021a). A comparative design of a campus microgrid considering a multi-scenario and multi-objective approach. *Energies, 14*, 2853.
Huang, Y., Yona, A., Takahashi, H., Hemeida, A. M., Mandal, P., Mikhaylov, A., Senjyu, T., & Lotfy, M. E. (2021b). Energy management system optimization of drug store operate electric vehicles charging station. *Sustainability, 14*, 1217836.
Khan, A. A., Shaikh, Z. A., Baitenova, L., Mutaliyeva, L., Moiseev, N., Mikhaylov, A., Laghari, A. A., Idris, S. A., & Alshazly, H. (2021). QoS-ledger: Smart contracts and metaheuristic for secure quality-of-service and cost-efficient scheduling of medical-data processing. *Electronics, 10*, 3083.
Kostis, P., Dinçer, H., & Yüksel, S. (2022). Knowledge-based energy investments of European economies and policy recommendations for sustainable development. *Journal of the Knowledge Economy*, 1–33.
Kou, G., Yüksel, S., & Dinçer, H. (2022). Inventive problem-solving map of innovative carbon emission strategies for solar energy-based transportation investment projects. *Applied Energy, 311*, 118680.
Li, J., Yüksel, S., Dınçer, H., Mikhaylov, A., & Barykin, S. E. (2022). Bipolar q-ROF hybrid decision making model with golden cut for analyzing the levelized cost of renewable energy alternatives. *IEEE Access, 10*, 42507–42517.
Liu, L., Kato, T., Mandal, P., Mikhaylov, A., Hemeida, A. M., & Senjyu, T. (2021a). Multi-area power system load frequency control by using model predictive control by introducing renewable energy sources. In *2021 International Conference on Science & Contemporary Technologies (ICSCT)* (pp. 1–6). https://doi.org/10.1109/ICSCT53883.2021.9642521
Liu, L., Kato, T., Mandal, P., Mikhaylov, A., Hemeida, A. M., Takahashi, H., & Tomonobu, S. (2021b). Two cases studies of model predictive control approach for hybrid renewable energy systems. *AIMS Energy, 9*(6), 1241–1259.
Liu, J., Lv, J., Dinçer, H., Yüksel, S., & Karakuş, H. (2021c). Selection of renewable energy alternatives for green blockchain investments: A hybrid IT2-based fuzzy modelling. *Archives of Computational Methods in Engineering, 28*(5), 3687–3701.
Liu, Z.-J., Panfilova, E., Mikhaylov, A., & Kurilova, A. (2022a). Assessing stability in relationship between parties in crowdfunding and crowdsourcing projects during the COVID-19 crisis. *Journal of Global Information Management, 30*(2), 1.
Liu, Z.-J., Panfilova, E., Mikhaylov, A., & Kurilova, A. (2022b). COVID-19 crisis impact on the stability between parties in crowdfunding and crowdsourcing. *Wireless Personal Communications, 122*, 915–930.
Meng, Y., Wu, H., Zhao, W., Chen, W., Dinçer, H., & Yüksel, S. (2021). A hybrid heterogeneous Pythagorean fuzzy group decision modelling for crowdfunding development process pathways of fintech-based clean energy investment projects. *Financial Innovation, 7*(1), 1–34.
Mikhaylov, A. (2018a). Volatility spillover effect between stock and exchange rate in oil exporting countries. *International Journal of Energy Economics and Policy, 8*(3), 321–326.
Mikhaylov, A. (2018b). Pricing in oil market and using probit model for analysis of stock market effects. *International Journal of Energy Economics and Policy, 8*(2), 69–73.
Mikhaylov, A. (2020a). Cryptocurrency market analysis from the open innovation perspective. *Journal of Open Innovation: Technology, Market, and Complexity, 6*(4), 197.

Mikhaylov, A. (2020b). Geothermal energy development in Iceland. *International Journal of Energy Economics and Policy, 10*(4), 31–35.
Mikhaylov, A. (2020c). Cryptocurrency market development: Hurst method. *Finance: Theory and Practice, 24*(3), 81–91.
Mikhaylov, A. (2021a). Development of Friedrich von Hayek's theory of private money and economic implications for digital currencies. *Terra Economicus, 19*(1), 53–62.
Mikhaylov, A. (2021b). Lichens as indicators of atmospheric pollution in urban ecosystems. *Israel Journal of Ecology & Evolution, 67*(1–2), 60–68. https://doi.org/10.1163/22244662-bja10016
Mikhaylov, A. (2022a). Efficiency of renewable energy generation in Russia. *Annals of the Brazilian Academy of Sciences, 94*(3).
Mikhaylov, A. (2022b). Sustainable development and renewable energy: A new view to a global problem. *Energies, 15*, 1397. https://doi.org/10.3390/en15041397
Mikhaylov, A., & Grilli, M. L. (2022). Machine learning methods and sustainable development: Metal oxides and multilayer metal-oxides. *Metals, 12*(4), 836.
Mikhaylov, A., & Tarakanov, S. (2020). Development of Levenberg-Marquardt theoretical approach for electric network. *Journal of Physics: Conference Series, 1515*, 052006.
Mikhaylov, A., Sokolinskaya, N., & Nyangarika, A. (2018). Optimal carry trade strategy based on currencies of energy and developed economies. *Journal of Reviews on Global Economics, 7*, 582–592.
Mikhaylov, A., Burakov, D., & Didenko, V. (2019). Relationship between oil price and macroeconomic indicators in Russia. *Finance: Theory and Practice, 23*(2), 105–116. https://doi.org/10.26794/2587-5671-2019-23-2-105-116
Mikhaylov, A., Yumashev, A., & Kolpak, E. (2022). Quality of life, anxiety and depressive disorders in patients with extrasystolic arrhythmia. *Archives of Medical Science, 18*(2), 328–335. https://doi.org/10.5114/aoms.2020.101359
Moiseev, N., Mikhaylov, A., Varyash, I., & Saqib, A. (2020). Investigating the relation of GDP per capita and corruption index. *Entrepreneurship and Sustainability Issues, 8*(1), 780–794.
Moiseev, N., Sorokin, A., Zvezdina, N., Mikhaylov, A., Khomyakova, L., & Danish, M. S. S. (2021). Credit risk theoretical model on the base of DCC-GARCH in time-varying parameters framework. *Mathematics, 9*, 2423. https://doi.org/10.3390/math9192423
Morkovkin, D., Lopatkin, D., Sadriddinov, M., Shushunova, T., Gibadullin, A., & Golikova, O. (2020a). Assessment of innovation activity in the countries of the world. *E3S Web of Conferences, 157*, 04015. https://doi.org/10.1051/e3sconf/202015704015
Morkovkin, D. E., Gibadullin, A. A., Kolosova, E. V., Semkina, N. S., & Fasehzoda, I. S. (2020b). Modern transformation of the production base in the conditions of industry 4.0: Problems and prospects. *Journal of Physics: Conference Series, 1515*, 032014.
Mukhametov, A., Bekhorashvili, A., Avdeenko, A., & Mikhaylov, A. (2021). The impact of growing legume plants under conditions of biologization and soil cultivation on Chernozem fertility and productivity of rotation crops. *Legume Research, 44*, 1219–1225.
Mukhtarov, S., Yüksel, S., & Dinçer, H. (2022). The impact of financial development on renewable energy consumption: Evidence from Turkey. *Renewable Energy, 187*, 169–176.
Mutalimov, V., Kovaleva, I., Mikhaylov, A., & Stepanova, D. (2021). Assessing regional growth of small business in Russia. *Entrepreneurial Business and Economics Review, 9*(3), 119–133. https://doi.org/10.15678/EBER.2021.090308
Nyangarika, A., Mikhaylov, A., & Tang, B.-J. (2018). Correlation of oil prices and gross domestic product in oil producing countries. *International Journal of Energy Economics and Policy, 8*(5), 42–48.
Nyangarika, A., Mikhaylov, A., & Richter, U. (2019a). Influence oil price towards economic indicators in Russia. *International Journal of Energy Economics and Policy, 9*(1), 123–129.
Nyangarika, A., Mikhaylov, A., & Richter, U. (2019b). Oil price factors: Forecasting on the base of modified auto-regressive integrated moving average model. *International Journal of Energy Economics and Policy, 9*(1), 149–159.

Saqib, A., Chan, T.-H., Mikhaylov, A., & Lean, H. H. (2021). Are the responses of sectoral energy imports asymmetric to exchange rate volatilities in Pakistan? Evidence from recent foreign exchange regime. *Frontiers in Energy Research, 9*, 614463. https://doi.org/10.3389/fenrg.2021.614463

Sediqi, M. M., Nakadomari, A., Mikhaylov, A., Krishnan, N., Lotfy, M. E., Yona, A., & Senjyu, T. (2022). Impact of time-of-use demand response program on optimal operation of Afghanistan real power system. *Energies, 15*, 296.

Serezli, E., Yüksel, S., Tamer, İ., & Dinçer, H. (2021). The role of innovative renewable energy investment strategies on macroeconomic stability. In *Financial strategies in competitive markets* (pp. 165–178). Springer.

Shaikh, Z. A., Moiseev, N., Mikhaylov, A., & Yüksel, S. (2021). Facile synthesis of copper oxide-cobalt oxide/nitrogen-doped carbon (Cu2O-Co3O4/CN) composite for efficient water splitting. *Applied Sciences, 11*, 9974. https://doi.org/10.3390/app11219974

Tamashiro, K., Alharbi, T., Mikhaylov, A., Hemeida, A. M., Krishnan, N., Lotfy, M. E., & Senjyu, T. (2021). Investigation of home energy management with advanced direct load control and optimal scheduling of controllable loads. *Energies, 14*, 7314. https://doi.org/10.3390/en14217314

Uyeh, D. D., Asem-Hiablie, S., Park, T., Kim, K.-M., Mikhaylov, A., Woo, S., & Ha, Y. (2021). Could japonica rice be an alternative variety for increased global food security and climate change mitigation? *Food, 10*, 1869. https://doi.org/10.3390/foods10081869

Varyash, I., Mikhaylov, A., Moiseev, N., & Aleshin, K. (2020). Triple bottom line and corporate social responsibility performance indicators for Russian companies. *Entrepreneurship and Sustainability Issues, 8*(1), 313–331.

Xie, Y., Zhou, Y., Peng, Y., Dinçer, H., Yüksel, S., & an Xiang, P. (2021). An extended Pythagorean fuzzy approach to group decision-making with incomplete preferences for analyzing balanced scorecard-based renewable energy investments. *IEEE Access, 9*, 43020–43035.

Yüksel, S., Mikhaylov, A., Ubay, G. G., & Uyeh, D. D. (2021a). The role of hydrogen in the Black Sea for the future energy supply security of Turkey. In *Handbook of research on strategic management for current energy investments* (pp. 1–15). IGI Global.

Yüksel, S., Mikhaylov, A., & Ubay, G. G. (2021b). Factors causing delay in the installation of nuclear power plants. In S. Yüksel & H. Dinçer (Eds.), *Strategic approaches to energy management. Contributions to management science*. Springer. https://doi.org/10.1007/978-3-030-76783-9_7

Yüksel, S., Mikhaylov, A., Ubay, G. G., & Uyeh, D. D. (2021c). The role of hydrogen in the Black Sea for the future energy supply security of Turkey. In S. Yüksel & H. Dinçer (Eds.), *Handbook of research on strategic management for current energy investments* (pp. 1–15). IGI Global. https://doi.org/10.4018/978-1-7998-8335-7.ch001

Yüksel, S., Dinçer, H., Mikhaylov, A., Adalı, Z., & Eti, S. (2022). Key issues for the improvements of shallow geothermal investments. In H. Dinçer & S. Yüksel (Eds.), *Sustainability in energy business and finance. Contributions to finance and accounting*. Springer. https://doi.org/10.1007/978-3-030-94051-5_16

Yumashev, A., & Mikhaylov, A. (2020). Development of polymer film coatings with high adhesion to steel alloys and high wear resistance. *Polymer Composites, 41*(7), 2875–2880.

Yumashev, A., Ślusarczyk, B., Kondrashev, S., & Mikhaylov, A. (2020). Global indicators of sustainable development: Evaluation of the influence of the human development index on consumption and quality of energy. *Energies, 13*, 2768.

Zhao, Q., Cherkasov, S., Avdeenko, A., Kondratenko, L., & Mikhaylov, A. (2021a). Integral estimate of the added value of agricultural crops in the synergetic agriculture on the example of Vicia faba (Vicia faba L.). *Polish Journal of Environmental Studies, 30*(5), 1–9. https://doi.org/10.15244/pjoes/131949

Zhao, Y., Xu, Y., Yüksel, S., Dinçer, H., & Ubay, G. G. (2021b). Hybrid IT2 fuzzy modelling with alpha cuts for hydrogen energy investments. *International Journal of Hydrogen Energy, 46*(13), 8835–8851.

Zhe, L., Yüksel, S., Dinçer, H., Mukhtarov, S., & Azizov, M. (2021). The positive influences of renewable energy consumption on financial development and economic growth. *SAGE Open, 11*(3), 21582440211040133.

Zhou, P., Luo, J., Cheng, F., Yüksel, S., & Dinçer, H. (2021). Analysis of risk priorities for renewable energy investment projects using a hybrid IT2 hesitant fuzzy decision-making approach with alpha cuts. *Energy, 224*, 120184.

Chapter 11
Optimal Share of Investing in Solar Energy Companies' Stocks and Bonds for Sustainable Growth

Andrey Kraykin, Artur Meynkhard, and Tomonobu Senjyu

Abstract The main purpose of the study is to study some of the world's largest companies engaged in the production of solar panels and to make a forecast of the exchange rate of their shares in the coming year based on the analysis of various economic indicators. The paper uses fundamental methods for analyzing the stock price, such as the ratio of capitalization and cash flow, the ratio of the company's value to its balance sheet, the ratio of borrowed funds to equity, the ratio of the market price of a share to net profit and based on changes in the volume of sales of companies, a trend equation was derived, which was subsequently adjusted in accordance with the above indicators. In the course of the study, the following results were obtained: forecasts of the value of shares of First Solar Inc. and Canadian Solar Inc., including the maximum and minimum values during the day, for the coming year were obtained. Based on the results obtained, conclusions were drawn: this method allows us to consider many approaches to stock valuation and make a single forecast based on them; however, this requires a lot of calculations and time costs. The issue of the global transition from non-renewable to green energy was widely discussed back in the twentieth century, not only because of the limited energy resources, but also because of global pollution and the greenhouse effect, which was increasingly manifested due to the growth of the required amount of energy and, as a result, an increase in the number of power plants that pollute the atmosphere. The most widespread issue of green energy was already in the twenty-first century, when global pollution began to be felt even more acutely. For example, last year the European Commission presented a plan to turn the European Union into a carbon-neutral zone by 2050. It is also worth noting that the main topic of the XXIV St. Petersburg International Economic Forum, held in 2021, was the issue of renewable energy. In terms of the number of agreements in the field of green energy, this forum broke the records of all previous ones, which indicates the global

A. Kraykin (✉) · A. Meynkhard
Financial University Under the Government of the Russian Federation, Moscow, Russia

T. Senjyu
University of the Ryukyus, Nishihara, Japan
e-mail: b985542@tec.u-ryukyu.acj

H. Dinçer, S. Yüksel (eds.), *Circular Economy and the Energy Market*,
Contributions to Economics, https://doi.org/10.1007/978-3-031-13146-2_11

importance of the issue of switching to renewable energy. The purpose of this work is to study some of the world's largest companies engaged in the production of solar panels and to make a forecast of the exchange rate of their shares.

Keywords Promotion · Company · Cost · Price · Forecast · Trend

11.1 Introduction

Multinational corporations are one of the main sponsors of R&D in their field, so their development will determine the development of the field as a whole. At the moment, solar energy is in the development stage, but due to the high cost of solar electricity production, the intervention of states is required for the effective development of this area.

Of course, the developing industry attracts the attention of investors and solar energy is no exception. Nevertheless, although investments in developing projects can bring more profit than in developed ones, however, the latter are more stable in terms of risks. One of the primary tasks of an investor is to determine the future of the industry in which investments are planned, since even stable industries can lose the value of their shares over time and even completely close. There are many cases in history when developing industries have completely displaced developed ones from the market. This has also happened in the energy sector, when steam engines have completely become a thing of the past due to low efficiency. The object of the study are the companies First Solar Inc. and Canadian Solar Inc. The subject of the study is the tools of fundamental analysis of companies.

The theoretical basis of this research is the work of international researchers in various fields related to the development of companies working in the field of alternative energy.

11.2 Literature Review

11.2.1 Forecasting of Solar Activity as a Tool for Improving the Efficiency of Solar Power Plants

When making a forecast for a company, we should not forget about the importance of analyzing the state of its customers, since they largely determine the future of the company. One of the largest buyers of solar panels are solar power plants, so the economic indicators of companies that produce solar panels. it is directly dependent on the economic indicators of solar power plants (Yüksel et al., 2022a, b; Adalı et al., 2022; An et al., 2021).

The forecast of solar electricity generation is also important for individual buildings that use solar panels as one of the main sources of electricity (Liu et al.,

2021a, b, c; Mukhtarov et al., 2022; Xie et al., 2021; Kou et al., 2022; Zhou et al., 2021; Zhe et al., 2021; Meng et al., 2021). For consumers who combine the use of solar energy with traditional sources of its generation, a short-term forecast is of great importance to counteract possible failures in the operation of the power system (Yakovlev et al., 2021; Kranina, 2021).

11.2.2 Demand Generation and Main Consumers

Throughout history, the energy needs of humanity have only increased. There are even a number of works proving the mutual dependence between energy consumption and economic growth. First of all, the growth in demand for electricity is caused by global demographic growth, since the number of people is directly proportional to the amount of energy they consume. The growth of electricity consumption makes it necessary to optimize its consumption in all sectors of production, even in those that are aimed at meeting basic human needs, for example, this issue is relevant in the industry engaged in the production of public catering products (Dinçer et al., 2022; Ding et al., 2021; Haiyun et al., 2021; Dong et al., 2022; Li et al., 2022; Zhao et al., 2021a, b; Dayong et al., 2020). However, optimization does not mean a reduction in the volume of electricity consumption on a global scale, and even more so, a complete rejection of electricity consumption. New industries are constantly emerging in the world that require significant energy costs, which has a positive impact on the development of the entire energy sector. So, cryptocurrencies have appeared relatively recently and have already become known not only for sharp changes in their value, but also for high electricity costs during their mining (Denisova et al., 2019; Mikhaylov et al., 2021; Mikhaylov, 2020a, b, c; Tamashiro et al., 2021).

This is how the algorithm of human development is formed, where almost always each new stage is more progressive than the previous one, since each new generation of people as a whole has higher knowledge than the previous one. It should also be remembered that each new generation consumes more and more energy, and the quality of energy is only improving, and this fact acts as an indicator of global sustainable development (Denisova et al., 2019; Nyangarika et al., 2019a; b; Huang et al., 2021a, b; Mikhaylov, 2018a, b, 2022a, b; Mikhaylov et al., 2019; Conteh et al., 2021; Sediqi et al., 2022; Khan et al., 2021; Bhuiyan et al., 2022a; Liu et al., 2021a, b; Daniali et al., 2021).

11.2.3 Investing in Energy

To invest in solar energy, many factors must be taken into account. For example, the interdependence between energy consumption and economic growth. This is important because economic growth, in turn, affects all industries, including solar energy. In the modern world, energy is aimed at obtaining energy in the safest way, that is, so that everything is systematized, and the work goes smoothly (Kostis et al., 2022; Serezli et al., 2021; Fang et al., 2021). Industries with the highest job security and, accordingly, the stability of systems are most likely to achieve uniform income growth. In such industries, there is a systematic growth in the shares of the largest companies, so it is important that projects that increase the safety and, accordingly, the stability of the industry are regularly implemented in the solar energy sector. For example, machine learning can be one of the tools for improving security (An et al., 2020a, b, c; Nie et al., 2020). Machine learning can also be widely used in investment forecasting issues (An et al., 2019a, b; Mikhaylov, 2018c; Mikhaylov et al., 2019).

Another important factor affecting the stability of the company is the professional management of the revenues of the power plant network in conditions of limited information. It is hardly possible to find an industry in which information would not be limited, so the conditions of limited information can be called a normal phenomenon in the energy sector (An et al., 2021; Maslov, 2021; Shkodinsky et al., 2021; Pishchik & Alekseev, 2021; Lukashov, 2021; Kudelich, 2021; Sinenko & Mitrofanov, 2021; Artemiev, 2021).

Energy has always been an industry where the most modern technologies were used. The emergence of new methods of generating electricity, increasing the efficiency of old methods of generating electricity, the development of new models of approaches and projects all this affects the investment attractiveness of a particular area of the energy (An et al., 2019a, b, 2020a, b, c; Mikhaylov, 2020a, b, c, 2021a; Mikhaylov & Tarakanov, 2020; Moiseev et al., 2020, 2021; Grilli et al., 2021; Gura et al., 2020; Dooyum et al., 2020; Mikhaylov et al., 2022; Varyash et al., 2020; Zhao et al., 2021a, b; An & Mikhaylov, 2020; Alwaelya et al., 2021; Yumashev & Mikhaylov, 2020; Yumashev et al., 2020; Mutalimov et al., 2021; Morkovkin et al., 2020a, b; An & Mikhaylov, 2021).

There are many different investment strategies in each industry, but it is important to choose the optimal one from this variety. The selection of the optimal investment strategy is a complex process that requires a long-term analysis of efficiency; in this regard, it is not surprising that there are many disputes about the optimal investment strategy. No matter how effective this or that investment strategy is, there will always be an investor who will use another strategy and consider it optimal (Mikhaylov et al., 2018; Nyangarika et al., 2018; Danish et al., 2020, 2021; An et al., 2021; Uyeh et al., 2021; Shaikh et al., 2021).

11.2.4 Competitors in the Field of Alternative Energy

In addition to solar energy, there are several other types of alternative energy. Some of them, such as hydropower and geothermal energy, require the presence of rivers, seas, and geysers for their use. Wind power is the most significant competitor to solar, as it requires similar conditions for the most efficient operation, that is, a flat surface, no barriers to wind or sun, as well as a warm climate.

There are also areas of land where solar energy is completely or almost completely suppressed by another type of alternative energy. Thus, geothermal energy in countries with high volcanic activity is a key alternative energy, since this type of energy is much more efficient than solar (Mikhaylov, 2020a, b, c; Ivanova & Fedosov, 2021; Milchakov, 2021; Bukharsky, 2021; Bakulina & Kuzmina, 2021; Timofeeva, 2021; Likhacheva, 2021; Tarasova & Fevraleva, 2021; Vasilyeva, 2021; Levina, 2021; Belousov & Timofeeva, 2021).

11.2.5 Competition with Traditional Energy

It is important not to forget that in addition to competitors in alternative energy, solar energy also has competitors in traditional energy. Moreover, for many developing countries, traditional energy brings a significant share of income, therefore, taking into account the high cost of generating electricity by alternative means, we can say that solar energy on a global scale cannot compete with traditional energy, and this fact must be taken into account when forecasting the prospects for the development of solar energy. (Mikhaylov, 2018a, b, c, 2019). It is also worth noting that the number of projects in the traditional energy sector is not decreasing. The assessment and prospects for the development of traditional energy are often even more relevant and large-scale than projects in alternative energy. This also confirms that solar energy constantly has to compete with traditional energy, and the latter is in the most favorable position (Bhuiyan et al., 2021; Dong et al., 2021, Mikhaylov, 2021b, c; Baboshkin et al., 2022; Barykin et al., 2022; Baig et al., 2022a, b; Liu et al., 2022a, b; Bhuiyan et al., 2022b; Danish et al., 2022; Saqib et al., 2021; Yüksel et al., 2021a, b, c; Mukhametov et al., 2021; Candila et al., 2021; Mikhaylov & Grilli, 2022).

A major advantage of solar energy over any type of traditional energy is the preservation of the environment. In general, the global environmental agenda has a positive impact on the development of all types of alternative energy, and the more environmental research is carried out, the more significant the transition to alternative energy sources becomes on a global scale (Mikhaylov, 2020a, b, c; Sannikova, 2021; Zhihua & Yu, 2021; Rezvanov, 2021; Mingaleva & Starkov, 2021; Bushukina, 2021; Arlashkin, 2021; Matveeva, 2021; Vinogradova, 2021; Lukyanova, 2021; Mrachek & Valyushitskaya, 2021).

11.2.6 Global Energy Issues

It is worth noting that energy issues are global in nature, so it is important to cooperate in this industry so that the share of traditional energy decreases on a global scale, and not only in individual, most developed countries. For example, developed countries can use their solar energy projects in underdeveloped countries.

This approach is effective in order to reduce greenhouse gas emissions and resolve global environmental issues, because most underdeveloped countries are located in zones south of the subtropical, which makes solar energy in these countries efficient, and the low level of technological development of these countries does not allow developing such projects independently (An & Mikhaylov, 2020).

There is also cooperation between advanced countries in the energy field and developing countries. This type of cooperation allows us to maintain energy security (Dooyum et al., 2020).

11.3 Materials and Methods

Since the shares in question belong to risky assets due to the specifics of the industry, it can be argued that their profitability is distributed in conditions of stochastic and abrupt price changes. The prices of these assets exhibit strong asymmetry relative to normal values. To describe the dynamics of the price of the shares in question, the following stochastic differential equation will be used:

$$\frac{\mathrm{d}P_t}{P_t} = (\mu_t - \lambda S)\mathrm{d}t + \sigma_t \mathrm{d}z_t + (\mathrm{e}^g - 1)\mathrm{d}V(\lambda) \tag{11.1}$$

where z_t—standard Brownian motion, σ_t—instantaneous mean square deviation of the asset price, μ_t—trend. In this formula $S = E(\mathrm{e}^g - 1)$, where E is the mathematical expectation operator. S shows the average contribution of jumps to the asset price per 1 jump, and u—this is a normally distributed quantity with N (μg, σ_g^2). d$V(\lambda)$ defines a random Poisson process with the intensity of jumps λ, at the same time, the probability of one jump in a small period of time dt corresponds to $\Pr(\mathrm{d}V = 1) = \lambda \mathrm{d}t$. The Poisson probability allows us to determine on the investment horizon the probability of n jumps. Taking into account what has already been said, the Poisson probability can be displayed by the formula:

$$\Pr_n(\tau) = \mathrm{e}^{-\lambda\tau}\frac{(\lambda\tau)^n}{n!} \tag{11.2}$$

A sharp change in stock prices is the cause of yield deviations from the norm. Since the trend is μ, so is the volatility σ—const, the mathematical expectation of profitability can be expressed by the formula:

$$\ln\frac{P(t+\tau)}{P(t)} \tag{11.3}$$

(It is quite logical that the logarithm of the relative strength of an asset is the profitability of a financial title over a period of time τ, nachislya eating continuously.). Thus, the mathematical expectation of profitability is:

$$\tau - \frac{\sigma^2 \tau}{2} - \lambda (S - \mu_g) \tau \tag{11.4}$$

when the length of the time horizon is τ. There is no difficulty in obtaining the inverse Kolgorov equation (11.2) for the characteristic function of profitability (Eq. 11.2), which determines the variance and the highest moments of profitability, if we use Ito's lemma from Eq. (11.1)

$$K_2 = \left[\sigma^2 + \lambda\left(\mu_g^2 + \sigma_g^2\right)\right]\tau; \quad K_3 = \lambda\mu_g\left[\mu_g^2 + 3\sigma_g^2\right)]\tau; \quad K_4 = \lambda\left(\mu_g^4 + 6\mu_g^2\sigma_g^2 + 3\sigma_g^4\right)]\tau \tag{11.5}$$

where $m_1 = K_2$; $m_3 = K_3$; $m_4 = K_4 + 3m_2^2$—the relation of the cumulant to the central moments of m_j. The asymmetry is the normalized third cumulant, and the excess is the fourth, respectively

$$\Upsilon_1 = \frac{\lambda\mu_g\left(\mu_g^2 + 3\sigma_g^2\right)}{\left[\sigma^2 + \lambda\left(\mu_g^2 + \sigma_g^2\right)\right]^{3/2}\sqrt{\tau}}; \quad \Upsilon_2 = \frac{\lambda\left(\mu_g^4 + 6\mu_g^2\sigma_g^2 + 3\sigma_g^4\right)}{\left[\sigma^2 + \lambda\left(\mu_g^2 + \sigma_g^2\right)\right]^2\tau}$$

Bond price dynamics:

$$\mathrm{d}B_t = B_t[(r_t + \lambda_1\sigma_{\mathrm{B}}(r_t, t))\mathrm{d}t + \sigma_{\mathrm{B}}(r_t, t)\mathrm{d}z_{1t} \tag{11.6}$$

$$\lambda_1 = \sigma_{\mathrm{B}}^1(\mu - r_t) \tag{11.7}$$

where $\lambda_1 = \sigma_{\mathrm{B}}^1(\mu - r_t)$—the market price of the risk induced by an exogenous perturbing process, z_1, μ—expected rate of return, σ_{B}—price volatility. For stocks, taking into account the absence of dividend payments (in this case, it means that all the company's profits go exclusively to its development), the price dynamics corresponds to the following stochastic equation:

$$\mathrm{d}S_t = S_t\left[(r_t + \Psi\sigma_S)\mathrm{d}t + p_{BS}\sigma_S\mathrm{d}z_{1t} + \sqrt{1 - p_{BS}^2}\sigma_S\mathrm{d}z_{2t}\right. \tag{11.8}$$

where p_{BS}—correlation between bond and stock market yields, Ψ—the Sharpe number for a stock, which is a constant, and z_2—wiener random process. And in general, the price dynamics can be displayed in the form of the following equation:

$$\begin{pmatrix} dB_t \\ dS_t \end{pmatrix} = \begin{pmatrix} B_t & 0 \\ 0 & S_t \end{pmatrix} \left[\left(r_t \begin{pmatrix} 1 \\ 1 \end{pmatrix} + \begin{pmatrix} \sigma_B(r_t, t) & 0 \\ p_{BS}\sigma_S & \sigma_S\sqrt{1-p_{BS}^2} \end{pmatrix} \begin{pmatrix} \lambda_1 \\ \lambda_2 \end{pmatrix} \right) dt + \begin{pmatrix} \sigma_B(r_t, t) & 0 \\ p_{BS}\sigma_S & \sigma_S\sqrt{1-p_{BS}^2} \end{pmatrix} \begin{pmatrix} dz_{1t} \\ dz_{2t} \end{pmatrix} \right] \tag{11.9}$$

where

$$\lambda_2 = (\Psi - p_{BS}\lambda_1)/\sqrt{1-p_{BS}^2} \tag{11.10}$$

11.4 Results

This section will show the results of calculations for each company, as well as a table and a graph of the predicted values of the company's stock prices over the next 365 days. The paper considered two global companies producing solar panels—First Solar Inc. and Canadian Solar Inc. Calculations for Canadian Solar Inc. will be presented first.

Now let's go directly to the consideration of the projected values of the stock price for the coming year, obtained after all calculations.

11.5 Conclusions

It is also worth noting that the lows and highs at First Solar Inc. are much closer to the closing prices than at Canadian Solar Inc., since the latter company has a higher risk. As mentioned earlier, the area formed by the minimum and maximum becomes smaller as the certainty in the behavior of prices of the future period increases. This issue was discussed within the framework of the trend stage and tipping points, but the same is true for stocks with more or less risk, in general. Thus, Canadian Solar, due to reports on the company's activities during the crisis period, seems to be a more unstable company compared to its direct competitor, although before the crisis it was the opposite. Moreover, this is the reason for the longer sideways movement of prices in the forecast for the coming year. If First Solar reports are generally positive compared to the previous pre-crisis period, then Canadian Solar has a number of negative data in some cases prevails over positive ones, however, do not forget that both companies are large businesses with a large number of reserves that allow them to support the company for a long time during the crisis, which is why Canadian Solar stock prices did not fall even lower during the current crisis.

References

Adalı, Z., Dinçer, H., Eti, S., Mikhaylov, A., & Yüksel, S. (2022). Identifying new perspectives on geothermal energy investments. In H. Dinçer & S. Yüksel (Eds.), *Multidimensional strategic outlook on global competitive energy economics and finance* (pp. 1–11). Emerald Publishing Limited. https://doi.org/10.1108/978-1-80117-898-320221002

Alwaelya, S. A., Yousif, N. B. A., & Mikhaylov, A. (2021). Emotional development in preschoolers and socialization. *Early Child Development and Care, 191*, 16.

An, J., & Mikhaylov, A. (2020). Russian energy projects in South Africa. *Journal of Energy in Southern Africa, 31*(3), 58–64.

An, J., & Mikhaylov, A. (2021). Analysis of energy projects financial efficiency and renewable energy generation in Russia. *Finance: Theory and Practice, 25*(5), 79–91.

An, J., Mikhaylov, A., & Moiseev, N. (2019a). Oil price predictors: Machine learning approach. *International Journal of Energy Economics and Policy, 9*(5), 1–6.

An, J., Mikhaylov, A., & Sokolinskaya, N. (2019b). Machine learning in economic planning: Ensembles of algorithms. *Journal of Physics: Conference Series, 1353*, 012126.

An, J., Mikhaylov, A., & Jung, S.-U. (2020a). The strategy of South Korea in the global oil market. *Energies, 13*(10), 2491.

An, J., Mikhaylov, A., & Kim, K. (2020b). Machine learning approach in heterogeneous group of algorithms for transport safety-critical system. *Applied Sciences, 10*(8), 2670.

An, J., Mikhaylov, A., & Richter, U. H. (2020c). Trade war effects: Evidence from sectors of energy and resources in Africa. *Heliyon, 6*, e05693. https://doi.org/10.1016/j.heliyon.2020.e05693

An, J., Mikhaylov, A., & Jung, S.-U. (2021). A linear programming approach for Robust network revenue management in the airline industry. *Journal of Air Transport Management, 91*, 101979.

Arlashkin, I. (2021). Clustering of Russian regions by level of debt sustainability. *Financial Journal, 13*(5), 108–124.

Artemiev, A. (2021). The flow of dividends to the seller: Customs valuation methodology. *Financial Journal, 13*(3), 104–115.

Baboshkin, P., Mikhaylov, A., & Shaikh, Z. A. (2022). Sustainable cryptocurrency growth is not possible? Impact of network power demand on bitcoin price. *Financial Journal, 14*(2), 39–55.

Baig, U., Hussain, B. M., Khan, A. A., Shaikh, Z. A., Mikhaylov, A., Chao, C.-C., & Barykin, S. E. (2022a). Research on investors of the reginal stock exchange: An influence of behavioral finance on investment decision making. *Risks, 10*(4), 116.

Baig, U., Khan, A. A., Abbas, M. G., Shaikh, Z. A., Mikhaylov, A., Laghari, A. A., & Hussain, B. M. (2022b). Crucial causes of delay in completion and performance management of the construction work: Study on the base of relative importance index. *Journal of Tianjin University Science and Technology, 55*(6), 75–102.

Bakulina, P., & Kuzmina, K. (2021). China's policy of economic sanctions: Legislation and enforcement. *Financial Journal, 13*(4), 24–38.

Barykin, S., Mikheev, A., Kiseleva, E., Putikhin, Y., Alekseeva, N., & Mikhaylov, A. (2022). An empirical analysis of Russian regions' debt sustainability. *Economies, 10*(4), 296.

Belousov, Y., & Timofeeva, O. (2021). Methodological aspects of compiling open budget rankings. *Financial Journal, 13*(4), 122–138.

Bhuiyan, M. A., An, J., Mikhaylov, A., Moiseev, N., & Danish, M. S. S. (2021). Renewable energy deployment and COVID-19 measures for sustainable development. *Sustainability, 13*, 4418.

Bhuiyan, M. A., Dinçer, H., Yüksel, S., Mikhaylov, A., Danish, M. S. S., Pinter, G., Uyeh, D. D., & Stepanova, D. (2022a). Economic indicators and bioenergy supply in developed economies: QROF-DEMATEL and random forest models. *Energy Reports, 8*, 561–570.

Bhuiyan, M. A., Khare, V., Mikhaylov, A., & Zhang, P. G. (2022b) Does renewable energy consumption affect economic growth? A systematic literature review. *Frontiers in Environmental Science.*

Bukharsky, V. (2021). Fiscal decentralization and incentives of local authorities in the Russian Federation. *Financial Journal, 13*(2), 114–129.

Bushukina, V. (2021). Specific features of renewable energy development in the world and Russia. *Financial Journal, 13*(5), 93–107.
Candila, V., Maximov, D., Mikhaylov, A., Moiseev, N., Senjyu, T., & Tryndina, N. (2021). On the relationship between oil and exchange rates of oil-exporting and oil-importing countries: From the great recession period to the Covid-19 era. *Energies, 14*, 8065.
Conteh, F., Takahashi, H., Hemeida, A. M., Krishnan, N., Mikhaylov, A., & Senjyu, T. (2021). Hybrid grid-connected renewable power generation for sustainable electricity supply in Sierra Leone: Case study lungi town. *Sustainability, 13*(18), 1–20.
Daniali, S. M., Barykin, S. E., Kapustina, I. V., Khortabi, F. M., Sergeev, S. M., Kalinina, O. V., Mikhaylov, A., Veynberg, R., Zasova, L., & Senjyu, T. (2021). Predicting volatility index according to technical index and economic indicators on the basis of deep learning algorithm. *Sustainability, 2021*(13), 14011.
Danish, M. S. S., Bhattacharya, A., Stepanova, D., Mikhaylov, A., Grilli, M. L., Khosravy, M., & Senjyu, T. (2020). A systematic review of metal oxide applications for energy and environmental sustainability. *Metals, 10*(12), 1604.
Danish, M. S. S., Senjyu, T., Sabory, N. R., Khosravy, M., Grilli, M. L., Mikhaylov, A., & Majidi, H. (2021). A forefront framework for sustainable aquaponics modeling and design. *Sustainability, 13*, 9313.
Danish, M. S. S., Estrella-Pajulas, L. L., Alemaida, I. M. A., Grilli, M. L., Mikhaylov, A., & Senjyu, T. (2022). Green synthesis of silver oxide nanoparticles for photocatalytic environmental remediation and biomedical applications. *Metals, 12*(4), 769.
Dayong, N., Mikhaylov, A., Bratanovsky, S., Shaikh, Z. A., & Stepanova, D. (2020). Mathematical modeling of the technological processes of catering products production. *Journal of Food Process Engineering, 43*(2), 1–9.
Denisova, V., Mikhaylov, A., & Lopatin, E. (2019). Blockchain infrastructure and growth of global power consumption. *International Journal of Energy Economics and Policy, 9*(4), 22–29.
Dinçer, H., Yüksel, S., & Martínez, L. (2022). Collaboration enhanced hybrid fuzzy decision-making approach to analyze the renewable energy investment projects. *Energy Reports, 8*, 377–389.
Ding, Z., Yüksel, S., & Dincer, H. (2021). An Integrated Pythagorean fuzzy soft computing approach to environmental management systems for sustainable energy pricing. *Energy Reports, 7*, 5575–5588.
Dong, B., Ikonnikova, I., Rogulin, R., Sakulyeva, T., & Mikhaylov, A. (2021). Environmental economic approach to optimization of transport communication in megacities. *Journal of Environmental Science and Health, Part A, 56*(6), 660–666.
Dong, W., Zhao, G., Yüksel, S., Dinçer, H., & Ubay, G. G. (2022). A novel hybrid decision making approach for the strategic selection of wind energy projects. *Renewable Energy, 185*, 321–337.
Dooyum, U. D., Mikhaylov, A., & Varyash, I. (2020). Energy security concept in Russia and South Korea. *International Journal of Energy Economics and Policy, 10*(4), 102–107.
Fang, S., Zhou, P., Dinçer, H., & Yüksel, S. (2021). Assessment of safety management system on energy investment risk using house of quality based on hybrid stochastic interval-valued intuitionistic fuzzy decision-making approach. *Safety Science, 141*, 105333.
Grilli, M. L., Valerini, D., Rizzo, A., Yilmaz, M., Song, C., Hu, G., Chierchia, R., Mikhaylov, A., & Rinaldi, A. (2021). A comparative study of the mechanical and tribological properties of thin Al2O3 coatings fabricated by atomic layer deposition and radiofrequency sputtering. *Physica Status Solidi (A), 218*(24), 1–25.
Gura, D., Mikhaylov, A., Glushkov, S., Zaikov, M., & Shaikh, Z. A. (2020). Model for estimating power dissipation along the interconnect length in single on-chip topology. *Evolutionary Intelligence*.
Haiyun, C., Zhixiong, H., Yüksel, S., & Dinçer, H. (2021). Analysis of the innovation strategies for green supply chain management in the energy industry using the QFD-based hybrid interval valued intuitionistic fuzzy decision approach. *Renewable and Sustainable Energy Reviews, 143*, 110844.

Huang, Y., Masrur, H., Shigenobu, R., Hemeida, A. M., Mikhaylov, A., & Senjyu, T. (2021a). A comparative design of a campus microgrid considering a multi-scenario and multi-objective approach. *Energies, 14*, 2853.

Huang, Y., Yona, A., Takahashi, H., Hemeida, A. M., Mandal, P., Mikhaylov, A., Senjyu, T., & Lotfy, M. E. (2021b). Energy management system optimization of drug store operate electric vehicles charging station. *Sustainability, 14*, 1217836.

Ivanova, N., & Fedosov, V. (2021). Goal setting of youth practices of participatory budgeting. *Financial Journal, 13*(2), 83–92.

Khan, A. A., Shaikh, Z. A., Baitenova, L., Mutaliyeva, L., Moiseev, N., Mikhaylov, A., Laghari, A. A., Idris, S. A., & Alshazly, H. (2021). QoS-ledger: Smart contracts and metaheuristic for secure quality-of-service and cost-efficient scheduling of medical-data processing. *Electronics, 10*, 3083.

Kostis, P., Dinçer, H., & Yüksel, S. (2022). Knowledge-based energy investments of European economies and policy recommendations for sustainable development. *Journal of the Knowledge Economy*, 1–33.

Kou, G., Yüksel, S., & Dinçer, H. (2022). Inventive problem-solving map of innovative carbon emission strategies for solar energy-based transportation investment projects. *Applied Energy, 311*, 118680.

Kranina, E. I. (2021). China on the way to achieving carbon neutrality. *Financial Journal, 13*(5), 51–61. https://doi.org/10.31107/2075-1990-2021-5-51-61

Kudelich, M. (2021). Problems of innovative science and technology center financing from budgetary funds. *Financial Journal, 13*(3), 76–87.

Levina, V. (2021). Problems of regional participatory budgeting practices. *Financial Journal, 13*(4), 110–121.

Li, J., Yüksel, S., Dınçer, H., Mikhaylov, A., & Barykin, S. E. (2022). Bipolar q-ROF hybrid decision making model with golden cut for analyzing the levelized cost of renewable energy alternatives. *IEEE Access, 10*, 42507–42517.

Likhacheva, A. (2021). On the strategic effects of unilateral sanctions: Russian experience. *Financial Journal, 13*(4), 52–66.

Liu, L., Kato, T., Mandal, P., Mikhaylov, A., Hemeida, A. M., & Senjyu, T. (2021a). Multi-area power system load frequency control by using model predictive control by introducing renewable energy sources. In *2021 International Conference on Science & Contemporary Technologies (ICSCT)* (pp. 1–6). https://doi.org/10.1109/ICSCT53883.2021.9642521.

Liu, L., Kato, T., Mandal, P., Mikhaylov, A., Hemeida, A. M., Takahashi, H., & Tomonobu, S. (2021b). Two cases studies of model predictive control approach for hybrid renewable energy systems. *AIMS Energy, 9*(6), 1241–1259.

Liu, J., Lv, J., Dinçer, H., Yüksel, S., & Karakuş, H. (2021c). Selection of renewable energy alternatives for green blockchain investments: A hybrid IT2-based fuzzy modelling. *Archives of Computational Methods in Engineering, 28*(5), 3687–3701.

Liu, Z.-J., Panfilova, E., Mikhaylov, A., & Kurilova, A. (2022a). Assessing stability in relationship between parties in crowdfunding and crowdsourcing projects during the COVID-19 crisis. *Journal of Global Information Management, 30*(2), 1.

Liu, Z.-J., Panfilova, E., Mikhaylov, A., & Kurilova, A. (2022b). COVID-19 crisis impact on the stability between parties in crowdfunding and crowdsourcing. *Wireless Personal Communications, 122*, 915–930.

Lukashov, A. (2021). Some directions of increasing the efficiency of public administration in the context of digitalization. *Financial Journal, 13*(3), 67–75.

Lukyanova, N. (2021). Saint Petersburg experience of participatory budgeting. *Financial Journal, 13*(2), 61–69.

Maslov, A. (2021). Development of new payment systems in Russia similar to a CLS analogue. *Financial Journal, 13*(3), 27–37.

Matveeva, N. (2021). Legislative regulation financial statement preparation by micro entities: International experience. *Financial Journal, 13*(5), 125–138.

Meng, Y., Wu, H., Zhao, W., Chen, W., Dinçer, H., & Yüksel, S. (2021). A hybrid heterogeneous Pythagorean fuzzy group decision modelling for crowdfunding development process pathways of fintech-based clean energy investment projects. *Financial Innovation, 7*(1), 1–34.

Mikhaylov, A. (2018a). Volatility spillover effect between stock and exchange rate in oil exporting countries. *International Journal of Energy Economics and Policy, 8*(3), 321–326.

Mikhaylov, A. (2018b). Pricing in oil market and using probit model for analysis of stock market effects. *International Journal of Energy Economics and Policy, 8*(2), 69–73.

Mikhaylov, A. (2018c). The yield of the carry trade strategy. *Finance: Theory and Practice, 22*(3), 52–63. https://doi.org/10.26794/2587-5671-2018-22-3-52-63

Mikhaylov, A. (2019). Oil and gas budget revenues in Russia after crisis in 2015. *International Journal of Energy Economics and Policy, 9*(2), 375–380.

Mikhaylov, A. (2020a). Cryptocurrency market analysis from the open innovation perspective. *Journal of Open Innovation: Technology, Market, and Complexity, 6*(4), 197.

Mikhaylov, A. (2020b). Geothermal energy development in Iceland. *International Journal of Energy Economics and Policy, 10*(4), 31–35.

Mikhaylov, A. (2020c). Cryptocurrency market development: Hurst method. *Finance: Theory and Practice, 24*(3), 81–91.

Mikhaylov, A. (2021a). Development of Friedrich von Hayek's theory of private money and economic implications for digital currencies. *Terra Economicus, 19*(1), 53–62.

Mikhaylov, A. (2021b). Lichens as indicators of atmospheric pollution in urban ecosystems. *Israel Journal of Ecology & Evolution, 67*(1–2), 60–68. https://doi.org/10.1163/22244662-bja10016

Mikhaylov, A. (2022a). Efficiency of renewable energy generation in Russia. *Annals of the Brazilian Academy of Sciences, 94*(3).

Mikhaylov, A. (2022b). Sustainable development and renewable energy: A new view to a global problem. *Energies, 15*, 1397. https://doi.org/10.3390/en15041397

Mikhaylov, A., & Grilli, M. L. (2022). Machine learning methods and sustainable development: Metal oxides and multilayer metal-oxides. *Metals, 12*(4), 836.

Mikhaylov, A., & Tarakanov, S. (2020). Development of Levenberg-Marquardt theoretical approach for electric network. *Journal of Physics: Conference Series, 1515*, 052006.

Mikhaylov, A., Sokolinskaya, N., & Nyangarika, A. (2018). Optimal carry trade strategy based on currencies of energy and developed economies. *Journal of Reviews on Global Economics, 7*, 582–592.

Mikhaylov, A., Burakov, D., & Didenko, V. (2019). Relationship between oil price and macroeconomic indicators in Russia. *Finance: Theory and Practice, 23*(2), 105–116. https://doi.org/10.26794/2587-5671-2019-23-2-105-116

Mikhaylov, A., Danish, M. S. S., & Senjyu, T. (2021). New stage in evolution of cryptocurrency market: Analysis by Hurst method. In H. Dincer & S. Yuksel (Eds.), *Strategic outlook in business and finance innovation: Multidimensional policies for emerging economies* (pp. 35–45). Emerald Publishing Limited. https://doi.org/10.1108/978-1-80043-444-820211004

Mikhaylov, A., Yumashev, A., & Kolpak, E. (2022). Quality of life, anxiety and depressive disorders in patients with extrasystolic arrhythmia. *Archives of Medical Science, 18*(2). https://doi.org/10.5114/aoms.2020.101359

Milchakov, M. (2021). Implementation of regional development priorities under the conditions of the COVID-19 pandemic. *Financial Journal, 13*(2), 93–113.

Mingaleva, Z., & Starkov, Y. (2021). The role of environmental innovation in green modernization of industrial enterprises. *Financial Journal, 13*(5), 79–92.

Moiseev, N., Mikhaylov, A., Varyash, I., & Saqib, A. (2020). Investigating the relation of GDP per capita and corruption index. *Entrepreneurship and Sustainability Issues, 8*(1), 780–794.

Moiseev, N., Sorokin, A., Zvezdina, N., Mikhaylov, A., Khomyakova, L., & Danish, M. S. S. (2021). Credit risk theoretical model on the base of DCC-GARCH in time-varying parameters framework. *Mathematics, 9*, 2423. https://doi.org/10.3390/math9192423

Morkovkin, D., Lopatkin, D., Sadriddinov, M., Shushunova, T., Gibadullin, A., & Golikova, O. (2020a). Assessment of innovation activity in the countries of the world. *E3S Web of Conferences, 157*, 04015. https://doi.org/10.1051/e3sconf/202015704015

Morkovkin, D. E., Gibadullin, A. A., Kolosova, E. V., Semkina, N. S., & Fasehzoda, I. S. (2020b). Modern transformation of the production base in the conditions of industry 4.0: Problems and prospects. *Journal of Physics: Conference Series, 1515*, 032014.

Mrachek, E., & Valyushitskaya, I. (2021). The role of project centers in the development of participatory budgeting: The practice of the Krasnoyarsk territory. *Financial Journal, 13*(2), 70–82.

Mukhametov, A., Bekhorashvili, A., Avdeenko, A., & Mikhaylov, A. (2021). The impact of growing legume plants under conditions of biologization and soil cultivation on Chernozem fertility and productivity of rotation crops. *Legume Research, 44*, 12.

Mukhtarov, S., Yüksel, S., & Dinçer, H. (2022). The impact of financial development on renewable energy consumption: Evidence from Turkey. *Renewable Energy, 187*, 169–176.

Mutalimov, V., Kovaleva, I., Mikhaylov, A., & Stepanova, D. (2021). Assessing regional growth of small business in Russia. *Entrepreneurial Business and Economics Review, 9*(3), 119–133. https://doi.org/10.15678/EBER.2021.090308

Nie, D., Panfilova, E., Samusenkov, V., & Mikhaylov, A. (2020). E-learning financing models in Russia for sustainable development. *Sustainability, 12*(11), 4412.

Nyangarika, A., Mikhaylov, A., & Tang, B.-J. (2018). Correlation of oil prices and gross domestic product in oil producing countries. *International Journal of Energy Economics and Policy, 8*(5), 42–48.

Nyangarika, A., Mikhaylov, A., & Richter, U. (2019a). Influence oil price towards economic indicators in Russia. *International Journal of Energy Economics and Policy, 9*(1), 123–129.

Nyangarika, A., Mikhaylov, A., & Richter, U. (2019b). Oil price factors: Forecasting on the base of modified auto-regressive integrated moving average model. *International Journal of Energy Economics and Policy, 9*(1), 149–159.

Pishchik, V., & Alekseev, P. (2021). Cybercrime as a key operational risk of the payment and settlement infrastructure of the global financial system and approaches to its regulation in the Eurasian Economic Union. *Financial Journal, 13*(3), 54–66.

Rezvanov, R. (2021). Implementation of international sustainable financing practices into the National Debt System. Can infrastructure loans become responsible? *Financial Journal, 13*(5), 62–78.

Sannikova, L. (2021). Legal framework for green finance in the EU and Russia. *Financial Journal, 13*(5), 29–43.

Saqib, A., Chan, T.-H., Mikhaylov, A., & Lean, H. H. (2021). Are the responses of sectoral energy imports asymmetric to exchange rate volatilities in Pakistan? Evidence from recent foreign exchange regime. *Frontiers in Energy Research, 9*, 614463. https://doi.org/10.3389/fenrg.2021.614463

Sediqi, M. M., Nakadomari, A., Mikhaylov, A., Krishnan, N., Lotfy, M. E., Yona, A., & Senjyu, T. (2022). Impact of time-of-use demand response program on optimal operation of Afghanistan real power system. *Energies, 15*, 296.

Serezli, E., Yüksel, S., Tamer, İ., & Dinçer, H. (2021). The role of innovative renewable energy investment strategies on macroeconomic stability. In *Financial strategies in competitive markets* (pp. 165–178). Springer.

Shaikh, Z. A., Moiseev, N., Mikhaylov, A., & Yüksel, S. (2021). Facile synthesis of copper oxide-cobalt oxide/nitrogen-doped carbon (Cu2O-Co3O4/CN) composite for efficient water splitting. *Applied Sciences, 11*, 9974. https://doi.org/10.3390/app11219974

Shkodinsky, S., Dudin, M., & Usmanov, D. (2021). Analysis and assessment of cyberthreats to the National Financial System of Russia in the digital economy. *Financial Journal, 13*(3), 38–53.

Sinenko, O., & Mitrofanov, T. (2021). Identification of signs of "business fragmentation" in Russian far eastern territories with special economic status. *Financial Journal, 13*(3), 88–103.

Tamashiro, K., Alharbi, T., Mikhaylov, A., Hemeida, A. M., Krishnan, N., Lotfy, M. E., & Senjyu, T. (2021). Investigation of home energy management with advanced direct load control and optimal scheduling of controllable loads. *Energies, 14*, 7314. https://doi.org/10.3390/en14217314

Tarasova, Y., & Fevraleva, E. (2021). Forecasting of bankruptcy: Evidence from insurance companies in Russia. *Financial Journal, 13*(4), 75–90.

Timofeeva, Y. (2021). US sanctions against financial companies: Key features. *Financial Journal, 13*(4), 39–51.

Uyeh, D. D., Asem-Hiablie, S., Park, T., Kim, K.-M., Mikhaylov, A., Woo, S., & Ha, Y. (2021). Could japonica rice be an alternative variety for increased global food security and climate change mitigation? *Food, 10*, 1869. https://doi.org/10.3390/foods10081869

Varyash, I., Mikhaylov, A., Moiseev, N., & Aleshin, K. (2020). Triple bottom line and corporate social responsibility performance indicators for Russian companies. *Entrepreneurship and Sustainability Issues, 8*(1), 313–331.

Vasilyeva, A. (2021). Approaches to modelling exposure at default for the entire life of the asset. *Financial Journal, 13*(4), 91–109.

Vinogradova, I. (2021). Participatory budgeting as a tool contributing to the achievement of the sustainable development goals. *Financial Journal, 13*(2), 46–60.

Xie, Y., Zhou, Y., Peng, Y., Dinçer, H., Yüksel, S., & an Xiang, P. (2021). An extended Pythagorean fuzzy approach to group decision-making with incomplete preferences for analyzing balanced scorecard-based renewable energy investments. *IEEE Access, 9*, 43020–43035.

Yakovlev, I. A., Kabir, L. S., & Nikulina, S. I. (2021). Changes in climate policies and financial strategies of their implementation in the EU and Russia. *Financial Journal, 13*(5), 11–28. https://doi.org/10.31107/2075-1990-2021-5-11-28

Yüksel, S., Mikhaylov, A., Ubay, G. G., & Uyeh, D. D. (2021a). The role of hydrogen in the Black Sea for the future energy supply security of Turkey. In *Handbook of research on strategic management for current energy investments* (pp. 1–15). IGI Global.

Yüksel, S., Mikhaylov, A., & Ubay, G. G. (2021b). Factors causing delay in the installation of nuclear power plants. In S. Yüksel & H. Dinçer (Eds.), *Strategic approaches to energy management. Contributions to management science*. Springer. https://doi.org/10.1007/978-3-030-76783-9_7

Yüksel, S., Mikhaylov, A., Ubay, G. G., & Uyeh, D. D. (2021c). The role of hydrogen in the black sea for the future energy supply security of Turkey. In S. Yüksel & H. Dinçer (Eds.), *Handbook of research on strategic management for current energy investments* (pp. 1–15). IGI Global. https://doi.org/10.4018/978-1-7998-8335-7.ch001

Yüksel, S., Dinçer, H., Çağlayan, Ç., Uluer, G. S., & Lisin, A. (2022a). Bitcoin mining with nuclear energy. In *Multidimensional strategic outlook on global competitive energy economics and finance*. Emerald Publishing Limited.

Yüksel, S., Dinçer, H., Mikhaylov, A., Adalı, Z., & Eti, S. (2022b). Key issues for the improvements of shallow geothermal investments. In H. Dinçer & S. Yüksel (Eds.), *Sustainability in energy business and finance. Contributions to finance and accounting*. Springer. https://doi.org/10.1007/978-3-030-94051-5_16

Yumashev, A., & Mikhaylov, A. (2020). Development of polymer film coatings with high adhesion to steel alloys and high wear resistance. *Polymer Composites, 41*(7), 2875–2880.

Yumashev, A., Ślusarczyk, B., Kondrashev, S., & Mikhaylov, A. (2020). Global indicators of sustainable development: Evaluation of the influence of the human development index on consumption and quality of energy. *Energies, 13*, 2768.

Zhao, Q., Cherkasov, S., Avdeenko, A., Kondratenko, L., & Mikhaylov, A. (2021a). Integral estimate of the added value of agricultural crops in the synergetic agriculture on the example of Vicia faba (Vicia faba L.). *Polish Journal of Environmental Studies, 30*(5), 1–9. https://doi.org/10.15244/pjoes/131949

Zhao, Y., Xu, Y., Yüksel, S., Dinçer, H., & Ubay, G. G. (2021b). Hybrid IT2 fuzzy modelling with alpha cuts for hydrogen energy investments. *International Journal of Hydrogen Energy, 46*(13), 8835–8851.

Zhe, L., Yüksel, S., Dinçer, H., Mukhtarov, S., & Azizov, M. (2021). The positive influences of renewable energy consumption on financial development and economic growth. *SAGE Open, 11*(3), 21582440211040133.

Zhihua, F., & Yu, C. (2021). Promoting green development in China's new development stage through tax reform. *Financial Journal, 13*(5), 44–50.

Zhou, P., Luo, J., Cheng, F., Yüksel, S., & Dinçer, H. (2021). Analysis of risk priorities for renewable energy investment projects using a hybrid IT2 hesitant fuzzy decision-making approach with alpha cuts. *Energy, 224*, 120184.

Chapter 12
Multifractal and Cross-correlation Analysis of Cryptocurrencies for Direct Green Investments

Ivan Udalov, Almakul Abdimomynova, and Svetlana Moldagulova

Abstract The article contains a comprehensive study of cryptocurrencies and digital currencies (crypto-yuan, bitcoin, ethereum, TRON, and Tether). Using the MF-X-DMA and DMCA methods, a statistical study of the 5-year dynamics of the closing prices in US dollars of the Chinese yuan and the above cryptocurrencies was carried out, which is part of the multifractal and cross-correlation analysis. The result of the study was to identify the relationship between the price dynamics of the Chinese yuan, ethereum, and TRON. The further analytical study and comparison of the characteristics of the objects, the study allowed us to conclude that the wider distribution of the digital version of the Chinese yuan in the international space may hypothetically affect the rate of TRON, Ethereum, and some other similar cryptocurrencies, the structure of which is based on their platforms. In addition, the results of the study suggest that the spread of the crypto-yuan will affect the platforms for international transfers in yuan, as well as affect the volume of settlements in the Chinese currency. The evolution of economic systems at the beginning of the twenty-first century led to the emergence of a new type of financial assets, which can be designated as digital "currency." Since the appearance of the first cryptocurrency, called Bitcoin, a lot of scientific research has been carried out concerning the nature of this phenomenon in the economy, its dynamics in financial markets, as well as the impact on economic systems in general. Most of the cryptocurrencies are based on the principle of decentralized emission, and their proliferation forced central banks to develop a set of measures to regulate the market for these assets. Several governments have adopted more stringent measures, limiting or prohibiting their circulation and use. As the study of cryptocurrencies, as well as their distribution, the positions of financial regulators changed. Few central banks have softened the conditions for the circulation of cryptocurrencies to achieve their own goals in monetary policy, while others have announced their intention to create

I. Udalov (✉)
Financial University Under the Government of the Russian Federation, Moscow, Russia

A. Abdimomynova · S. Moldagulova
Korkyt Ata Kyzylorda University, Kyzylorda, Kazakhstan

H. Dinçer, S. Yüksel (eds.), *Circular Economy and the Energy Market*,
Contributions to Economics, https://doi.org/10.1007/978-3-031-13146-2_12

their own counterparts. List of initiators includes the People's Bank of China and the Bank of England.

Keywords Cryptocurrencies · People's Bank of China · CBDC · Bitcoin · Ethereum · TRON · Yuan · DCEP

12.1 Introduction

The People's Republic of China pioneered the development of a national digital currency, experimenting with a digital version of the yuan in several provinces to collect party dues, travel payments, and other.

Prospects for the introduction of the digital currency of the Central Bank of China not only cover the domestic financial system of the country, but also, according to some researchers, include the construction of infrastructure for international payments and transfers, which in the future provides an opportunity for competition between China and other countries in the field of digital versions of national currencies, as well as US dollars and cryptocurrencies in the field of international exchange.

Interest in cryptocurrencies in the academic environment is stable and comprehensive due to the peculiarities of the structure of their emission systems, functionality for users, and so on. At the same time, there are significant gaps in theoretical research regarding cryptocurrencies and similar "digital currency units" (new articles in the review file). At the same time, the DCEP academic research considered in the preparation of this article focuses directly on the perspective of its development, characteristics, or certain common features with some cryptocurrencies. Interest in digital renminbi can be justified by its belonging to one of the most influential financial systems in the world. While digital currencies of small states, such as Cambodia or the Bahamas, serve to ensure the stability of national economies, the crypto-yuan claims to be an instrument in international financial transactions on a par with the US dollar and cryptocurrencies. This precedent is unique in international practice and requires separate consideration. An analytical review of the financial system of the PRC, in particular the money turnover within the country and abroad, expressed in yuan, will make it possible to make predictions about the prospects for further internationalization of the crypto-yuan and its impact on international money transfer systems.

The article will compile the characteristics of the digital currency of the People's Bank of China, the most common cryptocurrencies in international practice (bitcoin, ethereum, TRON), as well as the Tether cryptocurrency token (within the framework of the article, taken as a digital version of the US dollar). The data obtained will allow a comparison between the selected research objects, namely, to draw complex conclusions regarding their advantages and disadvantages relative to each other. This can serve to fill the gap in the comprehensive aggregate valuation of cryptocurrencies and the digital yuan. In the future, the results obtained can be useful for assessing the investment attractiveness of assets, as well as for conducting additional research on related issues.

Comparative statistical analysis of the dynamics of the closing prices of the Chinese yuan and the above cryptocurrencies will be carried out in parallel with the analytical study. This section of the study will be compiled using cross-correlation and multifractal analysis methods (MF-X-DMA method). The results of the calculations will complement the conclusions in terms of predicting the possible mutual influence of research objects in economic systems and their competitiveness. In addition, the results of the study will make it possible to define the place of the digital yuan more clearly in the international and intra-Chinese economic system, in particular, in the systems of financial transfers and transactions, than will contribute to the existing theoretical research base on the issue of mutual existence of cryptocurrencies and digital monetary units of central banks.

12.2 Literature Review

In 2016, in the United States, opinions were expressed that the emission of a "state cryptocurrency" can reduce the costs of maintaining the M0 money supply and create competition for existing cryptocurrencies. The prerequisites for this, according to Swedish experts, may be a high level of development of electronic payment systems and a drop in demand for cash.

One of the tasks of central banks is to maintain the stability of the financial system of the state by managing the key rate, issuing government securities and other instruments. Under certain conditions, the issuance of digital money can supplement the central bank's toolkit as a stimulator of GDP growth and a means of leveling the consequences of some economic difficulties.

The regulation of the turnover of digital monetary units, like the turnover of cash, is carried out according to generally accepted concepts. Monetarist theory holds that any government involvement in monetary policy should be minimized, since the market is economically self-sufficient. New Keynesians advocate the opposite position: central banks should be actively involved in maintaining the stability of the monetary system. The use of central bank digital currencies can facilitate the use of regulatory instruments, including wealth redistribution, inflation regulation, and price stability. Due to the limited volume of digital currency units in the economy, the regulator can more accurately plan its own monetary policy (Denisova et al., 2019; Nyangarika et al., 2019a, b; Huang et al., 2021a, b; Mikhaylov, 2018a, b, 2022a, b; Mikhaylov et al., 2019; Conteh et al., 2021; Sediqi et al., 2022; Khan et al., 2021; Bhuiyan et al., 2022a; Liu et al., 2021a, b; Daniali et al., 2021).

The blockchain platform, which is the functional basis of cryptocurrencies, in the future can be used to build emission systems for digital currencies, since it provides opportunities for storing information in branched databases protected from hacking, as well as developed mechanisms for implementing transactions and other factors (Yüksel et al., 2022; Adalı et al., 2022).

The introduction of the digital currency of central banks includes the issues of organizing reporting on bank accounts opened with the central bank and other transactions. A decentralized database with a single administrator (CB), with whose approval it is possible to make changes to one or another information block, etc., will simplify and make more transparent information about loans from commercial banks. According to another approach, the central bank will not be the only institution with access to data on transactions and editing data about them. Other government agencies or other users can act as validators of transactions, in which case the database of transactions will continue to function even in the hypothetical absence of the central bank, which has appointed other administrators. The approaches described above are applicable in the context of decentralized systems. However, in China, the system for issuing and managing the circulation of the digital yuan is based on centralized regulation, which, on the one hand, reduces the transparency of transactions made using CBDC and increases the system's vulnerability to technical failures and other problems related to the status of the central bank as a validator of transactions. To some extent, it increases the reliability of the system and reduces the risk of information leaks (An et al., 2019a, b, 2020a, b, c; Mikhaylov, 2021a, 2022a, b; Mikhaylov & Tarakanov, 2020; Moiseev et al., 2020, 2021; Grilli et al., 2021; Gura et al., 2020; Dooyum et al., 2020; Mikhaylov et al., 2022; Varyash et al., 2020; Zhao et al., 2021; An & Mikhaylov, 2020, 2021; Alwaelya et al., 2021; Yumashev & Mikhaylov, 2020; Yumashev et al., 2020; Mutalimov et al., 2021; Morkovkin et al., 2020a, b).

In decentralized platforms, it is almost impossible to track the path of a unit of cryptocurrency from one wallet to another, while the presence of a central authority allows you to track the path of a transaction and collect data about users. World Central Banks should work together to develop measures to effectively regulate the circulation of digital currency, including with respect to international transfers. The specificity of the legislation of individual countries, as well as the gap in the level of technological development, can create difficulties for carrying out financial transactions with CBDC. At the same time, the implementation of consistent actions towards the establishment of uniform measures to regulate the circulation of digital currency units can reduce the risks associated with criminogenic situations. Transferring money turnover to the digital sphere will reduce the scale of illegal financial transactions carried out by means of cash, the turnover of which is almost impossible to track, but will increase the risks of information leaks and hacks (Maslov, 2021; Shkodinsky et al., 2021; Pishchik & Alekseev, 2021; Lukashov, 2021; Kudelich, 2021; Sinenko & Mitrofanov, 2021; Artemiev, 2021).

The emergence of digital currencies and the opening of personal accounts of citizens in the central bank can provoke a sharp reformatting of the banking sector. The central bank will be able to accept deposits from the population. For commercial banks, the advancement of the central bank into the savings sector can turn into a crisis and a sharp reduction in the supply of various financial services or their replacement (for example, deposits can hypothetically be replaced by bonds or other securities). Moreover, the digital currency of the central bank can be used to replace government securities. The introduction of the digital currency of the central bank may hypothetically require additional investments in commercial banking since banks will need to install special equipment and software required to carry out transactions (Dayong et al., 2020; Mikhaylov et al., 2018; Nyangarika et al., 2018; Danish et al., 2020, 2021; An et al., 2021; Uyeh et al., 2021; Tamashiro et al., 2021; Shaikh et al., 2021; Yakovlev et al., 2021; Kranina, 2021).

A relevant issue for CBDC is the relationship between the factors of anonymity of transactions and compliance with the principles of legality. Of course, the regulator cannot guarantee complete confidentiality when making transactions, since in this case it will lose the instrument of control over criminal operations and influence on them. However, the correlation of the concepts of anonymity and legality (together with the principle of transparency) is a key factor in determining the investment attractiveness of a digital currency, especially in relation to decentralized cryptocurrencies (Bhuiyan et al., 2021, 2022b; Dong et al., 2021; Mikhaylov, 2021b; Baboshkin et al., 2022; Barykin et al., 2022; Baig et al., 2022a, b; Liu et al., 2022a, b; Danish et al., 2022; Saqib et al., 2021; Yuksel et al., 2021; Mukhametov et al., 2021; Candila et al., 2021; Mikhaylov & Grilli, 2022).

12.3 Results

Taking into account the results of past tests, we will put forward the following hypothesis: Based on the results of multifractal analysis, the correlation between the CNY and ETH series, as well as CNY and TRX, will be confirmed, while the test results will show the opposite or they will not be clear.

Based on the statistical research carried out, it is impossible to draw completely unambiguous conclusions about the relationship between the dynamics of the exchange rate of cryptocurrencies and the Chinese yuan; however, several tests showed results indicating the presence of a long-term correlation between the Chinese currency and cryptocurrencies, especially TRON and Ethereum. Thus, the calculations carried out confirmed the hypothesis put forward earlier. The determining factors of the revealed correlation can be the common functional features of the three cryptocurrencies (will be described in more detail below), as well as a hypothetically time factor. All three cryptocurrencies began to develop at about the same time: Ethereum and DCEP from 2015, and TRON from 2017. The Chinese authorities' encouragement to develop similar blockchain platforms could also strengthen the correlation between the time series studied.

If we take these results into account, what needs to be done after additional research is carried out, then we can assume that the further transition of the Chinese yuan to the digital environment will affect the cryptocurrency market the rate of Ethereum and TRON, since the TRX, ETH, and DCEP platforms have a lot in common. It can be assumed that in the long term, when the digital currency of the People's Bank of China enters the international market, this relationship may increase, since the PRC government shows an open and strong interest in TRON, having concluded an agreement with its developers. These three monetary units are based on the use of blockchain technology and can serve as a means of payment and a medium of exchange.

Similar studies can be carried out with respect to other digital monetary units of central banks, mainly those that have a large weight in the international economy (US dollar, pound Sterling, euro, or Japanese yen), since their turnover is comparable to the turnover of cryptocurrencies. The detection of a correlation between them can be caused both by the similarity of the platforms based on which they will be created, and by currency support.

12.4 Discussion and Conclusions

All compared platforms are based on the use of blockchain technology, which consists in distributing data over a certain number of isolated but connected blocks. The movement of data along the blockchain is carried out through transaction procedures in which two subjects participate: the transmitting and receiving.

The presented systems have differences in the issue of the fundamental principle of building the system. Chinese developers have created a centralized system in order to control the transactions and consolidate the role of the People's Bank of China as the sole issuer of the currency (for external users, DCEP will be a completely anonymous system). This significantly reduces the possibility of crypto-yuan speculation on cryptocurrency exchanges. Unlike the turnover of cryptocurrencies, which can be overestimated by influencing the financial market, the analogous indicator for the digital version of the monetary unit will be practically unaffected by this.

In this aspect, the thesis about the need for state control is becoming more relevant. In a number of aspects, DCEP is a more closed system: the source code of the digital currency of the Central Bank of China is not advertised, although it is known that the Chinese developers used the Ethereum platform as a prototype, and the developers of the TRON platform, which in some aspects is based on Ethereum, were involved in cooperation with the PRC as advisers. The closed nature of information can provoke a slowdown in the further development of the platform, but at the same time, it avoids information leakage that could lead to hacking or cyberattacks on structures using DCEP (Sannikova, 2021; Zhihua & Yu, 2021; Rezvanov, 2021; Mingaleva & Starkov, 2021; Bushukina, 2021; Arlashkin, 2021; Matveeva, 2021; Vinogradova, 2021; Lukyanova, 2021; Mrachek & Valyushitskaya, 2021).

The reliability of digital renminbi is strengthened by the availability of its backing with fiat money, which puts it in a similar position to the Tether token, which is secured by reserves of major currencies in the assets of the issuing organization (US dollar, Japanese yen, Chinese yuan, etc.). This quality of the digital yuan, despite the closed nature of the system, can increase its investment attractiveness, since its value will be less volatile compared to cryptocurrencies issued in a decentralized manner (Ivanova & Fedosov, 2021; Milchakov, 2021; Bukharsky,

2021; Bakulina & Kuzmina, 2021; Timofeeva, 2021; Likhacheva, 2021; Tarasova & Fevraleva, 2021; Vasilyeva, 2021; Levina, 2021; Belousov & Timofeeva, 2021).

The internationalization of the digital yuan could create problems for Alipay and WeChat pay, as DCEP is exchanged directly between users on a government platform, similar to the two previously named systems. However, this does not exclude the possibility of penetration of the digital yuan into private translation platforms. In addition, the introduction of the digital currency of the People's Bank of China may open prospects for increasing the scale of settlements in the national currency of the PRC, but for this, first, it is necessary to overcome the problems of the liquidity of the Chinese currency.

Green energy investments play a crucial role for the sustainable development of the countries. However, it is possible to mention some barriers of these projects (Liu et al., 2021a, b, c; Kou et al., 2022; Zhe et al., 2021; Dinçer et al., 2022). For example, the costs of these investments are quite higher in comparison to the fossil fuel investments (Mukhtarov et al., 2022; Xie et al., 2021; Zhou et al., 2021; Meng et al., 2021). Therefore, to handle this problem, necessary financial sources should be provided to these investors (Ding et al., 2021; Haiyun et al., 2021; Dong et al., 2022). Thus, by considering the issues stated below, it is understood that blockchain technology can be a solution to this problem.

References

Adalı, Z., Dinçer, H., Eti, S., Mikhaylov, A., & Yüksel, S. (2022). Identifying new perspectives on geothermal energy investments. In H. Dinçer & S. Yüksel (Eds.), *Multidimensional strategic outlook on global competitive energy economics and finance* (pp. 1–11). Emerald Publishing Limited. https://doi.org/10.1108/978-1-80117-898-320221002

Alwaelya, S. A., Yousif, N. B. A., & Mikhaylov, A. (2021). Emotional development in preschoolers and socialization. *Early Child Development and Care, 191*, 16.

An, J., & Mikhaylov, A. (2020). Russian energy projects in South Africa. *Journal of Energy in Southern Africa, 31*(3), 58–64.

An, J., & Mikhaylov, A. (2021). Analysis of energy projects financial efficiency and renewable energy generation in Russia. *Finance: Theory and Practice, 25*(5), 79–91.

An, J., Mikhaylov, A., & Moiseev, N. (2019a). Oil price predictors: Machine learning approach. *International Journal of Energy Economics and Policy, 9*(5), 1–6.

An, J., Mikhaylov, A., & Sokolinskaya, N. (2019b). Machine learning in economic planning: Ensembles of algorithms. *Journal of Physics: Conference Series, 1353*, 012126.

An, J., Mikhaylov, A., & Jung, S.-U. (2020a). The strategy of South Korea in the global oil market. *Energies, 13*(10), 2491.

An, J., Mikhaylov, A., & Kim, K. (2020b). Machine learning approach in heterogeneous group of algorithms for transport safety-critical system. *Applied Sciences, 10*(8), 2670.

An, J., Mikhaylov, A., & Richter, U. H. (2020c). Trade war effects: Evidence from sectors of energy and resources in Africa. *Heliyon, 6*, e05693. https://doi.org/10.1016/j.heliyon.2020.e05693

An, J., Mikhaylov, A., & Jung, S.-U. (2021). A linear programming approach for Robust network revenue management in the airline industry. *Journal of Air Transport Management, 91*, 101979.

Arlashkin, I. (2021). Clustering of Russian regions by level of debt sustainability. *Financial Journal, 13*(5), 108–124.

Artemiev, A. (2021). The flow of dividends to the seller: Customs valuation methodology. *Financial Journal, 13*(3), 104–115.
Baboshkin, P., Mikhaylov, A., & Shaikh, Z. A. (2022). Sustainable cryptocurrency growth is not possible? Impact of network power demand on bitcoin price. *Financial Journal, 14*(2), 39–55.
Baig, U., Hussain, B. M., Khan, A. A., Shaikh, Z. A., Mikhaylov, A., Chao, C.-C., & Barykin, S. E. (2022a). Research on investors of the reginal stock exchange: An influence of behavioral finance on investment decision making. *Risks, 10*(4), 116.
Baig, U., Khan, A. A., Abbas, M. G., Shaikh, Z. A., Mikhaylov, A., Laghari, A. A., & Hussain, B. M. (2022b). Crucial causes of delay in completion and performance management of the construction work: Study on the base of relative importance index. *Journal of Tianjin University Science and Technology, 55*(6).
Bakulina, P., & Kuzmina, K. (2021). China's policy of economic sanctions: Legislation and enforcement. *Financial Journal, 13*(4), 24–38.
Barykin, S., Mikheev, A., Kiseleva, E., Putikhin, Y., Alekseeva, N., & Mikhaylov, A. (2022). An empirical analysis of Russian regions' debt sustainability. *Economies, 10*(4), 296.
Belousov, Y., & Timofeeva, O. (2021). Methodological aspects of compiling open budget rankings. *Financial Journal, 13*(4), 122–138.
Bhuiyan, M. A., An, J., Mikhaylov, A., Moiseev, N., & Danish, M. S. S. (2021). Renewable energy deployment and COVID-19 measures for sustainable development. *Sustainability, 13*, 4418.
Bhuiyan, M. A., Dinçer, H., Yüksel, S., Mikhaylov, A., Danish, M. S. S., Pinter, G., Uyeh, D. D., & Stepanova, D. (2022a). Economic indicators and bioenergy supply in developed economies: QROF-DEMATEL and random forest models. *Energy Reports, 8*, 561–570.
Bhuiyan, M. A., Khare, V., Mikhaylov, A., Pinter G., & Zhang (2022b) Does renewable energy consumption affect economic growth? A systematic literature review. *Frontiers in Environmental Science.*
Bukharsky, V. (2021). Fiscal decentralization and incentives of local authorities in the Russian Federation. *Financial Journal, 13*(2), 114–129.
Bushukina, V. (2021). Specific features of renewable energy development in the world and Russia. *Financial Journal, 13*(5), 93–107.
Candila, V., Maximov, D., Mikhaylov, A., Moiseev, N., Senjyu, T., & Tryndina, N. (2021). On the relationship between oil and exchange rates of oil-exporting and oil-importing countries: From the great recession period to the Covid-19 era. *Energies, 14*, 8065.
Conteh, F., Takahashi, H., Hemeida, A. M., Krishnan, N., Mikhaylov, A., & Senjyu, T. (2021). Hybrid grid-connected renewable power generation for sustainable electricity supply in Sierra Leone: Case study lungi town. *Sustainability, 13*(18), 1–20.
Daniali, S. M., Barykin, S. E., Kapustina, I. V., Khortabi, F. M., Sergeev, S. M., Kalinina, O. V., Mikhaylov, A., Veynberg, R., Zasova, L., & Senjyu, T. (2021). Predicting volatility index according to technical index and economic indicators on the basis of deep learning algorithm. *Sustainability, 2021*(13), 14011.
Danish, M. S. S., Bhattacharya, A., Stepanova, D., Mikhaylov, A., Grilli, M. L., Khosravy, M., & Senjyu, T. (2020). A systematic review of metal oxide applications for energy and environmental sustainability. *Metals, 10*(12), 1604.
Danish, M. S. S., Senjyu, T., Sabory, N. R., Khosravy, M., Grilli, M. L., Mikhaylov, A., & Majidi, H. (2021). A forefront framework for sustainable aquaponics modeling and design. *Sustainability, 13*, 9313.
Danish, M. S. S., Estrella-Pajulas, L. L., Alemaida, I. M. A., Grilli, M. L., Mikhaylov, A., & Senjyu, T. (2022). Green synthesis of silver oxide nanoparticles for photocatalytic environmental remediation and biomedical applications. *Metals, 12*(4), 769.
Dayong, N., Mikhaylov, A., Bratanovsky, S., Shaikh, Z. A., & Stepanova, D. (2020). Mathematical modeling of the technological processes of catering products production. *Journal of Food Process Engineering, 43*(2), 1–9.
Denisova, V., Mikhaylov, A., & Lopatin, E. (2019). Blockchain infrastructure and growth of global power consumption. *International Journal of Energy Economics and Policy, 9*(4), 22–29.

Dinçer, H., Yüksel, S., & Martínez, L. (2022). Collaboration enhanced hybrid fuzzy decision-making approach to analyze the renewable energy investment projects. *Energy Reports, 8*, 377–389.

Ding, Z., Yüksel, S., & Dincer, H. (2021). An Integrated Pythagorean fuzzy soft computing approach to environmental management systems for sustainable energy pricing. *Energy Reports, 7*, 5575–5588.

Dong, B., Ikonnikova, I., Rogulin, R., Sakulyeva, T., & Mikhaylov, A. (2021). Environmental economic approach to optimization of transport communication in megacities. *Journal of Environmental Science and Health, Part A, 56*(6), 660–666.

Dong, W., Zhao, G., Yüksel, S., Dinçer, H., & Ubay, G. G. (2022). A novel hybrid decision making approach for the strategic selection of wind energy projects. *Renewable Energy, 185*, 321–337.

Dooyum, U. D., Mikhaylov, A., & Varyash, I. (2020). Energy security concept in Russia and South Korea. *International Journal of Energy Economics and Policy, 10*(4), 102–107.

Grilli, M. L., Valerini, D., Rizzo, A., Yilmaz, M., Song, C., Hu, G., Chierchia, R., Mikhaylov, A., & Rinaldi, A. (2021). A comparative study of the mechanical and tribological properties of thin Al2O3 coatings fabricated by atomic layer deposition and radiofrequency sputtering. *Physica Status Solidi (A), 218*(24), 1–25.

Gura, D., Mikhaylov, A., Glushkov, S., Zaikov, M., & Shaikh, Z. A. (2020). Model for estimating power dissipation along the interconnect length in single on-chip topology. *Evolutionary Intelligence.*

Haiyun, C., Zhixiong, H., Yüksel, S., & Dinçer, H. (2021). Analysis of the innovation strategies for green supply chain management in the energy industry using the QFD-based hybrid interval valued intuitionistic fuzzy decision approach. *Renewable and Sustainable Energy Reviews, 143*, 110844.

Huang, Y., Masrur, H., Shigenobu, R., Hemeida, A. M., Mikhaylov, A., & Senjyu, T. (2021a). A comparative design of a campus microgrid considering a multi-scenario and multi-objective approach. *Energies, 14*, 2853.

Huang, Y., Yona, A., Takahashi, H., Hemeida, A. M., Mandal, P., Mikhaylov, A., Senjyu, T., & Lotfy, M. E. (2021b). Energy management system optimization of drug store operate electric vehicles charging station. *Sustainability, 14*, 1217836.

Ivanova, N., & Fedosov, V. (2021). Goal setting of youth practices of participatory budgeting. *Financial Journal, 13*(2), 83–92.

Khan, A. A., Shaikh, Z. A., Baitenova, L., Mutaliyeva, L., Moiseev, N., Mikhaylov, A., Laghari, A. A., Idris, S. A., & Alshazly, H. (2021). QoS-ledger: Smart contracts and metaheuristic for secure quality-of-service and cost-efficient scheduling of medical-data processing. *Electronics, 10*, 3083.

Kou, G., Yüksel, S., & Dinçer, H. (2022). Inventive problem-solving map of innovative carbon emission strategies for solar energy-based transportation investment projects. *Applied Energy, 311*, 118680.

Kranina, E. I. (2021). China on the way to achieving carbon neutrality. *Financial Journal, 13*(5), 51–61. https://doi.org/10.31107/2075-1990-2021-5-51-61

Kudelich, M. (2021). Problems of innovative science and technology center financing from budgetary funds. *Financial Journal, 13*(3), 76–87.

Levina, V. (2021). Problems of regional participatory budgeting practices. *Financial Journal, 13*(4), 110–121.

Likhacheva, A. (2021). On the strategic effects of unilateral sanctions: Russian experience. *Financial Journal, 13*(4), 52–66.

Liu, L., Kato, T, Mandal, P., Mikhaylov, A., Hemeida, A. M., & Senjyu, T. (2021a). Multi-area power system load frequency control by using model predictive control by introducing renewable energy sources. In *2021 International Conference on Science & Contemporary Technologies (ICSCT)* (pp. 1–6). https://doi.org/10.1109/ICSCT53883.2021.9642521

Liu, L., Kato, T., Mandal, P., Mikhaylov, A., Hemeida, A. M., Takahashi, H., & Tomonobu, S. (2021b). Two cases studies of model predictive control approach for hybrid renewable energy systems. *AIMS Energy, 9*(6), 1241–1259.

Liu, J., Lv, J., Dinçer, H., Yüksel, S., & Karakuş, H. (2021c). Selection of renewable energy alternatives for green blockchain investments: A hybrid IT2-based fuzzy modelling. *Archives of Computational Methods in Engineering, 28*(5), 3687–3701.

Liu, Z.-J., Panfilova, E., Mikhaylov, A., & Kurilova, A. (2022a). COVID-19 crisis impact on the stability between parties in crowdfunding and crowdsourcing. *Wireless Personal Communications, 122*, 915–930.

Liu, Z.-J., Panfilova, E., Mikhaylov, A., & Kurilova, A. (2022b). Assessing stability in relationship between parties in crowdfunding and crowdsourcing projects during the COVID-19 crisis. *Journal of Global Information Management, 30*(2), 1.

Lukashov, A. (2021). Some directions of increasing the efficiency of public administration in the context of digitalization. *Financial Journal, 13*(3), 67–75.

Lukyanova, N. (2021). Saint Petersburg experience of participatory budgeting. *Financial Journal, 13*(2), 61–69.

Maslov, A. (2021). Development of new payment systems in Russia similar to a CLS analogue. *Financial Journal, 13*(3), 27–37.

Matveeva, N. (2021). Legislative regulation financial statement preparation by micro entities: International experience. *Financial Journal, 13*(5), 125–138.

Meng, Y., Wu, H., Zhao, W., Chen, W., Dinçer, H., & Yüksel, S. (2021). A hybrid heterogeneous Pythagorean fuzzy group decision modelling for crowdfunding development process pathways of fintech-based clean energy investment projects. *Financial Innovation, 7*(1), 1–34.

Mikhaylov, A. (2018a). Volatility spillover effect between stock and exchange rate in oil exporting countries. *International Journal of Energy Economics and Policy, 8*(3), 321–326.

Mikhaylov, A. (2018b). Pricing in oil market and using probit model for analysis of stock market effects. *International Journal of Energy Economics and Policy, 8*(2), 69–73.

Mikhaylov, A. (2021a). Development of Friedrich von Hayek's theory of private money and economic implications for digital currencies. *Terra Economicus, 19*(1), 53–62.

Mikhaylov, A. (2021b). Lichens as indicators of atmospheric pollution in urban ecosystems. *Israel Journal of Ecology & Evolution, 67*(1–2), 60–68. https://doi.org/10.1163/22244662-bja10016

Mikhaylov, A. (2022a). Efficiency of renewable energy generation in Russia. *Annals of the Brazilian Academy of Sciences, 94*(3).

Mikhaylov, A. (2022b). Sustainable development and renewable energy: A new view to a global problem. *Energies, 15*, 1397. https://doi.org/10.3390/en15041397

Mikhaylov, A., & Grilli, M. L. (2022). Machine learning methods and sustainable development: Metal oxides and multilayer metal-oxides. *Metals, 12*(4), 836.

Mikhaylov, A., & Tarakanov, S. (2020). Development of Levenberg-Marquardt theoretical approach for electric network. *Journal of Physics: Conference Series, 1515*, 052006.

Mikhaylov, A., Sokolinskaya, N., & Nyangarika, A. (2018). Optimal carry trade strategy based on currencies of energy and developed economies. *Journal of Reviews on Global Economics, 7*, 582–592.

Mikhaylov, A., Burakov, D., & Didenko, V. (2019). Relationship between oil price and macroeconomic indicators in Russia. *Finance: Theory and Practice, 23*(2), 105–116. https://doi.org/10.26794/2587-5671-2019-23-2-105-116

Mikhaylov, A., Yumashev, A., & Kolpak, E. (2022). Quality of life, anxiety and depressive disorders in patients with extrasystolic arrhythmia. *Archives of Medical Science, 18*(2), 328–335. https://doi.org/10.5114/aoms.2020.101359

Milchakov, M. (2021). Implementation of regional development priorities under the conditions of the COVID-19 pandemic. *Financial Journal, 13*(2), 93–113.

Mingaleva, Z., & Starkov, Y. (2021). The role of environmental innovation in green modernization of industrial enterprises. *Financial Journal, 13*(5), 79–92.

Moiseev, N., Mikhaylov, A., Varyash, I., & Saqib, A. (2020). Investigating the relation of GDP per capita and corruption index. *Entrepreneurship and Sustainability Issues, 8*(1), 780–794.

Moiseev, N., Sorokin, A., Zvezdina, N., Mikhaylov, A., Khomyakova, L., & Danish, M. S. S. (2021). Credit risk theoretical model on the base of DCC-GARCH in time-varying parameters framework. *Mathematics, 9*, 2423. https://doi.org/10.3390/math9192423

Morkovkin, D., Lopatkin, D., Sadriddinov, M., Shushunova, T., Gibadullin, A., & Golikova, O. (2020a). Assessment of innovation activity in the countries of the world. *E3S Web of Conferences, 157*, 04015. https://doi.org/10.1051/e3sconf/202015704015

Morkovkin, D. E., Gibadullin, A. A., Kolosova, E. V., Semkina, N. S., & Fasehzoda, I. S. (2020b). Modern transformation of the production base in the conditions of industry 4.0: Problems and prospects. *Journal of Physics: Conference Series, 1515*, 032014.

Mrachek, E., & Valyushitskaya, I. (2021). The role of project centers in the development of participatory budgeting: The practice of the Krasnoyarsk territory. *Financial Journal, 13*(2), 70–82.

Mukhametov, A., Bekhorashvili, A., Avdeenko, A., & Mikhaylov, A. (2021). The impact of growing legume plants under conditions of biologization and soil cultivation on Chernozem fertility and productivity of rotation crops. *Legume Research, 44*, 12.

Mukhtarov, S., Yüksel, S., & Dinçer, H. (2022). The impact of financial development on renewable energy consumption: Evidence from Turkey. *Renewable Energy, 187*, 169–176.

Mutalimov, V., Kovaleva, I., Mikhaylov, A., & Stepanova, D. (2021). Assessing regional growth of small business in Russia. *Entrepreneurial Business and Economics Review, 9*(3), 119–133. https://doi.org/10.15678/EBER.2021.090308

Nyangarika, A., Mikhaylov, A., & Tang, B.-J. (2018). Correlation of oil prices and gross domestic product in oil producing countries. *International Journal of Energy Economics and Policy, 8*(5), 42–48.

Nyangarika, A., Mikhaylov, A., & Richter, U. (2019a). Influence oil price towards economic indicators in Russia. *International Journal of Energy Economics and Policy, 9*(1), 123–129.

Nyangarika, A., Mikhaylov, A., & Richter, U. (2019b). Oil price factors: Forecasting on the base of modified auto-regressive integrated moving average model. *International Journal of Energy Economics and Policy, 9*(1), 149–159.

Pishchik, V., & Alekseev, P. (2021). Cybercrime as a key operational risk of the payment and settlement infrastructure of the global financial system and approaches to its regulation in the Eurasian Economic Union. *Financial Journal, 13*(3), 54–66.

Rezvanov, R. (2021). Implementation of international sustainable financing practices into the National Debt System. Can infrastructure loans become responsible? *Financial Journal, 13*(5), 62–78.

Sannikova, L. (2021). Legal framework for green finance in the EU and Russia. *Financial Journal, 13*(5), 29–43.

Saqib, A., Chan, T.-H., Mikhaylov, A., & Lean, H. H. (2021). Are the responses of sectoral energy imports asymmetric to exchange rate volatilities in Pakistan? Evidence from recent foreign exchange regime. *Frontiers in Energy Research, 9*, 614463. https://doi.org/10.3389/fenrg.2021.614463

Sediqi, M. M., Nakadomari, A., Mikhaylov, A., Krishnan, N., Lotfy, M. E., Yona, A., & Senjyu, T. (2022). Impact of time-of-use demand response program on optimal operation of Afghanistan real power system. *Energies, 15*, 296.

Shaikh, Z. A., Moiseev, N., Mikhaylov, A., & Yüksel, S. (2021). Facile synthesis of copper oxide-cobalt oxide/nitrogen-doped carbon (Cu2O-Co3O4/CN) composite for efficient water splitting. *Applied Sciences, 11*, 9974. https://doi.org/10.3390/app11219974

Shkodinsky, S., Dudin, M., & Usmanov, D. (2021). Analysis and assessment of cyberthreats to the National Financial System of Russia in the digital economy. *Financial Journal, 13*(3), 38–53.

Sinenko, O., & Mitrofanov, T. (2021). Identification of signs of "business fragmentation" in Russian far eastern territories with special economic status. *Financial Journal, 13*(3), 88–103.

Tamashiro, K., Alharbi, T., Mikhaylov, A., Hemeida, A. M., Krishnan, N., Lotfy, M. E., & Senjyu, T. (2021). Investigation of home energy management with advanced direct load control and optimal scheduling of controllable loads. *Energies, 14*, 7314. https://doi.org/10.3390/en14217314

Tarasova, Y., & Fevraleva, E. (2021). Forecasting of bankruptcy: Evidence from insurance companies in Russia. *Financial Journal, 13*(4), 75–90.

Timofeeva, Y. (2021). US sanctions against financial companies: Key features. *Financial Journal, 13*(4), 39–51.

Uyeh, D. D., Asem-Hiablie, S., Park, T., Kim, K.-M., Mikhaylov, A., Woo, S., & Ha, Y. (2021). Could japonica rice be an alternative variety for increased global food security and climate change mitigation? *Food, 10*, 1869. https://doi.org/10.3390/foods10081869

Varyash, I., Mikhaylov, A., Moiseev, N., & Aleshin, K. (2020). Triple bottom line and corporate social responsibility performance indicators for Russian companies. *Entrepreneurship and Sustainability Issues, 8*(1), 313–331.

Vasilyeva, A. (2021). Approaches to modelling exposure at default for the entire life of the asset. *Financial Journal, 13*(4), 91–109.

Vinogradova, I. (2021). Participatory budgeting as a tool contributing to the achievement of the sustainable development goals. *Financial Journal, 13*(2), 46–60.

Xie, Y., Zhou, Y., Peng, Y., Dinçer, H., Yüksel, S., & an Xiang, P. (2021). An extended Pythagorean fuzzy approach to group decision-making with incomplete preferences for analyzing balanced scorecard-based renewable energy investments. *IEEE Access, 9*, 43020–43035.

Yakovlev, I. A., Kabir, L. S., & Nikulina, S. I. (2021). Changes in climate policies and financial strategies of their implementation in the EU and Russia. *Financial Journal, 13*(5), 11–28. https://doi.org/10.31107/2075-1990-2021-5-11-28

Yuksel, S., Khomyakova, L., & Mikhaylov, A. (2021). Energy center selection in G7 industry with fuzzy MOORA. In S. Yüksel & H. Dinçer (Eds.), *Handbook of research on strategic management for current energy investments* (pp. 87–106). IGI Global. https://doi.org/10.4018/978-1-7998-8335-7.ch006

Yüksel, S., Dinçer, H., Mikhaylov, A., Adalı, Z., & Eti, S. (2022). Key issues for the improvements of shallow geothermal investments. In H. Dinçer & S. Yüksel (Eds.), *Sustainability in energy business and finance. Contributions to finance and accounting*. Springer. https://doi.org/10.1007/978-3-030-94051-5_16

Yumashev, A., & Mikhaylov, A. (2020). Development of polymer film coatings with high adhesion to steel alloys and high wear resistance. *Polymer Composites, 41*(7), 2875–2880.

Yumashev, A., Ślusarczyk, B., Kondrashev, S., & Mikhaylov, A. (2020). Global indicators of sustainable development: Evaluation of the influence of the human development index on consumption and quality of energy. *Energies, 13*, 2768.

Zhao, Q., Cherkasov, S., Avdeenko, A., Kondratenko, L., & Mikhaylov, A. (2021). Integral estimate of the added value of agricultural crops in the synergetic agriculture on the example of Vicia faba (Vicia faba L.). *Polish Journal of Environmental Studies, 30*(5), 1–9. https://doi.org/10.15244/pjoes/131949

Zhe, L., Yüksel, S., Dinçer, H., Mukhtarov, S., & Azizov, M. (2021). The positive influences of renewable energy consumption on financial development and economic growth. *SAGE Open, 11*(3), 21582440211040133.

Zhihua, F., & Yu, C. (2021). Promoting green development in China's new development stage through tax reform. *Financial Journal, 13*(5), 44–50.

Zhou, P., Luo, J., Cheng, F., Yüksel, S., & Dinçer, H. (2021). Analysis of risk priorities for renewable energy investment projects using a hybrid IT2 hesitant fuzzy decision-making approach with alpha cuts. *Energy, 224*, 120184.

Chapter 13
An Evaluation for the Use of Alternative Vehicle Technologies and Energy Resources in Logistic Sector with a Strategic Approach

Filiz Mızrak

Abstract Increasing global energy consumption results in important problems. The decrease in traditional energy resources such as oil, coal, and natural gas reveals the necessity of using these resources more efficiently. In this scope, being one of the most key functions in the workflow of most business, logistics activities should be taken into consideration since these activities have a direct impact on issues such as environment, air pollution, and climate change. It is known that 60% of the oil and 25% of the energy used in the world is consumed by the transportation sector. This situation directly concerns environmental sustainability. In this respect, the purpose of the study is to review the most recent literature to evaluate the alternative vehicle technologies and fuels for logistic activities and propose the most practical, environmental friendly, and cheapest technology. As a result of the evaluation, it has been found out that electrical vehicles can be the most convenient ones in terms of sustainable logistics activities despite some drawbacks. Thus, some strategies have been put forward to increase the use of these vehicles in the near future.

Keywords Alternative energy resources · Logistics · Strategy

13.1 Introduction

Logistics is one of the most key functions in a workflow. In this respect, the existence and good management of logistics activities are of great importance for many businesses. Logistics activities carried out in order to meet the needs of customers show us the most basic purpose of logistics. Logistics management is shaped around this purpose and is seen as an important part of the supply chain. The aim of logistics management is to manage the forward and reverse flow most effectively and efficiently in the whole process from the point of departure to the

F. Mızrak (✉)
The School of Business, İstanbul Medipol University, Istanbul, Turkey
e-mail: fmizrak@medipol.edu.tr

H. Dinçer, S. Yüksel (eds.), *Circular Economy and the Energy Market*,
Contributions to Economics, https://doi.org/10.1007/978-3-031-13146-2_13

place of consumption in order to meet the demands of the customers (Kherbach & Mocan, 2016).

People meet their needs thanks to the systems and applications they develop. Even if meeting these needs is seen as suitable for its purpose in the short term, it may have negative consequences for the next generations. These results require people and businesses that meet the needs of people to be aware of a common issue. This awareness emerges as the idea of sustainability. Today, it has become important for businesses to be able to produce efficiently by giving less damage to the environment with the idea of sustainability.

When this situation is evaluated in terms of the logistics sector, environmental sustainability and global warming emerged as the most important problems. Unconscious consumption of natural resources, deficiencies in waste management, increases in emission rates and individuals raised without environmental awareness have an important place in the emergence of global warming. Emission values are directly related to the carbon emissions of vehicles used in transportation. Since transportation is one of the most important components of the logistics sector, it can be said that the share of the sector in global warming is large. Considering that 60% of the total oil and 25% of the total energy used in the world is consumed by the transportation sector, the importance of the sector in terms of environmental sustainability can be better understood (Grzybowska & Awasthi, 2020).

The fact that people are conscious of environmental issues and experience negative consequences together gives clues about how important the concept of sustainability will be in the future. The understanding of sustainability can be applied in almost every sector, and it also has a wide area of influence in the logistics sector. When logistics activities are considered as a whole, it is seen that fossil resources are frequently used. Fossil resource use is among the causes of environmental problems to show itself in the top steps. As a result of the use of fossil resources, CO_2 emissions have a negative impact on the world today (García-Arca et al., 2020).

In this scope, the purpose of this study is to review the latest literature in order to evaluate the alternative vehicle technology and alternative fuels to be used in logistic activities, especially in road transport. The study is expected to contribute to literature well as it includes the review of the recent literature on sustainable logistics and alternative vehicle technologies. Thus, it could offer logistic companies a sustainable technology and ways to improve the efficiency and increase the use of it.

The study consists of four parts. In the following part, importance of logistics for enterprises as a business strategy has been stressed. Furthermore, sustainability for logistics has been discussed to create awareness for the necessity of taking action in the near future. Alternative vehicle technologies and fuels have been analyzed with all cons and pros in order to suggest the most practical, environmentally friendly, and cheapest technology. In conclusion part, electrical vehicles have been proposed to be the most convenient one despite some disadvantages. Moreover, some tactics and strategies to increase the use of electrical vehicles in logistics activities have been put forward.

13.2 Literature Review

13.2.1 Importance of Logistics

The logistics system itself is designed to benefit customers. However, it also provides several benefits to businesses that implement this system. Namely, the existence of an effective and efficient logistics system provides a competitive advantage to businesses thanks to the time and place benefit it provides to customers through effective product movement. In addition, logistics is an important business resource and capability that has an impact on the financial performance of the business. Logistics, which aims to deliver the right product at the right time to the right place undamaged, constitutes an important value-creating activity for products and services. Therefore, the logistics is a function that can provide both cost savings and strategic efficiency in the value chain and create a competitive advantage for businesses by performing it in accordance with business strategies (Tijan et al., 2019).

In addition to providing a strategic competitive advantage, logistics provides time and place utility. With a general definition, the aim of logistics activities is to have the right products and/or services available in the right quantities, in the right place, at the right time, and at the least cost. Within the scope of this definition, place utility is the transportation of products from places where they are of lower value to those where they are of higher value, thereby increasing the value of their location. This process also includes transportation costs. The time benefit is realized by storing the products until they are needed and making all processes more efficient. Logistics activities provide a better standard of living for humanity with the time and place benefit by creating a bridge between the space and time components of production and marketing (Martins et al., 2019).

13.2.2 Sustainable Logistics

Sustainability is based on the preservation of the natural order in nature and the life of human beings and the continuation of their normal functions. Sustainability, which can be briefly defined as the ability to be permanent, is the acceptance and application of business practices and tactics that allow the protection of natural and human resources that businesses will need in the future. Sustainability refers to an approach that aims at the protection and continuous use of natural resources and the environment, as well as an increase in quality and efficiency in production due to environmental problems as a result of production. Biodiversity, ecological, carbon and water footprints, greenhouse gases, carbon trade, carbon sequestration, reduction, and storage are among the important themes of sustainability (Yu, 2021).

Logistics activities of businesses have a direct impact on issues such as environment, air pollution, and climate change. It is known that 60% of the oil and 25% of the energy used in the world is consumed by the transportation sector. This is a situation that directly concerns environmental sustainability. The vehicles used for transportation cause air pollution, global warming, and an increase in emission values. Since transportation is a function of logistics, the damage caused by the logistics industry to the sustainable environment is quite high. This situation necessitates businesses to carry out their logistics activities with a sustainable understanding (Rashidi & Cullinane, 2019).

However, sustainable logistics should not be considered only from environmental perspective. In addition to environmental sustainability, it is necessary to adopt an understanding of sustainability in terms of social and economic aspects. While focusing on issues such as health, safety, equality, and access in socially sustainable logistics; Environmentally sustainable logistics focuses on issues such as air pollution, noise, biodiversity, land use, and waste management. In economically sustainable logistics, issues such as minimizing costs, maximizing profits, growth, development, and progress are on the agenda (Richnák & Gubová, 2021).

13.3 Alternative Vehicle Technologies and Alternative Fuels

Atmospheric emissions which result from the daily activities of human beings are a common problem in large, populated cities, and urban vehicle movement is the biggest source of this problem. Apart from carbon dioxide emissions, the increase in the number of vehicles increases the nitrogen oxide emission, while the air pollution caused by vehicle tire dust is increasing due to vehicle brake pads and friction on the roads. In addition, not using renewable resources in vehicles, particulate substances such as carbon monoxide, nitrogen oxide, sulfur dioxide, hydrocarbons, dioxin and benzene, nickel, cadmium, chrome carbon, zinc, and platinum directly cause air pollution (Liu et al., 2018).

From the 1970s, the idea of using alternative fuels in cars started to be discussed. Due to the oil crises in the world in the 1980s and 1990s, this idea gained importance. The most important criterion in alternative fuel research is the idea of low emissions. While reducing the negative effects of petroleum-based fuels used in conventional vehicles on the environment is the main objective, it is also aimed to protect energy resources (Stančin et al., 2020).

Below are the existing technologies in the production and use of low emission and sustainable vehicles (Chen et al., 2018):

- Internal combustion engines
- Hybrid vehicle systems
- Natural gas
- LPG technology
- Biofuels
- Fuel cell system

- Hydrogen energy
- Electric vehicles

13.3.1 Internal Combustion Engines

While engine features and technologies have changed significantly over the time, the basic operating principles of internal combustion engines, including efficiency and emissions improvements, have not changed significantly. Since alternative fuels are not considered, manufacturers are constantly striving for engine improvements because the transition to alternative fuel, integration with existing engines, and infrastructure solutions are considered both time consuming and costly (Halldórsson & Kovács, 2010).

In simple terms, internal combustion engines are systems that create linear power by converting chemical energy, which is formed by the combustion of petroleum-based fuel together with air, into mechanical energy. This linear power transmission is transmitted to the engine components and the vehicle moves. There are two main engine technologies of internal combustion engines, spark-ignition gasoline engines, and compression-ignition diesel engines. According to 2020 data, 54% of the vehicles used in the European Union countries are gasoline powered vehicles, 42% are diesel-powered vehicles, and 4% are alternative fuel and other vehicles. According to these data, approximately 96% of diesel-powered vehicles are medium and heavy commercial vehicles used in transportation (Zhang et al., 2011).

13.3.2 Hybrid Vehicles

Internal combustion engines operating with petroleum-based fuels provide a high energy density advantage and provide good performance and a long operating range. However, it has disadvantages such as low fuel economy and environmental pollution. Although battery electric vehicles seem advantageous compared to conventional vehicles due to their high fuel efficiency and environmental friendliness, they cannot be considered as a complete alternative due to factors such as battery life and cost, location of charging stations, and charging time (Pourhejazy et al., 2019).

Although hybrid electric vehicles do not have large-capacity batteries as in electric vehicles, small batteries are used to meet the power provided by the electric motor. These batteries are used to activate the electric motor. The use of internal combustion engine or electric motor in electric hybrid vehicles can be used as an automatic vehicle command system or manually, depending on the vehicle's performance. While the vehicle uses the electric motor in short-term and non-high-performance situations, it activates the internal combustion engine in situations that require high speed and high performance. Because the electric motor drive system of the vehicle cannot respond to vehicle movement that requires high performance (Taniguchi et al., 2016).

The right configurations to be made during the design of hybrid electric vehicles can positively affect the efficiency and performance expected from the vehicle and increase sustainability. Today, three different types of hybrid electric vehicles are used, namely the serial hybrid system, the parallel hybrid system, and the split hybrid system (Zhang et al., 2019).

13.3.3 Natural Gas

The commercial use and production of natural gas vehicles around the world began to take shape in the mid-1930s. The use of compressed natural gas in vehicles in transportation activities was carried out for the first time by Italy. As a result of the use of natural gas vehicles for the first time in the USA in 1969, approximately 30% of the city buses used in Los Angeles today consist of natural gas vehicles. Although natural gas can be used in all types of motor vehicles, it is predominantly used in buses worldwide. In terms of energy use, natural gas is the second most used alternative fuel type after liquefied petroleum gas. According to 2020 data, the number of natural gas vehicles used worldwide is around 24 million (Aktas et al., 2018).

In the studies, it has been determined that the usage costs of natural gas vehicles are 10% more economical than traditional vehicles. Assuming that the life of the car is 15 years, natural gas vehicles are 15% less costly when their production and usage costs are considered. Along with the technological developments, it is seen that the heavy natural gas vehicles used today show similar performances compared to the diesel engine vehicles. The low natural gas prices increase the demand for natural gas vehicle production and the need for infrastructure (Yüksel et al., 2021; Liu et al., 2021; Du et al., 2020). The resulting demand allows the creation of new markets by the equipment manufacturers used to convert diesel-powered vehicles to natural gas vehicles (Pfoser et al., 2018).

13.3.4 LPG Technology

LPG (Liquid Petroleum Gas) is the most widely used alternative motor fuel in the world. LPG used in automobiles outside the USA is generally referred to as Autogas. According to 2018 data, the number of LPG powered vehicles used all over the world is estimated to be around 25 million. It is known that close to 6 million of this figure is used in the region called the Asia Pacific. LPG is preferred because it has less negative impact on the environment and human health compared to fossil fuels. Today, China is taking guiding measures to deal with the negative effects of fossil fuels, such as reducing the prices of autogas vehicles, and free land allocation for the construction of autogas stations (Pourhejazy et al., 2019).

LPG engine system can be used in cars, buses, and light or heavy vehicles. LPG use can be made possible by changing the engine structures of existing gasoline or diesel-fueled vehicles. Vehicle manufacturers continue to design engines that allow LPG using vehicles to move with the same torque and horsepower without losing their performance. LPG can still be obtained cheaper than fossil fuels such as gasoline or diesel in many countries. For this reason, carriers and companies prefer to use this fuel type for long-term use, especially in urban logistics due to its low costs (Paczuski et al., 2016).

13.3.5 Biofuels

Biofuel is a general definition that refers to any liquid fuel produced from a biomass source. Biofuel is an efficient, environmentally friendly, and natural alternative fuel type as an alternative to petroleum fuels. Biofuels are preferred over fossil fuels because of their potential to be produced from different agricultural sources and their low emission characteristics. Ethanol and biodiesel, two different types of biofuels, can often be considered as a potential alternative fuels for road transport (Inkinen & Hämäläinen, 2020; Bhuiyan et al., 2022).

Ethanol, which is used as a raw material in the chemical industry and used in the production of pharmaceuticals and beverages, is widely thought to be used in motor vehicles. Ethanol is obtained in the sugar industry by fermenting and distilling molasses, a sugar residue. Vegetable sources with potential to produce ethanol are cassava, maize, rice, and potatoes. Biodiesel, on the other hand, refers to the pure ethyl structures of vegetable oils. Pure or purified oils of plants such as rapeseed, soybean, and sunflower are used as diesel fuel without any significant changes in the existing engine design. Since biofuel is a natural and clean fuel type, it causes 78% less carbon dioxide emissions compared to conventional diesel fuels. Ethanol and biodiesel are kept separately and mixed with fuel. Ethanol can be mixed with gasoline, but this ratio should not be more than two-third of the total fuel (Johnson et al., 2021).

13.3.6 Fuel Cells

Fuel cells produce electricity using an electrochemical process, the reaction between hydrogen and oxygen. Fuel cells are an efficient, nonpolluting, compact, modular, and reliable technology for power generation. Technological studies on fuel cell technologies still continue. Some of these systems are proton exchange source fuel cells, phosphoric acid fuel cells, molten carbonate fuel cells, solid oxide fuel cells, direct methanol fuel cells, and alkaline fuel cells (Wang et al., 2021).

Fuel cells work using hydrogen and oxygen from the air. The efficiency rate of fuel cell systems is approximately between 45% and 60%. This system offers high efficiency and low emissions. Fuel cells can be used for stationary/portable power generation and automotive applications. High conversion efficiency causes little or no emissions. Noiseless operation, high current density, and compactness are some of the advantages that make fuel cells an ideal power option for automotive applications (Hagen et al., 2019).

13.3.7 Hydrogen Energy

Hydrogen (H_2), which is called the fuel of the future, is an alternative fuel that does not contain carbon, has zero emissions, and only releases water when used in vehicles. Although hydrogen does not cause carbon or other emissions when used in vehicles, various amounts of greenhouse gas emissions occur during hydrogen production (Zhao et al., 2021; Zhu et al., 2020). Most of the world's hydrogen is found in water or hydrocarbons such as coal, oil, natural gas, and biomass. The amount of hydrogen obtained varies according to the source and technology used (Kurien & Mittal, 2022).

This situation also affects production costs differently and provides the freedom to use different sources and different technologies for manufacturers. In recent years, especially big countries such as America, Europe, and Japan have focused on hydrogen fuel cell electric vehicle production and technological research. The main purpose of the studies is to provide low-cost production, while at the same time, with the increasing number of vehicles, hydrogen is stored, transported, and delivered to the end user in the easiest way (Jelti et al., 2021).

Although hydrogen can be used in internal combustion engines, it is not preferred to be used in conventional motor vehicles since its efficiency cannot be achieved at the desired level when the range is covered according to the power density it produces and the amount of hydrogen burned. In order to get the expected efficiency from hydrogen, it should be used in fuel cell electric vehicles (Burchart-Korol et al., 2020).

Fuel cell electric vehicles use electrochemical devices that generate electricity from stored hydrogen instead of using batteries to store electricity. Among the various fuel cell technologies, proton exchange source fuel cells are considered the most suitable for vehicle applications due to their fast start-up response and high-power density. The benefit of hydrogen used in this method is high fuel economy and zero exhaust emissions (Anderhofstadt & Spinler, 2020).

13.3.8 Electric Vehicles

Electric vehicles began to be produced in the early 1900s. These are vehicles that are driven by an electric motor powered by batteries attached to it, moving the wheels through the mechanical equipment on the vehicle. When the batteries run out of energy, they must be charged from the mains (Kou et al., 2022). To be more widely used, electric vehicles must provide similar conveniences in performance, reliability, durability, and cost compared to petrol or diesel-powered vehicles. According to this idea, the batteries used in vehicles should have a long life (Juan et al., 2016).

Electric vehicles can be expressed as the most suitable alternative vehicle type for the zero-emission targets of the countries. Environmentally conscious logistics systems aim to change the transportation plan and a sustainable distribution network with less negative impact on the environment. With the increase in environmental and social awareness, the production, use, and spread of new generation electric vehicles have increased. In logistics, electric vehicles are now recognized as a serious alternative to conventional powered internal combustion vehicles (Duarte et al., 2016).

Considered as an alternative technology with its environmentally friendly feature, electric vehicles are seen to be more costly than traditional vehicles in many respects when evaluated in terms of acquisition and use. The costs are (Napoli et al., 2021):

- High procurement cost
- High repair cost
- Vehicle replacement cost
- Adding heating or cooling systems when requested
- Additional procurement cost
- Low operating cost
- Low maintenance cost

Although electric vehicles seem to be costly, their use will become much more common as the usage area becomes more widespread and production technologies develop. Positive decisions taken by local and national governments, such as tax reductions and providing free parking spaces, will also support this approach (Bac & Erdem, 2021).

When electric vehicles are examined in terms of production technology, engine type and usage, different vehicle types appear. These vehicles are designed entirely in line with the needs and to take advantage of the existing traditional vehicles because the existing conditions, infrastructure, and operating requirements for alternative vehicles are not yet at a sufficient level (İmre et al., 2021).

Considering that transportation activities account for more than 25% of the energy consumed in the world and that the energy production process also increases air pollution, these effects should be considered in order to ensure sustainable growth in transportation. It can be considered that increasing the use of electric vehicles and increasing the number of electric vehicle fleets will be primarily effective in reducing negative environmental factors such as air pollution, noise pollution, carbon emissions, and traffic congestion, which increase with the contribution of transportation and logistics activities (Lebeau et al., 2015).

Trucks used in urban transport generally have lower speeds, and electric motors provide higher efficiency at lower speeds. It is also very suitable for stopping and accelerating in urban traffic. Trucks move on the same road almost every day and return to their starting points. Looking at the flow, it can be considered that it would be appropriate to use electric motors in trucks as well. Although it has a very low emission value, it is difficult to compete with traditional motor vehicles in terms of high-cost features such as purchasing, operation, and fuel economy. Although this rate is slightly less in automobiles, it is quite high when compared to the capacity and freight frequency of commercial vehicles used in transportation (Ehrler et al., 2021).

13.4 Conclusion

Sustainability, which represents the understanding of not jeopardizing the needs of future generations while meeting the wishes and needs of people, is considered among the main priorities in all sectors, because today, customers' expectations from products and services are not just cheaper, faster, and higher quality. Along with these factors, customers now demand that products and services do not harm nature, the environment, society, and human health, and that the businesses they supply products and services from should be sensitive to these issues. In order to fulfill these demands, which can be expressed as sustainable life, businesses need to develop economically, socially, and environmentally sustainable strategies and tactics.

The increase in population in city centers has led to an increase in the number of vehicles used in logistics. In logistics, traditional vehicles are used to a large extent. However, considering the energy consumption of fossil fuel vehicles and their negative effects on the environment, it is necessary to consider the use of alternative fuels and alternative vehicle technologies. In this scope, this study discusses the alternative vehicle technologies and alternative energy sources in terms of sustainability benefiting from the latest literature.

As a result of the literature review, use of electrical vehicles in the logistic sector has been asserted as the most sustainable technology in terms of social, economic, and environmental aspects. Engine power, energy consumption cost, and environmental friendliness are the most important strengths of electric vehicles. The most important advantage of using electric vehicles is that it is environmental friendly. Since electric vehicles do not emit any harmful gases, they cause zero emissions. Compared to traditional vehicles, it is a very important issue for a livable environment. It is indisputably advantageous when compared to air and noise pollution caused by existing vehicles. The low maintenance frequency and maintenance cost of electric vehicles, lower failure rates compared to conventional vehicles, and low operating costs are the strengths that can be counted.

Considering that traditional vehicles are used in cities and areas with heavy traffic and the amount of fuel consumed is high, it is clearly seen that electric vehicles are more advantageous even if the range is short. In addition, the primary cause of air pollution in city centers is fossil fuel vehicles. The superiority of electric vehicles in terms of both sound and air pollution cannot be disputed. The use of electric vehicles is environmentally friendly, does not cause pollution, and has lower energy consumption.

Considering that the resources are decreasing, there will be no fuel for fossil fuel vehicles in the near future. Electric vehicles have a structure consisting of an electric motor and transmission organs, since there are not many mechanical parts that will cause malfunctions, they can be used for a long time without any problems if regular maintenance is done. When the conditions for the use of electric vehicles are mature and the infrastructures are made suitable, it will be more advantageous than traditional vehicles in terms of *b* cost, maintenance, and fuel consumption.

However, there are also downsides of electrical vehicles. The current sales prices of electric vehicles are high, the battery life is short, so the vehicle life is also short. Electric vehicle technologies are not yet at a sufficient level. The cost of using existing electric vehicles in logistics is very high. Besides, infrastructure deficiencies exist. If the existing infrastructures are not improved, it will take time to increase their use in logistics. The low number of vehicle charging stations, the lack of charging points for different vehicle types at vehicle charging stations, and long charging times are the weaknesses of the use of electric vehicles in logistics.

In this scope, since the purchase, replacement, and maintenance costs of vehicles are high, companies seem to have no choice but to continue their activities with their existing traditional vehicles. Considering these situations, electric vehicle manufacturers should focus on producing vehicles that can be used with lower costs or take measures to reduce current costs, which will increase the use of electric vehicles. Besides, increasing the battery capacities will increase the range and increase the vehicle usage of the companies. Last but not the least, shortening electric vehicle charging times and increasing the number of fast charging points will result in a shorter vehicle charging time.

The biggest obstacle to the use of electric vehicles by logistics companies is the cost barrier. Reducing costs can increase companies' orientation toward electric vehicles. Privileges such as interest-free loans and convenience in repayments or tax cuts can support the trend toward electric vehicle use. On the other hand, sanctions such as creating zero emission areas in city centers or reducing vehicle emission values with legal restrictions may increase the use of electric vehicles. In order to increase the use of electric vehicles in logistics, it would be a suitable approach to give priority to existing problems and to start implementing fast and effective solutions immediately.

References

Aktas, E., Bloemhof, J. M., Fransoo, J. C., Günther, H. O., & Jammernegg, W. (2018). Green logistics solutions. *Flexible Services and Manufacturing Journal, 30*(3), 363–365.

Anderhofstadt, B., & Spinler, S. (2020). Preferences for autonomous and alternative fuel-powered heavy-duty trucks in Germany. *Transportation Research Part D: Transport and Environment, 79*, 102232.
Bac, U., & Erdem, M. (2021). Optimization of electric vehicle recharge schedule and routing problem with time windows and partial recharge: A comparative study for an urban logistics fleet. *Sustainable Cities and Society, 70*, 102883.
Bhuiyan, M. A., Dinçer, H., Yüksel, S., Mikhaylov, A., Danish, M. S. S., Pinter, G., Uyeh, D. D., & Stepanova, D. (2022). Economic indicators and bioenergy supply in developed economies: QROF-DEMATEL and random forest models. *Energy Reports, 8*, 561–570.
Burchart-Korol, D., Gazda-Grzywacz, M., & Zarębska, K. (2020). Research and prospects for the development of alternative fuels in the transport sector in Poland: A review. *Energies, 13*(11), 2988.
Chen, Y., Ma, J., Han, B., Zhang, P., Hua, H., Chen, H., & Su, X. (2018). Emissions of automobiles fueled with alternative fuels based on engine technology: A review. *Journal of Traffic and Transportation Engineering (English Edition), 5*(4), 318–334.
Du, L., Dinçer, H., Ersin, İ., & Yüksel, S. (2020). IT2 fuzzy-based multidimensional evaluation of coal energy for sustainable economic development. *Energies, 13*(10), 2453.
Duarte, G., Rolim, C., & Baptista, P. (2016). How battery electric vehicles can contribute to sustainable urban logistics: A real-world application in Lisbon, Portugal. *Sustainable Energy Technologies and Assessments, 15*, 71–78.
Ehrler, V. C., Schöder, D., & Seidel, S. (2021). Challenges and perspectives for the use of electric vehicles for last mile logistics of grocery e-commerce—Findings from case studies in Germany. *Research in Transportation Economics, 87*, 100757.
García-Arca, J., Comesana-Benavides, J. A., González-Portela Garrido, A. T., & Prado-Prado, J. C. (2020). Rethinking the box for sustainable logistics. *Sustainability, 12*(5), 1870.
Grzybowska, K., & Awasthi, A. (2020). Literature review on sustainable logistics and sustainable production for industry 4.0. In *Sustainable logistics and production in industry 4.0* (pp. 1–18). Springer.
Hagen, A., Langnickel, H., & Sun, X. (2019). Operation of solid oxide fuel cells with alternative hydrogen carriers. *International Journal of Hydrogen Energy, 44*(33), 18382–18392.
Halldórsson, Á., & Kovács, G. (2010). The sustainable agenda and energy efficiency: Logistics solutions and supply chains in times of climate change. *International Journal of Physical Distribution & Logistics Management, 40*(1/2), 5–13.
İmre, Ş., Çelebi, D., & Koca, F. (2021). Understanding barriers and enablers of electric vehicles in urban freight transport: Addressing stakeholder needs in Turkey. *Sustainable Cities and Society, 68*, 102794.
Inkinen, T., & Hämäläinen, E. (2020). Reviewing truck logistics: Solutions for achieving low emission road freight transport. *Sustainability, 12*(17), 6714.
Jelti, F., Allouhi, A., Al-Ghamdi, S. G., Saadani, R., Jamil, A., & Rahmoune, M. (2021). Environmental life cycle assessment of alternative fuels for city buses: A case study in Oujda city, Morocco. *International Journal of Hydrogen Energy, 46*(49), 25308–25319.
Johnson, C., Moriarty, K., Alleman, T., & Santini, D. (2021). *History of ethanol fuel adoption in the United States: Policy, economics, and logistics* (No. NREL/TP-5400-76260). National Renewable Energy Lab (NREL).
Juan, A. A., Mendez, C. A., Faulin, J., De Armas, J., & Grasman, S. E. (2016). Electric vehicles in logistics and transportation: A survey on emerging environmental, strategic, and operational challenges. *Energies, 9*(2), 86.
Kherbach, O., & Mocan, M. L. (2016). The importance of logistics and supply chain management in the enhancement of Romanian SMEs. *Procedia-Social and Behavioral Sciences, 221*, 405–413.
Kou, G., Yüksel, S., & Dinçer, H. (2022). Inventive problem-solving map of innovative carbon emission strategies for solar energy-based transportation investment projects. *Applied Energy, 311*, 118680.

Kurien, C., & Mittal, M. (2022). Review on the production and utilization of green ammonia as an alternate fuel in dual-fuel compression ignition engines. *Energy Conversion and Management, 251*, 114990.

Lebeau, P., De Cauwer, C., Van Mierlo, J., Macharis, C., Verbeke, W., & Coosemans, T. (2015). Conventional, hybrid, or electric vehicles: Which technology for an urban distribution centre? *The Scientific World Journal, 2015*, 302867.

Liu, J., Yuan, C., Hafeez, M., & Yuan, Q. (2018). The relationship between environment and logistics performance: Evidence from Asian countries. *Journal of Cleaner Production, 204*, 282–291.

Liu, Y., Gong, X., Yüksel, S., Dinçer, H., & Aydın, R. (2021). A multidimensional outlook to energy investments for the countries with continental shelf in East Mediterranean region with hybrid decision making model based on IVIF logic. *Energy Reports, 7*, 158–173.

Martins, V. W., Anholon, R., Quelhas, O. L., & Leal Filho, W. (2019). Sustainable practices in logistics systems: An overview of companies in Brazil. *Sustainability, 11*(15), 4140.

Napoli, G., Polimeni, A., Micari, S., Dispenza, G., Antonucci, V., & Andaloro, L. (2021). Freight distribution with electric vehicles: A case study in Sicily. Delivery van development. *Transportation Engineering, 3*, 100048.

Paczuski, M., Marchwiany, M., Puławski, R., Pankowski, A., Kurpiel, K., & Przedlacki, M. (2016). Liquefied petroleum gas (LPG) as a fuel for internal combustion engines. In *Alternative fuels, technical and environmental conditions*. IntechOpen.

Pfoser, S., Schauer, O., & Costa, Y. (2018). Acceptance of LNG as an alternative fuel: Determinants and policy implications. *Energy Policy, 120*, 259–267.

Pourhejazy, P., Kwon, O. K., & Lim, H. (2019). Integrating sustainability into the optimization of fuel logistics networks. *KSCE Journal of Civil Engineering, 23*(3), 1369–1383.

Rashidi, K., & Cullinane, K. (2019). Evaluating the sustainability of national logistics performance using data envelopment analysis. *Transport Policy, 74*, 35–46.

Richnák, P., & Gubová, K. (2021). Green and reverse logistics in conditions of sustainable development in enterprises in Slovakia. *Sustainability, 13*(2), 581.

Stančin, H., Mikulčić, H., Wang, X., & Duić, N. (2020). A review on alternative fuels in future energy system. *Renewable and Sustainable Energy Reviews, 128*, 109927.

Taniguchi, E., Thompson, R. G., & Yamada, T. (2016). New opportunities and challenges for city logistics. *Transportation Research Procedia, 12*, 5–13.

Tijan, E., Aksentijević, S., Ivanić, K., & Jardas, M. (2019). Blockchain technology implementation in logistics. *Sustainability, 11*(4), 1185.

Wang, Y., Luo, S., Kwok, H. Y., Pan, W., Zhang, Y., Zhao, X., & Leung, D. Y. (2021). Microfluidic fuel cells with different types of fuels: A prospective review. *Renewable and Sustainable Energy Reviews, 141*, 110806.

Yu, Z. (2021). Sustainable logistics systems: A conceptual paper. *International Journal of Circular Economy and Waste Management (IJCEWM), 1*(2), 41–48.

Yüksel, S., Eti, S., Prosekov, S., & Uluer, G. S. (2021). A study on the energy problem in the eastern Mediterranean: Text mining and AHP-based strategy recommendations. In *Strategic approaches to energy management* (pp. 27–38). Springer.

Zhang, Y., Jiang, Y., Rui, W., & Thompson, R. G. (2019). Analyzing truck fleets' acceptance of alternative fuel freight vehicles in China. *Renewable Energy, 134*, 1148–1155.

Zhang, Y., Yu, Y., & Zou, B. (2011). Analyzing public awareness and acceptance of alternative fuel vehicles in China: The case of EV. *Energy Policy, 39*(11), 7015–7024.

Zhao, Y., Xu, Y., Yüksel, S., Dinçer, H., & Ubay, G. G. (2021). Hybrid IT2 fuzzy modelling with alpha cuts for hydrogen energy investments. *International Journal of Hydrogen Energy, 46*(13), 8835–8851.

Zhu, L., Hu, L., Yüksel, S., Dinçer, H., Karakuş, H., & Ubay, G. G. (2020). Analysis of strategic directions in sustainable hydrogen investment decisions. *Sustainability, 12*(11), 4581.

Chapter 14
Does Institutional Quality Affect Renewable Energy in Oil-Rich Developing Countries? Evidence from Azerbaijan

Shahriyar Mukhtarov, Javid Aliyev, and Shahin Maharramli

Abstract This study investigates the effect of government effectiveness as a proxy of institutional quality, CO_2 emissions, and economic growth on renewable energy consumption for Azerbaijan from 1996 to 2019, employing FMOLS method. Estimation results revealed that government effectiveness and CO_2 emissions both have statistically insignificant effect on renewable energy consumption. In addition, we found that economic growth has a statistically significant and positive influence on renewable energy consumption. According to empirical results, some policy recommendations for promoting renewable energy consumption are presented in this study.

Keywords Renewable energy · Government effectiveness · Institutional quality · FMOLS · Azerbaijan

---

S. Mukhtarov (✉)
Department of Economics, Baku Engineering University, Baku, Azerbaijan

Faculty of Economics and International Relations, Vistula University, Warsaw, Poland

UNEC Empirical Research Center, Azerbaijan State University of Economics (UNEC), Baku, Azerbaijan
e-mail: smuxtarov@beu.edu.az

J. Aliyev
Department of College of Islamic Studies, Islamic Finance and Economics, Hamad Bin Khalifa, Doha, Qatar
e-mail: jaal38861@hbku.edu.qa

S. Maharramli
Department of Tariff and Statistics, Azerbaijan Energy Regulatory Agency, Baku, Azerbaijan
e-mail: shahin.maharramli@regulator.gov.az

H. Dinçer, S. Yüksel (eds.), *Circular Economy and the Energy Market*,
Contributions to Economics, https://doi.org/10.1007/978-3-031-13146-2_14

14.1 Introduction

Currently, the environmental issues in the world get more severe and the ways to address these environmental problems are becoming harder. The main disastrous outcome of rising environmental problems is global warming and climate change (Mukhtarov et al., 2022). This is the eventual footprints of the world nations that utilized the "take, make waste" approach for years, therefore the level of pollution and greenhouse gas emissions skyrocketed thanks to their linear growth strategy which did not consider environmental responsibility (Troster et al., 2018). As a consequence of these, nowadays several troubles such as decreasing biodiversity, ocean acidification, land system change, and others are sharply rising (Hua et al., 2016). It was stated by Nordhaus (1975) that a 2 °C rise in world temperature could cause irreversible problems for the habitants of planet Earth. In this regard, many actions such as Paris and Kyoto agreements were adopted by world nations (Mukhtarov et al., 2022b). Furthermore, clean and renewable energy was promoted by UNDP as one of the sustainable development goals. Considering all of these, several actions including research and investigations should be taken by society with the purpose of eliminating the detrimental effects of global warming.

With regard to global warming, one of the main indicators of it is greenhouse gas emissions (Mukhtarov, 2022; Kumar et al., 2022; Huang et al., 2022). Therefore, taking into account the importance of finding ways to reduce greenhouse gas emissions, currently, many researchers are investigating this topic with the intention of discovering potential solutions to decrease them (Watari et al., 2022; Rüdisüli et al., 2022; Lamb et al., 2022). However, the measures and policy implications of those investigations should be implemented in a way that will not deteriorate the quality of life across countries. One of the best ways to reduce CO_2 is to shift toward the alternative energy (Mukhtarov et al., 2022; Liu et al., 2021; Xie et al., 2021). This is because this energy is a very valuable substitute for conventional energy. Moreover, it can be plausibly stated that the reason behind the claim which states the transition to renewable energy will cause to decline in greenhouse gas emissions is that the main sources of renewable energy are solar and hydropower that does not produce any harmful gases to the air (Zeng et al., 2017; Mukhtarov et al., 2020). Therefore, shifting toward renewable energy could lead to a decrease in harmful emission levels. In this regard, analyzing the factors affecting clean alternative energy will be of special value to the world (Kou et al., 2022; Zhou et al., 2021; Zhe et al., 2021; Meng et al., 2021).

However, as the linear growth model which concentrates on aggressive growth without considering environmental effects has been dominant all over the world for years, shifting to new and sustainable growth model through using renewable energy is tough. Therefore, there is no clear unanimously accepted consensus among all countries toward decreasing conventional energy use significantly (Shahzad et al., 2021). To help on this issue, international institutions such as the UN, the International Energy Agency (IEA) as well as local institutions are attempting to facilitate shifting from conventional to renewable energy.

The roles of institutions are very remarkable for the economic development of the country, as well as for the maintenance of high environmental standards (Salman et al., 2019). Especially, well-operating institutions will be very effective on this issue by formulating, regulating, and implementing rules and policies on renewable energy issues (Sinha et al., 2020). According to Mohsin et al. (2021), the difference in institutional quality among nations will lead to difference in the stage of economic development in these nations. Moreover, the qualitative development of a state can foster economic prosperity and environmental quality by encouraging alternative and clean energy (Smirnova et al., 2021).

This study has several contributions. Firstly, considering the literature, there are very few studies that focused on evaluating the effect of institutional quality on renewable energy transition. On the other hand, to the best of our knowledge, no study was pursued on this phenomenon in the case of Azerbaijan.

14.2 Renewable Energy in the World and Azerbaijan

Fluctuations in oil prices put pressure on Azerbaijan to diversify its economy. At present, the struggle of mankind against climate change is intensifying and globalizing. Reducing the amount of harmful emissions into the atmosphere and replacing them with "green energy" has become one of the most important issues on the world agenda. Countries around the world are making a number of plans to reduce the operation of nuclear power plants, as well as to replace coal and gas-fired power plants with "green energy" sources (Dinçer et al., 2022; Ding et al., 2021; Haiyun et al., 2021; Dong et al., 2022). Among energy sources, the only increase in 2020 was recorded in renewable energy sources. Although global energy demand fell by 5% last year due to the pandemic, the production of renewable energy sources rose by 7%. The International Energy Agency (IEA) forecasts that an average of $440 billion will be invested annually in the renewable energy sector over the next 10 years. Production of alternative energy sources will increase by 50% over the next 5 years to 33% of global electricity production in 2025.

Azerbaijan owns its significant development after 2000 to its oil and gas resources. A country has been at the center of main oil and gas projects and managed to attract large amounts of foreign investment in this area. According to the Ministry of Energy, in February 2022, daily oil production in Azerbaijan amounted to 684.1 thousand barrels. Adriatic Pipeline (TAP) also provided an uninterrupted flow of Azerbaijani natural gas to the European market in increasing volumes and a total of 10 billion cubic meters of natural gas from Azerbaijan entered Europe via the TAP.

GDP per capita (in current USD) increased from 663 USD in 2000 to 5400 USD in 2021. However, a significant plunge in oil prices starting from 2013, proved that economic growth is heavily dependent on oil prices. A continuous decrease in oil prices has led to the devaluation of Azerbaijani Manat. For the first time since 2000, GDP fell sharply, and in subsequent years, it never returned to the 75 billion USD level of 2014 (GDP was 55 billion USD in 2021).

Azerbaijan has huge untapped renewable energy potential. According to the Ministry of Energy and International Renewable Energy Agency, the potential of economically viable and technically feasible renewable energy sources of the country is estimated at 27,000 MW (3000 MW for wind energy, 23,000 MW for solar energy, 380 MW for bioenergy potential, and 520 MW for mountain rivers).

From the high fossil fuel-dominated energy mix of Azerbaijan, it can be said that the country has not used its vast renewable energy potential widely. As it is depicted in the table above, approximately 95% of the total electricity production comes from natural gas, while share of wind, solar, waste, and hydro are nearly 6% which is significantly lower than the world average (which is 28% according to BP statistical review).

Only 17% of the total installed capacity is renewable and hydropower plants. Azerbaijan is planning to add 1500 MW of new renewable energy capacity (till 2023 440 MW, 2023–2025 460 MW, 2026–2030 600 MW) in order to reduce carbon emission by 40% by 2050 in accordance with a new commitment adopted by Azerbaijan in November 2021, at the COP26 conference in Glasgow. According to the new target, share of the installed capacity of renewable energy in the country's overall energy balance will be 30%. Azerbaijan also took a commitment to create a "Netto Zero Emission" Zone in the liberated territories.

Azerbaijan has already started the implementation of several renewable energy projects through Power Purchase Agreement. In December last year, the Ministry of Energy and Azerenergy OJSC and ACWA Power of the Kingdom of Saudi Arabia signed an "Investment Agreement" for a wind power plant with a capacity of 240 MW and the groundbreaking ceremony of this plant (Khizi-Absheron Wind Power Plant) was held with the participation of President Ilham Aliyev on January 13. As a result of the first foreign-invested project, the wind farm will generate about 1 billion kWh of electricity per year, save 220 million cubic meters of gas and prevent the release of more than 400,000 tons of CO_2 into the atmosphere.

Moreover, in April 2021, the Ministry of Energy and Azerenergy OJSC and Masdar Company of the United Arab Emirates signed an "Investment Agreement" for a 230-MW solar power plant project. The agreement envisages the production of 500 million kWh of electricity per year, which, in turn, will save 110 million cubic meters of natural gas, reduce carbon emissions by 200,000 tons, create new jobs, as well as attract new investors to other projects. The foundation of this power plant is also expected to be laid in 2022.

Moreover, on June 3, 2021, the Republic of Azerbaijan's Ministry of Energy and bp signed an implementation agreement on cooperation in the field of project appraisal and execution for the construction of a 240-MW solar power plant in the Jabrayil region. The evaluation of the solar energy project from a technical and commercial standpoint, financial issues and the adoption of a final investment decision are all part of the implementation agreement's cooperation.

To define long-term growth directions and future targets Azerbaijan adopted a new strategical document namely "Azerbaijan 2030: National Priorities for Socio-economic Development." Fifth paragraph of this document deals with the promotion of renewable energy in all sectors of the economy, fighting against climate change.

Besides, law of the Republic of Azerbaijan "On the use of renewable energy sources in the production of electricity" which is approved on May 31, 2021, also played a vital role in the promotion of renewable energy projects and it will be a main reference point for the further developments.

14.3 Literature Review

Based on the result of literature review process, it can be stated that the empirical investigations on the association between institutional quality, environmental effects, and renewable energy are very few. An example of this could be the research by Sarkodie and Adams (2018). In this paper, the authors examined the effects of economic development and political institutional quality on environmental degradation in South Africa for the period 1971–2017. The outcome revealed that institutional quality has a crucial role on the environment, and it will be very effective in promoting renewable energy transition. On the other hand, Azam et al. (2021) did a similar investigation. By using the GMM method, the study attempted to find the influence of institutional quality on energy consumption and environment on 66 selected developing countries for the time span 1991–2017. The paper measured the institutional quality index by considering three main factors which are political stability, administrative capacity, and democratic accountability. The outcome revealed that institutional quality has a positive impact on energy utilization which comes from oil and fossil fuel.

Meanwhile, many studies have predicted that renewable energy will play a positive role in improving environmental quality through CO_2 emission reduction paths (Al-Mulali et al., 2016; Dogan & Ozturk, 2017; Li & Shao, 2021). Currently, most of the papers indicate the importance of including the institutional mechanism by introducing it as the key indicator for promoting renewable energy development (Kostis et al., 2022; Li et al., 2022; Zhao et al., 2021; Yüksel et al., 2021). Li and Shao (2021) revealed that three institutional indicators which are the legal structure of the country, property rights, and legal restrictions on transactions locally and internationally in credit, labor, and products market are a significant determinants of alternative and clean energy. Moreover, Opeyemi et al. (2019) revealed that a better legal system and good finance for private sector can lead to improved renewable energy for the sub-Saharan African countries. According to the other study which was conducted by Uzar (2020) for selected 38 nations, it was found that in the long-run institutional quality affects renewable energy use positively. On the other hand, a similar research was conducted by Mehrara et al. for Economic Cooperation Countries (ECO) for the time span 1992–2011. The outcome revealed that developing institutional circumstances and human capital would significantly and positively influence the renewable energy transition.

14.4 Model and Data

14.4.1 Data

This study uses the annual data period from 1996 to 2019 for empirical evaluation. The dependent variable is renewable energy (RE) consumption, which is measured as a proportion of total final energy consumption. The CO_2 emissions (CO_2) are expressed by kilotons (kt) of carbon dioxide per capita. Economic growth is indicated by real GDP per capita (US dollars at 2010 prices). Government effectiveness (GE) shows "perceptions of the quality of public services, the quality of the civil service and the degree of its independence from political pressures, the quality of policy formulation and implementation, and the credibility of the government's commitment to such policies". The data of RE and CO_2 are obtained from Our World in Data, accordingly. The data for *Y* and GE are taken from the World Bank database. In empirical analysis, all variables are used in logarithmic form.

14.4.2 Methodology

We analyze the effect of government effectiveness as an indicator of institutional quality, economic growth, and CO_2 emissions on renewable energy consumption using the FMOLS technique. The following steps will be covered in our empirical estimation. First, we will look at the variables' non-stationarity features employing the Augmented Dickey–Fuller unit root test (Dickey & Fuller, 1981, ADF).

Second, Park's Added Variables (Park, 1992) cointegration test is utilized to evaluate the cointegration relationship. Then, the Fully Modified Ordinary Least Squares (FMOLS; Phillips & Hansen, 1990) method is employed to see long-run effect of government effectiveness, economic growth, and CO_2 emissions on renewable energy consumption.

The above-mentioned approaches are widely utilized in many studies, and in order to conserve space and avoid confusing readers with econometric complexity, they are not discussed in this study. Dickey and Fuller (1981), Phillips and Hansen (1990), Park (1992), and others provide comprehensive information on these methods.

14.5 Empirical Results and Discussion

First, we need check the stationarity of the variables. For this, we employ the ADF unit root test. Table 14.1 shows the results of the unit root test. We found that the EG, GE, *Y*, and CO_2 are non-stationary at their levels but they are stationary at first

Table 14.1 Results of ADF unit root tests

	Panel A: level		Panel B: First difference		
Variable	*k*	Actual value	*k*	Actual value	Result
EG	0	−2.415	0	−5.764***	*I*(1)
GE	0	−0.360	0	−4.491**	*I*(1)
Y	1	−1.685	1	−2.746*	*I*(1)
CO_2	0	−1.645	0	−10.461***	*I*(1)

Notes: Maximum lag order is set to two and optimal lag order (*k*) is selected based on Schwarz criterion in the ADF test; *, **, and *** accordingly indicates rejection of null hypothesis at 10%, 5%, and 1% significance levels; critical values are taken from the table prepared by MacKinnonun. Time period: 1996–2019

Table 14.2 The results of FMOLS and cointegration test

	FMOLS			Park's added variables		
	Coefficient	*t*-statistic	*p*-values	Chi-squared	df	*p*-value
GE	−0.05	−0.1123	0.912	3.832	2	0.147
Y	0.92	4.4416	0.000			
CO_2	−0.37	−0.2802	0.782			

Notes: Dependent variables is RE

difference, being integrated of order one, *I*(1), therefore, we can test them for the cointegration.

For the testing cointegration link, we used Park's Added Variables test. The results are provided at the right side of Table 14.2. The cointegration test confirmed that the variables have a long-term link. As a result, we can say that the variables have a cointegrating relationship. Lastly, we apply the FMOLS technique to estimate the long-run coefficients. The estimation results of FMOLS are given at the left side of Table 14.2.

As can be seen from Table 14.2, the effect of government effectiveness as a proxy of institutional quality is to be found statistically insignificant. The insignificant influence of institutional quality on renewable energy consumption indicates that Azerbaijan, as a developing country, performs poorly on institutional quality indicators. As is widely known, bureaucrats in countries with low institutional quality who are trying to maximize their personal interests may fail to evaluate the environmental impact of certain authorized projects. Therefore, low institutional quality cannot avoid the loosening of environmental policies. As a result, renewable energy transition cannot be stimulated. In addition, the impact of real GDP per capita on renewable energy consumption is positive and statistically significant at the 1% level. This shows that a 1% increase in real GDP per capita results in 0.92% increase in renewable energy consumption. It implies that Azerbaijan's expanding revenues from traditional energy sources have been diverted to renewable energy sources. We also find that CO_2 emissions have a negative and statistically insignificant influence on renewable energy use. The insignificant influence of CO_2 emissions on renewable energy consumption also verifies the country's aversion to renewables. Rising CO_2

emissions and environmental deterioration do not compel the country to pursue a more ecologically friendly energy path.

14.6 Conclusion and Policy Recommendation

This study analyzes the influence of government effectiveness as an indicator of institutional quality, economic growth, and CO_2 emissions on renewable energy consumption in Azerbaijan. The results of ADF unit root test indicate all variables have the same integration order, which is $I(1)$. Therefore, the cointegration link between the variables can be evaluated. Long-run co-movement was evaluated employing Park's Added Variables and found a long-run cointegration relationship. The FMOLS method was utilized to evaluate possible long-run links. The empirical results stated that government effectiveness as a proxy of institutional quality, and CO_2 emissions are statistically insignificant. In addition, the impact of economic growth is revealed as positive and statistically significant.

Azerbaijan has made crucial steps in the implementation of utility-scale renewable energy scales through Power Purchase Agreement. The government is committed to purchasing the energy produced and offers investors a range of investments, tax breaks, and other favorable terms. Although Feed-in tariff is the most effective mechanism to promote production from renewable sources, it seems the government of Azerbaijan would not be inclined to implement this mechanism since it leads to a significant increase in retail prices. Or government has to subsidize a difference between retail and feed-in tariff prices. However, the development of small and micro-scale renewable energy projects is also vital and the country has to create a favorable environment for prosumers. Considering the European experience, the following suggestions on mechanisms to promote renewable energy production can be listed:

- **Net metering schemes**

  Under this scheme, excess electricity which is injected into the grid by the consumer can be used to offset electricity used by consumer when renewable energy system does not generate electricity. Current wholesale and retail tariffs, this system would be beneficial for consumers with higher consumption levels (monthly around 800–1000 kWh). If injected energy could be enumerated at retail tariffs instead of wholesale ones, typical households would also benefit from the scheme.
- **Reimbursement of a certain part of the initial investment cost (30–50%) by third parties (Energy Efficiency Fund, international organizations, and especially government)**

  In European practice, in many countries, prosumers are rewarded with a number of grants and subsidies for initial investment costs for renewable energy production facilities and energy storage batteries. Given that the cost of these facilities is high enough for those interested in becoming prosumer in Azerbaijan, some of these investment costs must be covered by the state or another third party.

- **Establishment of incentives mechanisms for the installation of energy storage batteries to reduce network loads and ensure system security**

  Energy storage batteries have a special place in the new energy directives of the European Union. Europe encourages prosumers to use more energy instead of injecting it to the grid. The additional energy produced can be used by the prosumers to operate heat pumps, air conditioners, and other equipment. Government can cover some or full part of battery investments (Serezli et al., 2021; Bhuiyan et al., 2022; Adalı et al., 2022; Fang et al., 2021; Yüksel et al., 2022).

- **Allocation of low-interest loans for renewable energy producers and tax exemptions**

  Considering higher level of interest rates in Azerbaijan, financial availability can be a serious problem for those willing to get prosumer status. Government or relevant state agencies have to provide low-interest loans. Renewable energy production facilities and sales revenue of prosumers from injecting electricity also have to be exempted from all taxes and duties.

References

Adalı, Z., Dinçer, H., Eti, S., Mikhaylov, A., & Yüksel, S. (2022). Identifying new perspectives on geothermal energy investments. In *Multidimensional strategic outlook on global competitive energy economics and finance*. Emerald Publishing Limited.

Al-Mulali, U., Ozturk, I., & Solarin, S. A. (2016). Investigating the environmental Kuznets curve hypothesis in seven regions: The role of renewable energy. *Ecological Indicators, 67*, 267–282. https://doi.org/10.1016/j.ecolind.2016.02.059

Azam, M., Liu, L., & Ahmad, N. (2021). Impact of institutional quality on environment and energy consumption: Evidence from developing world. *Environment, Development and Sustainability, 23*(2), 1646–1667. https://doi.org/10.1007/s10668-020-00644-x

Bhuiyan, M. A., Dinçer, H., Yüksel, S., Mikhaylov, A., Danish, M. S. S., Pinter, G., Uyeh, D. D., & Stepanova, D. (2022). Economic indicators and bioenergy supply in developed economies: QROF-DEMATEL and random forest models. *Energy Reports, 8*, 561–570.

Dickey, D., & Fuller, W. (1981). Likelihood ratio statistics for autoregressive time series with a unit root. *Econometrica, 49*, 1057–1072.

Dinçer, H., Yüksel, S., & Martínez, L. (2022). Collaboration enhanced hybrid fuzzy decision-making approach to analyze the renewable energy investment projects. *Energy Reports, 8*, 377–389.

Ding, Z., Yüksel, S., & Dincer, H. (2021). An Integrated Pythagorean fuzzy soft computing approach to environmental management systems for sustainable energy pricing. *Energy Reports, 7*, 5575–5588.

Dogan, E., & Ozturk, I. (2017). The influence of renewable and non-renewable energy consumption and real income on CO2 emissions in the USA: Evidence from structural break tests. *Environmental Science and Pollution Research, 24*(11), 10846–10854. https://doi.org/10.1007/s11356-017-8786-y

Dong, W., Zhao, G., Yüksel, S., Dinçer, H., & Ubay, G. G. (2022). A novel hybrid decision making approach for the strategic selection of wind energy projects. *Renewable Energy, 185*, 321–337.

Fang, S., Zhou, P., Dinçer, H., & Yüksel, S. (2021). Assessment of safety management system on energy investment risk using house of quality based on hybrid stochastic interval-valued intuitionistic fuzzy decision-making approach. *Safety Science, 141*, 105333.

Haiyun, C., Zhixiong, H., Yüksel, S., & Dinçer, H. (2021). Analysis of the innovation strategies for green supply chain management in the energy industry using the QFD-based hybrid interval valued intuitionistic fuzzy decision approach. *Renewable and Sustainable Energy Reviews, 143*, 110844.

Hua, Y., Oliphant, M., & Hu, E. J. (2016). Development of renewable energy in Australia and China: A comparison of policies and status, renew. *Energy, 85*, 1044–1051. https://doi.org/10.1016/j.renene.2015.07.060

Huang, D., Du, Y., Xu, Q., & Ko, J. H. (2022). Quantification and control of gaseous emissions from solid waste landfill surfaces. *Journal of Environmental Management, 302*, 114001.

Kostis, P., Dinçer, H., & Yüksel, S. (2022). Knowledge-based energy investments of European economies and policy recommendations for sustainable development. *Journal of the Knowledge Economy*, 1–33.

Kou, G., Yüksel, S., & Dinçer, H. (2022). Inventive problem-solving map of innovative carbon emission strategies for solar energy-based transportation investment projects. *Applied Energy, 311*, 118680.

Kumar, A., Singh, P., Raizada, P., & Hussain, C. M. (2022). Impact of COVID-19 on greenhouse gases emissions: A critical review. *Science of the Total Environment, 806*, 150349.

Lamb, W. F., Grubb, M., Diluiso, F., & Minx, J. C. (2022). Countries with sustained greenhouse gas emissions reductions: An analysis of trends and progress by sector. *Climate Policy, 22*(1), 1–17.

Li, J., Yüksel, S., Dınçer, H., Mikhaylov, A., & Barykin, S. E. (2022). Bipolar q-ROF hybrid decision making model with golden cut for analyzing the levelized cost of renewable energy alternatives. *IEEE Access, 10*, 42507–42517.

Li, S., & Shao, Q. (2021). Exploring the determinants of renewable energy innovation considering the institutional factors: A negative binomial analysis. *Technology in Society, 67*, 101680. https://doi.org/10.1016/j.techsoc.2021.101680

Liu, J., Lv, J., Dinçer, H., Yüksel, S., & Karakuş, H. (2021). Selection of renewable energy alternatives for green blockchain investments: A hybrid IT2-based fuzzy modelling. *Archives of Computational Methods in Engineering, 28*(5), 3687–3701.

Meng, Y., Wu, H., Zhao, W., Chen, W., Dinçer, H., & Yüksel, S. (2021). A hybrid heterogeneous Pythagorean fuzzy group decision modelling for crowdfunding development process pathways of fintech-based clean energy investment projects. *Financial Innovation, 7*(1), 1–34.

Mohsin, M., Kamran, H. W., Nawaz, M. A., Hussain, M. S., & Dahri, A. S. (2021). Assessing the impact of transition from nonrenewable to renewable energy consumption on economic growth-environmental nexus from developing Asian economies. *Journal of Environmental Management, 284*, 111999. https://doi.org/10.1016/j.jenvman.2021.111999

Mukhtarov, S. (2022). The impact of carbon pricing on international competitiveness in the case of Azerbaijan. *Environmental Science and Pollution Research, 29*(22), 33587–33594. https://doi.org/10.1007/s11356-022-18606-3

Mukhtarov, S., Mikayilov, J. I., Humbatova, S., & Muradov, V. (2020). Do high oil prices obstruct the transition to renewable energy consumption? *Sustainability, 12*(11), 4689.

Mukhtarov, S., Mikayilov, J. I., Maharramov, S., Aliyev, J., & Suleymanov, E. (2022b). Higher oil prices, are they good or bad for renewable energy consumption: The case of Iran? *Renewable Energy, 186*, 411–419. https://doi.org/10.1016/j.renene.2021.12.135

Mukhtarov, S., Yüksel, S., & Dinçer, H. (2022). The impact of financial development on renewable energy consumption: Evidence from Turkey. *Renewable Energy, 187*, 169–176.

Nordhaus, W. D. (1975). *Can we control carbon dioxide?* IIASA Working Paper. IIASA. Copyright, by the author(s). Retrieved from http://pure.iiasa.ac.at/365/

Opeyemi, A., Uchenna, E., Simplice, A., & Evans, O. (2019). Renewable energy, trade performance and the conditional role of finance and institutional capacity in sub-Sahara African countries. *Energy Policy, 132*, 490–498.

Park, J. (1992). Canonical cointegrating regressions. *Econometrica, 60*, 119–143.

Phillips, P., & Hansen, B. (1990). Statistical inference in instrumental variables regression with I (1) processes. *Review of Economic Studies, 57*, 99–125.

Rüdisüli, M., Bach, C., Bauer, C., Beloin-Saint-Pierre, D., Elber, U., Georges, G., Limpach, R., Pareschi, G., Kannan, R., & Teske, S. L. (2022). Prospective life-cycle assessment of greenhouse gas emissions of electricity-based mobility options. *Applied Energy, 306*, 118065.

Salman, M., Long, X., Dauda, L., & Mensah, C. N. (2019). The impact of institutional quality on economic growth and carbon emissions: Evidence from Indonesia, South Korea and Thailand. *Journal of Cleaner Production, 241*, 118331.

Sarkodie, S. A., & Adams, S. (2018). Renewable energy, nuclear energy, and environmental pollution: Accounting for political institutional quality in South Africa. *Science of the Total Environment, 643*, 1590–1601. https://doi.org/10.1016/j.scitotenv.2018.06.320

Serezli, E., Yüksel, S., Tamer, İ., & Dinçer, H. (2021). The role of innovative renewable energy investment strategies on macroeconomic stability. In *Financial strategies in competitive markets* (pp. 165–178). Springer.

Shahzad, U., Dogan, B., Sinha, A., & Fareed, Z. (2021). Does export product diversification help to reduce energy demand: Exploring the contextual evidences from the newly industrialized countries. *Energy, 214*, 118881. https://doi.org/10.1016/j.energy.2020.118881

Sinha, A., Sengupta, T., & Alvarado, R. (2020). Interplay between technological innovation and environmental quality: Formulating the SDG policies for next 11 economies. *Journal of Cleaner Production, 242*, 118549. https://doi.org/10.1016/j.jclepro.2019.118549

Smirnova, E., Szczepańska-Woszczyna, K., Yessetova, S., Samusenkov, V., & Rogulin, R. (2021). Supplying energy to vulnerable segments of the population: Macro-financial risks and public welfare. *Energies, 14*(7), 1834. https://doi.org/10.3390/en14071834

Troster, V., Shahbaz, M., & Uddin, G. S. (2018). Renewable energy, oil prices, and economic activity: A Granger-causality in quantiles analysis. *Energy Economics, 70*, 440–452.

Uzar, U. (2020). Political economy of renewable energy: Does institutional quality make a difference in renewable energy consumption? *Renewable Energy, 155*, 591–603. https://doi.org/10.1016/j.renene.2020.03.172

Watari, T., Northey, S., Giurco, D., Hata, S., Yokoi, R., Nansai, K., & Nakajima, K. (2022). Global copper cycles and greenhouse gas emissions in a 1.5 °C world. *Resources, Conservation and Recycling, 179*, 106118.

Xie, Y., Zhou, Y., Peng, Y., Dinçer, H., Yüksel, S., & an Xiang, P. (2021). An extended Pythagorean fuzzy approach to group decision-making with incomplete preferences for analyzing balanced scorecard-based renewable energy investments. *IEEE Access, 9*, 43020–43035.

Yüksel, S., Dinçer, H., Çağlayan, Ç., Uluer, G. S., & Lisin, A. (2022). Bitcoin mining with nuclear energy. In *Multidimensional strategic outlook on global competitive energy economics and finance*. Emerald Publishing Limited.

Yüksel, S., Mikhaylov, A., Ubay, G. G., & Uyeh, D. D. (2021). The role of hydrogen in the Black Sea for the future energy supply security of Turkey. In *Handbook of research on strategic management for current energy investments* (pp. 1–15). IGI Global.

Zeng, M., Li, C., & Zhou, L. S. (2017). Progress and prospective on the police system of renewable energy in China. *Renewable and Sustainable Energy Reviews, 20*, 36–44.

Zhao, Y., Xu, Y., Yüksel, S., Dinçer, H., & Ubay, G. G. (2021). Hybrid IT2 fuzzy modelling with alpha cuts for hydrogen energy investments. *International Journal of Hydrogen Energy, 46*(13), 8835–8851.

Zhe, L., Yüksel, S., Dinçer, H., Mukhtarov, S., & Azizov, M. (2021). The positive influences of renewable energy consumption on financial development and economic growth. *SAGE Open, 11*(3), 21582440211040133.

Zhou, P., Luo, J., Cheng, F., Yüksel, S., & Dinçer, H. (2021). Analysis of risk priorities for renewable energy investment projects using a hybrid IT2 hesitant fuzzy decision-making approach with alpha cuts. *Energy, 224*, 120184.

Chapter 15
Comparative Study of the Forecasting Solar Energy Generation in Istanbul

Kevser Şahinbaş

Abstract The importance of renewable energy sources makes it extremely important day by day due to the limited reserves of fossil fuels and the damage they cause to the environment. Fossil fuels play an important role in electrical energy production. This situation brings up the necessity of turning to alternative sources that cause the formation of renewable energies such as solar energy, which is one of the renewable energy sources. Solar energy is a renewable energy source with benefits such as ease of installation and use, as well as the fact that it does not pollute the environment or produce toxic waste. In the world and in our country, investments in solar power plants are increasing rapidly from year to year. In this study, the solar energy situation of our country was discussed and a model for solar energy generation forecasting was proposed by using RNN, LSTM, and GRU deep learning architecture using the İkitelli Solar Power Plant daily data of Istanbul between May 2018 and May 2019. Generation forecasting values for 5 days later were estimated with 0.0069 error and 0.92 R^2 values, which are accepted as one of the most important performance criteria by the LSTM model. The LSTM model's solar energy generation values are slightly greater than those of the other models, it can be concluded that the LSTM model is appropriate for forecasting solar energy generation.

Keywords Solar energy · Green energy · Energy consumption · Energy prediction

15.1 Introduction

Because of their low cost and huge contribution to carbon reduction, the power sector is transitioning toward renewable energy sources. Solar energy is swiftly establishing itself as one of the most promising sources of power for residential, commercial, and industrial applications. The energy needs of developing countries

K. Şahinbaş (✉)
The School of Business, İstanbul Medipol University, Istanbul, Turkey
e-mail: ksahinbas@medipol.edu.tr

H. Dinçer, S. Yüksel (eds.), *Circular Economy and the Energy Market*,
Contributions to Economics, https://doi.org/10.1007/978-3-031-13146-2_15

are increasing day by day. The energy required for this increasing need cannot be produced due to limited resources. For this reason, in order to meet its energy needs, it can meet its needs thanks to the energy it receives from different countries. However, it has to allocate a certain budget for the energy consumed in economic terms. For this reason, it may cause the country to weaken economically. In order for the budget not to be transferred to other countries, the country should prevent this situation by finding more economical and long-term solutions with its own internal resources. Otherwise, long-term dependence on foreign countries may bring some negativities for the country. Due to the increase in the need for energy, the sustainability of fossil fuel power plants is possible with different energy sources. However, due to the restricted usage of fossil fuels, sustainability may not be attainable. Furthermore, due to the finite reserves of fossil fuels and the environmental harm they create, it is necessary to diversify sources.

In parallel with the developing technology, it is possible to develop different alternative sources. These alternative energy sources, on the other hand, reveal different types of energy by making transformations thanks to different systems thanks to the energy they receive from the world. Solar energy systems, one of these systems, reveal an alternative energy source by converting the energy received from the sun into different energy forms. These energy forms are systems that convert solar energy into heat or electrical energy.

Solar panels convert direct sunlight to electrical energy. Thanks to the development of semiconductor technology, this energy can be converted into electrical energy thanks to diodes, which are solar energy semiconductor materials. In this way, it offers a more environmentally friendly energy alternative as an alternative to fossil fuel energy sources. Photovoltaic systems are preferred to be used because of their advantages such as being easy to install, environmentally friendly and safe (Doğanay, 2021).

Due to its geographic position, Turkey has a lot of potential for solar energy. The average annual total sunshine duration is 2741.07 h, and the average annual total radiation value is computed as 1527.46 kWh/m^2, according to the Turkey Solar Energy Potential Atlas (GEPA) (Yolcan & Ramazan, 2020).

The aim of this study is to demonstrate the forecasting solar production for Istanbul, İkitelli Solar Power Plant by using deep learning algorithms such as RNN, LSTM, and GRU. Experiments and findings are obtained and explained in detail.

In this chapter, we describe the solar energy potential in Turkey and İstanbul. We demonstrate the importance of the solar energy production. Section 15.2 includes methods for forecasting. In Sect. 15.3, Dataset and experiments are detailed. In Sect. 15.4, chapter is concluded.

15.2 Related Works

Huang et al. provide a model for predicting and analyzing electricity consumption data in Shanghai, Jiangsu, and Zhejiang using multilayer perceptron (MLP) and long short-term memory (LSTM) neural networks. During the control experiments, the accuracy of the prediction result is increased with the advanced algorithm. The proposed algorithm proves to be an effective method for PV power generation prediction. Adam and SDG are used to set the MLP and LSTM parameters. Log data of PV power generation is incorporated into monthly data and LSTM is utilized to forecast monthly data to further examine the forecast accuracy of PV power generation. The findings of the study demonstrate that both MLP and LSTM networks perform well when it comes to time series prediction.

Abu-Salih et al. propose multiple models for forecasting short-term renewable energy use and generation using real-time energy facts from smart meters via installed rooftop PV in Western Australia from August 2018 to April 2019. Findings from their study indicate that in forecasting both energy consumption and generation, the optimized deep learning-based Long-Term Short Memory (LSTM) model outperforms the basic model as well as alternative classical and machine learning methods (Abu-Salih et al., 2022).

Huang et al. examine the solar power generation prediction in a laboratory-level microgrid. ARMA and Persistence models are used for their applicability in a microgrid. The reasons for choosing the rigging and permanence models are their simplicity, low cost, and timely and accurate forecasting. The persistence model has been used because it is effective in very short-term forecasts. Historical solar radiation data from SolarAnywhere is obtained, and historical solar generation data is simulated by SAM. The ARMA model is implemented in the System Identification Toolbox, a MATLAB platform. The persistence model is used as a comparison in the paper by Huang et al. (2012a, b).

Zhu et al. (2021) propose a framework that directly takes the normal irradiance as the estimation target and proposes the SCNN-LSTM model to estimate the inter-clock DNI. The experiment was conducted using 2 years of historical observation data provided by NREL. The proposed Siamese Convolutional Neural Network has the advantage of CNN and Siamese Network. Experiments show that the SCNN-LSTM model has superior performance in estimating DNI 10 min ahead.

In the study of Pan et al. (2020), a very short-term solar production forecasting management based on TA-LSTM and LSTM is proposed. The LSTM prediction incorporates the temporal attention mechanism model to improve prediction accuracy. Experimental results have shown that the proposed method is effective. MAE and RMSE evaluation metrics are used for performance evaluation. TA-LSTM outperforms LSTM in terms of RMSE and MAE. In addition, the proposed method shows better prediction performance when compared to ANN.

15.3 Solar Energy Potential in Turkey

Because of its geographic location, Turkey has a large solar energy potential. According to the GEPA's general potential assessment and monthly average global radiation distribution, solar-based energy installed power was 6667 MW at the end of December 2020, accounting for 3.6% of total electricity production and its share in the installed power change and total electricity generation by years is as follows: Installed Power (MV) is 40 in 2014, 249 in 2015, 833 in 2016, 3421 in 2017, 5063 in 2018, 5995 in 2019, 6667 in 2020. Percentage share in total electricity production is 2014 It is 0.01 in 2015, 0.38 in 2016, 0.97 in 2017, 2.56 in 2018, 3.04 in 2019 and 3.66 in 2020 (https://enerji.gov.tr/eigm-yenilenebilir-enerji-kaynaklar-gunes).

While Istanbul is the most important city in Turkey with its historical significance, it is also among the most important cities in the world, both historically and geopolitically. According to 2019 data obtained from the Turkish Statistical Institute [TUIK] database, the Gross Domestic Product of Istanbul corresponds to 31% of the country's total (TUIK, 2019a). The population of Istanbul corresponds to 18.6% of Turkey's population (TUIK, 2019b). T.R. According to the Istanbul Governorship, the city has a 20.3% share in the Turkish workforce, 50.6% in exports, and 54.6% in imports (İstanbul Valiliği, 2021). These indicators reveal the economic value of Istanbul. According to 2016 year-end data, the share of Istanbul in Turkey's total electricity consumption is 17.39%. Considering the installed energy power in Istanbul, the ratio of production to consumption is 18%. In other words, Istanbul consumes more than five times as much electricity as it produces and provides the majority of its energy consumption with fossil fuels.

When renewable energy studies in Istanbul are examined, the prominent issue is the determination of the potential (Görgülü, 2019; Gün, 2019; Unan, 2019). In addition, evaluations in terms of combating climate change and decarbonization, economic and environmental analyzes over established renewable systems (Sulukan, 2020) and studies on increasing the weight of renewable energy in energy supply within the framework of the concept of "smart cities" (Yazıcı, 2019). In the literature review, almost no studies were found regarding the current situation of renewable energy in Istanbul and policy recommendations for increasing renewable resources in energy supply.

15.4 Methods

15.4.1 Recurrent Neural Network

Recurrent Neural Networks (RNNs) are a family of specialized neural networks for processing sequential data (Rumelhart et al., 1986). It is based on the logic of incorporating the information of the previous situation into the system along with the current situation.

15.4.1.1 Simple Recurrent Network

Simple Recurrent Network RNN subtype of the model. The hidden layer data (H_t) of the current state input (X_t) state of the SRN enters the next state. The following equations are used in the calculations of the model.

$$h_t = \tanh\left(W_{xh}x_t + W_{hh}h_{t-1} + b_h\right) \tag{15.1}$$

$$y_t = \tanh\left(W_{hy}h_t + b_y\right) \tag{15.2}$$

In the equations, the current input is shown as x_t, the hidden layer information from the previous moment is $ht - 1$, and the hidden layer information that will be used in this node and sent to the other node is shown as ht. W_{xh} is the W_{hh} and W_{hy} weight matrix. b_h and b_y bias vectors. The activation function tanh is the Hyperbolic Tangent Function.

Since the SRN model is known as the RNN model, the RNN nomenclature will be used in this study.

15.4.1.2 Long Short-Term Memory

This section contains information about the LSTM model used in the study. LSTM is a deep learning algorithm that can learn long-term dependencies (Wang et al., 2019). The LSTM algorithm is also used in areas such as text recognition, speech recognition, machine translation, as well as solving problems in the field of cyber security. The LSTM structure has input, output, and forget layers that are not in a recursive network structure. The first step in the LSTM structure is to decide whether to forget the data on the network. For example, when the forgetting layer is transferred from one environment to another, that environment is removed from the model if the old environment is not required for the model to run. In order to use the time series in the deep learning model, it must be converted to a supervised learning method. Sliding window method, time can be used to transform the series into a supervised learning approach. This method consists of using previous timesteps to estimate the value in the next timestep. The main purpose of using the sliding window method is to use deep learning algorithms when the output is precise according to the time series. The basic logic of this approach is to examine the value at the current time (t) and to predict the value at the next time t (t + 1).

In the RNN structure, the problem arises that the derivative of the activation function decreases and disappears or reaches very large values because of the use of large time series (Sherstinsky, 2020). As a solution to this disadvantage, computer scientists Hochreiter and Schmidhuber introduced the LSTM structure in 1997. In the LSTM structure, there are input, output and forgetting layers that are not in the recursive network structure (Hochreiter & Schmidhuber, 1997). The first step of the LSTM structure is to decide whether the data in the network can be forgotten or not. For example, when the forgetting layer is passed from one environment to another environment, that environment is removed from the model if the old environment is not necessary for the model to run.

Long Short-Term Memory (LSTM) is a subtype of the RNN architecture. The output and hidden layer parameters of LSTM are calculated using the following formulas:

$$i_t = \sigma(W_{xi}x_t + W_{hi}h_{t-1} + W_{ci}c_{t-1} + b_i) \tag{15.3}$$

$$f_t = \sigma(W_{xf}x_t + W_{hf}h_{t-1} + W_{cf}c_{t-1} + b_f) \tag{15.4}$$

$$c_t = f_t c_{t-1} + i_t \tanh(W_{xc}x_t + W_{hc}h_{t-1} + b_c) \tag{15.5}$$

$$o_t = \sigma(W_{xo}x_t + W_{ho}h_{t-1} + W_{co}c_t + b_o) \tag{15.6}$$

$$h_t = o_t \tanh(C_t)$$

Equation of the structure consisting of entrance gate(i), forget gate(f), exit gate (o), and cell state(c). The expression t indicates the current state and the expression t1 indicates the previous state. In Eq. (15.3), W_{xi}, W_{hi}, W_{ci} express the weight matrix and the b_i bias vector.

In Eq. (15.4), W_{xf}, W_{hf}, W_{cf} denotes the weight matrix and b_f the bias vector. In Eq. (15.5), W_{xc} denotes the weight matrix W_{hc} and b_c the bias vector. W_{xo} represents the W_{ho}, W_{co} weight matrix, and b_o bias vector. In equations σ is the sigmoid function. tanh is the Hyperbolic Tangent Function.

15.4.1.3 Gated Recurrent Units

Gated Recurrent Units (GRU) is a subtype of RNN, which is a simplified version of the LSTM system. When the GRU structure is examined, the difference of the method from LSTM is that a single gate unit controls both the forget factor and the update decision of the state unit at the same time (Goodfellow et al., 2018). The GRU structure consists of the update unit (z_t) and the delete unit (r_t), which are used as forget and state units. The equations of the GRU architecture are given between Eqs. (15.8) and (15.11) (Cho et al., 2014). As seen in the equations, t represents the current time, the previous time ($t - 1$), the hidden layer h_t, the current input x_t. W_{ir}, W_{hr}, W_{iz}, W_{hz}, W_{in}, W_{hn} represent the weight matrix. b_{ir}, b_{hr}, b_{iz}, b_{hz}, b_{in}, b_{hn} are bias vectors.

σ is the sigmoid function, tanh is the Hyperbolic Tangent Function.

$$r_t = \sigma(W_{ir}x_t + b_{ir} + W_{hr}h_{(t-1)} + b_{hr}) \tag{15.7}$$

$$z_t = \sigma(W_{iz}x_t + b_{iz} + W_{hz}h_{(t-1)} + b_{hz}) \tag{15.8}$$

$$\tilde{h}_t = \tanh\left(W_{in}x_t + b_{in} + r_t * \left(W_{hn}h_{(t-1)} + b_{hn}\right)\right) \tag{15.9}$$

$$h_t = (1 - z_t) * \tilde{h}_t + z_t * h_{(t-1)} \tag{15.10}$$

15.4.2 Error Metrics

Conventional error indicators RMSE (Root Mean Square Error), MAPE (Mean Absolute Percentage Error), and MAE (Mean) are used to evaluate the results of applications developed for solar power generation forecasting. Absolute Error and R^2 error metrics are used. Error rates are calculated by considering the difference between each predictive value ($\overline{y}_i$) and the actual value (y_i) for an array with n elements. The calculation equations for RMSE, MAPE, MAE, and R^2 are shown in the following equations, respectively (Willmott, 1982):

$$\text{RMSE} = \sqrt{\frac{1}{n}\sum_{i=1}^{n}\left(\overline{y_i} - y_i\right)^2} \tag{15.11}$$

$$\text{MAPE} = \frac{1}{n}\sum_{i=1}^{n}\frac{|\overline{y_i} - y_i|}{y_i} \tag{15.12}$$

$$\text{MAE} = \sum_{i=1}^{n}\frac{|\overline{y_i} - y_i|}{y_i} \tag{15.13}$$

$$R^2 = \frac{\sum(x - \overline{x})(y - \overline{y})}{\sum(x - \overline{x})^2 \sum(y - \overline{y})^2} \tag{15.14}$$

15.5 Dataset

IETT İkitelli Factory Solar Power Plant (GES) is located in the İkitelli region of Küçükçekmece district of Istanbul. Operated by IETT, a subsidiary of IETT, the power plant is Turkey's 1993 and Istanbul's 57th largest power plant with an installed power of 9.24 kWe. The solar power plant is also Turkey's 584th largest. With an average of 13.490 kWh electricity production, the IETT Kitelli Factory Solar Power Plant can cover all of the electrical energy needs of 4 people in their everyday lives (such as home, industry, metro transportation, government offices, and environmental lighting). When solely domestic electricity usage is considered, the IETT İkitelli Factory Solar Power Plant provides enough electricity to cover the demands of five households.

The dataset about Electricity Generation Quantities from the İkitelli Solar Power Plant is obtained from the IBB website.[1] The dataset includes daily 15-min 20.216 data for the 1200-kWp solar power plant in the İkitelli Drinking Water Treatment Facility of the Istanbul Water and Sewerage Administration (İSKİ) from May 2018 to May 2019. Electricity amounts were produced in May, June, August, September, November, December 2018 and February, March, April, May 2019.

15.6 Experiments and Findings

In this section, RNN, LSTM, and GRU algorithms that are frequently preferred in time series analysis, on solar generation data has been used and the findings obtained as a result of the analysis are shown in detail. Analysis processes were carried out with the Spyder interface on the Anaconda platform using the Python programming language, which offers a rich library for deep learning models.

15.6.1 Data Preprocessing

The column with Date has been converted to date format with format = '%Y-%m-%d %H: %M: %S'. After converting to Date format, the appearance of the data is as shown below:

Date	Generation_kWh
2018-05-01 07:30:00	10.0
2018-05-01 07:45:00	20.0
2018-05-01 08:00:00	0.0
2018-05-01 08:15:00	0.0
2018-05-01 08:30:00	20.0
2018-05-01 08:45:00	20.0
2018-05-01 09:00:00	30.0
2018-05-01 09:15:00	70.0
2018-05-01 09:30:00	40.0
2018-05-01 09:45:00	70.0

Production time consists of 15 min of data. For analysis, 15 min of data were collected and converted into 1-h data. Aggregation code: data = data.resample (rule='H', closed='left', label ='right').sum().

[1] https://data.ibb.gov.tr/dataset/ikitelli-gunes-enerjisi-santrali-elektrik-uretim-miktarlari

The appearance of the data is as follows:

Date	Generation_kWh
2018-05-01 08:00:00	30.0
2018-05-01 09:00:00	40.0
2018-05-01 10:00:00	210.0
2018-05-01 11:00:00	390.0
2018-05-01 12:00:00	660.0
2018-05-01 13:00:00	910.0
2018-05-01 14:00:00	970.0
2018-05-01 15:00:00	900.0

The missing value is filled with the mean method.

15.6.2 Normalizer Filter

The data were then normalized. The large differences between the data affect the learning accuracy of some classification methods. The purpose of applying normalization is to facilitate the comparison of data by eliminating the differences between mathematical operations and data. In this study, the data were normalized using the Standard Scaler in the Python programming language sklearn. Preprocessing library in RNN, LSTM, and GRU algorithms.

15.6.3 Splitting Data into Training and Testing

In order for the created model to learn, the data is divided into certain proportions. Some of them are for learning and the rest is for testing what they have learned. The percentage separation (Holdout cross validation) method used in this study also serves this purpose. With the help of this method, the data were divided into 2 different groups, X and Y data, of which 80% was learning data and 20% was test data. The purpose of doing this is when the model is used to retest the data we trained with the learning dataset. Measuring success will not yield accurate results. When we give the model to a dataset that the model has not encountered before, the measurement of the learning success of the model will give a result close to the truth. Sixteen thousand data trains and 2986 data were used for testing.

15.6.4 Hyperparameters of RNN, LSTM, and GRU

After the data preprocessing process was completed, RNN and LSTM models were established. The models use many parameters. The values of these hyperparameters can change the performance of the models. The hyperparameters used in the models are explained below:

- Feature Extraction: The production estimation is seq_len = 5 days. For the data, matrices such as the following matrices were created. For example, to estimate the solar energy on the 6th day, it is estimated by taking the values of 1, 2, 3, 4, and 5 days.
  # [[[1], [2], [3], [4], [5]]] [6]
  # [[[2], [3], [4], [5], [6]]] [7]
  # [[[3], [4], [5], [6], [7]]] [8]
- Number of Layers: 40 layers in RNN, LSTM, and GRU models used.
- Number of Nodes: 512 nodes are used in each layer in RNN, LSTM, and GRU models.
- Training Cycle (Epoch): Each study was run for 50 cycles by trial and error.
- Learning rate: It used 0.0001 learning steps in our experiments.
- Training and Test Ratio: 16,000 of each dataset is reserved for train and 2986 for testing.
- Batch Size: Group size in each trial.
- It was taken as 1000.
- Activation Function: relu is used as the activation function.
- Hidden Layers is 3.
- Optimizer is Adam.
- After each layer, the normalization process and the line.
- Dropout process has been applied.
- Error rate: MSE, RMSE, MAE, and R^2 values are used to find the error rate.

15.6.5 Results

In the LSTM, RNN, and GRU models; various methods were tried by changing Epochs (Parameters showing how many iterations the algorithm will be trained with the dataset), Batch (the amount taken at once) and Neuron numbers, and the best result was found in the experiment with 50 epochs, 32 batches, and 64 neurons. With these parameters used in the training of the network, the closest estimation values to the real values were obtained. However, the error criteria calculated in the estimation with RNN, LSTM, and GRU are RMSE, MSE, MAE, and R^2.

Table 15.1 Performance of the RNN-based model in terms of RMSE, MSE, and MAE

Model	RMSE	MSE	MAE	R^2
RNN	0.09475	0.00897	0.060581	0.8966

15.6.5.1 RNN Results

A small part of the values for each epoch is indicated below:

Epoch 45/50

8000/8000 [====================] – 1s 177us/sample – loss : 0.0042

Epoch 46/50

8000/8000 [====================] – 1s 168us/sample – loss : 0.0043

Epoch 47/50

8000/8000 [====================] – 1s 184us/sample – loss : 0.0043

Epoch 48/50

8000/8000 [====================] – 1s 175us/sample – loss : 0.0043

Epoch 49/50

8000/8000 [====================] – 1s 169us/sample – loss : 0.0042

Epoch 50/50

8000/8000 [====================] – 1s 172us/sample – loss : 0.0042

The performance of the RNN model was calculated, and the results are shown in Table 15.1. According to RNN performance values, RMSE (0.09475), MSE (0.00897), MAE (0.060581), and R^2 (0.89) scores were obtained. It is seen that in Table 15.1 the solar generation forecast values are close to the real values as a result of the analysis made with the deep learning model RNN.

15.6.5.2 LSTM Results

Many researches in the literature review suggest that the LSTM model is very useful in time series problems. The model's epoch value is set to 50. An example of the values for each epoch is indicated below:

Epoch 45/50

8000/8000 [====================] – 2s 210us/sample – loss : 0.0033

Table 15.2 Performance of the RNN-based model in terms of RMSE, MSE, and MAE

Model	RMSE	MSE	MAE	R^2
LTSM	0.08329	0.006937	0.04726	0.92

Epoch 46/50

8000/8000 [====================] – 2s 261us/sample – loss : 0.0032

Epoch 47/50

8000/8000 [====================] – 2s 202us/sample – loss : 0.0032

Epoch 48/50

8000/8000 [====================] – 2s 201us/sample – loss : 0.0032

Epoch 49/50

8000/8000 [====================] – 2s 233us/sample – loss : 0.0032

Epoch 50/50

8000/8000 [====================] – 2s 237us/sample – loss : 0.0032

The LSTM model structure consists of 64 neurons with 4 hidden layers. It has been observed that the prediction values follow the generation values successfully. The RMSE, MSE, MAE, and R^2 values of the data analyzed with LSTM are 0.08329, 0.006937, 0.04726, and 0.92, respectively. It is seen that the model has a very successful prediction rate (Table 15.2).

15.6.5.3 GRU Results

The epoch value of the GRU model is set to 50. An example of the values for each epoch is indicated below:

Epoch 45/508000/8000[====================] – 1s 177us/sample – loss : 0.0036 – root_mean_squared_error : 0.0601

Epoch 46/508000/8000[====================] – 1s 143us/sample – loss : 0.0036 – root_mean_squared_error : 0.0600

Epoch 47/508000/8000[====================] – 1s 141us/sample – loss : 0.0036 – root_mean_squared_error : 0.0599

Epoch 48/508000/8000[====================] – 1s 137us/sample – loss : 0.0036 – root_mean_squared_error : 0.0598

Table 15.3 Performance of the GRU-based model in terms of RMSE, MSE, and MAE

Model	RMSE	MSE	MAE	R^2
GRU	0.08518	0.00725	0.05062	0.9164

Table 15.4 Comparison of performance of RNN, LSTM, and GRU algorithms

Model	RMSE	MSE	MAE	R^2
RNN	0.09475	0.00897	0.060581	0.8966
LTSM	0.08329	0.006937	0.04726	0.92
GRU	0.08518	0.00725	0.05062	0.9164

$$\text{Epoch } 49/508000/8000[=====================] - 1\text{s } 137\text{us/sample} \\ - \text{loss} : 0.0036 - \text{root\_mean\_squared\_error} : 0.0598$$

$$\text{Epoch } 49/508000/8000[=====================] - 1\text{s } 140\text{us/sample} \\ - \text{loss} : 0.0036 - \text{root\_mean\_squared\_error} : 0.0597$$

Table 15.3 indicates the GRU performance values. RMSE is 0.08518, MSE is 0.00725, MAE is 0.05062, and R^2 is 0.91. The model has a very successful prediction rate.

It is seen that the R^2 score value is 0.963 in deep LSTM networks. If the R^2 value is close to 0, it indicates that the available data are not suitable for the model used. If such an inconsistency is detected, the model must be changed. If the R^2 score value is close to 1, it can be concluded that the fit of the model is appropriate, and the next step of the inferential control analysis is passed. It is seen that this value is close to one in three models used in the study.

The findings from Table 15.4 indicate that the LSTM algorithm gives better results because the MAE, MSE, and RMSE values are higher and R^2 values are lower than the LSTM algorithm values in the forecasting using the RNN and GRU algorithms. Since the solar generation values of the LSTM model are slightly higher than the other models, it can be concluded that the LSTM model is suitable to be used for solar generation.

15.7 Conclusion and Discussion

In this study, a model for solar energy generation forecasting was proposed by using RNN, LSTM, and GRU deep learning architecture using the Ikitelli Solar Generation 20,216 daily data of Istanbul between May 2018 and May 2019. The Spyder interface running on the Anaconda platform has been studied for training, testing, and future prediction of RNN, LSTM, and GRU models, which are frequently used in forecasting studies. Generation forecasting values for 5 days later were estimated with 0.0069 error and 0.92 R^2 using values that are accepted as one of the most important performance criteria by the LSTM model. The LSTM model's solar energy production numbers are slightly greater than those of the other models, it can be concluded that the LSTM model is appropriate for forecasting solar energy generation.

Measuring the renewable energy potential of Istanbul up-to-date and sharing it with the public will both support the emergence of a healthy communication environment and feed the investment appetite. It is necessary to determine the resource-based renewable energy potential and to make a suitable resource classification for the city. The current values of infrastructure and grid capacities should be measured and shared with the public in order to integrate the electricity generation, which has increased due to the development in renewable energy technologies and progress in the market, into the grid system in Istanbul. These values should be constantly updated, the capacities of transformers should be announced regularly where appropriate, the regular publication of reports showing a healthy measurement of the current situation of Istanbul, the implementation and regulations that take into account the unique characteristics of the city of Istanbul, Developments such as preparation and implementation should be carried out quickly.

Urban transformation offers a great opportunity to regulate the sources of energy consumption from buildings in Istanbul. Zoning plans should be enriched with regulations that will encourage the use of renewable energy. While providing financial advantages to constructions in terms of renewable energy supply and energy efficiency practices is a method, making it mandatory to meet energy supply from renewable energy sources at certain rates is the most effective way to popularize the use of renewable resources.

According to the results, it is suggested that as the training dataset increases, the model is better established, and the predictions are more consistent. In future studies, it is planned to examine more parameterized and layered models with more datasets.

References

Abu-Salih, B., Wongthongtham, P., Morrison, G., Coutinho, K., Al-Okaily, M., & Huneiti, A. (2022). Short-term renewable energy consumption and generation forecasting: A case study of Western Australia. *Heliyon, 8*(3), e09152.

Cho, K., Van Merriënboer, B., Bahdanau, D., & Bengio, Y. (2014). *On the properties of neural machine translation: Encoder-decoder approaches*. arXiv preprint arXiv:1409.1259.

Doğanay, M. M. (2021). MARDİN BÖLGESİ GÜNEŞ (FOTOVOLTAİK) ENERJİSİ POTANSİYEL ANALİZİ. *Uluslararası Batı Karadeniz Mühendislik ve Fen Bilimleri Dergisi, 3*(1), 91–125.

Goodfellow, I., Bengio, Y., & Courville, A. (2018). *Derin Öğrenme*. Buzdağı Yayınevi.

Görgülü, S. (2019). Atatürk Havalimanı verileri kullanılarak rayleigh dağılım yöntemiyle İstanbul'un rüzgâr karakteristiğinin tahmini. *Avrupa Bilim ve Teknoloji Dergisi, 17*, 103–108. https://doi.org/10.31590/ejosat.604739

Gün, E. (2019). *İstanbul ve çevresinde rüzgar-güneş hibrit sisteminin karşılama oranlarının belirlenerek Anfis tabanlı modellenmesi (Yayımlanmamış yüksek lisans tezi)*. İstanbul Üniversitesi Fen Bilimleri Enstitüsü.

Hochreiter, S., & Schmidhuber, J. (1997). Long short-term memory. *Neural Computation, 9*(8), 1735–1780.

Huang, D., et al. (2012a). Prediction of solar photovoltaic power generation based on MLP and LSTM neural networks. In *2020 IEEE 4th Conference on Energy Internet and Energy System Integration (EI2)*, 2020 (pp. 2744–2748). https://doi.org/10.1109/EI250167.2020.9347223

Huang, R., Huang, T., Gadh, R., & Li, N. (2012b). Solar generation prediction using the ARMA model in a laboratory-level micro-grid. In *2012 IEEE Third International Conference on Smart Grid Communications (SmartGridComm)*, 2012 (pp. 528–533). https://doi.org/10.1109/SmartGridComm.2012.6486039

İstanbul Valiliği, T. C. (2021). *Türkiye'nin ticaret, iş, yatırım, finans ve turizm başkenti: İstanbul.* Erişim adresi: https://www.istanbul.gov.tr/turkiyenin-ticaret-is-yatirimfinans-ve-turizm-baskenti-istanbul

Pan, C., Tan, J., Feng, D., & Li, Y. (2020). Very short-term solar generation forecasting based on LSTM with temporal attention mechanism. In *2019 IEEE 5th International Conference on Computer and Communications (ICCC)*, 2019 (pp. 267–271). https://doi.org/10.1109/ICCC47050.2019.9064298

Rumelhart, D., Hinton, G., & Williams, R. (1986). Learning representations by back-propagating errors. *Nature, 323*, 533–536.

Sherstinsky, A. (2020). Fundamentals of recurrent neural network (RNN) and long short-term memory (LSTM) network. *Physica D: Nonlinear Phenomena, 404*, 132306.

Sulukan, E. (2020). İstanbul'da bir fotovoltaik sistemin tekno-ekonomik ve çevresel analizi. *Pamukkale Üniversitesi Mühendislik Bilimleri Dergisi, 26*(1), 127–132. https://doi.org/10.5505/pajes.2019.24022

TÜİK (Türkiye İstatistik Kurumu). (2019a). *İl bazında gayrisafi yurt içi hasıla, iktisadi faaliyet kollarına göre, cari fiyatlarla, 2004–2018.* Erişim adresi: https://data.tuik.gov.tr/Bulten/Index?p=Gross-Domestic-Product-by-Provinces-2019-3366

TÜİK (Türkiye İstatistik Kurumu). (2019b). *Yıllara göre il nüfusları, 2000-2019.* Erişim adresi: https://data.tuik.gov.tr/Bulten/Index?p=The-Results-of-Address-BasedPopulation-Registration-System-2020-37210

Unan, A. (2019). *Küresel iklim değişikliği sürecinde güneş enerjisi potansiyelinin belirlenmesi: Ankara, Antalya ve İstanbul örneği(Yayımlanmamış yüksek lisans tezi).* İstanbul Teknik Üniversitesi, Fen Bilimleri Enstitüsü.

Wang, Y., Zhang, D., Liu, Y., Dai, B., & Lee, L. H. (2019). Enhancing transportation systems via deep learning: A survey. *Transportation Research, Part C: Emerging Technologies, 99*, 144–163.

Willmott, C. J. (1982). Some comments on the evaluation of model performance. *Bulletin of the American Meteorological Society, 63*, 1309–1313.

Yazıcı, F. (2019). *İstanbul ili için önerilen akıllı şebekenin modellenmesi ve benzetimi (Yayımlanmamış yüksek lisans tezi).* Kocaeli Üniversitesi Fen Bilimleri Enstitüsü.

Yolcan, O. O., & Ramazan, K. Ö. S. E. (2020). TÜRKİYE'NİN GÜNEŞ ENERJİSİ DURUMU VE GÜNEŞ ENERJİSİ SANTRALİ KURULUMUNDA ÖNEMLİ PARAMETRELER. *Kırklareli Üniversitesi Mühendislik ve Fen Bilimleri Dergisi, 6*(2), 196–215.

Zhu, T., Guo, Y., Li, Z., & Wang, C. (2021). Solar radiation prediction based on convolution neural network and long short-term memory. *Energies, 14*(24), 8498. https://doi.org/10.3390/en14248498

Chapter 16
Green Human Resources Management Integration with Employee Performance and Training Development Function of the Energy Sector: Strategy Recommendations

Pelin Vardarlıer and Abdullah Türk

Abstract In this study, the subject of green human resource management is evaluated. By making a comprehensive analysis, it is aimed to generate strategies for the companies to increase the performance of the human resources. In this respect, the first practical strategy proposal of the study is that human resources management should both teach and learn individual behavior changes that will encourage an environmental corporate culture. In this framework, necessary investments should be made in training and development activities that will bring a collective awareness, and by supporting employee participation. It is understood that the philosophy of green human resources management is one of the essential management practices for an energy sector and this philosophy should be evaluated within the shared values through human resources management.

Keywords Green HR · Human resources · Human quality · Personnel motivation

16.1 Introduction

Basically, with the training programs applied in enterprises, it is aimed to increase employee productivity, product or service quality, ensure effective communication, develop team skills, prevent occupational accidents, and increase employee motivation. However, this goal is not easy to achieve. Today, the more intensive use of technology has changed the role of the human factor. These changes have also diversified the studies on human resources management day by day. On the one

P. Vardarlıer (✉)
The School of Business, İstanbul Medipol University, Istanbul, Turkey
e-mail: pvardarlier@medipol.edu.tr

A. Türk
School of Civil Aviation, İstanbul Bilgi University, Istanbul, Turkey
e-mail: abdullah.turk@bilgi.edu.tr

H. Dinçer, S. Yüksel (eds.), *Circular Economy and the Energy Market*,
Contributions to Economics, https://doi.org/10.1007/978-3-031-13146-2_16

hand, businesses continue their efforts to increase organizational performance and on the other hand, they pay attention to the least amount of resource use. In addition, sustainability in the field of business brings concepts such as environmental management, green employee movement, green value chain, and green offices to the forefront. In order for this new management philosophy, which emerged in the name of corporate sustainability, to produce practical strategies, it is necessary to increase the level of awareness of employees. However, especially in the Energy sector, people often take on the role of the controller of the whole with improved systems. At this point, there is a need for a new institutional strategy for corporate sustainability in terms of both economic, social, and environmental aspects in the effective role of human resources in the process. In order to realize these strategies and to achieve the desired performance levels, the training development department stands out in the harmonization of human resources. In order to ensure the sustainability of its performance and to compete, it is vital to ensure and increase the training and development efficiency in human resources management. In particular, the fact that all green practices need awareness on the basis of awareness-raising and encouragement covers an important area for the future as the use of new policies to promote the sustainable use of resources within the enterprise, as green human resources management refers not only to awareness of environmental issues but also to the social and economic well-being of both the enterprise and employees. Although the philosophy of green human resources management in many sectors is a management strategy that will create value in the long term, the adaptation urgency of each sector is of the same weight and importance. In this respect, the perspective of the study is that the integration of green human resources management in the energy sector is based on the necessity rather than the responsibility of corporate sustainability. This integration has been tried to be based on the relationship between training development and employee performance functions. At this point, while proposing "green" strategy for the energy sector by conducting literature research, the issue was discussed in the light of the triple performance model put forward by Dyllick and Hockerts (2002). This model is examined under the headings of "institutional sustainability from an economic point of view," "corporate sustainability from a social point of view," and "institutional sustainability from an environmental point of view." In this study, which was tried to be explained with the performance approach, firstly, the "Green Human Resources Management" strategy suggestions were conveyed through the relevant model by considering the relationship between Performance and Training development in terms of employees and businesses.

16.2 Theoretical Information

One of the most important problems encountered in organizations today is to determine the extent to which the tasks assigned to employees are fulfilled. This problem caused the concept of performance to gain importance, especially in organizations. According to Başaran (2000); Performance is called a function of the connection between what a person should do in his work and the expectations about what he actually does. Performance, which is of primary importance for organizations, is personal performance. Job performance is defined as the value of a series of employee behaviors that contribute positively or negatively to organizational goal success (Colquitt et al., 2011). Although employee performance and job performance are used together, they are actually separated by a small nuance. At this point, employee performance is the harmony of the employees at the corporate level and a total corporate macro output, while job performance is the microlevel output of the behavior that the employee demonstrates individually while doing his/her "job." However, when these micro outputs are collected, they are discussed together in some studies, as they affect the total performance score of all employees in the company.

At this point, when the TR Index is scanned, in a bibliometric study on employee performance (Tekin & Türk, 2021), the concepts of "employee performance," "employee performance," and "job performance" were defined as headings. The title of the studies, the summary of the studies, and the keywords of the studies were included in the analysis. For this reason, although employee performance and job performance differ in definition, they are used together because they treat the total impact on the same basis, but they still have basic conceptual differences. Currently, job performance is a subdimension that constitutes employee performance in terms of task performance.

Basically, it is argued that employee performance is everything an employee does or does not do. Performance that demonstrates how much the employee contributes to the organization includes: amount of output, quality of output, timeliness of output, presence in the workplace, and collaboration (Mathis & Jackson, 2000). From this point of view, it is important that many factors play a role in ensuring employee performance. At this point, the morale and motivation of the employee, the desired wage level, the timely implementation of the promotion system, the faultless functioning of the necessary reward and bonus mechanisms, the recognition of social rights and opportunities, the showing of sincerity and sincerity, and the attention to the participation of the employee can be counted (İraz & Akgün, 2014). In general, it is seen that these dimensions are divided into two. The first is job performance and the other is contextual performance (Jawahar & Carr, 2007). Job performance is the type of performance that ensures that the work that needs to be done is done in accordance with the rules. This type of performance includes tasks that reveal significant differences between the jobs of employees. Contextual performance, on the other hand, refers to the attitudes and behavior patterns that support psychological and social contexts while working in the working environment (Borman & Motowidlo, 1997). From this point of view, it can be said that the point of interest of contextual performance is related to the ability to act together with other employees within the social work area while performing tasks differently from the compliance with the rules and rules that the task requires. When both subdimensions are taken together, a role model is created and information about the direction of organizational performance can be presented.

The performance of the individual is an important factor for organizations, and the performance and success of the employee determine the effectiveness of the organization. According to Sonnentag and Serbest (2002), organizations need high-performing employees in their jobs in order to achieve their goals and gain sustainable competitiveness. The ability of employees to produce efficiently by using resources effectively and to work at high performance depends on many factors within and outside the organization.

Investing in people, the most important resource of businesses, helps them stay active at all times. At this point, it has been stated that the training and development function in human resources management has benefits such as improving the level of understanding of the individual's roles and responsibilities in the organization, increasing the skills of individuals, and increasing the motivation of the individual to do his/her job well (Wexley & Latham, 2002). Training and development activities are an investment in building a sustainable organizational structure for businesses. Effective and planned development of human resources is the result of studies that increase the training and development of employees. Continuous and systematic training of human resources is extremely important in terms of ensuring the future and sustainability of the business and is an investment made by trained employees in their own future. In this way, businesses update themselves for corporate sustainability and develop an adaptation tolerance to the ecosystem.

In addition to the economic goals of the enterprises, they have only organizational goals in line with the objectives of the organization. These are; to accelerate production and to increase the total quality and to prevent occupational accidents, to provide motivation, and to accelerate the adaptation of the employee to change. Training is not only a process that serves the economic purposes of the enterprise. At the same time, training enables the individual to understand his/her roles and responsibilities in the organization, increases the individual's skills in the field of expertise, and increases the motivation of the individual to do his/her job correctly (Bingöl, 2010). Training in enterprises has an important function in terms of providing professional development on employees and thus supporting the increase of organizational efficiency. Within this understanding, each enterprise should plan and implement training activities to meet the needs of its employees and the organization in order to increase the effectiveness of human resources. In short, the training activities applied in the enterprise mean investment in people. In this respect, training and development play an important role in increasing employee and work efficiency. With the rapid change in technology, training, and development activities have become vital for the continuity of enterprises and supported the performance output role. Trainings are important sources of contribution in cases where it is thought that the lack of individual performance is due to lack of knowledge. These trainings play a performance-enhancing role, especially for employees who have problems doing their jobs even though they know. Therefore, if the reasons for the low individual performance are determined correctly and the correct trainings are selected and applied effectively, performance will be increased in individual and organizational terms (Barutçugil, 2002). At this point, some positive effects of a good training and development program on the performance of the employee are to teach new jobs to newcomers and former employees in a very short time, to increase the success of implementation, to see the results faster, to accelerate the adaptation and adaptation process, to increase the awareness about the job, to minimize mistakes and to increase skills, to provide the employee with self-confidence about the job, to contribute to the solution of the problem, to strengthen the sense of belonging, and to support the effectiveness and efficiency of existing practices.

16.3 Training Development and Performance Relationship in Human Resources Management

Performance-related training is related to the requirements of the business. While these requirements are developing and expanding the interests of the organization, introducing new products and services to the market, finding a new market and work systems, and implementing new technology, it is necessary to ensure that employees have the necessary knowledge and skills to undertake new tasks with training. As is known, today's rapidly changing market conditions, technology, socioeconomic and cultural environment, legal structures and policy, external variables such as external variables cause the information and skills to lose their currentity and validity in a short time. For this reason, employees need continuous training in order to be useful within the enterprise (Barutçugil, 2002). At this point, training and development activities aim to ensure that employees and indirectly businesses can easily adapt to changing environmental conditions and cope with uncertainties. Training is both a management tool that motivates employees and plays an important role in the skills, knowledge, talent, and employee development (Herzberg, 2004). Conscious businesses increase performance and motivation by meeting the training needs of their employees.

It is aimed to increase organizational performance through training and development practices. In this respect, when the results of the studies conducted in different sectors are examined, it is seen that the effect of training on performance is positive. In the study conducted by Boylu and Karakaş (2011) at the airport company, it was stated that there are many factors affecting the performance of employees. Trainings provided within the company, especially orientation training, are seen as one of these factors. According to the results of the research, the implementation of orientation training, which provides the information they need about their companies and business, increases the performance of employees and increases their commitment to the company. Training programs affect employee performance, job satisfaction, productivity, and profitability as well as loyalty and productivity processes.

Özyurt (2013) researched the effect of training and development on employee satisfaction and performance, job satisfaction, and performance. As a result of the research, it was determined that the training and development given to the employees had a positive effect on employee satisfaction and performance. Using four leading companies in the technology sector, Uyar (2010) found that commitment, continuity, and desire to receive training are associated with performance. Some researchers (Uyar, 2010; Kaptangil, 2010; Özbay, 2017) focused on a similar relationship in different sectors, and it was determined that the positive feedbacks put forward in the opportunities related to training and development were employee performance and also increased motivation. His/her approach to the relationship between performance and training establishes a relationship, especially between requirements. For employees, this means filling the gap between what they know and what they can do and what they need to know and what they can do. An understanding of performance based on training development is revealed as organizational development, designing new products and services, finding different working systems and new markets, implementing new technology, and taking initiative by employees in supporting their knowledge and skills.

16.4 Green Human Resources Management Proposal with Triple Performance Approach Basis

The triple performance model is mainly handled on the basis of corporate sustainability. According to this model, it is explained which antecedents stand out in achieving a sustainable structure of institutions. This model tries to explain the ability of enterprises to act in the face of change with certain practices in terms of basic principles.

According to this approach put forward by Dyllick and Hockerts (2002), it is foreseen that in order for institutions to adapt to the changing environment and to survive, the approaches that are divided as economic, social, and environmental should come together in a holistic perspective. From this point of view, in order to achieve the corporate sustainability goal, institutions need to protect and strengthen their economic, social, and environmental capital bases. At this point, the sustainability of institutions is based on a number of internal and external factors. Among these; leadership, shared values, corporate resources and reducing costs, moral and ethical values, and corporate sustainability reporting are internal factors; while laws and regulations, increasing social awareness, customer demands and expectations, environmental and social crises are considered as external factors (Lozano, 2013). All of the corporate sustainability definitions are based on a triple hair foot. Among these, economic sustainability is based on the management of various economic capital of the enterprise such as financial, tangible, and intangible capital, providing sufficient liquidity to its stakeholders, while guaranteeing a permanent cash flow (Dyllick & Hockerts, 2002). Socially sustainable businesses are considered on the basis of adding value to society by increasing human capital and increasing social capital as well as adding value to the society in which they operate (Dyllick & Hockerts, 2002). Therefore, the social dimension of sustainability includes supporting issues such as development, increasing training standards, public health, maintaining cultural diversity, and social justice. It evaluates the environmental dimension of sustainability within the scope of environmental adaptation and change management. Accordingly, an organization's environmental sustainability efforts are a balancing act that creates an element and comfort that prevents it from being exposed to institutional inertia. Therefore, it is a requirement for the survival of businesses (Imada, 2008). Sustainability policies put forward by institutions are generally tried to be read over costs. However, this has often been claimed by opposing views. Schaltegger and Synnestvedt (2002) explain the opposite thinking about this environmental and economic performance relationship as follows: "In one view, improved environmental performance essentially causes extra costs for the business and thus reduces profitability. However, the opposite view argues that improved environmental performance will save costs and increase sales, thus improving economic performance." At this point, sustainability can be considered as a valuable investment that enables the business to continue its life and differentiate from its competitors in the long term, even though it produces outputs that can increase costs in the short term for institutions.

Dyllick and Hockerts (2002) argue that environmental sustainability and environmental/natural capital are related to social sustainability and social capital, and that the difference between book value and market value stems from these types of claims. From this point of view, it can be said that the sustainability strategy is an attempt to increase the market value of companies. According to the estimates made within the scope of environmental sustainability, it is stated that 200 million people will become refugees due to floods and drought if temperatures increase by 2–3 degrees by 2050. In addition, if carbon emissions continue to rise at this level, it is stated that insurance claims will reach $320 billion due to storms and floods, deforestation will reduce crop yield in Africa by 33%, hunger will increase, and the melting ice layer will increase the sea level by 5 m and many coastlines will be flooded (Fisk, 2010). For this reason, it is recommended that businesses create awareness and consciousness at the corporate level by putting environmental sustainability issues on the agenda. It should not be forgotten that every awareness developed at the corporate level has a counterpart for the consumer. This awareness should first be taken with the human resources strategy; measurement and reporting of sustainability performance should be encouraged. Currently, there are compulsory situations that push institutions to these incentives. These include legal obligations and liabilities, reducing future costs, improving stakeholder relations and perceived corporate reputation, the concern that the lack of an effective environmental management of the company causes the questioning of the legitimacy of the company, social responsibility, and the need to adhere to social rules (Turhan et al., 2018). The problem of legitimacy, which is among these obligations, can have devastating consequences, especially when public health is under threat. The profitability criterion, which is often considered to achieve the best results with the least resources, is seen as the focus on the difference between the value created and resource consumption when viewed by the institutional contributions of sustainability practices. At this point, Figge and Hahn (2004) suggest a Sustainable Value Added approach to realize corporate sustainability performance with a focus on opportunity cost.

Sustainable Value Added measures how much value an institution creates by evaluating the economic, social, and environmental performances of that institution simultaneously. The reason for this is that all three dimensions are separate sources of capital and it is not possible to substitute these resources with each other (Figge & Hahn, 2004). Accordingly, a loss that may be in question in any of these capital resources cannot be compensated by the excess in another; in other words, the excess of one capital resource cannot replace the loss in another capital resource. For this reason, the economic, environmental, and social dimensions that constitute the three dimensions of corporate sustainability should be evaluated simultaneously, in a balanced and holistic approach.

When the literature on corporate sustainability is examined, it is seen that the researchers agree that separate indicators should be determined for economic, environmental, and social dimensions to determine sustainability performance. In the researchers conducted, the most emphasized economic indicators; Callens and Tyteca (1999) can be stated as net sales or turnover in the short term, the sum of salaries and aids paid, the cost of all goods, services, and materials purchased (Skouloudis & Evangelinos, 2009) and long-term indicators are stated as profitability, competitiveness, market shares, product durability, R&D efforts. Environmental indicators are focused on the goal of conservation of natural resources and air and water pollution, energy use amount, greenhouse gas emissions, (Diesendorf, 2000); biodiversity, renewable and nonrenewable resources, and fuel use amounts are considered (Mukhtarov et al., 2022; Liu et al., 2021; Xie et al., 2021; Kou et al., 2022). Mentioning the integration of corporate sustainability with the Corporate Performance Scorecard method developed by Kaplan and Norton (1996) on corporate sustainability performance measurement, he emphasized the four dimensions of the performance scorecard of the economic, social, and environmental dimensions, which are the three basic dimensions of corporate sustainability, together with financial, customer, internal process, learning, and development dimensions. This situation shows that businesses need a systematic integration in corporate sustainability. At this point, Renwick et al., in their study, emphasized the importance of establishing an environmental training system in the organization and listed the stages of this. Accordingly, it is necessary to supervise the activities and resources of current training systems, to establish an institutional environmental committee accompanied by professionals and experts, especially in human resources management and environmental management, to analyze the tasks in order to produce job descriptions covering the environment, to provide environmental awareness trainings as a part of workplace adaptation training, to increase efficiency and quality, to use performance management systems to observe the performance related to wastes, accidents, and environmental impacts. In order for this scope to be successful, while companies need to bring their awareness level and awareness to the level of green human resources management, its effective implementation requires the acceptance and importance of employees. One of the most important ways to ensure this is the training and development activities of human resources (Liyin et al., 2006).

Today, many global companies provide green trainings to their employees both in production processes and at other stages. In Germany, all Siemens employees receive some environmental training. These trainings cover the improvement processes received from experts in the field of hazardous wastes. Another goal of enterprises to realize sustainability and environmentally friendly practices through green training and development activities is to obtain better capital in the long term (Kola-Olusanya, 2013).

This stage, which has a connection with human resources management in terms of sustainability, is explained in two dimensions, macro and micro, in Ehnert's study. According to the macro-level statement, the relations of enterprises with the economic environment and social environment affect the society and the natural environment. For this reason, sustainability has also come to the fore in human resources. The explanation at the micro level is related to the relationship of the enterprise with its internal environment. It increases its commitment to qualified human resources, one of the most valuable assets of the organization, for reasons such as health problems, difficulties in working life, and ensuring employee participation in the fight against environmental problems. Therefore, it is based on the idea that sustainability studies should be carried out in human resources management (Uslu & Kedikli, 2017). Attention should be paid to the link between the triple performance model put forward by Dyllick and Hockerts in terms of the sustainability of the hair feet and human resources management. It lies on a parallel line in the economic, social, and environmental dimensions. At this point, it is necessary to correctly understand the objectives of green human resources management. Green human resources aim to minimize damage to environmental issues and increase awareness in this field. From this point of view, green human resources management refers to a number of practices that businesses adopt in order to achieve their green goals and to improve the green performance of their employees in their workplaces (Hervani et al. 2005; Jackson & Seo, 2010). In this direction, it aims to employ talented personnel, develop job design based on the development and participation of employees, green human resources practices, and reward and evaluation systems related to environmental performance (Kenar & Ceyhan, 2020). However, the business has goals that contribute to the development of an ecological working environment, continuity, and environmentally responsible employee behaviors and attitudes. In the last analysis, the length of the economic life of the enterprises progresses in direct proportion to their degree of compatibility with the ecosystem in which they are located. The length of the economic life of businesses that do not support their stakeholders socially is always an issue that remains open to discussion. At the sectoral level, the companies that have to observe the balance between the value they produce and the resource they spend are closed to short-term solutions as they fulfill their environmental responsibilities as part of the social and economic cycle. Today, when the change is very rapid, the activities of businesses are very open to supervision not only legally but also in the eyes of the society, especially with the contribution of developments in communication technology. The return of mistakes made due to lack of information confronts businesses with the problem of legitimacy and causes loss of reputation. For this reason, training development investments, especially at the sectoral level, are of great importance in terms of adapting the employee to changing conditions and resetting the errors that will occur due to performance reinforcement and lack of knowledge. According to a study conducted by Karakul (2016) in the energy sector, it is of great importance that employees in the energy sector enter the green-collar group, and especially those who serve in this sector can create an environmentally friendly sustainable service structure. In a different study, green-collar employee employment is encouraged at both sectoral and public levels, while green-collar trainings are currently mentioned for employees (Lund, 2009). Although the main purpose of the training development function is to keep the information about the job up to date, it also has a motivational role (Türk, 2021). Businesses want to protect the talents they have at their disposal. The triple performance approach addresses Sustainability strategically. At this point, it is natural for institutions to expect high performance from employees who will guide these strategies. At this point, green talent management processes can also lead to a performance relationship by supporting employees with training development (Acet & Vardarlıer, 2022). Currently, the need for this is essential for businesses. As a matter of fact, one of the practical results of a study conducted by Gardas et al. (2019) in the energy sector shows that the continuity of sustainability policies of energy companies is related to green human resources management functions. At this point, the role of training and development function in managing and directing information is very critical for performance improvement. The energy sector differs from other sectors, especially due to the burden of its responsibilities (Zhou et al., 2021; Zhe et al., 2021; Meng et al., 2021; Dinçer et al., 2022). Employee behavior that will contribute to sustainability in the sector is both essential and very strategic because controlling environmental impact should be seen as a responsibility for all employees, and the role of knowledge stands out at this point (Florea et al., 2013). The situation is basically the same on an employee basis as institutions have to approach sustainability from a total perspective. The empirical results of Rayner and Morgan (2018) in the relevant sector are in parallel with this situation. According to the findings, in order to be sustainable in the energy sector, green human resources management should be adopted better, and it is important to determine the level of green consciousness of the employees who will be employed for the first time, while investigating the necessity of trainings to support green employee behavior and how other functions should be coordinated with each other in order to improve performance (Ding et al., 2021; Haiyun et al., 2021; Dong et al., 2022; Kostis et al., 2022). With the green training development activities provided in the context of green human resources management, providing employees with information, skills, and competence-enhancing trainings on environmental issues increases their performance. Research shows that green training development and green learning have a significant positive effect on the environmental performance of individuals in the organization and the green performance of the organization (Bhutto & Auranzeb, 2016). As a matter of fact, among the process recommendations of management scientists such as Milliman and Clair (2017) for the implementation of Green WBS in enterprises, training of employees, and other stakeholders according to the environmental vision of the enterprise and evaluation of the performance of employees on the basis of environmentally friendly behaviors are included. In general terms, it is understood that the literature conceptually green human resources management practices will show an increase in performance with awareness-raising activities at a certain level by encouraging employees' green behaviors in the workplace (Jabbour, 2011; Jiang et al., 2012; Renwick et al., 2013).

16.5 Conclusion and Recommendations

Today, the success level of enterprises that develop proactive policies against the environment and try to use environmental resources most effectively is directly related to the internal stakeholders of the enterprises. There are some essential issues for sectors that have a level of environmental impact, especially in the energy sector. Institutions can never be considered independent of their employees because their success in achieving their goals depends on the attitudes and behaviors of their employees. In this direction, in order for businesses to achieve their environmental goals, first of all, employees should be made aware of this issue and the desired attitudes and behaviors should be gained to the employees. At this point, human resources functions of enterprises play a major role. Managing businesses with a common mind is a necessity of the age today. It is possible to adapt to change and to see all kinds of opportunities and threats with a transient memory. The social capital of the enterprise should both encourage and support the intellectual accumulation of employees in this direction. As evaluated from a collective perspective, these shared values are an investment in corporate culture.

In this respect, the first practical strategy proposal of the study is that human resources management, which focuses on collective and individual abilities to reveal green behaviors, should both teach and learn individual behavioral changes that will encourage an environmental corporate culture by investing in training and development activities that will bring a collective awareness, and by supporting employee participation. He/she should create a passive memory by revealing his/her collective mind and should not only encourage his/her employees, but also encourage them with a green collar suitable for the changing structure of the business, starting from the recruitment function to career development. If it is not only in businesses but also in the general society, changes within the structure are always subject to a certain level of resistance. At this point, the training participation and communication trio will have the opportunity to be used in an effect that will break this resistance to change. These practices, which can be considered as an investment in corporate culture, are needed at the maximum level, especially in the energy sector, in order to prevent waste and to follow innovations. At this point, training development has the task of adding a mission and creating a vision, as well as setting a standard for the employee and the institution. In fact, employees within the organization are evaluated according to these standards.

At this point, another practical strategy suggestion of the study is that businesses should set green targets for employees and create green performance standards that will enable these targets to be transformed into a collective action plan for the whole workforce and integrate these standards with the career management system, in order to improve environmental performance.

In the last analysis, it was understood that the philosophy of green human resources management is one of the essential management practices for an energy sector and this philosophy should be evaluated within the shared values through human resources management. At this point, it has been reiterated that creating green consciousness is not only a managerial responsibility but also the responsibility of everyone within the business. Although it is understood that sustainability in the energy sector has a key role in creating an economic, social, and environmental performance balance, it is understood that the performance relationship of each employee serves as a bridge with the training development activities that support collective consciousness according to the direction of change in ensuring this balance.

References

Acet, G. T., & Vardarlıer, P. (2022). Strategic talent perception in the energy sector. In *Sustainability in energy business and finance* (pp. 61–70). Springer.

Barutçugil, İ. (2002). *Eğiticinin Eğitimi, 1*. Kariyer Yayıncılık.

Başaran, İ. E. (2000). *Örgütsel Davranış: İnsanın Üretim Gücü* (p. 3). Ankara.

Bhutto, S. A., & Auranzeb, Z. (2016). Effects of green human resources management on firm performance: An empirical study on Pakistani firms. *European Journal of Business and Management, 8*, 119–125.

Bingöl, D. (2010). İnsan Kaynakları Yönetimi. In M. M. Üner (Ed.), *Genel İşletmecilik içinde* (ss. 281–332). 2. Baskı. Detay Yayıncılık.

Borman, W. C., & Motowidlo, S. J. (1997). Görev Performansı ve Bağlamsal Performans: Personel Seçimi Araştırmasının Anlamı. *İnsan Performansı, 10*, 99–109.

Boylu, Y., & Karakaş, A. (2011). İşe eğitimlerinin yetiştirilmesine yönelik başvuru yerlerine uygun bir eğitim. *Ankara Hacı Bayram Veli Üniversitesi Turizm Fakültesi Dergisi, 1*, 61–75.

Callens, I., & Tyteca, D. (1999). Towards indicators of sustainable development for firms: A productive efficiency perspective. *Ecological Economics, 28*(1), 41–53.

Colquitt, J., Lepin, J. A., & Wesson, M. (2011). Örgütsel Davranış: İşyerinde Performansı Ve Bağlılığı Geliştirmek.

Diesendorf, M. (2000). Sustainability and sustainable development. In *Sustainability: The corporate challenge of the 21st century* (Vol. 2, pp. 19–37). Allen & Unwin.

Dinçer, H., Yüksel, S., & Martínez, L. (2022). Collaboration enhanced hybrid fuzzy decision-making approach to analyze the renewable energy investment projects. *Energy Reports, 8*, 377–389.

Ding, Z., Yüksel, S., & Dincer, H. (2021). An Integrated Pythagorean fuzzy soft computing approach to environmental management systems for sustainable energy pricing. *Energy Reports, 7*, 5575–5588.

Dong, W., Zhao, G., Yüksel, S., Dinçer, H., & Ubay, G. G. (2022). A novel hybrid decision making approach for the strategic selection of wind energy projects. *Renewable Energy, 185*, 321–337.

Dyllick, T., & Hockerts, K. (2002). Beyond the business case for corporate sustainability. *Business Strategy and the Environment, 11*(2), 130–141.

Figge, F., & Hahn, T. (2004). Sustainable value added—Measuring corporate contributions to sustainability beyond eco-efficiency. *Ecological Economics, 48*(2), 173–187.

Fisk, P. (2010). *Sürdürülebilir büyüme; insanlar, gezegen ve kâr.* MediaCat, Çeviri, Evren Yıldırım.

Florea, L., Cheung, Y. H., & Herndon, N. C. (2013). For all good reasons: Role of values in organizational sustainability. *Journal of Business Ethics, 114*(3), 393–408.

Gardas, B. B., Mangla, S. K., Raut, R. D., Narkhede, B., & Luthra, S. (2019). Green talent management to unlock sustainability in the oil and gas sector. *Journal of Cleaner Production, 229*, 850–862.

Haiyun, C., Zhixiong, H., Yüksel, S., & Dinçer, H. (2021). Analysis of the innovation strategies for green supply chain management in the energy industry using the QFD-based hybrid interval valued intuitionistic fuzzy decision approach. *Renewable and Sustainable Energy Reviews, 143*, 110844.

Hervani, A. A., Helms, M. M., & Sarkis, J. (2005). Performance measurement for green supply chain management. *Benchmarking: An International Journal, 12*(4), 330–353.

Herzberg, F. (2004). *Bir Kere Daha: Çalışanları Nasıl Motive Edersiniz ?* (pp. 51–74). Leyla Aslan, MESS Yayınları.

Imada, A. S. (2008). Achieving sustainability through macroergonomic change management and participation. In *Corporate sustainability as a challenge for comprehensive management* (pp. 129–138). Physica-Verlag HD.

İraz, R., & Akgün, Ö. (2014). Örgütsel bağlılığın çalıştırılmak üzere yönlendiriliriye yönelik bir çalışma. *Selçuk Üniversitesi Sosyal Bilimler Meslek Yüksekokulu Dergisi, 14*(1–2), 201–224.

Jabbour, C. J. C. (2011). How green are HRM practices, organizational culture, learning and teamwork? A Brazilian study. *Industrial and Commercial Training, 43*(2), 98–105.

Jackson, S. E., & Seo, J. (2010). The greening of strategic HRM scholarship. *Organization Management Journal, 7*(4), 278–290.

Jawahar, I. M., & ve Carr D. (2007). Vicdanlılık ve Bağlamsal Performans Algılanan Örgütsel Destek ve Lider-Üye Değişiminin Telafi Edici Etkileri. *Yönetim Psikolojisi Dergisi, 22*, 330–349.

Jiang, K., Lepak, D. P., Han, K., Hong, Y., Kim, A., & Winkler, A. L. (2012). Clarifying the construct of human resource systems: Relating human resource management to employee performance. *Human Resource Management Review, 22*(2), 73–85.

Kaplan, R. S., & Norton, D. P. (1996). Using the balanced scorecard as a strategic management system. *Harvard Business Review, 74*(1), 75–85.

Kaptangil, K. (2010). *İşletmelerde insan kaynaklarına yönelik iyileştirmelerin iyileştirmeleri* (Yayınlanmamış doktora tezi). Ankara Üniversitesi, Sosyal Bilimler Enstitüsü.

Karakul, A. K. (2016). Educating labour force for a green economy and renewable energy jobs in Turkey: A quantitave approach. *Renewable and Sustainable Energy Reviews, 63*, 568–578.

Kenar, G., & Ceyhan, S. (2020). Yeşil İnsan Kaynakları Yönetimi Uygulamaları İşe Adanmışlığın Öncülü Olabilir Mi? *Parion Akademik Bakış Dergisi, 1*(1), 65–80.

Kola-Olusanya, A. (2013). Embedding environmental sustainability competencies in human capital training and development. *Mediterranean Journal of Social Sciences, 4*(4), 65.

Kostis, P., Dinçer, H., & Yüksel, S. (2022). Knowledge-based energy investments of European economies and policy recommendations for sustainable development. *Journal of the Knowledge Economy*, 1–33.

Kou, G., Yüksel, S., & Dinçer, H. (2022). Inventive problem-solving map of innovative carbon emission strategies for solar energy-based transportation investment projects. *Applied Energy, 311*, 118680.

Liu, J., Lv, J., Dinçer, H., Yüksel, S., & Karakuş, H. (2021). Selection of renewable energy alternatives for green blockchain investments: A hybrid IT2-based fuzzy modelling. *Archives of Computational Methods in Engineering, 28*(5), 3687–3701.

Liyin, S., Hong, Y., & Griffith, A. (2006). Improving environmental performance by means of empowerment of contractors. *Management of Environmental Quality, 17*(3), 242–257.

Lozano, R. (2013). Are companies planning their organisational changes for corporate sustainability? An analysis of three case studies on resistance to change and their strategies to overcome it. *Corporate Social Responsibility and Environmental Management, 20*(5), 275–295.
Lund, P. D. (2009). Effects of energy policies on industry expansion in renewable energy. *Renewable Energy, 34*(1), 53–64.
Mathis, R. L., & Jackson, J. H. (2000). *İnsan Kaynakları Yönetimi, 9. baskı*. SouthWestern College Yayıncılık.
Meng, Y., Wu, H., Zhao, W., Chen, W., Dinçer, H., & Yüksel, S. (2021). A hybrid heterogeneous Pythagorean fuzzy group decision modelling for crowdfunding development process pathways of fintech-based clean energy investment projects. *Financial Innovation, 7*(1), 1–34.
Milliman, J., & Clair, J. (2017). Best environmental HRM practices in the US. In *Greening people* (pp. 49–73). Routledge.
Mukhtarov, S., Yüksel, S., & Dinçer, H. (2022). The impact of financial development on renewable energy consumption: Evidence from Turkey. *Renewable Energy, 187*, 169–176.
Özbay, B. (2017). *İşletmelerde eğitim ile algılanan performans ilişkileriyle ilgili bir araştırma* (Yayınlanmamış lisans tezi). Maltepe Üniversitesi, Sosyal Bilimler Enstitüsü.
Özyurt, N. (2013). *İnsan Kaynaklarında Eğitim ve Geliştirme* (Yayınlanmamış lisans tezi). Beykent Üniversitesi, Sosyal Bilimler Enstitüsü.
Rayner, J., & Morgan, D. (2018). An empirical study of 'green' workplace behaviours: Ability, motivation and opportunity. *Asia Pacific Journal of Human Resources, 56*(1), 56–78.
Renwick, D. W., Redman, T., & Maguire, S. (2013). Green human resource management: A review and research agenda. *International Journal of Management Reviews, 15*(1), 1–14.
Schaltegger, S., & Synnestvedt, T. (2002). The link between 'green' and economic success: Environmental management as the crucial trigger between environmental and economic performance. *Journal of Environmental Management, 65*(4), 339–346.
Skouloudis, A., & Evangelinos, K. I. (2009). Sustainability reporting in Greece: Are we there yet? *Environmental Quality Management, 19*(1), 43–60.
Sonnentag, S., & Serbest, M. (2002). Performans Kavramları Ve Performans Teorisi. *Bireysel Performansın Psikolojik Yönetimi, 23*(1), 3–25.
Tekin, İ. Ç., & Türk, A. (2021). 2000'li Yıllarda Çalışan Performansı Konusunda Yapılan Ulusal Makalelerin (Tr Dizin) Bibliyometrik Analizi. *Elektronik Türkçe Çalışmaları, 16*(2).
Turhan, G. D., Özen, T., & Albayrak, R. S. (2018). Kurumsal sürdürülebilirlik kavrami, stratejik önemi ve sürdürülebilirlik performansi ölçümü. *Ege Stratejik Araştırmalar Dergisi, 9*(1), 17–37.
Türk, A. (2021). Güncel Ve Teknolojik Gelişmeler Işığında İnsan Kaynakları Yönetimi. *Eğitim ve Geliştirme*, (ed: dr. İlknur çevik tekin).
Uslu, Y. D., & Kedikli, E. (2017). *Sürdürülebilirlik kapsamında yeşil insan kaynakları yönetimine genel bir bakış*. Üçüncü Sektör Sosyal Ekonomi.
Uyar, B. (2010). *İşletmelerde Eğitim Geliştirme ve Performans İlişkileri ve Türk Telekomünikasyon Sektöründe Bir Araştırma* (Yayımlanmamış Yüksek Lisans Tezi). Marmara Üniversitesi, Sosyal Bilimler Enstitüsü.
Wexley, K. N., & Latham, G. P. (2002). *Developing and training human resources in organizations* (3rd ed.). Prentice Hall.
Xie, Y., Zhou, Y., Peng, Y., Dinçer, H., Yüksel, S., & an Xiang, P. (2021). An extended Pythagorean fuzzy approach to group decision-making with incomplete preferences for analyzing balanced scorecard-based renewable energy investments. *IEEE Access, 9*, 43020–43035.
Zhe, L., Yüksel, S., Dinçer, H., Mukhtarov, S., & Azizov, M. (2021). The positive influences of renewable energy consumption on financial development and economic growth. *SAGE Open, 11*(3), 21582440211040133.
Zhou, P., Luo, J., Cheng, F., Yüksel, S., & Dinçer, H. (2021). Analysis of risk priorities for renewable energy investment projects using a hybrid IT2 hesitant fuzzy decision-making approach with alpha cuts. *Energy, 224*, 120184.

Chapter 17
Energy Production from Waste: Biomass Energy

Halil İbrahim Uzun

Abstract In the world, fossil fuels such as coal and oil are clustered in certain regions and existing resources are rapidly depleting. However, the negative effects of fossil fuels on the environment and animal health make renewable energy sources more important. Renewable energy sources have advantages such as sustainability, less negative environmental impacts than fossil fuels, and their availability in almost every region. Biomass, which appears to be an environmental burden but has great potential, is also one of the renewable energy sources. Biomass; It forms the basis for many secondary energy sources such as biogas, biochar, biohydrogen, and biodiesel. Biomass energy is a source that can provide continuous energy, not intermittently like wind and sun. The easy storage of biomass energy provides an advantage over other renewable energy sources. As a result of storing the endless energy of the sun in plants, biomass energy based on agriculture is offered for use with various technologies. In this study, first of all, the definition of biomass energy, its sources and secondary energy sources produced from biomass energy are mentioned. Afterward, production methods for secondary energy sources and processes such as product purification are mentioned. Finally, some suggestions have been expressed in the context of the energy production approach from biomass.

Keywords Biomass energy · Energy production · Clean energy · Energy investments · Unemployment

17.1 Introduction

Energy is one of the most important sources in the provision of primary and secondary needs of people. Especially in the last century, it is seen that fossil fuels such as coal, oil, and natural gas are being used in energy supply (Bhuiyan et al., 2022; Fang et al., 2021). As a result of the combustion of fossil fuels, various

H. İ. Uzun (✉)
The Faculty of Engineering and Architecture, Mus Alparslan University, Mus, Turkey
e-mail: ha.uzun@alparslan.edu.tr

H. Dinçer, S. Yüksel (eds.), *Circular Economy and the Energy Market*,
Contributions to Economics, https://doi.org/10.1007/978-3-031-13146-2_17

gaseous pollutants are released, especially gases defined as greenhouse gases such as carbon dioxide (CO_2), nitrogen oxides (NO_x), sulfur oxide (SO_x), and particulate matter. These gases, which are released and released into the environment, are shown as the most important actors in climate change (Adalı et al., 2022; Yüksel et al., 2022). In addition, these toxic gaseous pollutants harm human health and cause chronic respiratory diseases, strokes, and heart attacks (Sinharoy & Pakshirajan, 2020). Due to technological developments and the increase in population, the demand for energy has also increased. The scarcity of fossil fuels has increased interest in new energy production methods to meet energy needs (Saravanan et al., 2021).

Interest in alternative energy sources has been on the agenda of scientists for a long time. In particular, it is important that alternative energy sources have less damage to the environment, be renewable and low cost. In this sense, so far; Alternative energies such as wind, hydraulic, hydrogen, biomass, geothermal, and ocean thermal energy have been produced (Dinçer et al., 2022; Mukhtarov et al., 2022; Liu et al., 2021; Xie et al., 2021). However, the solution that has the criteria such as efficiency, low cost, and suitability for purpose at the optimum level will always be valid. Although it is included in the energy issue, the subject that needs to be emphasized is transportation. Today, transportation is still very heavily supplied by fossil fuels. There is also an alternative fuel requirement for vehicles. For this purpose, research studies on the use of electricity, solar, and hydrogen energy in vehicles are carried out all over the world (Kou et al., 2022; Zhou et al., 2021; Zhe et al., 2021; Meng et al., 2021). In studies, hybrid vehicles can play an intermediary role in the process of adapting to these new technologies. For this purpose, major automotive companies all over the world put forward perspectives for intensive R&D, prototype production, and even mass production (Uzun, 2021).

17.2 Biomass Energy

Among the different types of renewable energy that are increasing their share in energy supply day by day, biomass energy is considered as a promising energy source due to its economic feasibility and relatively easy availability. Biohydrogen, which is obtained from natural organic materials (biomass), defined as biomass, is shown as an important alternative as a low-carbon fuel. Since biomass is a plant-based fuel, it will continue to exist as long as the sun and other natural cycles exist. Biomass; It can be defined as the total amount of mass possessed by living organisms belonging to a species or a community of different species at a given time. The roots and whole trunks of trees in forest areas are defined as forest biomass. Approximately 90% of the total biomass in the world originates from forests (Yilmaz et al., 2017). Biomass energy obtained from biomass is divided into two classes, traditional and modern. Wood from forests and residues from other plants and animals can be defined as conventional biomass energy. Modern biomass energy is; energy from forestry, forest-wood industry wastes, vegetable waste in agriculture, urban waste, and agriculture-based industrial waste. Today, a method called energy agriculture is being used. In this method, instead of C_3 plants, C_4 plants with high carbon sequestration efficiency (sugarcane, corn, sweet millet, etc.) are grown. Biomass-based energy products can be changed into solid, liquid, and gas forms according to the need. The storability of these forms also provides an advantage to biomass energy when compared with other renewable energy sources. Biomass energy can be converted into energy by methods such as direct combustion, gasification, pyrolysis, anaerobic digestion, and co-firing (Yilmaz et al., 2017).

The aim of biomass production is to obtain modern biomass fuel raw materials from energy forests and energy agriculture. The basis of this aquaculture, which is based on forestry and agriculture, is the fact that plants store solar energy in their bodies through photosynthesis, and the emphasis is on plants that grow quickly with fast photosynthesis (Karayilmazlar et al., 2011).

Today, fast-growing trees such as black poplar, balsam poplar, aspen, willow, eucalyptus, and cynara as semiarid area plants are grown for energy purposes. These trees can grow in quite different climates and soil conditions. At the same time, their growth rate varies between 10 and 20 times faster compared to other trees. Today, the growth rate of energy trees can be increased even more with biotechnological methods. These trees are usually pruned every 5 years to allow them to grow back, and the harvested branches are used as a source of biomass. The average annual yield from energy forests is around 22 tons of biomass per hectare. The calculations show that approximately seven million tons of biomass energy can be obtained annually from the energy forests to be established on one million hectares. This amount is equivalent to approximately 30 million barrels of crude oil. As can be seen, it is possible to protect existing forests and reduce environmental pollution with energy trees (Ar et al., 2004).

In recent years, studies on energy plants, which have high growth rates and can grow even on very infertile soils, have intensified. With these plants, a new type of agriculture has been developed that can be done with annual or perennial plants and can be defined as energy agriculture today. The seeds of some of the plants used in energy agriculture are developed with the help of genetic engineering. Energy plants are called C_4-type plants (Panicum Pennisetum, sugarcane, corn, sugar beet, sweet sorghum, and miscanthus, which are not well known in our country). General characteristics of C_4 plants can be given as follows:

- They can live in low carbon dioxide environments.
- They necessitate high temperatures.
- Uses less water.
- They are resistant to seasonal drought.
- At first, they bind to organic molecules containing four carbon atoms.
- Their ability to use light intensity is high.

Some plants cannot respire when the carbon dioxide concentration in the air falls below a certain level. However, one of the most important features of C_4 plants is that they can absorb every carbon dioxide molecule in the atmosphere. Compared to other cultivated plants, they can evaluate and use carbon dioxide better in photosynthesis. C_4 crops are the main raw material for numerous energy products. In recent years, it has attracted a lot of attention from developed countries due to its use in different industries. Among these energy products are ethanol, pyrrhoetic oil, fuels of improved quality, barbecue, synthetic gas, and cellulosic substances obtained from the pulp part of the plant from which water and sugar have been removed. The most promising form of application for energy generation from biomass and derivative fuels is to generate electricity. The cost of electricity generation by burning biomass can be greatly reduced by higher yields from planting C_4 crops (Acaroğlu, 2003).

17.3 Biogas

Biogas is a gas produced from biomass. In an anaerobic environment, the microbiological flora converts biomass into CO_2 and CH_4. Other biological wastes remaining as a result of fermentation can be evaluated as qualified fertilizers for the soil.Biogas production takes place in three phases: hydrolysis, acid formation, and methane formation. In the first stage, the waste is dissolved by enzymes secreted by microorganisms. At this stage, polysaccharides are converted into monosaccharides, proteins into peptides, and amino acids. In the next step, acid-forming bacteria step in and turn these substances into small-structured substances such as acetic acid. In the final stage, these substances are converted into biogas by methane-forming bacteria (Onursal et al., 2011).

The gas formed as a result of biogas production is not pure. The content of this gas is approximately 55–75% CH_4 gas, 25–45% CO_2 gas, 1–10% hydrogen gas (H_2), 0–0.3% nitrogen (N_2) gas, and 0–3% hydrogen sulfide gas (H_2S). Biogas has a lower energy content than other gaseous energy sources other than hydrogen. It does not precipitate on the bottom when air is present. Therefore, it mixes with the air faster and its ratio in the air decreases. This reduces the risk of a sudden explosion and fire. The high ignition temperature should be considered an important advantage in this respect. The combustion velocity in air (0.25 m/s) is low. This is because it contains CO_2. In order for it to burn, it must be present in the air for at least 5%. One cubic meter of biogas to 5.7 m^3 of air is required (Onursal et al., 2011).

Animal and vegetable organic waste/residue materials are mostly either burned directly or given to agricultural land as fertilizer. It is more common to use such waste in heat generation, especially by incineration. In this way, the desired quality of heat cannot be produced, and it is not possible to use the wastes as fertilizer after heat production. Biogas technology, on the other hand, allows both to obtain energy from organic-based waste/residue materials and to bring the wastes to the soil.

- It is an easily accessible, inexpensive, and environmentally friendly energy source. Waste can be used as qualified fertilizer at the end of fermentation.

- As a result of biogas production, bad odor is reduced in cattle, sheep, and poultry manure. Disease factors that will negatively affect water, soil, and living life are reduced (Engler et al., 1999).

Animal manure is very important for biogas production. On average, approximately 33 m^3 biogas can be produced from 1 ton of cattle manure, 58 m^3 from 1 ton of sheep manure, and 78 m^3 from 1 ton of poultry manure. Animal manure is both a source of nutrients for plants and a soil conditioner that regulates the physical, chemical, and biological properties of the soil. Fermented animal manure facilitates the cultivation of the soil. It makes the soil suitable for plant growth. In sandy soils, it ensures that the soil sticks together. Poultry manure contains pathogenic microorganisms. The inadequacy of evaluation methods and the high cost of drying techniques cause poultry farms to have negative effects on the environment. Biomass resources for biogas production (Rutz & Janssen, 2013).

Urban solid waste, wastewater, and sludge from wastewater have great potential for biogas production. There are two general methods of producing biogas from urban waste. The first method is to separate the organic parts of these municipal solid wastes from the other parts and to produce oxygen-free fermentation biogas from these organic parts. This method is called biomethanization. Because the source of the produced gas is only organic horses. The second method is biogas production by direct oxygen-free fermentation by accumulating these urban solid wastes in waste storage. The gas produced in this way is called LFG gas (landfill gas) or landfill gas. Wastewater contains organic matter, nutrients, heavy metals, and pathogenic microorganisms. Biogas content obtained from wastewater treatment sludge; 60–70% CH_4, 30–35% CO_2, 1–2% H_2S, and 0.3–3% N_2. The methane percentage of the gas formed from wastewater treatment sludge is approximately 65%. The heating value of the gas formed is 22.4 MJ/m^3 on average (Rutz & Janssen, 2013).

Wastes arising directly from agricultural activities or resulting from the industrial processes of agricultural products (sugar beet pulp, peanut shell, olive pulp, olive black water, etc.) are an important source of pollution. Such waste is usually incinerated and causes air pollution. Agricultural waste can be converted into biogas by anaerobic fermentation (Rutz & Janssen, 2013).

17.4 Biodiesel

Biodiesel is a fuel equivalent to diesel, produced by the reaction of vegetable oils obtained from oilseed plants such as canola (rapeseed), sunflower, soybean, safflower, and cotton with a short-chain alcohol (methanol or ethanol) accompanied by a catalyst. Domestically used frying oils and animal fats can also be used as biodiesel raw materials. However, biodiesel does not contain petroleum; therefore, it can be used as a fuel in any place where diesel oil is used, either pure or mixed with petroleum-based diesel in any proportion. It can be produced using domestic resources and domestic industry. Small-scale and local production is possible (Ar et al., 2004).

Biodiesel can be used without making any technical changes to engines using diesel fuel or by making minor modifications to some vehicles, and can be stored in the conditions and places where diesel fuel is stored. Due to this feature, it is widely used in the transportation sector. It has strategic importance in the defense industry. The properties of biodiesel allow the use of alternative fuels as a fuel other than diesel engines. Besides being used as generator fuel and heating fuel, biodiesel is also possible in greenhouses, mines, and all branches of industry (Ar et al., 2004).

Today, the most important environmental problem in the world is global warming, caused by the greenhouse effect. Global warming is the result of other harmful emissions such as SO_x and NO_x, especially CO_2 emissions resulting from combustion. Since biodiesel converts carbon dioxide through photosynthesis within the biological carbon cycle and accelerates the carbon cycle, it has no effect on increasing the greenhouse effect. In addition, it has been proven that CO_2, SO_x emissions, and unburned hydrocarbons (HC) are released less (Ar et al., 2004).

17.5 Biohydrogen

Biohydrogen obtained from natural organic materials (biomass) has a high energy efficiency (about 2.75 times greater) compared to fossil and other carbon-based combustion fuels. Also, no toxic air pollutants or greenhouse gases are released as a result of hydrogen combustion. As a by-product, only water is produced (Kumar et al., 2017). Along with plant sources of biomass, especially both domestic and industrial, wastewater is an important energy source that cannot be evaluated. A significant amount of water is released into the environment as a result of anthropogenic and industrial activities. Combining the disposal of wastewater, which is an ecological threat, with the production of hydrogen from this water will be an effective environmental protection method. Wastewater contains high organic content. Various biological technologies such as biohydrogen, biophotolysis, microbial electrolysis, and fermentation can convert organic materials into hydrogen energy (Oceguera-Contreras et al., 2019).

Biohydrogen is used in a wide variety of industrial applications as a material for the production of valuable compounds. Hydrogen production from both nonrenewable and renewable sources can be accomplished using a thermochemical or biological technique. Renewable sources for hydrogen production include biomass, urban effluents, and all wastewater, primarily industrial wastewater (Saratale et al., 2019). Organic waste is a low-cost resource that is widely used as a raw material to produce biohydrogen. Organic waste can originate from waste generated in the industrial processes of agricultural and agricultural products, wood waste, animal waste, urban waste, food waste, waste, activated sludge, and wastewater from industries (Urbaniec & Bakker, 2015). Converting organic waste to energy or fuel has a dual role in waste management and clean energy generation (Salem et al.,

2018). Organic waste serves as a suitable raw material for the production of biohydrogen, as it is plentiful, inexpensive, and rich in carbohydrates, proteins, and nutrients. Products enriched in carbohydrates and sugars for hydrogen production are defined as first-generation biomass feedstock, lignocellulosic biomass, second-generation biomass feedstock, agricultural waste, animal waste, forest residues, and wastewater), as well as third-generation biomass feedstock including algal biomass (Nagarajan et al., 2021).

Agricultural waste is the waste obtained from the output of agricultural activities. Agricultural waste is easy to dispose of and is a plentiful, low cost, and environmentally friendly resource. Since agricultural wastes are rich in carbohydrates, they serve as a very good carbon source for biohydrogen production. Agricultural waste contains lignocellulose, a complex carbohydrate polymer composed of cellulose, hemicellulose, and lignin as its main components (Kumari & Singh, 2018). Lignocellulosic biomass needs to be pre-treated to achieve high conversion efficiency. The pretreatment aids the dissolution and subsequent hydrolysis of the cellulose and hemicelluloses contained in the lignocellulosic biomass (Khoo et al., 2021). Pretreatments can be physical, chemical, or biological. When NaOH is used as a suitable alkaline agent and lignocellulosic biomass is fermented, highly fermentable sugars can be produced. Biohydrogen production is mainly affected by the source of organic wastes due to the presence of sulfur and ammonia. However, it has been suggested that pretreatment of organic wastes can significantly increase the efficiency of biohydrogen production (Chen et al., 2008).

Food waste is formed during the production, processing, retail sale, and consumption of food. Food waste is ideal for biohydrogen production due to its nutritional value, biodegradability, moisture content, and high volatile solids content (Abubackar et al., 2019). Fruit and vegetable wastes contain high amounts of sugar and protein that can be converted to hydrogen biologically. Re-pretreatment is required to increase the production of fermentable sugars, which are easily broken down by H_2-producing microorganisms for biohydrogen production. Domestic and industrial wastewater is generated as a result of anthropogenic and industrial activities. Common industrial wastewater that can be used for biohydrogen production is water with a high organic load, such as milk, beverage, pharmaceutical, textile processing, and food processing water. Wastewater is easily accessible, low cost, and organically rich. It is a suitable source for biohydrogen production as long as it does not contain toxic substances such as low pH, high salt content, or heavy metals (Sivagurunathan et al., 2015). The use of wastewater for hydrogen production helps to protect the environment by simultaneously producing biofuels. There are studies in the literature on the use of wastewater as a raw material for biohydrogen production (Ramos & Silva, 2018). Sugar industry wastewater with high carbohydrate content (Arimi et al., 2015), palm oil industry wastewater (Mohammadi et al., 2011), food processing wastewater that is highly rich in carbohydrates and residual lignocellulose content (Amorim et al., 2014), dairy industry wastewater (Gadhe et al., 2015), wastewater from the textile industry during bleaching and washing processes (Lay et al., 2012) are some of the sources whose biohydrogen production potential has been investigated.

Chemical absorption, membrane separation, cryogenic separation, and adsorption are widely used for biohydrogen purification (Sazali, 2020). High purity biohydrogen can be obtained by chemical absorption, but solvent costs and corrosion problems are disadvantages of chemical adsorption (Azira & Aisah, 2019). The membrane separation approach has advantages such as low investment, operating and maintenance costs, high adaptability, and easy operation (Aasadnia et al., 2021). Hydrogen is a clean and efficient fuel source, especially for vehicles (Yüksel et al., 2021; Serezli et al., 2021; Zhao et al., 2021; Li et al., 2022). Since the biohydrogen fuel cell does not require any high energy input, such as a high temperature, it is shown as a sustainable and environmentally friendly electricity generation method. Biohydrogen can be combined with biogas as a fuel to improve the combustion process and reduce carbon dioxide emissions (Rahman et al., 2016).

Ensuring high biohydrogen production and yield from biomass remains one of the main challenges. Today, industrial biohydrogen production from biomass sources has not been achieved yet. The need for pretreatment of some substrates is another challenge in biohydrogen production. It may be necessary to use valuable chemicals as agents or direct solvents (Shao et al., 2020). In addition to the process conditions, biohydrogen production performance is affected by the substrate, the microorganisms used, and the operational conditions. Some volatile fatty acids and residual substrates inhibit microbial biohydrogen production by causing inhibition (Wainaina et al., 2019). Although photofermentative processes produce hydrogen in high yield, the high input light energy requirement makes the process unsuitable for industrial scale. Therefore, it is necessary to develop new microbial species with improved light conversion capability and to develop more efficient light source technologies (Mishra et al., 2019). Although it is known that the addition of nanoparticles to the fermentation medium increases the biohydrogen yield, the stimulating effect of nanoparticles is highly dependent on the microorganisms used and the dosage of the nanoparticles. High nanoparticle concentrations can cause high oxidative stress in bacteria. This causes inhibition of bacterial growth and hydrogen production. In order to prevent the toxicity caused by inorganic nanoparticles, studies on the development and use of microbial or biological nanoparticles in the fermentation process should be expanded. In order to reduce the cost of H_2 production, reduce environmental waste, and also achieve the goal of a circular economy, it is necessary to select the appropriate waste feedstock for biohydrogen production. Finally, nanocatalysts can also be used to increase the production of biofuels, including hydrogen (Jayabalan et al., 2021).

Dark fermentation is a fermentative process in which organic and inorganic substances are converted into biohydrogen by anaerobic bacteria in the absence of light. Dark fermentation is an inexpensive, high rate of hydrogen production that can be integrated into wastewater treatment (Lay et al., 2012).

Photofermentation is a fermentative, light-dependent process in which the organic substrate is converted to hydrogen by photosynthetic bacteria (Hoàng et al., 2021). Hydrogen production by photofermentation is also called photo-heterotrophic hydrogen production (Oh et al., 2013). Purple sulfur bacteria, purple non-sulfur bacteria, and green sulfur bacteria are photosynthetic bacteria that produce hydrogen using light and organic wastes. Purple non-sulfur bacteria are photosynthetic bacteria commonly used for photofermentation (Brentner et al., 2010).

Biomass can be used as a substrate to produce biohydrogen, and microorganisms called thermophiles, which can thrive at high temperatures, can digest biomass to produce hydrogen. This fermentation mode has several advantages, as it operates at higher temperatures. These advantages can be expressed as lower pollution risk, no need for mixing, higher reaction rates, and no need for cooling water. Apart from these, thermophiles have enzymes that increase biohydrogen production as they can withstand higher temperatures. *Clostridium thermocellum*, *Thermoanaerobacterium thermostercus*, *Clostridium thermolacticum*, *Thermobrachium celere*, and *Thermoanaerobacterium saccharolyticum* are some of the thermophiles used for biohydrogen production. Thermophilic fermentation is preferred for biohydrogen production. Because in order to provide mesophilic conditions in hydrogen fermentation, it is necessary to cool or wait for the cooling of the wastes. Hot industrial waste can be fermented directly to produce biohydrogen without any restrictions on thermophilic fermentation. High hydrogen production rates, elimination of pathogens, and less end product variety are other benefits of thermophilic fermentation (Zeldes et al., 2015).

With biophotolysis, water is broken down into molecular hydrogen and oxygen under special conditions by using cyanobacteria and green microalgae with the help of sunlight. Biophotolysis can be carried out in two ways, direct, and indirect (Rahman et al., 2016).

Solar energy and algae are used in the photosynthesis system to convert water into chemical energy. Organisms involving direct biophotolysis are *Chlamydomonas reinhardtii* from the green algae and *Synechocystis* from the cyanobacteria. In these processes, hydrogen production is successful if the oxygen content is kept below 0.1%. The advantage of these processes is that they are easily accessible and inexpensive. The disadvantage is its low efficiency (about 5%). In recent studies, it has been produced by microalgae mutants of microorganisms such as Scenedesmus obliquus. It increased hydrogen production by showing a better effect in the presence of oxygen, which negatively affects the hydrogen production of mutants (Rahman et al., 2016).

It is a two-step process applied to convert solar energy into hydrogen in the photosynthesis system using water, cyanobacteria, and microalgae. The first step is the production of large amounts of biomass by photosynthesis to increase the carbohydrate-rich biomass. The second stage is hydrogen production using carbohydrate-rich biomass stored in fermentation (Rahman et al., 2016).

Another way to oxidize acetate (or dark fermentation output) to produce hydrogen is to provide external energy in the form of electricity instead of solar energy. In this approach, acetate is located in the anodic compartment of the electrolysis cell, and the protons and electrons produced by bacteria are collected at the cathode (the cathode is the platinum electrode that catalyzes the hydrogen generation reaction). About 100 mV is required to produce hydrogen at the cathode. At 250 mV, 2.9 mol of H_2 are produced for every mole of acetate. Algae and photosynthetic bacteria can use daylight to autotrophically produce hydrogen gas from water, but their efficiency is low. Carbohydrates such as glucose and polysaccharides such as starch and cellulose can ferment into hydrogen gas at an average rate of 2.5 $\pm$ 4.3 m^3/m^3 per day. The conversion of organic by-products dissolved in fermentation to hydrogen occurs by an endothermic reaction. These molecules cannot be converted into hydrogen without the addition of external energy. The method used by the bacteria depends on sunlight. It has emerged that electrolysis-type processes based on microbial fuel cells (MFC) can be used to produce hydrogen gas. In MFC, bacteria oxidize organic matter, releasing CO_2 and protons into the solution, and releasing electrons to the electrode (anode). Electrons flow from the anode to the cathode. At the cathode, the electrons are depleted in the reduction of oxygen. When oxygen is present at the cathode, current can be produced, but in the absence of oxygen, current generation does not occur spontaneously (Manish & Banerjee, 2008).

They are mixed systems that combine the fermentative and photofermentation processes either directly or in a serial configuration. In the complete breakdown of 1 mol of glucose, 12 mol of hydrogen are produced. However, the complete breakdown of glucose into hydrogen and carbon dioxide is not possible because it is thermodynamically impossible for this reaction to occur. With an external energy source (photon energy in photofermentation), it can theoretically produce 12 mol of hydrogen per 1 mol of glucose. However, this process cannot be operated in the absence of light. On the other hand, in the absence of external energy (in the case of dark fermentation), a maximum of 4 mol of hydrogen and some by-products are formed by the oxidation of 1 mol of glucose by fermentative bacteria. Acetate produced in the dark fermentation stage can be oxidized to produce hydrogen by photosynthetic bacteria. Therefore, continuous hydrogen production at the highest yield can be achieved by combining dark and photofermentation methods (Manish & Banerjee, 2008).

According to ISO standards, biohydrogen must have a minimum H_2 purity of 99% in order to be used as a fuel source (Aasadnia et al., 2021). Chemical absorption, membrane separation, cryogenic separation, and adsorption are widely used for biohydrogen purification (Sazali, 2020). High purity biohydrogen can be obtained by chemical absorption, but solvent costs and corrosion problems are disadvantages of chemical adsorption (Azira & Aisah, 2019). The membrane separation approach has advantages such as low investment, operating and maintenance costs, high adaptability, and easy operation (Aasadnia et al., 2021).

17.6 Conclusion

Energy, which is the most important factor in meeting people's primary and secondary needs, is now heavily reliant on fossil fuels. As a result of the combustion of fossil fuels, pollutants such as carbon dioxide, nitrogen oxides, sulfur oxides, and particulate matter are released into the environment. These pollutants released into nature are known as "greenhouse gases," which have been shown to be the cause of global climate change. On the other hand, these pollutants, directly and indirectly, threaten the health of living things. The expansion of industry, technological developments, and population growth naturally increase the demand for energy. Factors such as the negative effects of fossil fuels on the environment, the commitments made by countries within the framework of international agreements, and the scarcity of fossil fuels drive societies to alternative energy sources (Ding et al., 2021; Haiyun et al., 2021; Dong et al., 2022; Kostis et al., 2022).

Biomass energy, one of the renewable energy types, is increasing its share of the energy supply day by day. Biomass energy is considered a promising energy source due to its economics, contribution to sustainability and economic feasibility, and relatively easy availability. Since it is based on plant and animal waste, biomass will continue to exist as long as the sun and other natural cycles exist. This means an almost endless source of energy. Biogas obtained from biomass has great advantages in terms of recovering organic matter and some minerals. In addition, in the process of biogas production, wastes are disposed of, organic and qualified fertilizers are obtained, and energy is produced. The world has a large source of biomass. Most of these resources cannot be converted into energy, and these organic wastes cause environmental pollution. There is a need for increasing biogas production facilities, developing research on biogas, and providing financial support, especially for the establishment of biogas facilities. In addition to clean energy production, the biogas facilities to be established will provide political and economic benefits, especially for foreign-dependent countries in energy production. Since organic materials are not included in the biogas production process, 590–880 million tons of methane gas are thrown into the atmosphere every year as a result of the breakdown of organic materials by anaerobic microorganisms. Biogenic sources constitute 90% of the methane gas released into the atmosphere. The rest comes from fossil fuels. The methane concentration in the atmosphere in the northern hemisphere is approximately 1.65 ppm. Methane gas has 21 times more global warming potential than carbon dioxide. The greenhouse effect of methane gas on earth is 15%.

Another important source obtained from biomass is biohydrogen. In practice, operating an efficient and economically viable hydrogen production process is of the utmost importance. H_2 production by dark fermentative conversion of organic substrates or by photobiological processing is very important because of its two functions (substrate removal and H_2 production). The production of H_2 by fermentation is accompanied by the formation of organic acids as a metabolic product, but these microorganisms cannot break down acids. The formation and accumulation of these soluble acid metabolites cause the pH to drop excessively in the system and inhibits the H_2 production process. Acidophilic conditions suppress the methanogenic process and energy conversion from organic sources in the form of H_2 remains at only 15%. The use of carbon sources not used in wastewater for additional hydrogen production will support the practical applicability of the process. Among biological methods, dark fermentation is an effective way to produce renewable hydrogen. The reactor required for biohydrogen production is simple in design and uses a technology based on a well-known anaerobic treatment. For the operation of this process under the most suitable conditions, analysis of bioprocess parameters should be carried out; competitive reactions should be prevented. H_2 partial pressure should be reduced, and the use of thermophilic species should be encouraged. The low efficiency and production rates of biological hydrogen production processes constitute a major obstacle to the practical application of these processes. Two-thirds of the carbon and protons in the substrate are converted to other products. The development of new techniques for the production of hydrogen-producing bacteria, the intensification of studies on unusual microorganisms and enzyme species, and the increase in hydrogen production efficiency with modern biotechnology are promising innovations for the future of hydrogen energy. Large-scale applicability will increase with the operation of biological hydrogen production processes at high hydrogen efficiency using a wide range of renewable substrate sources. Hydrogen is considered a renewable, clean energy carrier if it is produced from renewable biomass. In this context, especially agricultural waste, domestic and domestic industrial waste should be considered primarily. Food processing waste has great potential for alternative energy production due to its high carbohydrate, protein, and lipid contents. However, for the effective use of food processing waste, careful analysis of the main components of the waste and economic analysis of possible conversion processes such as thermal, chemical, and biological energy processes should be carried out. All possible problems and additional costs that may occur should be considered when designing the recycling process for waste. In order to select a process that provides both economic and environmental benefits, economic analysis should be performed in the process design. When the energy conversion method is to be determined, the best option among the different energy forms should be analyzed to optimize the potential of the waste. Hydrogen fermentation and gasification methods with high protein and/or fatty acid-containing wastes will be more suitable than ethanol and methane production. A combination of different processes can be considered to maximize energy production efficiency and minimize potential problems.

In the production of biodiesel from biomass, especially the farmers who plant oilseed plants, will be indirectly supported and the marketing problems of their products will be eliminated. New business areas will be opened in the production and consumption stages of biodiesel, and migration to big cities will be prevented. The socio-economic structure of the rural areas will improve, foreign dependency on oil will decrease, and added value will be created for the country's economy. Switching to the use of modern biomass energy is important for the country's economy and environmental pollution. Every country in the world needs to provide an alternative energy source from the most suitable and economical agricultural and forest products according to its ecological conditions.

References

Aasadnia, M., Mehrpooya, M., & Ghorbani, B. (2021). A novel integrated structure for hydrogen purification using the cryogenic method. *Journal of Cleaner Production, 278*, 123872.

Abubackar, H. N., Keskin, T., Yazgin, O., Gunay, B., Arslan, K., & Azbar, N. (2019). Biohydrogen production from autoclaved fruit and vegetable wastes by dry fermentation under thermophilic condition. *International Journal of Hydrogen Energy, 44*(34), 18776–18784.

Acaroğlu, M. (2003). Alternatif Enerji Kaynaklar, Atlas Yayn Dağtm, \.Istanbul, Temmuz.

Adalı, Z., Dinçer, H., Eti, S., Mikhaylov, A., & Yüksel, S. (2022). Identifying new perspectives on geothermal energy investments. In *Multidimensional strategic outlook on global competitive energy economics and finance*. Emerald Publishing Limited.

Amorim, N. C. S., Alves, I., Martins, J. S., & Amorim, E. L. C. (2014). Biohydrogen production from cassava wastewater in an anaerobic fluidized bed reactor. *Brazilian Journal of Chemical Engineering, 31*(3), 603–612.

Ar, F. F. I., Akdağ, F., Malkoç, Y., & Çalşkan, M. (2004). Biyokütle enerjisi ve biyomotorin. Biyoenerji–Biyomotorin, E\.IE \.Idaresi Genel Müdürlüğü, Ankara (pp. 583–594).

Arimi, M. M., Knodel, J., Kiprop, A., Namango, S. S., Zhang, Y., & Geißen, S.-U. (2015). Strategies for improvement of biohydrogen production from organic-rich wastewater: A review. *Biomass and Bioenergy, 75*, 101–118.

Azira, A. M. N., & Aisah, A. U. (2019). Purification of biohydrogen from fermentation gas mixture using two-stage chemical absorption. *E3S Web of Conferences, 90*, 1012.

Bhuiyan, M. A., Dinçer, H., Yüksel, S., Mikhaylov, A., Danish, M. S. S., Pinter, G., et al. (2022). Economic indicators and bioenergy supply in developed economies: QROF-DEMATEL and random forest models. *Energy Reports, 8*, 561–570.

Brentner, L. B., Peccia, J., & Zimmerman, J. B. (2010). Challenges in developing biohydrogen as a sustainable energy source: Implications for a research agenda. *Environmental Science & Technology, 44*(7), 2243–2254.

Chen, C.-Y., Yang, M.-H., Yeh, K.-L., Liu, C.-H., & Chang, J.-S. (2008). Biohydrogen production using sequential two-stage dark and photo fermentation processes. *International Journal of Hydrogen Energy, 33*(18), 4755–4762.

Dinçer, H., Yüksel, S., & Martínez, L. (2022). Collaboration enhanced hybrid fuzzy decision-making approach to analyze the renewable energy investment projects. *Energy Reports, 8*, 377–389.

Ding, Z., Yüksel, S., & Dincer, H. (2021). An Integrated Pythagorean fuzzy soft computing approach to environmental management systems for sustainable energy pricing. *Energy Reports, 7*, 5575–5588.

Dong, W., Zhao, G., Yüksel, S., Dinçer, H., & Ubay, G. G. (2022). A novel hybrid decision making approach for the strategic selection of wind energy projects. *Renewable Energy, 185*, 321–337.

Engler, C. R., Jordan, E. R., McFarland, M. J., & Lacewell, R. D. (1999). *Economics and environmental impact of biogas production as a manure management strategy*. Biological & Agricultural Engineering, Texas A & M.

Fang, S., Zhou, P., Dinçer, H., & Yüksel, S. (2021). Assessment of safety management system on energy investment risk using house of quality based on hybrid stochastic interval-valued intuitionistic fuzzy decision-making approach. *Safety Science, 141*, 105333.

Gadhe, A., Sonawane, S. S., & Varma, M. N. (2015). Enhancement effect of hematite and nickel nanoparticles on biohydrogen production from dairy wastewater. *International Journal of Hydrogen Energy, 40*(13), 4502–4511.

Haiyun, C., Zhixiong, H., Yüksel, S., & Dinçer, H. (2021). Analysis of the innovation strategies for green supply chain management in the energy industry using the QFD-based hybrid interval valued intuitionistic fuzzy decision approach. *Renewable and Sustainable Energy Reviews, 143*, 110844.

Hoàng, T. Y., Khoo, K. S., Ngọc, H. L. T., Thu, Q. T. T., Thị, T. Đ., Thu, H. Đ. T., Hoàng, H. C., Chinthalapati, S., Lay, C.-H., & Show, P. L. (2021). Sustainable cultivation via waste soybean extract for higher vaccenic acid production by purple non-sulfur bacteria. *Clean Technologies and Environmental Policy, 23*(1), 103–112.

Jayabalan, T., Matheswaran, M., Radhakrishnan, T. K., & Mohamed, S. N. (2021). Influence of nickel molybdate nanocatalyst for enhancing biohydrogen production in microbial electrolysis cell utilizing sugar industrial effluent. *Bioresource Technology, 320*, 124284.

Karayilmazlar, S., Saraçoğlu, N., Çabuk, Y., & Rfat, K. (2011). Biyokütlenin Türkiye'de enerji üretiminde değerlendirilmesi. *Bartn Orman Fakültesi Dergisi, 13*(19), 63–75.

Khoo, K. S., Tan, X., Ooi, C. W., Chew, K. W., Leong, W. H., Chai, Y. H., Ho, S.-H., & Show, P. L. (2021). How does ionic liquid play a role in sustainability of biomass processing? *Journal of Cleaner Production, 284*, 124772.

Kostis, P., Dinçer, H., & Yüksel, S. (2022). Knowledge-based energy investments of European economies and policy recommendations for sustainable development. *Journal of the Knowledge Economy*, 1–33.

Kou, G., Yüksel, S., & Dinçer, H. (2022). Inventive problem-solving map of innovative carbon emission strategies for solar energy-based transportation investment projects. *Applied Energy, 311*, 118680.

Kumar, G., Park, J.-H., Sivagurunathan, P., Lee, S.-H., Park, H.-D., & Kim, S.-H. (2017). Microbial responses to various process disturbances in a continuous hydrogen reactor fed with galactose. *Journal of Bioscience and Bioengineering, 123*(2), 216–222.

Kumari, D., & Singh, R. (2018). Pretreatment of lignocellulosic wastes for biofuel production: A critical review. *Renewable and Sustainable Energy Reviews, 90*, 877–891.

Lay, C.-H., Kuo, S.-Y., Sen, B., Chen, C.-C., Chang, J.-S., & Lin, C.-Y. (2012). Fermentative biohydrogen production from starch-containing textile wastewater. *International Journal of Hydrogen Energy, 37*(2), 2050–2057.

Li, J., Yüksel, S., Dınçer, H., Mikhaylov, A., & Barykin, S. E. (2022). Bipolar q-ROF hybrid decision making model with golden cut for analyzing the levelized cost of renewable energy alternatives. *IEEE Access, 10*, 42507–42517.

Liu, J., Lv, J., Dinçer, H., Yüksel, S., & Karakuş, H. (2021). Selection of renewable energy alternatives for green blockchain investments: A hybrid IT2-based fuzzy modelling. *Archives of Computational Methods in Engineering, 28*(5), 3687–3701.

Manish, S., & Banerjee, R. (2008). Comparison of biohydrogen production processes. *International Journal of Hydrogen Energy, 33*(1), 279–286.

Meng, Y., Wu, H., Zhao, W., Chen, W., Dinçer, H., & Yüksel, S. (2021). A hybrid heterogeneous Pythagorean fuzzy group decision modelling for crowdfunding development process pathways of fintech-based clean energy investment projects. *Financial Innovation, 7*(1), 1–34.

Mishra, P., Krishnan, S., Rana, S., Singh, L., Sakinah, M., & Ab Wahid, Z. (2019). Outlook of fermentative hydrogen production techniques: An overview of dark, photo and integrated dark-photo fermentative approach to biomass. *Energy Strategy Reviews, 24*, 27–37.

Mohammadi, P., Ibrahim, S., Annuar, M. S. M., & Law, S. (2011). Effects of different pretreatment methods on anaerobic mixed microflora for hydrogen production and COD reduction from palm oil mill effluent. *Journal of Cleaner Production, 19*(14), 1654–1658.

Mukhtarov, S., Yüksel, S., & Dinçer, H. (2022). The impact of financial development on renewable energy consumption: Evidence from Turkey. *Renewable Energy, 187*, 169–176.

Nagarajan, D., Dong, C.-D., Chen, C.-Y., Lee, D.-J., & Chang, J.-S. (2021). Biohydrogen production from microalgae—Major bottlenecks and future research perspectives. *Biotechnology Journal, 16*(5), 2000124.

Oceguera-Contreras, E., Aguilar-Juárez, O., Oseguera-Galindo, D., Macías-Barragán, J., Bolaños-Rosales, R., Mena-Enríquez, M., Arias-García, A., Montoya-Buelna, M., Graciano-Machuca, O., & de León-Rodríguez, A. (2019). Biohydrogen production by vermihumus-associated microorganisms using agro industrial wastes as substrate. *International Journal of Hydrogen Energy, 44*(20), 9856–9865.

Oh, Y.-K., Raj, S. M., Jung, G. Y., & Park, S. (2013). Metabolic engineering of microorganisms for biohydrogen production. In *Biohydrogen* (pp. 45–65). Elsevier.

Onursal, E., Oechsner, H., & Ekici, K. (2011). Biogas production potential of rose oil processing wastes and quail manure in Turkiye: Assessment by Hohenheim Batch Test. *Tarm Makinalar Bilimi Dergisi, 7*(4), 393–398.

Rahman, S. N. A., Masdar, M. S., Rosli, M. I., Majlan, E. H., Husaini, T., Kamarudin, S. K., & Daud, W. R. W. (2016). Overview biohydrogen technologies and application in fuel cell technology. *Renewable and Sustainable Energy Reviews, 66*, 137–162.

Ramos, L. R., & Silva, E. L. (2018). Continuous hydrogen production from cofermentation of sugarcane vinasse and cheese whey in a thermophilic anaerobic fluidized bed reactor. *International Journal of Hydrogen Energy, 43*(29), 13081–13089.

Rutz, D., & Janssen, R. (2013). Biomass resources for biogas production. In *The biogas handbook: Science, production and applications* (p. 19). Elsevier.

Salem, A. H., Brunstermann, R., Mietzel, T., & Widmann, R. (2018). Effect of pre-treatment and hydraulic retention time on biohydrogen production from organic wastes. *International Journal of Hydrogen Energy, 43*(10), 4856–4865.

Saratale, G. D., Saratale, R. G., Banu, J. R., & Chang, J.-S. (2019). Biohydrogen production from renewable biomass resources. In *Biohydrogen* (pp. 247–277). Elsevier.

Saravanan, A., Kumar, P. S., Khoo, K. S., Show, P.-L., Carolin, C. F., Jackulin, C. F., Jeevanantham, S., Karishma, S., Show, K.-Y., Lee, D.-J., & Chang, J.-S. (2021). Biohydrogen from organic wastes as a clean and environment-friendly energy source: Production pathways, feedstock types, and future prospects. *Bioresource Technology, 342*, 126021.

Sazali, N. (2020). Emerging technologies by hydrogen: A review. *International Journal of Hydrogen Energy, 45*(38), 18753–18771.

Serezli, E., Yüksel, S., Tamer, İ., & Dinçer, H. (2021). The role of innovative renewable energy investment strategies on macroeconomic stability. In *Financial strategies in competitive markets* (pp. 165–178). Springer.

Shao, W., Wang, Q., Rupani, P. F., Krishnan, S., Ahmad, F., Rezania, S., Rashid, M. A., Sha, C., & Din, M. F. M. (2020). Biohydrogen production via thermophilic fermentation: A prospective application of Thermotoga species. *Energy, 197*, 117199.

Sinharoy, A., & Pakshirajan, K. (2020). A novel application of biologically synthesized nanoparticles for enhanced biohydrogen production and carbon monoxide bioconversion. *Renewable Energy, 147*, 864–873.

Sivagurunathan, P., Sen, B., & Lin, C.-Y. (2015). High-rate fermentative hydrogen production from beverage wastewater. *Applied Energy, 147*, 1–9.

Urbaniec, K., & Bakker, R. R. (2015). Biomass residues as raw material for dark hydrogen fermentation—A review. *International Journal of Hydrogen Energy, 40*(9), 3648–3658.

Uzun, H. İ. (2021). Renewable energy and environment in the context of sustainability. In *Strategic approaches to energy management* (pp. 257–269). Springer.

Wainaina, S., Lukitawesa, Kumar Awasthi, M., & Taherzadeh, M. J. (2019). Bioengineering of anaerobic digestion for volatile fatty acids, hydrogen or methane production: A critical review. *Bioengineered, 10*(1), 437–458.

Xie, Y., Zhou, Y., Peng, Y., Dinçer, H., Yüksel, S., & an Xiang, P. (2021). An extended Pythagorean fuzzy approach to group decision-making with incomplete preferences for analyzing balanced scorecard-based renewable energy investments. *IEEE Access, 9*, 43020–43035.

Yilmaz, A., Ünvar, S., Tufan, K., & Koçer, A. (2017). Türkiye'de Biyogaz Üretimi ve Biyogaz Üretimi Istatistik Bilgileri. *Technological Applied Sciences, 12*(4), 218–232.

Yüksel, S., Dinçer, H., Çağlayan, Ç., Uluer, G. S., & Lisin, A. (2022). Bitcoin mining with nuclear energy. In *Multidimensional strategic outlook on global competitive energy economics and finance*. Emerald Publishing Limited.

Yüksel, S., Mikhaylov, A., Ubay, G. G., & Uyeh, D. D. (2021). The role of hydrogen in the Black Sea for the future energy supply security of Turkey. In *Handbook of research on strategic management for current energy investments* (pp. 1–15). IGI Global.

Zeldes, B. M., Keller, M. W., Loder, A. J., Straub, C. T., Adams, M. W. W., & Kelly, R. M. (2015). Extremely thermophilic microorganisms as metabolic engineering platforms for production of fuels and industrial chemicals. *Frontiers in Microbiology, 6*, 1209.

Zhao, Y., Xu, Y., Yüksel, S., Dinçer, H., & Ubay, G. G. (2021). Hybrid IT2 fuzzy modelling with alpha cuts for hydrogen energy investments. *International Journal of Hydrogen Energy, 46*(13), 8835–8851.

Zhe, L., Yüksel, S., Dinçer, H., Mukhtarov, S., & Azizov, M. (2021). The positive influences of renewable energy consumption on financial development and economic growth. *SAGE Open, 11*(3), 21582440211040133.

Zhou, P., Luo, J., Cheng, F., Yüksel, S., & Dinçer, H. (2021). Analysis of risk priorities for renewable energy investment projects using a hybrid IT2 hesitant fuzzy decision-making approach with alpha cuts. *Energy, 224*, 120184.

Chapter 18
Renewable Energy Investments and Unemployment Problem

Hakan Kaya

Abstract Renewable energy is important to reduce the global climate threat, ensuring energy security, and minimizing environmental risks. Although the renewable energy sector has entered a rapid development process in recent years, many countries still depend on traditional energy sources. Environmental degradation caused by the intensive use of traditional energy sources creates serious employment losses on a global scale. Policy makers turn to renewable energy investments in the face of both the negative effects of environmental degradation and employment losses shows the existence of the potential to eliminate these externalities in the long term. In the study, which deals with the effects of developments in the renewable energy sector on employment, it is evaluated how employment conditions evolve depending on the increase in renewable energy investments in the short, medium, and long term. The direct, indirect, and induced effects of renewable energy investments on employment show different employment balances in the short, medium, and long term. In this study, in which renewable energy sources are presented, renewable energy investments and employment relations are evaluated, it has been concluded that the precondition for the continuity of employment depends on the adaptation of human capital to the development in the renewable energy sector and the production of policies suitable for this development in a way that covers the entire society.

Keywords Renewable energy · Unemployment · Clean energy · Macroeconomics

18.1 Introduction

Renewable energy investments are one of the most effective factors for sustainable development and economic growth. In recent years, many countries consider the strategies of increasing efficiency in production and reducing greenhouse gas (GHG)

H. Kaya (✉)
The School of Business, Bitlis Eren University, Bitlis, Turkey
e-mail: hkaya@beu.edu.tr

H. Dinçer, S. Yüksel (eds.), *Circular Economy and the Energy Market*,
Contributions to Economics, https://doi.org/10.1007/978-3-031-13146-2_18

emissions through renewable energy investments as an important part of their growth and development processes (Dinçer, 2000; Goldemberg & Coelho, 2004; Bergmann et al., 2006). Considering the dependence of the global system on energy supply, renewable energy investments make up the first stage of the transition to sustainable energy (Xie et al., 2021; Ding et al., 2021; Liu et al., 2021; Li et al., 2021). Sustainable energy, which includes the balance of energy production and consumption, provides social and economic advantages to countries while minimizing environmental negative externalities (Strantzali & Aravossis, 2016). Therefore, renewable energy investments driven by government-supported programs (subsidies, tax credits, and various incentives) have made renewable energy sources competitive with traditional energy sources in many countries (Bhattacharya et al., 2016). The impact of the said competition plays an important role in the optimization process of social benefit by contributing to the development of high energy efficiency, high economic growth, and low carbon energy technologies (Dai et al., 2016; Zhou et al., 2021; Meng et al., 2021).

The effect of renewable energy investments on employment is an important factor that should be considered in terms of social benefits. Increasing production costs because of the intensive use of traditional energy factors, loss of productivity, and employment losses because of environmental degradation, and high unemployment rates arising from the global labor market are among the issues that policymakers should consider (Nasirov et al., 2021). In this context, high unemployment rates and environmental degradation caused by energy production through traditional energy sources lead policy makers to policies that can solve both problems at the same time. The increase in support for these policies, which are described as green jobs and draw attention to the employment creation capability of renewable energy, has increased the interest in renewable energy investments in many countries, especially in developing countries (Rivers, 2013; Zhe et al., 2021; Haiyun et al., 2021; Yüksel et al., 2021). In the literature, the effects of renewable energy investments on labor markets and employment have been investigated in many countries and country groups. Studies using the input-output analysis method, panel data analysis, and computable general equilibrium models to estimate the direct, indirect, and induced employment effects of renewable energy investments have got different results. For example, Hillebrand et al. (2006) argue that the renewable energy support policy in the German economy will have a positive effect on employment in the short term and a negative effect in the medium and long term. Unlike Hillebrand et al., Lehr et al. (2008) argue that the net effect of the support policies provided to the renewable energy sector in the German economy is positive and increases employment in the long run. Tourkolias and Mirasgedis (2011) argue that the increase in renewable energy investments in the Greek energy sector will have a positive impact on economic development and employment, as well as create significant environmental improvements. Rivers (2013), in his study, in which the effect of renewable energy support programs on employment is handled within the framework of the three-sector general equilibrium model; He argues that renewable electricity support policies can reduce the equilibrium unemployment rate where the elasticity of substitution between capital and labor is low; the capital is not mobile at the international level, and the labor intensity of production through renewable energy sources is higher than conventional production. According to Rivers's results, a 10% reduction in renewable electricity sector emissions will cause an increase in employment by approximately 0.1–0.3%. Heinbach et al. (2014) point out that renewable energy investments have the potential to create added value and employment in Germany's existing renewable energy sector and even in regions where there is no manufacturing industry. Apergis and Salim (2015) argue that high and large-capacity investments to be made in the renewable energy sector will have a direct and positive impact on employment in the relevant sectors. Dvorak et al. (2017) found that the ability of renewable energy investments to create jobs in the Czech Republic is high in the short run, but in the long run, the said effect depends on the continuity of financial incentives. Peltier (2017) emphasizes that by transferring the investment made in fossil energy resources to the renewable energy sector, there will be an employment increase of 5% for each million dollars. Mu et al. (2018) argue that the increase in solar PV and wind energy investments will create direct and indirect employment, but the expansion in green jobs with the increase in renewable energy investments may lead to net employment losses in the entire economy. Mu et al. (2018) reached similar results with Dvorak et al. (2017). According to Mu et al. (2018), the impact of the increase in renewable energy investments on the development of green jobs and employment depends on the type of renewable energy to which investment will be expanded, subsidies, financing mechanism, and employment conditions. According to Chen (2018), who evaluates the employment creation capability of renewable energy investments in China, a million dollar expenditure on renewable energy investments tends to create approximately 162.3 green jobs compared to fossil resources. According to Chen, the increased efficiency with the development of the renewable energy sector has the potential to significantly reduce the employment creation capacity of traditional energy sources.

As theoretical and empirical studies show, the ability of renewable energy investments to create employment varies according to the physical and human characteristics of countries. Substituting traditional energy sources for renewable energy sources in the production processes of countries brings with it an important socio-economic transformation (Fang et al., 2021; Yuan et al., 2021; Serezli et al., 2021). The employment creation capacity of the renewable energy sector develops in direct proportion to the increase in the amount of investment, and the permanence of employment is related to the continuity of support and incentives. In this context, the study focuses on the effects of renewable energy in the short and medium term, rather than its long-term positive effects. The main argument that the study focuses on is the hypothesis that renewable energy investments, which are described as green jobs, will create more environmentally friendly business lines by increasing efficiency in production. Therefore, in the following section first, renewable energy sources and their types are discussed. In the second part, renewable energy investments are defined. The third section deals with the employment creation capacity of renewable energy sources. This section, which deals with the sectoral effects of renewable energy, especially the direct, indirect, and induced effects of investments in the renewable energy sector, tries to explain how employment opportunities develop depending on the developments in the renewable energy sector. The fourth and last part of the study includes the conclusion and evaluation part.

18.2 Renewable Energy Sources

Renewable energy sources play an important role both in meeting the world's future energy demand and in reducing environmental damage (Ottinger & Williams, 2002). Energy resources are divided into three categories: fossil fuels, renewable resources, and nuclear resources. Fossil fuels refer to traditional energy sources. Traditional energy sources, which are described as derivatives of fossil fuels such as oil, coal, and natural gas, are the main energy sources for transportation, heating, and electricity generation in many countries (Wright, 2010). Although these traditional energy sources are the main key to growth in many countries' economies, they decrease rapidly, become exhaustible, and create negative externalities on the environment during production and use (OECD, 2022). For this reason, negative externalities created by traditional energy sources and policies aimed at ensuring energy supply and security lead policy makers to policies toward reducing dependency on traditional energy sources and increasing the use of renewable energy sources. Renewable energy sources are the type of energy that does not run out after being used and can produce energy again and again (Shang et al., 2021; Kou et al., 2022; Mukhtarov et al., 2022). This type of energy, which is got from natural sources such as hydroelectric, solar energy, wind energy, biomass energy, and geothermal energy, is often called alternative energy sources. Renewable energy technologies differ. This difference requires the use of different mechanisms in the phase of obtaining energy from renewable energy sources (Edenhofer et al., 2013).

18.2.1 Hydropower

Hydroelectricity is the most widely used renewable energy type in the world. Hydroelectricity transforms the energy got from running water beds into electricity (Herzog et al., 2001). Conventional hydroelectricity uses the potential and kinetic energy of the precipitation collected in a high basin or the water source stored from the stream sources. Hydroelectric power plants, which provide energy in proportion to the flow volume, are a source type dependent on precipitation. Therefore, it is subject to fluctuations in energy production from season to season and from year to year (Laughton, 2003). Although hydroelectricity is an efficient energy source in terms of energy production, this resource is got through large dams that flood large lands, create environmental problems and displace agricultural lands clustered around streams. For this reason, it appears to be an energy source with a high hydroelectric power generation capacity, but also has environmental disadvantages (Maczullak, 2010, p. 109). In addition, approximately 40% of hydroelectric power plants that have been in use since the 1960s in many developed economies need modernization to improve their performance and increase their efficiency. There is a loss of between 5% and 10% in the energy capacity of old power plants that do not complete the modernization phase. In this context, the renewal of large equipment such as turbines and generators is important to sustain energy supply through hydroelectricity. Hydroelectric production increased by 3% in 2020 and reached 4418 TWh. With this statistic, hydroelectricity produced more energy than any other renewable energy source. The hydroelectric generation capacity, which is projected to increase to 5870 TWh by 2050, is expected to contribute significantly to the global zero carbon emission scenario (IEA, 2021a, b).

18.2.2 Solar Energy

Another renewable energy source is solar energy. Solar energy is defined as a renewable and/or sustainable energy source as long as the sun exists. Solar energy, which provides a great advantage in reducing energy costs, especially for developing countries, has the feature of contributing to the provision of basic services such as cooling, irrigation, communication, and lighting in rural areas where electricity networks are not available (Ottinger & Williams, 2002). The most widely used form of solar technology, which used the power from the sun to produce heat, light, and power, is photovoltaic (PV) technology (Krozer, 2022, p. 101), which converts daylight directly into electricity. Photovoltaic cells capture the energy in the sun's radiation called photons and produce electric current by separating electrons (Maczullak, 2010, p. 102). Besides eliminating the high cost and negative externalities of fossil fuels, PV technology is more efficient than existing energy sources (Dinçer et al., 2022; Kostis et al., 2022). The energy produced by PV technology is an important source for meeting the large energy demands of the domestic, agricultural, industrial and commercial sectors. Solar energy technology is a clean energy source because it does not create negative environmental externalities during the energy production phase. Therefore, solar energy capacity is important in terms of energy sustainability (Li et al., 2020; Yüksel et al., 2020).

18.2.3 Wind Energy

Wind energy is widely used in many parts of the world for electricity generation after solar energy. As an installed renewable energy technology, wind energy, which is the most common energy source after hydroelectricity, plays an important role in expanding installed capacity and mitigating climate change. Wind technology converts the energy in the wind into electricity or mechanical power with the help of wind turbines. The power got in this way depends on the rotation of the wind turbines and the generation of energy as long as there is wind. Wind energy is a noncompetitive technology in energy production and has almost no pollution in terms of emissions (Panwar et al., 2011). While the seasonal and seasonal differences caused by climate, changes benefit the wind energy industry, other changes may have negative effects on the efficiency and development of that energy. The benefit level, which emerges because of the geographical location of the country, makes wind energy an important alternative energy source to meet low-level energy needs (Liu et al., 2020; Du et al., 2020). Compared to solar PV technologies, which cannot generate power at night, wind energy can produce electricity continuously as long as there is wind (Demirbaş, 2006). Wind energy is a good alternative energy source, especially for developing countries that have difficulties in maintaining the energy supply and demand balance. The ability of the turbines that convert wind energy into energy to be installed even in inaccessible and hilly areas provides a significant flexibility between alternative energy sources. The energy produced by wind technology is inexhaustible, significantly reducing the dependence on traditional energy sources and contributing to the minimization of emissions (Panwar et al., 2011). Compared to 2020, the wind industry grew by 1.8%. New investments of 93.6 GW in 2021 increased global energy capacity by 12%. New installations of onshore wind turbines in Europe, Latin America and Africa, and the Middle East increased by 19%, 27%, and 120%, respectively (Zhao, 2022).

18.2.4 Bioenergy

Bioenergy is considered an interesting energy source in terms of its contribution to sustainable development and energy security (Hoogwijk, 2004, p. 26). Bioenergy is a type of energy got from organic substances found in nature. The main sources of bioenergy are ethanol produced from cereal crops; methanol produced from natural gas, or solid organic waste called biomass; biogas comprises methane and carbon dioxide (CO_2) mixture and vegetable oils (Maczullak, 2010, p. 57). Biomass energy or bioenergy got through the collection and storage of solar energy through photosynthesis converting biomass into energy such as heat, electricity, and liquid fuels (Herzog et al., 2001). Biomass is an important energy source, especially for developing countries, as it uses local raw materials and the workforce. Agricultural wastes, cellulosic biomass, and crops grown to be used as inputs in the energy sector are converted into usable energy for industry and households because of simple combustion and gasification processes. Bioenergy has a positive effect on reducing greenhouse gas emissions and degraded soil structures. While adding organic matter to the soil contributes to the recovery of degraded land, the sustainable production and use of bioenergy contribute to the balancing of greenhouse gas emissions from fossil fuels (Hoogwijk, 2004, p. 26). The distribution of renewable energy resources varies according to the geographical characteristics of the country and has different efficiency levels. Solar energy, wind energy, and hydropower have the ability to generate energy in all locations around the world, albeit at different levels. This wide accessibility makes renewable energy sources an alternative to traditional energy sources in many geographical areas, especially in developing countries. The energy densities of these energy sources, measured by the energy content per area or mass unit, are low. For this reason, they need to spread over a large area per renewable energy generation. Although this wide spread is not a problem in rural areas, it causes spatial problems in the execution of energy-intensive activities in cities (in densely populated areas). In other words, renewable energy sources with high energy density are under spatial constraints. In addition, the energy production capacities of these renewable energy sources show seasonal differences depending on seasonal changes, weather conditions, and day and night time intervals. This situation, which is defined as intermittent energy supply, causes the volatility in energy prices to increase due to interruptions in energy supply from time to time or decrease in energy intensity. Efficiency losses caused by wide spread, low energy density, and geographical conditions require diversification of energy resources (Krozer, 2022, pp. 27–29). Renewable energy sources are still in the development stage compared to the energy obtained from traditional energy sources. However, it offers various opportunities to all countries, especially developing countries, to reduce energy dependence, sustainability, and reduce environmental externalities.

18.2.5 Geothermal Energy

Geothermal energy has a wide range of uses because of its low cost and has been used for many years. Geothermal energy is fed from the natural and continuous heat source at the center of the earth. Although geothermal energy is a renewable resource, it is accepted that the energy got from a certain area will run out after a while. Using geothermal energy is limited by economic and technical factors. The basis of these limits lies in the development of practical and economical mechanisms to make available the intense but diffuse thermal energy represented by the heat flow (Laughton, 2003). Because the acquisition of geothermal energy is the drilling of costly boreholes and the erosion of the materials used in the production phase. Sometimes, these costs (because of deeper drilling and more expensive equipment) are higher than the cost of heat plants. Since geothermal energy depends on the temperature of the groundwater, the hot water used in summer must be cooled, and in winter it must be heated by heat pumps. Considering the cost-efficiency balance of these processes, the great potential of geothermal energy limits the spread of low efficiency (Krozer, 2022). Geothermal wells from which geothermal energy is got release greenhouse gases trapped underground. Compared with emissions from traditional fossil fuels, however, this trend has a lower impact on fossil fuel combustion. In this respect, the widespread use of geothermal technology can support the reduction of global warming (Tran, 2018, p. 43).

18.3 Renewable Energy Investments

Renewable energy investments form the basis of a sustainable green economy. The main purpose of the green economy is to reduce energy consumption because of fossil fuel use, increase energy efficiency and savings, minimize emissions, and finally benefit from economic growth and environmental optimization. The investment behaviors of renewable energy enterprises, which make up an important branch of economic activities, are based on making profits by minimizing environmental risks. The capacity of enterprises to consider environmental concerns in their investment and production decisions has the potential to directly affect the development level of the green economy (He et al., 2019). Because of the increasing world population and modernization, it is predicted that the global energy demand will more than double in the first half of the twenty-first century and more than triple at the end of the century (Curley, 2014). Considering the reduction of traditional energy sources and the climate problems caused by carbon emissions, renewable energy technologies will play an important role in the supply of sufficient, clean, and sustainable energy sources soon (Foster et al., 2010). In this context, renewable energy investments, which include the development of renewable energy technologies, have an important share in reducing the threat of climate change through renewable energy support mechanisms and minimizing negative externalities, which are characterized as market failure (Raikar & Adamson, 2019, pp. 9–10). Renewable energy investments should be considered in two aspects. The first of these is the improvements to be made in the existing renewable energy sector, and the other is the investments to be made in the renewable energy sector. Improvements in the renewable energy sector include the modernization process of existing energy sources. Modernization processes aiming to increase the production flexibility of aging facilities or technologies with decreasing efficiency are the process of combining old technology with new technology. Improvements and investments to make the energy sector more efficient depend on the R&D capacities of the countries. Investments to be made in the renewable energy sector in countries with high R&D capacity will contribute to increasing the efficiency of existing renewable energy resources and enable the creation of energy policies according to the dynamics of the country. In most market economies, new energy infrastructures are financed by the private sector rather than governments. Considering that private sector capital finances more than 90% of renewable energy investments on a global scale, it is understood that the role of the state is to contribute to the creation of market regulatory regulations and to direct investments to optimal areas. Large-scale renewable energy projects require larger capital investments compared to investments in traditional energy sources. The realization of such investments in the project's context is subject to certain preconditions. First, investors should allocate resources to renewable energy investments, believe that the average price of the energy produced will be high enough to cover the investment rate and that the income from the investment will be stable enough to cover the operating costs of the project (interest costs, debt repayment, etc.). Especially with large-scale renewable energy investments, energy purchase agreements (PPA) arrangements are applied that fix the price of the energy sold for a certain period. Such mechanisms are considered within policy mechanisms that support renewable energy, since renewable energy is more expensive than traditional energy sources. Thanks to these policy support, the development of renewable energy sources speeds up and the rate of resources allocated to renewable energy investments increases (Raikar & Adamson, 2019, pp. 1–9). However; unlike traditional technologies, renewable energy technologies produce an indefinite amount of energy. The main reason for this problem is that seasonal disruptions caused by climate changes change the direction and amount of resources that power renewable energy resources. The decisions and regulations taken by policy makers and the international climate and energy communities vary over time between countries and often create great uncertainties in establishing the energy supply and demand balance. Even though the investment costs for renewable energy technologies decrease, this uncertainty prevents the stereotypes of countries from breaking down at the level of abandoning traditional energy sources. The reason for this situation is that the traditional power generation facilities that countries already own benefit from relatively lower investment and operation-maintenance costs (Reuter et al., 2012). In this context, the future growth of the energy sector depends on policy makers encouragement of renewable energy investments and the use of renewable energy technologies. Promoting renewable energy technologies will create market opportunities both to innovate through R&D and to exploit emerging energy markets. The development, use, and diversity of renewable energy resources will help to provide sustainable energy resources in the long term, reduce local and global emission rates, and contribute to economic growth by reducing energy dependence, especially in developing countries (Herzog et al., 2001). The negative framework created by the COVID-19 pandemic, especially supply chain disruptions, construction delays, and increase in raw material and commodity prices has also caused renewable energy investments on a global scale to be less than expected. Although renewable energy capacity additions increased by 6% in 2021, this rate remained below the estimates of organizations that put forward many projections for the future of the renewable energy sector, especially the IEA. While the 17% decline in wind technology investments in 2021 was balanced by the growth in solar power plants and hydroelectric power plants; The level of investment in bioenergy and geothermal energy resources remained stable in 2021 compared to the previous year. However, renewable energy capacities are expected to increase by 8% in 2022 compared to 2021.

18.4 Renewable Energy Investments Employment Relationship

Renewable energy technologies are more labor-intensive when compared to traditional energy sources, and because of this feature, their ability to increase employment is high. It is argued that the increase in renewable energy investments, especially in underdeveloped and developing countries with high dependence on foreign energy, will provide positive benefits to these countries in the long run (ILO, 2011). However, the short and medium-term effects of renewable energy investments contain both positive and negative effects. The effects of renewable energy investments on employment are discussed in three groups as direct, indirect, and induced effects. The direct employment effect is a function of overall investment in the renewable energy sector. The intensive labor force needed in the production, installation, and preparation of renewable energy equipment directly creates an employment increase. However, such an increase in employment is not permanent. Employment conditions will improve as long as sustainability is ensured in renewable energy investments. In this context, increasing employment conditions during the transition from traditional energy sources to renewable energy does not offer a permanent solution to the problem of reducing unemployment. Another effect of renewable energy investments on employment is indirect. The indirect employment effect operates as a subset of the direct effects and covers the secondary industries that provide input to the primary sector in making renewable energy available for use. The need for additional employment, which arises during the production, planning, and construction of materials to be used in renewable energy investment, will have a positive impact on employment rates. Finally, the positive effect of renewable energy on employment is evaluated within the induced employment effect. The induced employment effect is defined as the increase in the taxable income level of renewable energy expenditures and the increase in additional income in the economy with the multiplier effect of additional employment, which is the total function of the direct and indirect effects of renewable energy investments. The negative effects of renewable energy investments on employment are observed during the transition period from traditional energy sources to renewable energy sources. Factors such as the replacement of many sectors that produce with traditional energy sources with less green jobs, employment losses in coal mining because of the decrease in the demand for fossil fuels, and the closure of production facilities that highly depend on traditional energy sources in reducing environmental externalities with renewable energy may cause employment losses (IRENA & ILO, 2021; Yılancı et al., 2020; ILO, 2011). The fact that renewable energy sources are more costly than traditional energy sources and the possible technological and human adaptation problem in the transition phase of production forces to new technology is another factor that may adversely affect the employment creation capacity of renewable energy sources seen as the cause. The differences in the geographical locations of the countries bring up the problem that not every renewable energy source is suitable for every country, and therefore different investment costs vary depending on the suitability of different renewable energy sources. Meeting the costs of renewable energy investments is an important problem, especially for underdeveloped and developing countries. Considering that investments are financed with debt in countries with low capital accumulation, it is possible that the increase in renewable energy investments will impose additional borrowing costs on countries. In this context, the relationship between renewable energy investments and employment points to the existence of a multidimensional, complex, and controversial system. With the increase in investments in the renewable energy sector, the ability of the renewable energy sector to create employment is constantly increasing. According to IRENA and ILO (2021), while the renewable energy sector directly or indirectly employed 11.5 million people in 2019, this figure reached 12 million in 2020. The PV, bioenergy, hydroelectric, and wind energy industries are among the sectors that create the most employment (IRENA & ILO, 2021). The ability of renewable energy investments to create employment depends on the level of development of national and international markets. In the context of technological leadership, applied industrial policies, local energy requirements, and the effects of the supply chain, the renewable energy sector develops, and its employment creation capacity increases. At this stage, the shaping and transformation of human capital according to the current conditions of the country is decisive. Ensuring the skill-based supply and demand balance in the industry is important in terms of creating a skilled workforce. Creating sustainable employment conditions for a larger and more skilled workforce within the scope of green growth is possible with the coordination of optimal education policies, policy makers, and education and training institutions. In this context, the fact that employment conditions cover the whole society during the transition from economies in which traditional energy resources are used intensively to green economy, which is the return of renewable energy use, is based on the diversification of the country's talent line. As the renewable energy sector expands, individuals with technical, commercial, administrative, economic, legal, and other skills will become more important in ensuring sustainable employment. The opposite situation indicates that the renewable energy sector will have difficulties in employing well-educated and experienced personnel, even if wages rise. For this reason, the steps to be taken to increase the existing human capital of the country and the steps to be taken to cover the whole society of the renewable energy sector will not only represent a great opportunity for the renewable energy sector, but also contribute to increasing direct, indirect, and induced employment.

18.5 Discussion and Conclusion

The most important factor determining the growth and development levels of countries is energy consumption and energy efficiency. In addition to increasing carbon emissions due to the intense use of traditional energy resources, which are scarce in nature, resource conflicts and energy crises are frequently seen on a global scale. Macroeconomic variables such as production and employment, especially the balance of payments of countries that are dependent on foreign energy, are adversely affected by fluctuations in energy prices. For this reason, the possibility that resources such as natural gas and oil, which are already scarce, may become even more scarce and expensive in the future, requires replacing traditional energy sources with renewable energy sources or increasing their share in total energy use. Countries that have renewable energy resources or develop renewable energy systems gain advantages in terms of ensuring energy supply security, improving living standards, increasing the level of employment, and ensuring sustainable economic growth and development. The renewable energy sector is still under development in most countries. Projections drawn for the future indicate that the energy demand, which is expected to increase in the future, will be met by renewable energy technologies. As the renewable energy sector develops, employment conditions change significantly. As discussed in the study, while the ability of renewable energy technologies to create employment is high in the short and medium term, it depends on the adaptation of human capital to the renewable energy sector in the long term. Decisions to be taken to expand this harmonization to include the whole society will increase the qualifications of the country's potential workforce and contribute to the supply–demand balance in the total workforce.

References

Apergis, N., & Salim, R. (2015). Renewable energy consumption and unemployment: Evidence from a sample of 80 countries and nonlinear estimates. *Applied Economics, 47*(52), 1–20.

Bergmann, A., Hanley, N., & Wright, R. (2006). Valuing the attributes of renewable energy investments. *Energy Policy, 34*(9), 1004–1014.

Bhattacharya, M., Paramati, S. R., Ozturk, I., & Bhattacharya, S. (2016). The effect of renewable energy consumption on economic growth: Evidence from top 38 countries. *Applied Energy, 162*, 733–741.

Chen, Y. (2018). Renewable energy investment and employment in China. *International Review and Applied Economics, 33*(3), 314–334.

Curley, M. (2014). *Finance policy for renewable energy and a sustainable environment*. CRC Press.

Dai, H., Xie, X., Xie, Y., Liu, J., & Masui, T. (2016). Green growth: The economic impacts of large-scale renewable energy development in China. *Applied Energy, 162*, 435–449.

Demirbaş, A. (2006). Global renewable energy resources. *Energy Sources, Part A: Recovery, Utilization, and Environmental Effects, 28*(8), 779–792.

Dinçer, H., Yüksel, S., & Martínez, L. (2022). Collaboration enhanced hybrid fuzzy decision-making approach to analyze the renewable energy investment projects. *Energy Reports, 8*, 377–389.

Dinçer, İ. (2000). Renewable energy and sustainable development: A crucial review. *Renewable and Sustainable Energy Reviews, 4*(2), 157–175.

Ding, Z., Yüksel, S., & Dincer, H. (2021). An Integrated Pythagorean fuzzy soft computing approach to environmental management systems for sustainable energy pricing. *Energy Reports, 7*, 5575–5588.

Du, L., Dinçer, H., Ersin, İ., & Yüksel, S. (2020). IT2 fuzzy-based multidimensional evaluation of coal energy for sustainable economic development. *Energies, 13*(10), 2453.

Dvorak, P., Martinal, S., Horst, D. V., Frantal, B., & Tureckova, K. (2017). Renewable energy investment and job creation; a cross-sectoral assessment for the Czech Republic with reference to EU benchmarks. *Renewable and Sustainable Energy Reviews, 69*, 360–368.

Edenhofer, O., Seyboth, K., Creutzig, F., & Schlömer, S. (2013). On the sustainability of renewable energy sources. *The Annual Review of Environment and Resources, 38*, 169–200.

Fang, S., Zhou, P., Dinçer, H., & Yüksel, S. (2021). Assessment of safety management system on energy investment risk using house of quality based on hybrid stochastic interval-valued intuitionistic fuzzy decision-making approach. *Safety Science, 141*, 105333.

Foster, R., Ghassemi, M., & Cota, A. (2010). *Solar energy: Renewable energy and the environment*. CRC Press.

Goldemberg, J., & Coelho, S. T. (2004). Renewable energy—Traditional biomass vs. modern biomass. *Energy Policy, 32*(6), 711–714.

Haiyun, C., Zhixiong, H., Yüksel, S., & Dinçer, H. (2021). Analysis of the innovation strategies for green supply chain management in the energy industry using the QFD-based hybrid interval valued intuitionistic fuzzy decision approach. *Renewable and Sustainable Energy Reviews, 143*, 110844.

He, L., Zhang, L., Zhong, Z., Wang, D., & Wang, F. (2019). Green credit, renewable energy investment and green economy development: Empirical analysis based on 150 listed companies of China. *Journal of Clean Production., 28*, 363–372.

Heinbach, K., Aretz, A., Hirschl, B., Prahl, A., & Salecki, S. (2014). Renewable energies and their impact on local value added and employment. *Energy, Sustainability and Society, 4*(1), 1.

Herzog, A. V., Lipman, T. E., & Kammen, D. M. (2001). Renewable energy: A viable choice. *Environment Science and Policy for Sustainable Development, 43*(10), 8–20.

Hillebrand, B., Buttermann, H. G., Behringer, J. M., & Bleuel, M. (2006). The expansion of renewable energies and employment effects in Germany. *Energy Policy, 34*, 3484–3494.

Hoogwijk, M. M. (2004). *On the global and regional potential of renewable energy sources* [Thesis/Dissertation]. Faculty of Chemistry, Utrecht University.

IEA. (2021a). *Hydropower*. IEA. Retrieved from https://www.iea.org/reports/hydropower

IEA. (2021b). *Renewables: Analysis and forecast to 2026*. International Energy Agency.

International Labour Office (ILO). (2011). Investment in renewable energy generates jobs. Supply of skilled workforce needs to catch up. In *Skills and occupational needs in renewable energy*. International Labour Organization.

International Renewable Energy Agency (IRENA), & International Labour Office (ILO). (2021). Renewable energy and jobs. In *Annual review 2021*. Special edition: Labour and policy perspectives, Abu Dhabi, Geneva.

Kostis, P., Dinçer, H., & Yüksel, S. (2022). Knowledge-based energy investments of European economies and policy recommendations for sustainable development. *Journal of the Knowledge Economy*, 1–33.

Kou, G., Yüksel, S., & Dinçer, H. (2022). Inventive problem-solving map of innovative carbon emission strategies for solar energy-based transportation investment projects. *Applied Energy, 311*, 118680.

Krozer, Y. (2022). *Economics of renewable energy: An assessment of innovations with statistical data*. Springer International Publishing AG.

Laughton, M. A. (2003). *Renewable energy sources*. Taylor & Francis Books.

Lehr, U., Nitsch, J., Kratzat, M., Lutz, C., & Edler, D. (2008). Renewable energy and employment in Germany. *Energy Policy, 36*(1), 108–117.

Li, X., Zhu, S., Yüksel, S., Dinçer, H., & Ubay, G. G. (2020). Kano-based mapping of innovation strategies for renewable energy alternatives using hybrid interval type-2 fuzzy decision-making approach. *Energy, 211*, 118679.

Li, Y. X., Wu, Z. X., Dinçer, H., Kalkavan, H., & Yüksel, S. (2021). Analyzing TRIZ-based strategic priorities of customer expectations for renewable energy investments with interval type-2 fuzzy modeling. *Energy Reports, 7*, 95–108.

Liu, H., Yüksel, S., & Dinçer, H. (2020). Analyzing the criteria of efficient carbon capture and separation technologies for sustainable clean energy usage. *Energies, 13*(10), 2592.
Liu, J., Lv, J., Dinçer, H., Yüksel, S., & Karakuş, H. (2021). Selection of renewable energy alternatives for green blockchain investments: A hybrid IT2-based fuzzy modelling. *Archives of Computational Methods in Engineering, 28*(5), 3687–3701.
Maczullak, A. E. (2010). *Renewable energy: Sources and methods*. Facts on File, Inc.
Meng, Y., Wu, H., Zhao, W., Chen, W., Dinçer, H., & Yüksel, S. (2021). A hybrid heterogeneous Pythagorean fuzzy group decision modelling for crowdfunding development process pathways of fintech-based clean energy investment projects. *Financial Innovation, 7*(1), 1–34.
Mu, Y., Cai, W., Evans, S., Wang, C., & Holst, D. R. (2018). Employment impacts of renewable energy policies in China: A decomposition analysis based on a CGE modeling framework. *Applied Energy, 210*, 256–267.
Mukhtarov, S., Yüksel, S., & Dinçer, H. (2022). The impact of financial development on renewable energy consumption: Evidence from Turkey. *Renewable Energy, 187*, 169–176.
Nasirov, S., Girard, A., Pena, C., Salazar, F. & Simon, F. (2021). Renewable energy in Chile: Analysis of the effects on employment. *Energy*, 226.
OECD. (2022), *Renewable energy (indicator)*. Retrieved June 14, 2022, from https://doi.org/10.1787/aac7c3f1-en.
Ottinger, R. L., & Williams, R. (2002). Renewable energy sources for development. *Environmental Law, 32*(2), 331–368.
Panwar, N. L., Kaushik, S. C., & Kothari, S. (2011). Role of renewable energy sources in environmental protection: A review. *Renewable and Sustainable Energy Reviews, 15*(3), 1513–1524.
Peltier, H. G. (2017). Green versus brown: Comparing the employment impacts of energy efficiency, renewable energy, and fossil fuels using an input-output model. *Economic Modelling, 61*, 39–447.
Raikar, S., & Adamson, S. (2019). Renewable energy finance: Theory and practice. In *Business and economics industries*. Elsevier Academic Press.
Reuter, W. H., Szolgayova, J., Fuss, S., & Obersteiner, M. (2012). Renewable energy investment: Policy and market impacts. *Applied Energy, 97*, 249–254.
Rivers, N. (2013). Renewable energy and unemployment: A general equilibrium analysis. *Resource and Energy Economics, 35*, 467–485.
Serezli, E., Yüksel, S., Tamer, İ., & Dinçer, H. (2021). The role of innovative renewable energy investment strategies on macroeconomic stability. In *Financial strategies in competitive markets* (pp. 165–178). Springer.
Shang, H., Su, F., Yüksel, S., & Dinçer, H. (2021). Identifying the strategic priorities of the technical factors for the sustainable low carbon industry based on macroeconomic conditions. *SAGE Open, 11*(2), 21582440211016345.
Strantzali, E., & Aravossis, K. (2016). Decision making in renewable energy investments: A review. *Renewable and Sustainable Energy Reviews, 55*, 885–898.
Tourkolias, C., & Mirasgedis, S. (2011). Quantification and monetization of employment benefits associated with renewable energy technologies in Greece. *Renewable and Sustainable Energy Reviews, 15*(6), 2876–2886.
Tran, N. H. (2018). Renewable energy in achieving sustainable development goals (SDGS) and nationally determined contribution (NDC) of Vietnam. In *Green energy and technology, renewable energy in developing countries: Local development and techno-economic aspects*. Springer International Publishing AG.
Wright, P. D. (2010). *Renewable energy and the public: From NIMBY to participation*. Earthscan Publications Ltd.
Xie, Y., Zhou, Y., Peng, Y., Dinçer, H., Yüksel, S., & an Xiang, P. (2021). An extended Pythagorean fuzzy approach to group decision-making with incomplete preferences for analyzing balanced scorecard-based renewable energy investments. *IEEE Access, 9*, 43020–43035.

Yılancı, V., İslamoğlu, E., Yıldırımalp, S., & Candan, G.(2020). The relationship between unemployment rates and renewable energy consumption: Evidence from Fourier ADL cointegration test. *Alphanumeric Journal, 8*(1).

Yuan, G., Xie, F., Dinçer, H., & Yüksel, S. (2021). The theory of inventive problem solving (TRIZ)-based strategic mapping of green nuclear energy investments with spherical fuzzy group decision-making approach. *International Journal of Energy Research, 45*(8), 12284–12300.

Yüksel, S., Dinçer, H., & Uluer, G. S. (2020). The role of technological development on renewable energy usage: An econometric analysis for G7 countries. In *Handbook of research on sustainable supply chain management for the global economy* (pp. 136–153). IGI Global.

Yüksel, S., Mikhaylov, A., Ubay, G. G., & Uyeh, D. D. (2021). The role of hydrogen in the Black Sea for the future energy supply security of Turkey. In *Handbook of research on strategic management for current energy investments* (pp. 1–15). IGI Global.

Zhao, F. (2022). The data: 2021 was the wind industry's second-best year. In *Global wind report 2022*. GWEC.

Zhe, L., Yüksel, S., Dinçer, H., Mukhtarov, S., & Azizov, M. (2021). The positive influences of renewable energy consumption on financial development and economic growth. *SAGE Open, 11*(3), 21582440211040133.

Zhou, P., Luo, J., Cheng, F., Yüksel, S., & Dinçer, H. (2021). Analysis of risk priorities for renewable energy investment projects using a hybrid IT2 hesitant fuzzy decision-making approach with alpha cuts. *Energy, 224*, 120184.

The manufacturer's authorised representative in the EU is Springer Nature Customer Service Centre GmbH, Europaplatz 3, 69115 Heidelberg, Germany. If you have any concerns regarding our products, please contact ProductSafety@springernature.com

Printed and bound by CPI Group (UK) Ltd, Croydon, CR0 4YY
30/09/2026
02225228-0008